The Vocation of Anglican Theology

The Vocation of Anglican Theology

Edited by
Ralph McMichael

scm press

© The Editors and Contributors 2014

Published in 2014 by SCM Press
Editorial office
3rd Floor Invicta House
108-114 Golden Lane
London EC1Y OTG

SCM Press is an imprint of Hymns Ancient & Modern Ltd (a registered charity)
13A Hellesdon Park Road
Norwich NR6 5DR, UK

www.scmpress.co.uk

All rights reserved. No part of this publication may be reproduced,
stored in a retrieval system, or transmitted,
in any form or by any means, electronic, mechanical,
photocopying or otherwise, without the prior permission of
the publisher, SCM Press.

The Authors have asserted their right under the Copyright, Designs and Patents
Act, 1988, to be identified as the Authors of this Work

British Library Cataloguing in Publication data

A catalogue record for this book is available
from the British Library

978 0 334 02973 1

Typeset by Manila Typesetting Company
Printed and bound by
CPI Group (UK) Ltd, Croydon

In Memoriam:
Richard Norris and Kenneth Stevenson

Contents

Contributors		ix
Introduction		xi
1	What does Canterbury have to do with Jerusalem? The Vocation of Anglican Theology *Ralph McMichael*	1
2	The Trinity *Richard Norris*	35
3	Christology *Rowan Williams*	77
4	Theological Anthropology *Kathryn Tanner*	111
5	The Church *Mark D. Chapman*	153
6	The Beauty of Holiness: Practical Divinity *Ellen T. Charry*	196
7	The Sacraments *Kenneth Stevenson*	244
8	Eschatology *Christopher A. Beeley*	280
Select Bibliography		311
Index		313

Contributors

Christopher A. Beeley is the Walter H. Gray Associate Professor of Anglican Studies and Patristics at Yale Divinity School. He teaches early Christian theology and history and modern Anglican tradition. Dr Beeley is the author of *Leading God's People: Wisdom from the Early Church for Today* (2012), *The Unity of Christ: Continuity and Conflict in Patristic Tradition* (2012), and *Gregory of Nazianzus on the Trinity and the Knowledge of God* (2008). An Episcopal priest, he has served parishes in Connecticut, Indiana, Texas and Virginia.

Mark D. Chapman is Dean of College and Lecturer in Systematic Theology at Ripon College Cuddesdon, where he teaches modern church history, theology, ecclesiology and Anglicanism, as well as being a reader in modern theology in the University of Oxford. He has written and edited books in many different areas of theology and church history. Dr Chapman's many publications include *Anglicanism: A Very Short Introduction* (2006), *Anglican Theology* (2012) and *The Fantasy of Reunion: Anglicans, Catholics, and Ecumenism 1833–1882* (2014).

Ellen T. Charry is the Margaret W. Harmon Professor of Theology at Princeton Theological Seminary. Her interest is in human flourishing in Christian perspective. Her monographs are *Franz Rosenzweig and the Freedom of God* (1987), *By the Renewing of your Minds* (1997) and *God and the Art of Happiness* (2010). She is past editor of *Theology Today* (1997–2004), and was a member of the Theology Committee of the House of Bishops of the Episcopal Church (1998–2010). Dr Charry has served on the editorial boards of the *Scottish Journal of Theology* and *Pro Ecclesia*.

Ralph McMichael is Director and Founder of the Center for the Eucharist located in St. Louis, Missouri, USA. Dr McMichael has been an Anglican priest for over 30 years, having served as a seminary professor, dean of a diocesan school for ministry, canon for ministry formation and in parish ministry. Author of two books and editor of another one, he has written, taught and lectured extensively on the history, theology and practice of the Eucharist. His newest book, *Eucharist: A Guide for the Perplexed* was published in 2010.

Richard Norris was a professor at Union Theological Seminary, New York City (1978–96), and was Professor Emeritus there and Honorary Canon Theologian of the Episcopal Diocese of New York upon his death in 2009. Dr Norris was the author of many distinguished volumes in church history and theology. His most recent work was a large collection of translated commentaries on the Song of Songs, from the early and medieval Church. Earlier works included *Manhood and Christ* (1963), *God and World in Early Christian Theology* (1965) and *The Christological Controversy* (1980).

Kenneth Stevenson was the Bishop of Portsmouth (1995–2009), Rector of Holy Trinity, Guildford (1986–95) and Chaplain and Lecturer at the University of Manchester (1980–86). Dr Stevenson authored and edited numerous publications in the areas of liturgics, sacramental theology and Anglicanism. These works include co-editing *Love's Redeeming Work* (2004), co-writing *The Mystery of the Eucharist in the Anglican Tradition* (2012), authoring *The Mystery of Baptism in the Anglican Tradition* (1998) and *Covenant of Grace Renewed: Vision of the Eucharist in the Seventeenth Century* (1994). Bishop Stevenson died in 2011.

Kathryn Tanner is Frederick Marquand Professor of Systematic Theology at Yale Divinity School. Her research relates the history of Christian thought to contemporary issues of theological concern using social, cultural and feminist theory. Dr Tanner's publications include *The Politics of God: Christian Theologies and Social Justice* (1992), *Jesus, Humanity and the Trinity: A Brief Systematic Theology* (2001), *Economy of Grace* (2005) and *Christ the Key* (2010). For eight years she has been a member of the Theology Committee that advises the Episcopal Church's House of Bishops. In 2015–16, she will deliver the Gifford Lectures at the University of Edinburgh in Scotland.

Rowan Williams is Master of Magdalene College, University of Cambridge, after serving as the Archbishop of Canterbury (2002–12). Dr Williams has taught theology, patristics and ascetical theology in a variety of institutions including the Universities of Oxford and Cambridge. He has authored several volumes representing a wide scope of interests including poetry, Russian literature, spirituality, early Christian theology as well as the relationship between faith and culture. A widely sought after speaker, Dr Williams gave the Gifford Lectures in 2013. Some of his publications are *On Christian Theology* (2000), *Anglican Identities* (2004), *Resurrection* (1982) and *The Wound of Knowledge* (1979).

Introduction

The Anglican Communion is under strain, if not fragmentation, depending upon who is making the observation. An appraisal of the state of the Anglican Communion, as well as how it got into this 'state', issues from a theological perspective, whether explicitly acknowledged or not. Some might point to particular decisions and actions within the Anglican Communion as the provocation for this ecclesial and theological instability. Others might trace a theological instability to the beginnings of what became Anglicanism. That is, as a hybrid of Protestantism and Roman Catholicism, with a little Eastern Orthodoxy thrown in for good measure, Anglicanism has always been on the brink of an identity crisis, and now under postmodern pressure, the canonical, theological or liturgical glue that held it together has melted, and the whole thing has fallen apart. Is this a time for lament or rejoicing; is it a time for nostalgia or renewal? However one answers these questions, or wherever one is on the theological and ecclesial spectrum of the Anglican Communion, it is time for a deep, habitual and pervasive engagement with our common theological tradition as Anglicans.

This volume of new essays by Anglican theologians, along with excerpts from the work of Anglican theologians from the tradition, is one effort towards a theological renewal within Anglicanism. It is an invitation to inhabit the Anglican theological imagination. Any authentic renewal begins with the basics, and this volume contains essays on some of the basic subjects of theology: Trinity, Jesus Christ, humanity, grace, the Church, sacraments and eschatology. The sources sections of this volume include excerpts drawn not only from the typical theological treatise but from sermons, poems, prayers and hymns, which collectively tell us something about the nature of Anglican theology. Renewal starts at the centre of faith and works it way out from there. So, while the reader will find treatment of the basics of the Christian faith as presented by Anglican theologians, she or he will not find either a comprehensive survey of theology or one representative of the diversity of Anglicanism. This volume cannot stand alone, and the reader or student of Anglican theology is encouraged to locate and delve into an ever-increasing array of books and materials on Anglicanism in all of its maddening and delightful diversity.

The purpose of this volume is twofold: to introduce the student to the basics of Christian theology, as articulated by Anglicans, and to invite the reader into a serious and intentional study of the Anglican theological tradition and of the contemporary efforts of Anglican theologians. Thus, this volume is offered for use in courses on Anglican theology, hopefully found within the required curriculum of every Anglican seminary and theological college. Also, as so many Anglicans do not come to the study of theology within an Anglican institution, this volume serves as a text that they can adopt for their theological formation. Likewise, since theology is increasingly done not in ecclesial and confessional isolation, this volume can provide the non-Anglican with an introduction to the essentials of theology as viewed from the work of Anglican theologians.

The production of this volume is a tale that would be long in the telling, and even a little confusing. However, here it is, finally. The patience and perseverance of the successive representatives of SCM Press is gratefully acknowledged, and in this regard Dr Natalie Watson has primary place. I am grateful for her guidance, encouragement and exceptional patience as this volume progressed. Also, I have great appreciation and gratitude for the contributors to this volume, who either stuck with it years after turning in their work, or who took up the challenge of writing in a more compressed period of time. I would like to acknowledge the contribution of Mark McIntosh as a co-worker on this project for many years. Two of the contributors have passed into the fullness of theology since submitting their work, and so this volume is in memory of Richard Norris and Kenneth Stevenson. As this introduction is written on Ash Wednesday, the beginning of the season of renewal, may we lay aside our distractions, purge our anxieties and give up our fixation on issues, and enter into that theological place where true joys are to be found, the place where our dead thinking and understanding is brought out of the tombs of our making and into the life God creates anew each time we go to worship, praise and adore the glorious Trinity: Father, Son and Holy Spirit.

Ralph McMichael
Ash Wednesday 2014

I

What does Canterbury have to do with Jerusalem?

The Vocation of Anglican Theology

RALPH MCMICHAEL

Theology is about God. This may seem, at first, a fairly obvious thing to say. However, what often is called theology does not sustain the effort directed to its proper subject. In the actual doing, theology quickly becomes the effort to think and speak about a lot of other things besides God. Directed towards other topics, theology might not only betray its true vocation by not considering primarily God; it might distort its proper subject once it turns towards God. God can become a fixture of a house already built, something or someone that now fits or belongs in this place. God can be put to use in order that our 'theological' world runs more efficiently or is more intelligible. There is at least the presumption that theology eventually will say something about God. And yet, we need to acknowledge that Christian thought, understanding and reflection is not always theological. We engage in all sorts of intellectual endeavours for the sake of purposes or 'agendas' that do not pretend towards the theological. Ruminations on how best to do things, to accomplish certain goals, to understand or analyse congregational dynamics, to find new ways to bolster stagnant views or to become a persuasive expositor of the latest trend in the Church, are all activities that not only crowd out any time and space for theology, but also create obstacles to it. You cannot do theology and do anything else at the same time and in the same way.

The performance of theology is comprehensive; it involves the whole person, the whole community, directed towards the wholeness of God's nature and will, God's presence. Theology proper abides within the catholic vocation to speak the whole truth of the whole God for the whole world. Note the word 'abide'. Doing theology is living theologically in an enduring, patient, habituated and disciplined way, eschewing all temptations to fashion the ultimate moment or the definitive change. In order to speak appropriately about God, one lives in the presence of God; one speaks and thinks within and from this presence. So the theological question begins with the theological habits. Thinking about God is not the same as thinking about any other object or subject of thought. God is not an object in the world in at least two ways. One way is that God is not an object in the sense of something that is there and only there. God is not one thing in one place that remains this one. Who God is cannot be located contingently. Even heaven is not an identifiable place of God's identity; God is not the one who lives in heaven because God created heaven. The second way that God is not an object in the world is that we cannot make an unqualified and direct correspondence between God and objects in the world. God cannot be conceptually related to anything or anyone else without remainder. All such comparisons stand under the judgement of the infinite and absolute difference between God and the world, between the Creator and creation. We do not approach God the way we approach all other possible objects of study or subjects within the curriculum of our knowledge. Thinking about God involves knowing God, and knowing God issues from being in the presence of God. As such, anyone who wishes to do theology, to study it, will embark on an intentional life involving prayer, worship, acts of charity and the reading of, and meditating on, Scripture. One does not set out only to acquire the skills of analysing theological writings or to develop one's own theological voice; one enters into the disciplined formation required of a theologian. Thus, the nature and exercise of theology inextricably involves formation of the theologian; the knower is adapted to the known, and knowledge is revealed through relationship.

However, to state that God is not an object within the panoply of all other possible objects of human study and knowledge is not to fall into an inevitable subjectivity whereby theology becomes an analysis of ourselves before God issuing in discourses primarily concerned with our experience, spirituality or consciousness. That is, theology cannot be reduced to a faithful anthropology. Acknowledging the difference between God and ourselves does not mean that we are enclosed epistemologically within our side of this relationship, that we cannot say or know anything about God, because we are not God. Theological formation is not the fine-tuning of our self-reflective skills; it is training in attentiveness to God's active presence that breaks open all our enclosures of space and time to receive God's gift of life, which we then know and experience as gift. The abiding fulcrum of any viable theological endeavour is the resurrection of Jesus. By reflecting on the resurrection of Jesus, we are introduced to the mystery of theology and to its claims on the theologian.

While theology is indeed about God, it is not about an idea or an ideal of God. Christian theology is underappreciated when it becomes one more effort to think about God. Likewise, theology is not the projection of an absolute and infinite or transcendent ideal that we then call God. Thinking and projecting, the enterprise of ideas and ideals, easily come under the judgement that we are really speaking about ourselves, about the workings of the human mind and will. In the history of human thought, God is a contested reality. This is why theology will look in the direction of God's history. However, this history is not established alongside our history. God enters our history in order to make it God's own. Consequently, we do not escape our lives in order to do theology; we do not seek to dwell in a parallel history where God resides. Theology occurs within our lives, history and cultures, because this is where God *happens* to be; this is where God acts always for the purpose of our transformation in the presence of God. Theology *happens* in the wake of God's act; theology exists in the presence of God's otherness.

The resurrection of Jesus was preceded by a life seemingly located within the contours of human history as well as located within a particular religious tradition. However, neither this history nor this tradition could receive the resurrection without being transformed by it. Human history (the customary course of events) and a religious tradition (conventional theology) are both confronted by the resurrection of Jesus. God lays down the epistemological, ontological and historical gauntlet when Jesus shows up in places other than where our historical fixations and our traditional fidelities have located him. Jesus appears where his disciples are, where some of them have returned to the consolations of familiarity, and they are confused and afraid. Confusion and fear can now mark the path of theological fidelity. Jesus is with them, but he is not there as they are. The ways that the disciples know reality, their modes of navigating life, have been definitively and irreversibly disrupted. All of their intellectual, historical, religious and experiential directions are now blocked by the appearance of Jesus. The risen Jesus stands in the way of all our paths to theological understanding. Although there have been and will continue to be intellectual and historical efforts to put Jesus back where human history and religious traditions can find him, where the consolations of the familiar can be renewed, theology proper will repent of all such efforts.

Who we are, where we are and how we live cannot be understood by ourselves within our various and specific locations, whether they be intellectual, traditional, cultural or historical. Theologically, we always have to reckon with the strange appearance of Jesus, with how his presence disrupts ours. The risen presence of Jesus always introduces instability into our theological worlds, and consequently theological objectivity and subjectivity will remain *sui generis*. The implications of this instability for the nature and study of theology are manifold. One such implication is that we cannot adopt a method or rationality from another intellectual discipline and deem it a theological method. The justification for the place and exercise of theology is never an appeal to kindred spirits. However, this does not entail sealing theology off from other disciplines of study and understanding. Theology can incorporate some of the concerns and skills of these disciplines without making them surrogates for the proper theological task. We should not ignore that theology is done by humans located in various worlds, and yet theology exists before, and for the sake of, the presence of God. Since this presence is never static as well as being other than our presence, the adaptation of investigative methods and theoretical concepts by theology will have an enduring critical dynamic. Theology always has its own proper questions to ask, its own purpose to pursue.

Likewise, another implication of the inherent instability of theology is that it should never become an exercise in ecclesial self-justification. Just as our minds, wills and experiences of the world should never become enclosed and self-referential theological places, neither should the Church. That is, theology can become the way the Church seeks to justify its specific structures and characteristic actions, its way of saying and doing things. This is not to refrain from having a theological rationale for what the Church says and does; this rationale is imperative. Rather, what betrays the nature of theology is making it solely how we justify and defend our ecclesial selves. Theology does not exist to justify or explain the Church. Theology exists because God shows up, and any theological endeavour that ignores or occludes God's surprising and disturbing appearance will betray and distort its true nature. The appearance of God destabilizes all of our attempts to locate our certainties and securities in any putative stability residing in our minds, our wills, our worlds or our churches. Stability as a theological reality is a reflection of, or witness to, the fidelity of God's appearance in Word and Sacrament. Thus, theological stability is rooted in theological fidelity to God's arriving presence in those places and modes created by God's promise. Theology is inherently a covenanted relationship, a mutuality of sacrificial presence: God will arrive where we are, and where we are will be the event of God's presence. Theology seeks to act and speak truthfully of God from this presence, from where we are in the presence of God.

Given the argument thus far regarding the nature of theology and the theologian, the study of theology is not a purely objective intellectual discipline. While we do learn what questions to ask of our sources, we are not to forget that God can question us through these same sources. That is, theological and liturgical texts are not just the deposit left to us by historically and culturally located minds but witnesses of an engagement between fellow believers and God. The appreciation of sources and witnesses does not invalidate critical study, but it does extend the critical scope of study to include us. In this way, we are not able to draw or maintain impermeable boundaries around what constitutes the subject and the object of theology. Likewise, neither the subjectivity of ourselves nor the objectivity of our sources can be allowed to render our interpretative orientation towards one direction. We cannot become so subjective that theology is only an interpretation of our experience or so objective that theology becomes the constellation of timeless truths formulated into inalterable propositions. Both of these subjective and objective extremes suffer from the same theological malady: they seek a stability and a solidity away from God's destabilizing presence. Language and experience are indeed found in the presence of God, but the danger is to treat the sign as the thing signified.

The distinction and the relationship between God and us is the abiding dynamic of theology, and how we understand this distinction and this relationship is crucial to all other possible theological concerns and expositions. God's movement towards us and our reception of it, our search for God along with God's will to be found, comprise the underlying themes of such major theological relationships as between revelation and faith, Creator and creation and nature and grace, especially as these relationships are understood in terms of the person and work of Jesus Christ. It is not my purpose in this chapter to explicate each of these relationships, which would result in a more comprehensive display of the appropriate content of theology. Rather, I wish to explore in more depth the relationship between the nature and work of theology and the vocation of theology and of theologians. Furthermore, witnesses from the Anglican theological tradition will guide this exploration, and as such I will pose the question of an Anglican theological vocation.

Formation of the Theologian: Three Anglican Witnesses

We begin the exploration of the theological relationship between God and ourselves, which can be transcribed as the relationship between theology and theologians, by attending to how three theologians located within the Anglican theological tradition approach the task of theology. Each of these three witnesses assigns a foundational role to the formation of the theologian for any authentic performance of theology. In contrast to a preponderance of modern theologians, they do not begin their respective theological tasks arguing for a proper theological method, whose propriety accords with the perceived demands of a reigning epistemology, a historical relevance or a cultural context. Instead, they address the conversion of the theologian as the basis for apprehending any possible content of theology. Doing theology, knowing something of God, requires the disciplines of the theological life.

Anselm of Canterbury

Anselm was the Archbishop of Canterbury from 1093 to 1109, and hence he pre-dates the Reformation of the sixteenth century and the separation of the Church of England from the Roman Catholic Church. While he certainly did not engage in any proleptic Anglican apologetic, his work exists within the theological tradition that continued and developed through those theologians who lived and worked in a self-consciously Anglican ecclesial environment. That is, the Anglican theological tradition is a tradition that did not begin in the sixteenth century. As will be presented below, a characteristic of the Anglican apologetic that did emerge was an appeal to the undivided Church, to the normative tradition of ancient and primitive catholicism. So, while Anselm was not a historically identified Anglican, he is recognized as part of this tradition by later identifiable Anglican theologians.

In his book *Proslogion*,[1] Anselm argues for the existence of God as 'that-than-which-a-greater-cannot-be-thought', the so-called ontological argument. What concerns us here is not the substance of this argument, but how Anselm begins and concludes this book. The first and the last chapters of this book convey Anselm's own sense of the vocation of the theologian. In this first chapter, 'A rousing of the mind to the contemplation of God', he comes to define theology as 'faith seeking understanding', a definition that culminates his extended prayer to God for this undertaking. Anselm begins his prayer with an exhortation to abandon every thought and concern that is not directly involved in the task of seeking God. For him, seeking God is not an exercise in intellectual virtuosity; it requires God's direction: 'Come then, Lord my God, teach my heart where and how to seek You, where and how to find You.'[2] The theological task of seeking God fulfils the purpose of created humanity. However, due to the fall of Adam, we are not able to seek God on our own because, unlike Adam, who initially enjoyed the abundant presence of God, we begin our seeking from a place characterized by God's absence. Thus Anselm prays that God would bridge this chasm:

---

1 The text referenced here is taken from *Anselm of Canterbury: The Major Works*, Brian Davies and G. R. Evans (eds), Oxford: Oxford University Press, 1998.
2 *The Major Works*, pp. 84–5.

> Teach me to seek You, and reveal Yourself to me as I seek, because I can neither seek You if You do not teach me how, nor find You unless You reveal Yourself. Let me seek You in desiring You; let me desire You in seeking You; let me find You in loving You; let me love You in finding You.[3]

The basis of this seeking of God, of this desire to see God, is belief in God. Anselm's quest to understand God is rooted in his prior belief in God. He wishes to understand the truth of God, which he already 'believes and loves'. While Anselm spends the bulk of the *Proslogion* in what we would designate as philosophical theology, he does not regard this work as a purely rational effort, a speculation that strives *towards* saying something 'meaningful' about God. Theology here is not a dispassionate or objective endeavour, one that eschews any prior commitments or convictions. Theology begins in a relationship with God, one in which God teaches, one in which the theologian requires formation for what lies ahead.

While the theological task begins with laying aside all distractions and praying that God will teach the theologian how to seek God, Anselm describes the fulfilment of this task as entering 'the joy of the Lord' (Matt. 25.21). Theology begins in prayer before the presence of God and concludes as life within this presence. As such, Anselm traces the theological endeavour of knowing and loving God from its earthly hope to its heavenly abundance. Theology is the theologian's faithful movement into the life of God, the life that both fulfils and transcends all pure human desires and joys: 'The whole of that joy, then, will not enter into those who rejoice, but those who rejoice will enter wholly into that joy.'[4] God is not an object for human understanding but a destiny for human transformation. Understanding is not the location of God within the mind of the theologian; it is a movement of the whole self into the 'ever-greater' life of God through participation in the truth of God, and one knows this truth when one's joy is complete (John 16.24). Anselm concludes the *Proslogion* with this petition:

> God of truth, I ask that I may receive so that my 'joy may be complete'. Until then let my mind meditate on it, let my tongue speak of it, let my heart love it, let my mouth preach it. Let my soul hunger for it, let my flesh thirst for it, my whole being desire it, until I enter into the 'joy of the Lord', who is God, Three in One, 'blessed forever. Amen.'[5]

In order to pursue theology, the theologian commits the whole self to a life not one's own. Truly understood, theology is not so much a product of the theologian's work, but the reality that forms the theologian.

Jeremy Taylor

Jeremy Taylor (1613–67) lived through a period of great conflict in both Church and State. Having served as chaplain to Charles I, with Archbishop William

---

3 *The Major Works*, pp. 86–7.
4 *The Major Works*, p. 103.
5 *The Major Works*, p. 104.

Laud as his patron, Taylor was not permitted any public role or formal ministry during the Commonwealth led by Oliver Cromwell. He was imprisoned three times and at the Restoration became a bishop in Ireland, where he died. Thus, Taylor is a theologian who knew well the divisions of theology and politics, as he sought to fashion and convey a theological ethos that would characterize Anglicanism for future generations. While he was Bishop of Down and Connor and Vice-Chancellor of the University of Dublin, he preached to the students and faculty of Trinity College, Dublin in 1662. Taylor took John 7.17 as his text, calling his sermon *Via Intelligentiae*, the 'way of understanding'.[6] He accounts for the various ways that churches and theologians have sought to maintain both truth and peace, and he exhorts and instructs his listeners regarding the proper way to apprehend God's truth, and therefore for establishing peace among all Christians.

According to Taylor, there have been five ways that churches and theologians have sought to perceive and protect truth and thereby to establish peace among Christians. The first approach upholds 'one true way'. There is one denomination or church that establishes an absolute 'system or collective body of articles' that express the truth, and this expression will not permit other faithful formularies. Likewise, this church is understood as the true one, and 'out of this church they will hardly allow salvation'. The second path to truth and peace is 'submission to an infallible guide'. There is an authoritative group or person who decides what is the truth during occasions of confusion and controversy. Taylor identifies the Church of Rome as having this mode of discerning and enforcing the truth. A more pliable sensibility characterizes Taylor's description of a third way. Conflict or division among Christians could be overcome by seeking moderation among all parties. The strategy is to 'join in common terms and phrases of accommodation'. Instead of accentuating the differences, or bolstering each church's perceived unique claim to truth, common ground is sought, which becomes the basis of agreed truth and shared peace. Similarly, the fourth way to dissipate conflict among churches is to reformulate the controversial language or the entrenched doctrinal positions that couch the disputed issues. The hope is that if the question were stated more clearly, intelligible to all parties, then disputes would dissolve. Lastly, Taylor speaks of an approach that privileges peace over truth. Adherents of this way consider all doctrinal disputes to be expression of 'opinions', and as such, all differing views should be tolerated.[7] While he may be describing the ebb and flow of Christianity in the West during the sixteenth and seventeenth centuries, Taylor's typology of approaches to truth and peace (what we might call later 'ecumenism') certainly resonates within the twenty-first century, especially regarding the Anglican Communion.

In Taylor's estimation, all of these efforts to maintain truth and peace within Christianity have failed, and now it is time to engage the one faithful way to God's truth and peace: 'Let us go to the truth itself, to Christ, and He will tell us an easy way of ending all of our quarrels.'[8] He argues that God's truth can

---

6 The text of the sermon referenced here is taken from *Jeremy Taylor: Selected Works*, Thomas K. Carroll (ed.), New York: Paulist Press, 1990.

7 *Selected Works*, pp. 356–9.

8 *Selected Works*, p. 356.

only be obtained from direct engagement with God, for God is the teacher of this truth. Referring to his scriptural text (John 7.17), Taylor contends that only those who do God's will know God's truth. How we live for God determines our capacity to discern God's teaching and our ability to understand it. He locates the animation of theology as follows:

> [T]heology is rather a divine life than a divine knowledge. In heaven indeed we shall first see, and then love; but here on earth we must first love, and love will open our eyes as well as our hearts, and we shall then see and perceive and understand.[9]

Loving God and the doing of theology do not come naturally. We are to undergo a conversion of our desires and of our affections. In Taylor's assessment, a sinful life is the basis for ignorance of God, and only after repenting of sin can one hope to know and understand the content of theology, what God would teach us. No matter how learned someone might be, this naturally acquired knowledge will never be sufficient for the task of theology unless one's passions are directed solely to God. In order to be a true theologian, Taylor directs us to the crucifixion.

> Passionate men . . . must begin again at Christ's cross; they must learn true mortification and crucifixion of their anger and desires, before they can be good scholars in Christ's school, or be admitted into the more secret enquiries of religion, or profit in spiritual understanding.[10]

Repentance of sin, conversion of life, allows us to become theologians, to have the capacity to be taught by God. Thus, for Taylor, the closer we are to God, the more knowledge we can acquire from God; the more the truth of God takes hold of our lives, the more we can know it.[11]

In Taylor's estimation, the primary characteristic of a theologian, one who grows nearer to God for God's teaching, is holiness: 'to the direct demonstration of the article in question, that holiness is the only way of truth and understanding'.[12] Doing God's will, loving God, will yield knowledge of God's truth that is otherwise unavailable to us. Holiness grants a perception of God all its own. While we might know some things of God by diligent study, this knowledge exists in the 'shadow' of God, a place where disputes arise.[13] Furthermore, Taylor emphasizes the role of holiness in discerning what aspiring Christian scholars or theologians should study. He tells his listeners that not every subject or question of theological study is to be pursued. There are some scholarly investigations that do not develop the life of holiness, that do not bring us closer to God. That is, our studies can become a distraction from true

---

9 *Selected Works*, p. 361.
10 *Selected Works*, p. 367.
11 *Selected Works*, pp. 361–9.
12 *Selected Works*, p. 361.
13 *Selected Works*, p. 374.

theology. This discernment of what to study takes place when the 'Spirit of God' is our teacher, when we are converted from being our own teachers.[14]

> But there is no satisfactory knowledge of the blessed Trinity but this; and therefore whatever thing is spoken of God metaphysically, there is no knowledge of God theologically, and as He ought to be known, but by the measures of holiness, and the proper light of the Spirit of God.[15]

Taylor concludes his sermon by addressing directly future clergy, telling them that the path to wisdom and through all the disputations of Christianity is not paved by reading a lot of books, by surveying commentaries or by following metaphysical logic, but only 'by the proportions of holiness: and when all books are read, and all arguments examined, and all authorities alleged, nothing can be found to be true that is unholy'.[16] Those who strive to share God's holiness gain knowledge of God, and this striving transforms the mind and the passions of the knower. Taylor does not reject the exercise of reason or the hard work of study. He spent years acquiring knowledge of the patristic writings, but he does say that such reason and study are not ends in themselves. Unless our studies are directed towards God, animated by the purified desire to know, love and see God, chiefly characterized by holiness, then we are not fulfilling our vocation as theologians.

Studying God involves openness to God's act on oneself, the willingness to be directed by God's will and the desire to become what God would make of you. Theologians are transformed persons. That is, to be a theologian of the Christian faith, one will be a Christian. Although theology is about God, it is not about an idea or an abstract reality remaining exterior to thought and to life. Furthermore, there is a specificity about this God, a history of divine action, which presents not only a narrative for interpretation, but a narrative that is to overcome the theologian's life. The life, death and resurrection of Jesus Christ is not only the subject of theological thought. It subjects the theologian to its reality and responsibilities. In order to say and know something truthful about God, the theologian is called to repentance, to endure the cross of Christ.

Michael Ramsey

Such is the perspective to theology, to the formation of the theologian, of our third Anglican witness, Arthur Michael Ramsey, the 100th Archbishop of Canterbury. As a young priest and teacher at Lincoln Theological College, Ramsey wrote his *magnum opus* in 1936: *The Gospel and the Catholic Church*.[17] While this book roots the catholic ordering of the Church as episcopal and liturgical in the New Testament, as the normative expression of the gospel itself, Ramsey

---

14 *Selected Works*, pp. 378–9.
15 *Selected Works*, p. 383.
16 *Selected Works*, p. 386.
17 *The Gospel and the Catholic Church*, 2nd edn, London: Longmans, 1956. Henceforth, *Gospel*.

speaks to the nature of Christian theology, to the place of the theologian in the Church, when he expounds the essence of liturgy and our engagement with the truth of God. He writes, 'The Church's perilous office of teaching is inseparable from the Church's worship of the mystery whereby it exists.'[18] The teachers of the Church are formed within its liturgical life, because it is there, in the liturgy, that they encounter the subject of their work, the saving act of God. For Ramsey, 'All life, therefore is, for a Christian, eucharistic; and the worship does not start with common needs, but with the divine action of the redeemer, and into this action it brings all common life.'[19] God has a history of acting, and the definitive events of this history are the death and resurrection of Jesus, which are unique and unrepeatable. However, this history, these events, are there not only to be contemplated but to be active *within* Christians.[20] Worship is an event of divine power and action whereby God acts on and within the gathered worshippers. Ramsey presses the point that worship is fundamentally not our act but Christ's redemptive act in us, Christ himself acting in us.

> Christ in His Body glorifies the Father, and His members share in what He does. The Holy Spirit prays within the Christians. It is as though a stream of love flows forth from God to mankind and returns to God through Christ; the Christians cast themselves into the stream, and while their own efforts are called forth in full measure, the stream, which is the essence of worship and prayer, is that of God himself.[21]

As the centre of worship, this movement of the Triune God is the revelation of God's 'eternal truths'. Thus, the liturgy itself, its language and structure, will signify God's action in the death and resurrection of Jesus and will not signify the transient and trendy attributes of our lives. Through worship and its divine movement, God's saving acts, Christians share a history located in heaven and in the Church because its 'centre is the High Priestly act of Jesus Christ in heaven and in history'.[22] Furthermore, the centrality of Christ's action means that worship is a corporate act and reality: 'The voice of the single Christian is drawn into the voice of the Body and represents the Body.'[23] As members of the Body of Christ, Christians are called to speak the language of this Body, a language that becomes theirs in worship. They speak as those who have been acted upon by the Father through Christ in the Holy Spirit; our Christian speech is always already responsorial. For the Church, and for its theologians, the truth of God is revealed primarily by God's saving act in Christ and not by the speculative adventures of the human mind. God's truth is a liturgical reality and event.

Having explored the liturgical relationship between God and Christians, Ramsey turns directly to the nature and understanding of the 'truth of God': 'what

---

18 *Gospel*, p. 126.
19 *Gospel*, p. 89.
20 *Gospel*, p. 91.
21 *Gospel*, p. 93.
22 *Gospel*, p. 95.
23 *Gospel*, p. 95.

does the "truth" mean on the lips of the Church's teachers?'[24] For these teachers, for theologians and for all Christians, the truth of God is not so much located within the Church or within Scripture. Rather, we are to encounter the truth that has 'created' the Church and Scripture; again, the truth of God is revealed in our encounter with God, an encounter that happens as and in the Body of Christ. However, we learn the nature of this truth by examining the word for truth (*aletheia*) in the New Testament. Ramsey's study of this word leads to his assertion that truth is spoken in God's saving act through Christ, and therefore learning this truth requires not only intellectual work but also repentance of life. We receive the truth of God in our thinking and in our living: 'For God's Truth is not an abstract value to be contemplated: it is active to save in Christ.'[25] Likewise, learning God's truth in this way has implications for the nature of theology.

> Christian knowledge (*gnosis*) and Christian love (*agape*) lie close together, and Christian theology is not only a detached exercise of the Christian intellect; it is the life of the one Body in which Truth is thought out and lived out.[26]

Christian theology is the self-understanding of the Body of Christ, a Body whose intellect is not separate from its liturgical mode of living, whose life begins at the cross of Christ through the penitential turning to God: 'Crucifixion–Truth–the life of holiness, all these are linked.'[27] Since God's truth is known as God's saving act, whose epistemological centre of gravity is always the death and resurrection of Christ, it follows for Ramsey that we can never claim a comprehensive understanding of this truth.[28] The truth of God, the truth that creates the Church and created Scripture, belongs to God alone and not to us. We share this truth as we share God's life, as God's life animates and transforms our life as members of the Body of Christ. As such, those who embark on the vocation of theology will do so for the sake of God's truth offered to the penitent and signified by holiness of life.

What then is the principal work of a theologian? What do they do? The answer Ramsey commends, and indeed models in *The Gospel and the Catholic Church*, is that theologians 'dig' rather than build. He borrows this concept of theological digging from another Anglican theologian, F. D. Maurice (d.1872). For although Maurice is often appreciated as well as derided as a 'modern' theologian, one whose work bore the marks of nineteenth-century modernism and its positive regard for science, social concerns and critical thought, Ramsey argues that Maurice fashioned his thoughts not on the tides of the day but from the wellspring of the past, by taking the tradition seriously. Of Maurice's 'pioneering' theology, Ramsey states:

> But he was able to be a pioneer precisely because he refused to succumb to the modernisms of this time, and because he drank deeply from a theology

---

24 *Gospel*, p. 120.
25 *Gospel*, p. 122.
26 *Gospel*, p. 124.
27 *Gospel*, p. 122.
28 *Gospel*, p. 126.

learnt from the Greek Fathers, from the Catholic order, from St. John, and from the Gospel of God. He enabled others to build because he chose himself to 'dig'.[29]

Ramsey is well aware that there are contemporary challenges to theology, including the reinterpretation of doctrine in light of the developments in science and philosophy and of Christian life with regard to changing social and economic realities. Yet, for him, the way to engage these challenges is not by imitating their methods, or by finding equivalents in the Church, but by 'digging' 'down to its own foundations, which are the Gospel of God, the sacramental life, and the soundest learning that its clergy and laity can possess'.[30] In this study of the Church from its New Testament origins and the Church's foundation on the crucifixion and resurrection of Christ, Ramsey 'has attempted to share in the work of digging'.[31]

The formation of theologians, as articulated by these three Anglican witnesses, leads to the question of what is the proper activity of theologians. Ramsey speaks of the task of the theologian as one of digging, a theological sensibility characterized more by exploration than speculation, the renewal of theological sources more than their rehabilitation in contemporary idioms of epistemology and human agency. Consequently, our attention is now drawn from the theologian to theology itself, from the question of who to the questions of how and what. Thus, we now turn directly to the question of Anglican theology itself.

The Question of Anglican Theology

What is Anglican theology? Any forthright consideration of Anglican theology will face this question as an enduring and inescapable provocation. It is a question that will not go away, and its answer cannot be located within an assured and assumed topography of historical theology or confessional documentation. It can even be argued that it is the nature of Anglican theology to remain a question, a question open to a variety of answers or a question that always transcends any attempt to provide an answer. It is a question that permits many answers, or it is a question that resists any answer, definitive or otherwise. Yet, the question of Anglican theology can lead us to some thematic content. Many theologians have sought to describe or project the content or the form, the doctrine or the methodology, of Anglican theology. It has been argued that Anglican theology does not have a normative content, but instead a distinctive (not unique) methodology or perspective. In contrast to this approach, the claim is made that Anglican theology has a constitutive Anglican doctrine, and furthermore, that Anglican theologians should engage this teaching systematically. Another way to pose this question is to ask whether Anglican theology is theology done by Anglicans and/or is it theologians doing identifiable Anglican theology?

---

29 *Gospel*, p. 216.
30 *Gospel*, p. 216.
31 *Gospel*, p. 221.

I will not explore every facet of these questions. Rather I will consider briefly how three theologians sought to answer directly the question of Anglican theology. The creation of an autonomous church in England with its declared departure from the Roman Catholic Church, within the theological context of the Reformation, provoked basic questions of ecclesial and theological identity, all of which were posed within a contested political landscape. It is no surprise then that the initial efforts at proclaiming, describing and defining what would be a distinctive Anglican theology were pursued in the idiom of argument, apology or polemic. That is, stating what is Anglican theology was done by saying what it is not, by articulating how it differs from other theological perspectives or doctrinal structures, principally in opposition to Puritans or Roman Catholics. Roughly, against the Puritans, Anglicans contended for the place of tradition in the Church's life and teaching, and contrary to the Roman Catholic Church, Anglicans appealed to a tradition uncorrupted by later accretions. While Richard Hooker's *Laws of Ecclesiastical Polity* (Books I–IV 1594, Book V 1597) provides an abiding reference for subsequent approaches to the exposition of Anglican theology, John Jewel's *An Apology for the Church of England* (1562) sharpens the argument for what constitutes this theology, what serves as its normative boundaries.

John Jewel

John Jewel (1522–71), Bishop of Salisbury (1560–71), led the defence and the defining of an Anglican theological consensus emerging from the Elizabethan Settlement, and he did so primarily by drawing the differences between the Church of England and the Roman Catholic Church. In his *Apology*, Jewel turns to a variety of ecclesial subjects in order to show how the Church of England remains a faithful steward of Scripture and the ancient tradition, while the Roman Catholic Church has departed from this same Scripture and tradition. For him, the test of an authentic faith and ecclesial practice is whether it is 'confirmed by the words of Christ, by the writings of the apostles, by the testimonies of the catholic fathers, and by the example of many ages'.[32] Again, he states, 'Surely we have ever judged the primitive church of Christ's time, of the apostles, and of the holy fathers, to be the catholic church.'[33] One example of Jewel's appeal to the ancient tradition over against the 'heresies' of Rome, is the area of eucharistic practices. He denounces private Masses, Communion of the bread alone and adoration of the sacrament without Communion as clearly against both the scriptural witness and the testimony of the patristic Church. These are the criteria for whether a belief or practice can be regarded as catholic, and in Jewel's mind it is evident that the Church of England is a catholic church. In the 'Recapitulation' section of the *Apology*, he summarizes the basic theme of this work:

> [W]e have declared at large unto you the very whole manner of our religion, what our faith is of God the Father, of his only Son Jesus Christ, of the Holy

---

[32] John Jewel, *An Apology of the Church of England*, J. E. Booty (ed.), Ithaca, NY: Cornell University Press, 1963, p. 21.
[33] *Apology*, p. 65.

Ghost, of the church, of the sacraments, of the ministry, of the Scriptures, of ceremonies, and of every part of Christian belief . . . and that we have searched out of the Holy Bible, which we are sure cannot deceive, one sure form of religion, and have returned again unto the primitive church of the ancient fathers and apostles, that is to say, to the first ground and beginning of things, as unto the very foundations and headsprings of Christ's church.[34]

Thus, for Jewel and for many subsequent Anglican apologists, the separation from the Roman Church, and the establishment of the Church of England, was a return not only to the scriptural witness but also to its proximate tradition. This appeal to Scripture and the ancient tradition has two corollaries within the body of Anglican theology: the views that Anglicanism does not have its own distinctive doctrine and that the primary concern of Anglican theology is for the essentials of Christian faith. This appeal is to a *common* tradition and to an age when the essentials of the faith were being expressed in credal forms.

Lancelot Andrewes

The appeal to the ancient or primitive tradition of Christian theology becomes an abiding theme in Anglican theology, whether in theory or in practice. Perhaps the definitive articulation of this appeal is provided by Lancelot Andrewes (1555–1626). After referencing Jewel's *Apology*, he offers this summation of Anglican theology:

One canon reduced to writing by God himself, two testaments, three creeds, four general councils, five centuries, and the series of Fathers in that period – the centuries that is, before Constantine, and two after, determine the boundary of our faith.[35]

For Andrewes, this period was not only formative for Christian theology in general, and for Anglican theology in particular, it was the basis for his own formation as a theologian and preacher. Throughout his life, he was an indefatigable student of the patristic era and of its languages. His sermons exhibited an easy and focused employment of patristic texts through allusions or direct quotations, which can only emerge from a life of deep learning. While he considers the ancient tradition to be the foundation for Anglican theology, he does not advocate an antiquarian theological method, one that retreats to quoting something from the past in order to dispense with an issue or question in the present. Andrewes's theological formation granted him a perspective that would eschew attempts to promote definitive statements on all manner of topics in Christian theology and life. That is, being steeped in the essentials of theology, he is able to recognize what is essential and not essential, or what is foundational and

---

34 *Apology*, pp. 134–5.
35 As quoted and translated in Stephen Sykes and John Booty (eds), *The Study of Anglicanism*, London: SPCK, 1988, p. 267. Original text found in *Opuscula quaedam Posthuma*, Library of Anglo-Catholic Theology, Oxford: Parker, 1853, p. 91.

secondary.[36] There is a role for reason in exploring this ancient tradition and in addressing contemporary questions. Or as Andrewes once put it: 'we do not innovate; it may be we renovate what was customary among the ancients'.[37] The premise of this assertion is not that the Church of England, or Anglican theology, duplicates the primitive Church and its theological development. Rather, Andrewes and like-minded Anglican apologists contend that there is a fundamental continuity between the patristic period and their contemporary Church with its doctrine and liturgy.

John Keble

The appeal to the patristic Church for guidance and direction during times of theological and ecclesial controversy was a principal tenet of the Oxford Movement (1833–45). An example of this appeal, and of the argument that the primitive tradition accompanies the authority of Scripture, is found in a sermon by John Keble (1792–1866). Taking as his text 'that good thing which was committed unto thee keep by the Holy Ghost which dwelleth in us' (2 Tim. 1.14), Keble addresses a climate in the Church characterized by 'anxious discussions' that require the clergy to refrain from 'drawing back from responsibility' and to 'endeavor to see our own way'.[38] He examines carefully the question of what constituted the 'treasure' entrusted to Timothy, by asking whether what was given to Timothy included material not explicitly found in Scripture:

> that it contained, besides the substance of Christian doctrine, a certain form, arrangement, selection, methodizing the whole, and distinguishing fundamentals; and also a certain system of church practice, both in government, discipline, and worship; of which, whatever portion we can prove to be still remaining, ought to be religious guarded by us, even for the same reason we reverence and retain that which is more properly scriptural, both being portion of the same divine treasure.[39]

Keble rehearses how in the primitive Church there was an apostolic tradition prior to the development and determination of the New Testament, and that even after the New Testament existed as such there was still a role for tradition in its interpretation and extrapolation. The authoritative existence of the canon of Scripture did not extinguish the apostolic tradition. There are practices and doctrines of the early Church, while 'confirmed from Scripture, are yet ascertainable parts of the primitive, unwritten system, of which we yet enjoy the

---

36 See H. R. McAdoo's treatment of Andrewes's 'appeal to antiquity' in *The Spirit of Anglicanism: A Survey of Anglican Theological Method in the Seventeenth Century*, London: Black, 1967, especially pp. 316–36.

37 As quoted in McAdoo, p. 334 from Andrewes's *Tortura*, L.A.C.T., p. 96.

38 John Keble, *Primitive Tradition Recognised in Holy Scripture: A Sermon preached in Cathedral Church of Winchester . . . September 27, 1836*, third edition, with a postscript London: J. G. & F. Rivington, 1837, p. 21. 'Project Canterbury', anglicanhistory.org/keble/primitive.html.

39 *Primitive Tradition*, pp. 6–7.

benefit'.[40] Furthermore, Keble argues that without appeal to primitive tradition or 'Catholic tradition', the Church cannot continue to 'advance satisfactorily or safely' in its basic teachings, the interpretation of Scripture and its practice. He acknowledges that there is diversity or variety among the teachings and practices of the patristic period. However, what constitutes the 'primitive Catholic tradition' are those teachings, interpretations and practices found in all places of this tradition, what is the common tradition to all subsequent developments and diversities.[41]

After having argued for the necessary mutuality between Scripture and the common primitive tradition, Keble turns to the question of the present and future Church, of how this 'deposit of the faith' is entrusted to the ministry of the Church. He contends that the Holy Spirit that dwelt in Paul and in Timothy is imparted to their apostolic successors, to the bishops of the Church of England. These bishops received at their ordination the gift of the Holy Spirit, which enables them to guard the original faith of the Church. While there are many duties and responsibilities facing the ordained ministry, they are secondary to maintaining 'the integrity of the good deposit, the orthodox faith, the Creed of the Apostolical Church, guaranteed to us by Holy Scripture, and by the consent of pure antiquity'.[42] Furthermore, Keble cautions against upholding either Scripture or tradition in isolation from the accountability of each other. For focusing on Scripture without the tradition of its interpretation, or referring to tradition without rooting it in Scripture, leads to impoverishing the integrity of both Scripture and tradition. Keble proceeds to warn his hearers against 'novelty' in theology. By novelty, he does not mean something that appears new or different to the contemporary Church. Rather, he wishes to avoid any novelty arising from a deviation from the common or Catholic tradition, the primitive church. For he acknowledges that when one explores this common tradition, there are teachings or practices that can be experienced as new in the present; and therefore, the established present is disturbed and challenged. Theology is guided by faithful engagement with Scripture and the primitive tradition and not by the temptations of treating theology as one more human science, one in which we expect to continue to progress in our knowledge from one generation to the next. Keble exhorts theologians to protect the mystery of faith from the temptations of confining it to the conventions of language or of rationality.[43]

For the three Anglican theologians considered, Anglican theology is identified by the intentional and focused engagement with the common and ancient tradition of the Christian faith and Church. Such an engagement is neither an imitation of prior theological efforts nor a repetition of past propositions as closed arguments. That is, theology is not ahistorical or atemporal, while we can yet speak of continuity with this tradition as well as an enabled discernment between essentials and non-essentials, between what is foundational and what is secondary to the Christian faith. While rooted in the ancient tradition, the identity of Anglican theology is lived in the present and is alive to the possibilities of a

---

40 *Primitive Tradition*, p. 10.
41 *Primitive Tradition*, pp. 12–13.
42 *Primitive Tradition*, p. 14.
43 *Primitive Tradition*, pp. 14–16.

faithful future. Perhaps posing the question of the identity of Anglican theology only introduces us to an enterprise that cannot be contained by this question. The idiom of identity, of what is identifiable as such, while it may indeed be appropriate for theology of any sort, is not *really* and *truly* adequate.

The Vocation of Anglican Theology

Exploration of the question of Anglican theology has brought us to a place that can be characterized as both identifiable and ambiguous. Identifiable, because we can speak of enduring themes and a persistent array of attributes. Identifying the roles and relationships among Scripture, tradition and reason has provided a recurring reference. The effort to distinguish between what is fundamental and secondary, or essential and non-essential, continues within the life and thought of the Anglican Communion. Yet, however we identify Anglican theology, we are not able to resolve the inherent ambiguity of this identification. This is so for two basic reasons. The first reason is reflected in the heritage of Anglican theology itself. Different theologians, events and developments within the life of Anglicanism have sought to solidify and shape Anglican identity in various ways. While Scripture, tradition and reason all receive notice, they are not employed in the same way by all Anglicans at all times. Each of these terms can and does receive an array of treatments, and each of them can be the optic through which to regard the other two. Furthermore, each of these concepts, or theological coordinates, can be understood in conflicting ways. Reason is not a univocal operation on a transparent reality, nor does the appeal to Scripture yield a uniformity of faith. Anglicans can have their own versions of Anglican theology and their own representative Anglican theologians. Thus, there is an inherent ambiguity to the question of the identity of Anglican theology.

The second basic reason we are faced with ambiguity when striving for an identifiable Anglican theology resides not so much in the past as with the present. Diversity marks both the ecclesial and theological climate of the contemporary Anglican Communion. The vanguard of inclusion purchases fragmentation, and the fashioning of more putative, definitive and authoritative confessional strands escalates the perception of increasing apostasy in the ranks of Anglicans. Theology as an intellectual pursuit, an academic subject, or as an expression of faith is shaped by a greater awareness of contexts, cultures and personal or corporate experiences. That is, what is going on in the world shapes what is going on in the Church's thought about itself and about the world. The proliferation of post-sensibilities and critical strategies suffocates any possibility of expressing or espousing an Anglican theology that is coherently and comprehensively identifiable as such by all Anglicans. Of course, one could argue that the lack of a comprehensive identifiable Anglican theology is itself the identity – comprehensiveness serves not as an accountable boundary but as an ever-expansive collection of the views of all Anglicans: comprehensiveness as description rather than prescription. We are left with two countervailing theological forces: the drive towards a more coherent and focused confession or towards a more diverse arrangement of perspectives. Is Anglican theology the identifiable self-understanding of a corporate faith, or is it the existence of what

Anglicans believe? It is no theological surprise that this contemporary Anglican exhibition of the mystery of, or conundrum between, the one and the many often finds its justification in versions of Christology (the one) or in versions of pneumatology (the many): those who speak of Christ as the basis for accountable unity, and those who speak of the Spirit as a rationale for diversity. Direct theological associations can serve to bolster an already articulated argument or conceptual construct. However, this direct appeal to theological vocabulary and categories may not have generated the argument or perspective.

What does one do with this inherent ambiguity of an Anglican theological identity or with this contemporary diversity of theologies or theological perspectives? Again, one can either move towards a more definitive or confessional identity or continue to re-describe diversity itself as the Anglican identity. Authentic theology requires the rejection of both of these Anglican trajectories or scenarios.

Asking what is Anglican theology leads to an array of answers that could, however, retain one commonality among them: the idiom of acknowledgement. What is Anglican theology is acknowledged as such due to a set of characteristics, circumstances or presumed authority. Knowledge of Anglican theology is preceded by its existence in some form or expression. This theology is what Anglicans have done or are doing, and we are able to acknowledge that this is the case. Furthermore, this acknowledgement is enabled by a prior assumption of what identifies Anglican theology as such. There is the identity known as Anglican, and there are the identifiers of its theology. There are subjective and objective identifiers: subjects that identify, and objects that are identified. Identity is an existence that can be acknowledged and maintained, and it serves to locate ourselves within the possibilities of other locations, other ways to be oneself, to belong somewhere else. My identity allows me to claim a specific existence with its appropriate narrative, the history that has made this place for me and the history of how I came to be located here. Likewise, this existence, with its place and history, enables others to acknowledge my identity. Thus, identity is a construct of self-reference made possible by a history that can be told in such a way that others can acknowledge that I am who I say I am. I have an identity, and I am identified by it. The acknowledgement or construction of an identity presumes the primacy of human agency, our capacity to know who we are, or what something is, as well as to make it so. Identities are acknowledged, established or maintained by those who have them. Thus, Anglican theology is identified by Anglicans who acknowledge, establish or maintain a theology that is theirs or that belongs to them. For this identification by non-Anglicans would require a familiarity with Anglicans and their history such that the act of identification is reasonable and plausible. Anglican theology is a theology recognized as Anglican; this theology represents what we know already about Anglicans and their theology. However, what if we pose the question of Anglican theology outside the confines of the primacy of human agency, identifiable history and mutual recognition? What if who is here, what is the case and how this is done become questions not of self-identification but the inauguration of revelation? In other words, who we are, what something is and how it got to be here are not products of human agency or of human cogitation.

What *happens* when identity is associated with claims for the existence, nature and will of God? This is a more consequential question than asking what it *means* for our identity, or for the identity of anything, that there is a God. While intellectual associations can be, and are appropriately, drawn between the existence of humanity and of divinity, our initial question emphasizes a dynamic between our efforts at self-designation and the presence of God. Identity is not something that we might investigate or extrapolate in reference to the existence of God. Such an effort could render God an extension of the self, a hermeneutic of the self or an explanation of why things are the way they are. Investigations, explanations, affirmations and associations still operate within the idiom of acknowledgement with the currency of what is as it is. However, an association with claims for the existence, nature and will of God, with the presence of God, will not permit identity to be a cipher for the status quo, or a desire to improve the self or to make progress in the Church and in the world. For God not only has an existence (God is), a nature (God who) but a will (God, how and why). In the presence of God, being entails becoming, and becoming bridges the difference between God and us, God and the world, through renunciation and annunciation, through sacrifice and gift and through death and resurrection(In this way, *theologically* speaking, identity yields to vocation, and vocation operates within the idiom of revelation.)

Vocation is the calling of God to and on us. God is a calling God, and we are a called humanity. We are called within this world, which itself is called to become other than its contemporary existence. That is, vocation is always already the possibility of being transformed. Vocation is the creation of a re-newed (born again) person; it is the knowledge and direction that is received, that takes place, in the presence of God. As called by God, we come to know the difference God makes when our lives, the Church and the world are open to God's presence, are capable of hearing the invitation to love God with all our 'hearts, minds, and bodies'. We were not created and then told to figure out the meaning of life the best we can, what might 'work' for us. We are called *into* the knowledge and love of God. Truly knowing the world and ourselves will involve knowledge of God, and the knowledge of God will lead to the knowing of the true self. In the presence of God, identity becomes vocation.

As a dynamic reality, an always-present call issued by the irreducible Other, vocation is characterized by movement. Movement is constituted by the mover, the moved and the motion, the actual moving from one place to another place. Thus, movement is realized through activities of dis-placement and re-placement, a going from somewhere towards and into a promised place, the location of a renewal wrought by the mover upon the moved. However, this vocation, realized in the presence of God, is not a linear progression from place to place stretched out over the temporal canon of past, present and future. We do not leave the past behind, while hurrying to vacate the present in order to achieve the self-fulfilled future. Time is not the stage where vocation is played out; time itself has a part in this drama. Time exists in the presence of God. In this presence, the past is never absent, even though it has happened; the past is always distinguished from the present. The past has a presence without being present, which is taking place now. The future is the place towards which the present is taking us. Therefore, we can say that the present has an origin and a destiny, which are demarcated not only by past and future, but also by the movement from place towards another place, a type of temporal and spatial movement that occurs in the presence of God and as this presence. The vocation of time and place reflects and is realized ultimately by the movement of God. Since this origin and destiny of vocation is in the presence of God, we would not say that origin is ever separated from destiny; they both remain distinctive but not absent from each other. The origin of vocation always has the horizon of destiny, while this vocational destiny always has its generative origin. Can we then name such a place, a place that abides as origin and destiny in the presence of God? A place where past, present and future chart the vocational movement without ever leaving it behind in the annals of an objectivist history? A place where past, present and future always belong, never absent, but also never subsumed into one defining moment? Located in such a place, our present theological speech and activity would explore the promise of the past and proclaim the fidelity of the future. There is such a place where the vocation of Christian theology can be located; this place is called Jerusalem.

Jerusalem: Origin of Vocation

The origin of God's call to life is, in a sense, located initially within God – the Triune 'vocation' to be God: the movement of the divine persons from and towards each other within God is the nature of God, and thus this nature is constituted as both origin and destiny. However, the call of God into God's life to those who do not already have this life, who are alienated from its vocational potential, is issued in a place marked by a time and a history that cannot be accounted for without speaking of God. Such a place is Jerusalem, a place with its accustomed patterns of speaking of God, and where these patterns are fulfilled and disrupted by God's own speech in the life, death and resurrection of Jesus of Nazareth. Theology originates where our patterns of speech about God and about ourselves and the world are fulfilled and disrupted by God's Word, and where we then learn to speak again of God, of ourselves and of the world in ways that are transparent to God's now Word-ed presence. What Jerusalem was, and what it represented, is the location for the origin of theology. Furthermore, as Jerusalem served as the central place in the temple tradition for the epiphany of the presence of God, the place where all other places are to receive their vocation, Jerusalem remains the central place for theology, the original location of faithful speech. However, when speaking of and from Jerusalem, we are not engaged in a fantasy of ideas or in a putative normative nominalism. Rather, we are confronted with a history, with speech that happened, with events that cannot be separated from their original narration and somehow re-located (demythologized) within the familiarity that belongs to the places of our various origins. The primary and principal example of this original and originating narration is the resurrection of Jesus. If we want to talk about the resurrection of Jesus in a contemporary idiom, whatever that might be, we cannot do so faithfully without learning the narrative(s) of the original event, without practising speaking in that way. We cannot speak faithfully of the resurrection without allowing the resurrection to speak as itself. This does not mean that nothing else can ever be said about the resurrection except what is found in the original narratives (one would then cease to do theology). What it does mean is that when we speak of the resurrection of Jesus, we are truly and really speaking of *that* resurrection in all its narrative and historical specificity. Indeed, one would not be faithful to the original event unless its narrative availability both shaped and provoked our contemporary theological efforts, our speaking of God. The resurrection of Jesus is the origin of the resurrection of theological narrative and history. To retreat once again into our own minds, stories, events and cultures, to elide God's disruption, is to re-enter the empty tomb and to analyse and speculate as to its meaning and possible truth-claims. The vocation found in God's presence cannot be heard in the echo chamber of our own voices and minds. God is found where God finds us, where God's life is both eternal and historical, comprehensive and particular, universal and local, where we freely (sacrificially) inhabit God's freedom for us.

The resurrection of Jesus presented a series of questions: what does this event mean for Jesus, for God, for us and for the world? The Church came to exist as the embodiment of answering these questions, and theology originated as the attempt to provide the answers. Thus, we could say that the origination and development of the New Testament is located where the risen Jesus appeared, his living presence initiated a narrative telling others who this is, and who God truly is, and who we are as called to stand in this presence. Furthermore, what came to be deemed the Old Testament was received as a necessary companion to the New Testament, because we cannot tell who Jesus is (telling as both recognition and proclamation) without it. Scripture is not exclusively then a text, or a collection of texts, for ever-sophisticated analysis. Rather, Scripture is the textual witness to the presence and agency of God; Scripture exists within the relational tension and paradox between God and ourselves. For theology, Scripture is that book we discover when we inhabit the strange territory where the risen Jesus appears, showing us that his presence cannot be found in that place where we talk about persons who can no longer speak for themselves. The 'meaning' of Scripture is not located within the tombs to which we assign it through the 'pure act' of our minds and wills. That is, the theological appreciation of Scripture does not reside within the empty tomb but within the mystery of witness and presence that takes place on the road to Emmaus. Theological exploration is not the typology of the familiar; it is the perception of God's surprising presence. We read, hear and study Scripture in order to encounter God, and this encounter opens before us a vision of ourselves and of the world that has an abiding witness in Scripture itself. Theology is neither the product of textual analysis nor a prisoner of textual propositions. Scripture makes theology possible because it displays a world existing in the presence of God. The vocation of theology is entering this imaginative world and exiting the tombs of our self-referential storytelling. Scripture then is not so much a text(s) given to understanding and repetition; it grounds the imaginative place before the presence of God. Scripture conveys the territory where Jesus is known to appear, where God makes things happen and where lives are transparent to God's transformative will for us and for the world.

As witness to God's saving presence, Scripture is the source of theology. The vocation of theology originates in the contemplation of Scripture, within our attentive presence to God's abiding textual presence. The origin of theology is the place where we listen for God's address, where we are formed into an expectant life. While Scripture is the source of theology, it is never theologically left behind. The theologian and the Church are called always to return to this originating source, inhabiting the imaginative place created by the presence of God. Theology moves from this place without ever exiting it.

There is more to the theological life than engaging Scripture, for this life not only has a source; it has a shape. This shape is called tradition. For Anglican theology, tradition is not a distinctive source of God's revelation; tradition is never an appeal to itself. Rather, as source of theology, Scripture has a tradition of its interpretation and of its employment for the development of the Church's authoritative teaching. Scripture does not stand alone without a scriptural and ecclesial tradition. The Anglican referral to the primitive Church, or to the ancient tradition, constitutes its appeal to Scripture. This is the recognition that Scripture is the traditional source of theology; we do not approach Scripture without entering the tradition of its own constitution and consequences. That is, our theological relationship to Scripture eschews any approach that would isolate the individual interpreter from the body of believers, and from the recognizable patterns of this body's behaviour. As the source of theology, Scripture belongs to a corporate life, a normative gathering for the sake of hearing and embodying the Word of God. Scripture is not a phase of theological discourse; we do not speak of Scripture and *then* tradition, a past yielding to an ever-new (novel?) present. Tradition is the way Scripture is present in this theological moment.

Tradition provides theology with recognizable patterns of fidelity, with normative belief, teaching and behaviour that manifest both the reality and the possibility of a corporate life accountable to the Triune agency of God, i.e. the ecclesial Body of Christ. The handing on of this belief, teaching and behaviour takes place within this Body, and as this Body. In order then to speak of God, theology will inhabit this Body, turning to its generative source (Scripture) and taking the shape of its faithful life (tradition). However, this habitation of theology is not a fixed location, a place confined to the temporal boundaries of an institution. Being placed within the tradition of this Body is being taken up into the movement of vocation, into the imaginative world before the presence of God, a world that will not rest until it finds its comprehensive repose in that divine presence.

Jerusalem: Destiny of Vocation

Theology is a movement, and tradition is its trajectory. A vision of where we are going is obtained from where we are and by what brought us to this place. Tradition is the abiding structures, disciplines and beliefs that continually place us in the presence of God and at the mercy of God's agency. Thus, tradition is more of a vulnerable and risky venture than a repetitive achievement of stability and inevitability. Traditional structures, disciplines and beliefs remove our perennial temptations to make things happen, to seek solace in our own agency. Rather, traditional beliefs and behaviours are the ways to escape the realm of ourselves as first causes and as foundational principles. Tradition provides the coordinates of the space where we find the capacity to repent of self-generation and discover the willingness to receive new life. This is why true traditional theology, or theological tradition, is never the practice of restoration but of renewal. We are not called to go back to the beginnings of history; we are called to inhabit God's future for us, God as our common future. Tradition is our map to the Promised Land.

The Anglican appeal to the ancient tradition of the Church is not an exercise in theological nostalgia; it is a provocation to reflect on what is common to all later traditions of ecclesial identities and differences. An appeal to a common tradition is an anamnetic act, a call to remember that all churches and Christians have a common destiny. The remembrance of the historical Jerusalem as origin of vocation should provoke the expectation, and the kenotic realization, of common destiny in the heavenly Jerusalem. This is a purgative remembrance that allows for the illuminative perception of God's common vocation for us: 'your will be done on earth as it is in heaven'. Tradition then is not the servant of our efforts to maintain the distinctive boundaries between our various ecclesial and doctrinal territories. The Body of Christ does not have multiple futures; it has one common future for all of its members, and we are baptized into that common future. The celebration of the Eucharist is not the maintenance of distinctive ecclesial identities; it is the sacrament of heaven. The vocation of theology is accountable to the imaginative fulfilment of God's will for us, for the Church and for the life of the world. Vocation is going somewhere, to a place of God's transparent presence and unmediated agency.

While Scripture is the source, and tradition the shape, of the vocation of theology, reason is its imaginative disposition, thinking in the presence of God. Thus reason is not an act with its own inherent purpose and direction; there is always already the one thinking and that about which one is thinking. Reason does not escape the cogitative continuum between the subjective and the objective. Reason is not a sanctuary protected from Scripture and tradition. Returning to the above reflection on the formation of the theologian, reason undergoes formation; we are formed as thinkers in the presence of God. How we live shapes how we think; what we live for directs our thinking towards its desired object/subject. For theology, reason is both disposition and desire. Theology places us in the presence of God, and this presence is always a movement from its textual witness in Scripture and is recognized by its traditional shape. Reason operates within this place ordered to its imaginative actuality and fulfilment. This is why, for the vocation of theology, reason is not essentially for attaining knowledge for its own sake, or for the practical possibilities for its utility. Reason is how we desire the knowledge of God, the desire born from the love of God. All theological thinking, all methodologies, are destined for the contemplation of God's presence; analysis is subsumed into doxology. Orthodoxy is inhabiting the place where and whereby we are moving into the presence of God the Father, the presence offered to us in God the Son and by God the Holy Spirit. Orthodoxy is being moved in the right direction, towards the doxological destiny of the heavenly Jerusalem, the place where God's agency is the freedom of thought and behaviour for which we have longed, the freedom found beyond the tomb. Ultimately, reason is beholding the mystery of God and knowing ourselves made in God's image in the face of Jesus Christ. The vocation of Anglican theology has its source in Scripture, its shape within tradition and its imaginative future through reason. The vocation of Anglican theology is to bring people into the presence of God, and then to see what happens.

Introduction to the Sources

When we ask what are the sources of Anglican theology, we are faced with two basic considerations. First, we enquire regarding the sources of theology itself. That is, with the Anglican custom in mind of not claiming to have its own distinctive theology, but rather a theology rooted in Scripture, with a form relying on the heritage of the early Church, along with the exercise of reason, we can delve into the basic, non-unique, sources of Christian theology. However, there is an Anglican theological tradition, and this tradition does have texts of various kinds that have served to nurture and direct faithful Anglicans and the several churches that now comprise the global Anglican Communion. While not having a confessional or magisterial structure, this tradition does have distinctive contours and habitual references. Anglicans will refer to the different Books of Common Prayer, the Thirty-Nine Articles, the Book of Homilies and to theologians such as Richard Hooker, Lancelot Andrewes or Charles Gore. There are sources of the Anglican tradition that were formative in the constitution of this tradition as such, and then there are Anglican theologians that are influential to particular groups within the Anglican theological orbit. In other words, certain groups of Anglicans refer to certain Anglican theologians as authoritative; not all Anglicans doing theology will reference the same Anglican theologians. The further we get away from the sixteenth century, the more these references become distinctive of the perspective of various gatherings and theological concerns of Anglicans. That is, the question of Anglican theological sources can become as partisan as the Anglicans asking this question.

What is the question behind the question of theological sources, whether distinctively Anglican or not? It is the question of truth, which for theology is always already the question of God. Furthermore, this question of truth as a proper theological question is never posed in the abstract; it is never a question that exists in a vacuum. The question is asked because we as theologians find ourselves within a conceptual, historical, linguistic and liturgical tradition in which truth is spoken, present, obeyed and adored. When it comes to asking 'What is truth?' we share the position of Pilate before the presence of Jesus, but we do not share his place within the philosophical, religious and civil authorities of that moment of asking. We are members of the Body of Christ, and to ask this question is to ask ourselves whether we live and believe truly. Truth is the presence of Christ, realized by the Holy Spirit, where and whereby we find ourselves before the Father.

Each of the following excerpts from Anglican theologians addresses the nature of the truth, and how this truth is lived and known. The trajectory of their arguments begins in Christ but then reaches out towards a comprehensive vision of truth in which we meet science, philosophy, religions and all of humanity. It is an apprehension of truth that is catholic, because it is Christological, comprehensive, because it is pneumatological, and ecclesial, because it is sacramental. Knowing the truth is rooted in the knowledge of Christ made possible by the Holy Spirit, but knowing this truth is not confined to the boundaries of the Church or of dogma. Likewise, knowing this truth issues from living the truth through discipline and worship. Hence, the work of theology cannot be extradited from the formation of the theologian.

Sources

Jeremy Taylor, 'Via Intelligentiae', in *Jeremy Taylor: Classics of Western Spirituality*, Thomas K. Carroll (ed.), New York: Paulist Press, 1990, pp. 355–88.

But therefore since we are so miserable, and are in error, and have wandered very far, we must do as wandering travellers use to do, go back just to that place from whence they wandered, and begin upon a new account. Let us go to the truth itself, to Christ, and He will tell us an easy way of ending all our quarrels: for we shall find Christianity to be the easiest and the hardest thing in the world: it is like a secret in arithmetic, infinitely hard till it be found out by a right operation, and then it is so plain, we wonder we did not understand earlier.

I know I am in an auditory of inquisitive persons, whose business is to study for truth, that they may find it for themselves and teach it unto others: I am in a school of prophets and prophets' sons, who all ask Pilate's question, 'What is truth?' You look for it in your books, and you tug hard for it in your disputations, and you derive it from the cisterns of the fathers, and you enquire after the old ways, and sometimes are taken with new appearances, and you rejoice in false lights, or are delighted with little umbrages and peep of day. But where is there a man, or a society of men, that can be at rest in his enquiry, and is sure he understands all the truths of God?

And this is the only way which Christ hath taught us: if you ask, 'What is truth?' you must not do as Pilate did, ask the question, and then go away from Him that only can give you an answer: for as God is the author of truth, so He is the teacher of it; and the way to learn it is this of my text: for so saith our blessed Lord, 'If any man will do His will, he shall know of the doctrine whether it be of God or no.'

The way to judge of religion is by doing of our duty; and theology is rather a divine life than a divine knowledge. In heaven indeed we shall first see, and then love; but here on earth we must first love, and love will open our eyes as well as our hearts, and we shall then see and perceive and understand. Holiness is the only way of truth and understanding.

It remains therefore that we enquire what is that immediate principle or means by which we shall certainly and infallibly be led into all truth, and be taught the mind of God, and understand all His secrets; and this is worth our knowledge. I cannot say that this will end your labours, and put a period to your studies, and make your learning easy; it may possibly increase your labour, but it will make it profitable; it will not end your studies, but it will direct them; it will not make human learning easy, but it will make it wise unto salvation, and conduct it into true notices and ways of wisdom.

I am now to describe to you the right way of knowledge: *Qui facit voluntatem Patris mei*, saith Christ, that's the way; 'do God's will, and you shall understand God's word.'

Now in this enquiry I must take one thing for a *præcognitum*, that every good man is 'taught of God': and indeed unless He teach us, we shall make but ill scholars ourselves, and worse guides to others.

There is in every righteous man a new vital principle; the Spirit of grace is the Spirit of wisdom, and teaches us by secret inspiration, by proper arguments, by actual persuasions, by personal applications, by effects and energies: and as the soul of a man is the cause of all his vital operations, so is the Spirit of God the life of that life, and the cause of all actions and productions spiritual.

Charity makes the best scholars. No sermons can edify you, no scriptures can build you up a holy building to God, unless the love of God be in your hearts.

But that we may speak not only things mysterious, but things intelligible; how does it come to pass, by what means and what economy is it effected, that a holy life is the best determination of all questions, and the surest way of knowledge? Is it to be supposed that a godly man is better enabled to determine the questions of purgatory or transubstantiation? Is the gift of chastity the best way to reconcile Thomas and Scotus? and is a temperate man always a better scholar than a drunkard? To this I answer, that in all things in which true wisdom consists, holiness, which is the best wisdom, is the surest way of understanding them.

For that which we are taught by the holy Spirit of God, this new nature, this vital principle within us, it is that which is worth our learning; not vain and empty, idle and insignificant notions, in which when you have laboured till your eyes are fixed in their orbs, and your flesh unfixed from its bones, you are no better and no wiser. If the Spirit of God be your teacher, He will teach you such truths as will make you know and love God, and become like to Him, and enjoy Him for ever, by passing from similitude to union and eternal fruition.

Too many scholars have lived upon air and empty notions for many ages past, and troubled themselves with tying and untying knots, like hypochondriacs in a fit of melancholy, thinking of nothing, and troubling themselves with nothing, and falling out about nothings, and being very wise and very learned in things that are not and work not, and were never planted in paradise by the finger of God. Men's notions are too often like the mules, begotten by equivocal and unnatural generations; but they make no species: they are begotten, but they can beget nothing; they are the effects of long study, but they can do no good when they are produced: they are not that which Solomon calls *via intelligentiæ*, 'the way of understanding'. If the Spirit of God be our teacher, we shall learn to avoid evil, and to do good, to be wise and to be holy, to be profitable and careful: and they that walk in this way shall find more peace in their consciences, more skill in the scriptures, more satisfaction in their doubts, than can be obtained by all the polemical and impertinent disputations of the world.

It is not by reading multitudes of books, but by studying the truth of God: it is not by laborious commentaries of the doctors that you can finish your work, but by the expositions of the Spirit of God: it is not by the rules of metaphysics, but by the proportions of holiness: and when all books are read, and all arguments examined, and all authorities alleged, nothing can be found to be true that is unholy.

F. J. A. Hort, *The Way, The Truth, and The Life (1871)*, Cambridge: Cambridge University Press, 2009, pp. 75–94.

Nor is the character of truth changed by the form in which it is originally acquired: it is no merely verbal bond which unites truth of revelation to truth of discovery. Whether God might be expected to bestow, and whether as a matter of fact He has bestowed, a truth beyond discovery, are legitimate enquiries; though all consistent Christian faith implies the answer. But neither these enquiries, nor any attempts to determine the limits of a revelation, can alter the relations of discovered and revealed truth, supposing both to exist. Truth of discovery is received by every one except the discoverer as much from without as if it were revealed. Truth of revelation remains inert till it has been appropriated by a human working of recognition which it is hard to distinguish from that of discovery. Its initial authority is the first step in a commendation of itself to the conscience and reason, if not of each and at once, yet of many and part by part; in which experience of what lies within the domain of experience becomes in turn the legitimate assurance of what lies above experience.

Once more, theological truth is not divided from other truth by the inscrutable nature of its subject matter. If the revealed knowledge of God receives its form from the limits and peculiarities of human faculty, yet no kind of human knowledge is exempt from the same condition. Theological reflexion does but disturb the habitual unconsciousness which deludes us as to what is involved in the apprehension of any object whatever by finite beings. In like manner the special contradictions which are found to beset all thought on things Divine have their counterparts in every province of knowledge, the moment we lift our eyes from the ground which surrounds our own feet to look into the vanishing distance before and behind. The truth of God revealed in Christ calls not for the separate exercise of an unique faculty, but for the cooperation of every power by which we can read ourselves, and hold converse with whatever is not ourselves. Christian theology has in it indeed an element which other knowledge has not; but it embraces all elements that are scattered elsewhere.

In the Christian revelation, as we have already seen, the knowledge of truth was for the first time set in its proper place as necessary to sound life and rightful action. But further its own proper subject was the knowledge of God, and this was the knowledge which it set before mankind to be learned first. The whole range of truth contained in Christ was, so to speak, opened from above: the first truth disclosed in Him was the truth of God. This truth alone was essential to the most indispensable of the gifts given in Christ, the life of the spirit in faith, hope, and love, and thus to the constraining of all lower things into the service of life. As the fear of God is the beginning of all wisdom, so the knowledge of God is the surest entrance into all knowledge. Through the primacy of the theology all the parts of knowledge are best maintained in their true place, and knowledge itself holds its true place amidst that which is not knowledge.

For, as we stand between things above and things below, and our knowledge like our nature partakes of both, the truth which we recognize must lead us either upwards or downwards. It has always been hard for man to stand erect while discarding the truth of God sent down from heaven. It was hard of old, while he seemed to himself to be an independent being, severed by an impassable chasm from all lower things, and therefore able to pursue a separate perfection. But now, as the chasm closes, and the earth's full force permitted to act on man, it becomes impossible for him to lift up his head in his ancient dignity unless there be a countervailing force from on high. No god-like thoughts or feelings within, no conjectured or fabricated divinities without, can restore him to himself, much less raise him to the better self towards which he fain would still aspire. When once he has learned to know truth, he cannot be permanently sustained by any power which is separate from truth. Nothing less will avail than the true God in the heavens, truly known, as He is known to His Church in His Son Jesus Christ our Lord. If the children of God find it a hard struggle to resist the fostering earth when she draws them down in the might of her own partial truth, yet He who said 'I am the Truth' said also 'I if I be lifted up out of the earth will draw all men unto Myself.'

As we can seldom bathe ourselves in the freshness of living things without coming forth with purified and brightened hearts, even such let us believe may be the effect of the truth of nature on our thoughts of God Himself. The substance of our faith in Him can come only from that one Life and Death and Resurrection into the fellowship of which we as men are permitted to enter; and the primary lore through which our faith is deepened and enlarged is always the human lore, the knowledge of what men have done and thought and felt, and above all of their words, the most comprehensive treasure-house of their experience. But the earth as well as the heaven is full of God's glory, and His visible glory is but the garment of His truth; so that every addition to truth becomes a fresh opportunity for adoration.

Thus the strictest sense of Christ's words 'I am the Truth' is also the most comprehensive: it answers alike to the requirements of the hour when it was spoken, and to the gradual fulfilment of the Divine kingdom. It points first to that manifestation of the unseen God of which He spoke when He said 'He that hath seen me hath seen the Father'; while it includes in its ultimate scope all creation, the world of nature of which He is the Life, and the world of man whom He redeemed out of nature, and of whom He is both the Life and the Light. This second declaration like the first spoke comfort and hope to the faint-hearted disciples by disclosing to them the depth and range of the Lord's own permanent working, and therefore of the work which they were to carry forward in His name. It speaks comfort and hope in like manner to all at any time who find themselves perplexed by the presence of truth not before known. It warns of the danger of suffering truth to lose its rightful place in work and devotion. It marks every truth which seems alien to Christ as a sign that the time is come for a better knowledge of Christ, since no truth can be alien to Him who is the Truth. It points to Him in His eternal fulness as the one sufficient measure by which all truth may find its proper station.

This at least let us who have been taught by the Gospel believe, that no faith founded on truth can ever die except that it may rise to a better life. Believed or not believed, known or not known, it abides for ever in heaven till the hour appointed by the Father. In so far as we have hitherto been content not to know Him whom we have believed, let us thankfully learn to know Him better now, for so only shall we be persuaded that He is able to guard that which He has committed to our charge, and committed it for stewardship and distribution, and not for hoard.

The pursuit of truth begins in a sense of freedom. We almost make truth itself the symbol of freedom for the workings of our minds. We are slow to learn that truth is never that which we choose to believe, but always that which we are under a necessity to believe. In proportion to the earnestness of the pursuit we discover that we must needs be servants where we thought to be masters. A life devoted to truth is a life of vanities abased and ambitions forsworn. We have to advance far in the willing servitude before we recognise that it is creating for us a new and another freedom. The early dream was not false: only freedom comes last, not first. The order of experience corresponds with the order of the Lord's promises which He offered to those who had begun to believe Him: 'If ye abide in my word, ye are truly disciples of mine', and then 'ye shall know the truth, and' then 'the truth shall make you free'.

Charles Gore, *'What is Truth?' A Sermon Preached at S. Barnabas, Oxford, on Trinity Sunday, 1879*, Oxford: James Parker and Co., 1880, pp. 3–16.

Christian faith, my brethren, is not primarily faith in a system or a doctrine, or a creed, but in something which lies behind all these and gives them their meaning: it is faith in Jesus Christ, a living Person divine and human. When He appeared teaching and working among men, they were drawn to Him, not because He preached a doctrine and proved it by a miracle, but because of *what He was*.

If indeed the Church had always been made up of faithful Christians we might have done without the Athanasian Creed; but as things actually were, if the realities of Christian life do, as in fact they do, depend upon the conscious and clear communion with God the Father, the Incarnate Son, and the Indwelling Spirit, to preserve the recognition of those realities intact through barbaric confusion and the intellectual strife of tongues, needed nothing less than such a formula as the Athanasian Creed. For, look at it. What is it? Omitting for the moment the warning – miscalled 'damnatory' – clauses, how is it made up? It asserts that the Father is God, the Only-begotten Son is God, and the Holy Ghost proceeding from them is God, and that the three are yet one God, – that the Son remaining God was made perfectly man, and died for us, and rose and ascended, and will come in judgment. This is absolutely all: and of all this nothing is abstract, nothing far off from us; it is just the alphabet of the Christian religion.

The Creed is only an explicit expression in a dogmatic formula of what every worshipper of Christ and the Holy Ghost must acknowledge; and he who has so expressed his faith in a formula, or acknowledged it so expressed, is in a better position than he was before that process, just as we are in a better position as regards any subject when we have thought what we meant by it than we were before.

This central faith in Father, Son, and Spirit is all the Creed expresses. Why then is it so long? It is not the love of defining, but the love of contemplating and adoring Divine Truth which makes the Creed so long; and the more we love to contemplate and adore it, the more we come to realize and live it, to know and to rejoice in it, the more we shall find this Creed the natural expression of our feelings. The Creed does little in the way of defining; all the ideas of uncreatedness, incomprehensibility, and the rest are included in the idea of God: if Christ and the Holy Spirit are God, they are of necessity and confessedly also eternal, coequal, uncreate, incomprehensible, almighty, Lord; and when the Creed comes to express the relation between the Divine Person, with a reverent caution as stepping on holy ground, it uses simply the words of Scripture, 'begotten', 'proceeding', without any attempt at explaining. Thus the Creed expresses this spirit only – a humble, simple Christian faith in a living, loving Person, which has been forced to explain and guard itself by the rise of false doctrines destructive of the foundation of its life and worship, and which in doing this has tried simply to be clear and unmistakeable, without argument or philosophical reasoning, while at the same time it loves in adoring contemplation to dwell upon and to reiterate the truths it is stating.

What is Christianity? It is God's final and absolute revelation of himself on earth. God all along has been revealing Himself, all along the Light has been coming into the world, 'in many parts and many manners'. He has spoken to the Jew pre-eminently, but also in conscience and religion in a measure to all the nations of the earth. But all these other religions stand to Christianity (at the best) as the partial to the complete, as the transitory to the final, as the local to the universal, as what is dim and veiled to what is clear and revealed. Christ came as the final and authoritative revelation of God – the supreme Light.

The Creed, first of all, does *not* say that a heathen who has never heard of Christ is lost: if he has never heard *of* Christ, yet if he is living up to the light of conscience, he has *heard Christ*: for Christ is present and working (let us never forget it) in Nature as in Grace: He speaks in Nature as in Grace. Implicitly then in the life of such a heathen is involved faith in Christ, which is faith in the Trinity. It is there in him, only circumstances prevent it from expressing itself in this life; and in the next he will recognise the truth as it is.

In all such cases let us think this – if a man is obeying the call of God, listening to the claim of God, however in conscience or religion it comes to him, that man is, though he know it not, *believing Christ*: and that man, though not now, shall consciously at last *'think rightly'* of the Trinity. Upon his eyes after death shall break the vision of God, and he having welcomed the truth all along shall welcome it then.

And he who loves the light here in humility and self-surrender is living in faith; and if not here in knowledge too, yet, if it be not by his own choice, that too shall come before the day of judgment.

But we must return, finally, to ourselves. What for us is the message of Trinity Sunday? It comes to tell us what truth is and bid us reverence it. 'I am the truth', says Christ. It comes with the appeal of perfect love and the claim of absolute authority, not as something which belongs to us, which we possess, something to be proud of and to boast ourselves in. Oh, no! It possesses us, not we it: it comes from above upon us in might and in love: it comes in the conscience, see we reverence it; it comes in Nature, see we recognise it: but it comes, above all, in Christ: He claims the reverence, the faith, the love of our whole heart and soul and will and intellect for Himself. Listen, then, to His appeal as it comes with the confirmation, if any be needed, of the great cloud of witnesses, of all who from the beginning have washed their robes and made them white in the blood of the Lamb, who through faith have pleased God. Recognise that appeal, and – not blindly, but counting the costs – yield yourselves to it with a whole-hearted love. It comes, true, with warning, if you like, with threats: but do we call it a threat in a father if he sees his child by the precipice's edge and bids it clutch tight his hand or it will fall over? Such is the threat of the Athanasian Creed. It is the threat of truth, that, if we reject her, we perish; a threat which is all love. Accept, then, the Truth: welcome it: rejoice in it: do not be ashamed of it. And then, above all, go out and live it; live in its magnificent possibilities, in its ennobling privileges, in its splendid traditions: so shall ye know the Truth, and ever more and more shall it make you free; free from the lusts which so beset us, free from the tyranny of the world, free from the snares of the devil, free, through hard struggling, but free at last. Go out in its power! Go out in its love! for 'this is the victory that overcometh the world, even our faith: who is he that overcometh the world but he that believeth that Jesus is the Son of God?' Faith and life are closely bound up; nay, they are the same thing from different sides. Do not forget that.

Arthur Michael Ramsey, *The Gospel and the Catholic Church*, London: Longmans, second edition; 1956, pp. 120–35.

JESUS CHRIST is not only the Way and the Life. He is also the Truth; and the Church, which is His Body, is commissioned to teach the Truth. How shall the Church know where to find what is true, and, how, after finding it, shall the Church assimilate it so as to proclaim it with authority to men?

The answer to these questions has, in Christian history, been sought specially in two phrases, 'the authority of the Bible' and 'the authority of the Church'. Some have turned to the Bible as a whole or to the New Testament, and have said in effect, 'Propositions about God which we find here are true; those which we do not find here are unwarranted or false.' Others have turned to the Church as a divine institution and have said in effect, 'This institution is divinely inspired. What it teaches (semper et ubique et ab omnibus) is true.' We are not to say that either of these methods is wrong; but neither of them goes deep enough. The deeper questions are these. What does the Bible mean by 'Truth'? What did our Lord mean when He said 'I am the Truth'? and what does the word 'truth' mean on the lips of the Church's teachers? It is not enough, and it may be even misleading to assert that Truth is found in the Bible and in the Church. We must ask, 'What is this Truth which has created both the Church and the Bible?'

In the light of the meaning of the words 'Truth' and 'Wisdom' in the New Testament the nature of the Church's doctrine and authority becomes plain. These facts emerge inescapably from our biblical study.

(1) The Wisdom of God is working through all created life, and far and wide is the sustainer and the inspirer of the thought and the endeavour of men. The Church will therefore reverence every honest activity of the minds of men; it will perceive that therein the Spirit of God is moving, and it will tremble lest by denying this, in word or in action, it blaspheme the Spirit of God. But Wisdom cannot be thus learnt in all its fulnesss. The mind and the eye of man are distorted by sin and self-worship; and the Wisdom which the Spirit of God unfolds throughout the world can lead to blindness and to deceit unless men face the fact of sin and the need for redemption.

Hence, (2) the Church proclaims the Wisdom of God, set forth in its very essence in the crucifixion of Jesus Christ, a Wisdom learnt when men are brought to the crisis of repentance and to the resulting knowledge of self and of God. The Wisdom of the Cross seems at first to deny the wisdom of the Spirit of God in the created world; it scandalizes men's sense of the good and the beautiful. But the Christians, who have first faced the scandal, discover in the Cross a key to the meaning of all creation. The Cross unlocks its secrets and its sorrows, and interprets them in terms of the power of God.

Thus (3), the Wisdom uttered in the Cross has created the Church and is expressed through the Church's whole life as the Body of Christ crucified and risen. The Church's work in thinking and interpreting and teaching is inseparable from the Church's life in Christ. Its authority is Christ Himself, known in the building up of the one Body in Truth and in Love. Hence 'orthodoxy' means not only 'right opinion', but also 'right worship' or 'true glory', after the Biblical meaning of the word *doxa*; for life and thought and worship are inseparable activities in the body of Christ. *kai etheasametha ten doxan autou.*

In these three ways the Church will be faithful to the Biblical meaning of Truth, by reverencing the works of God everywhere and the Spirit of God manifested in the endeavours of men's minds; by keeping before itself and before men the scandal of the Cross; and by remembering that orthodoxy means not only correct propositions about God, but the life of the One Body of Christ in the due working of all its members.

It follows that the Church can never be said to have apprehended the truth. Rather is the Truth the divine action which apprehends the Church. Dimly it understands what it teaches. For the more the Church learns of God, the more it is aware of the incomprehensible mystery of His being, in creation and in transcendence and on the Cross.

Ineffable, therefore, is the revelation of God, which creates and which uses the teaching Church. Human languages can never express it. Yet the Church, like its Lord, must partly commit it to human speech and thought, and is indeed commissioned to do this in every age and civilization. Hence have appeared the Canon of Scripture and the Creeds; both express and both control the Church's teaching. But, since Truth and life and worship are inseparable, the Scriptures and the Creeds are not given for use in isolation. They form, with the ministry and the sacraments, one close-knit structure which points the Christians to the historical facts wherein God is revealed, and to the life and experience of the universal society. The Creeds, therefore, have authority not as scholastic definitions of Christianity, but as a part of the structure which points behind scholasticism and philosophy to the Messianic work of Jesus. They point away from speculative theories which would swamp the Gospel, and from partial or ephemeral definitions which would distort its proportions. But the Creeds are not in themselves the Christian Faith; Christians do not 'believe in the Creeds,' but, with the Creeds to help them, they believe in God.

We began with the Bible. The books of the old covenant disclose a Church and a Passion; Jesus Christ fulfils them both, and in His Passion the Church of the new covenant is born. In the midst of this Church His saving work is known through a new access of men to God. This access is in one Spirit and in one Body, and the outward order of the Church points to the events whence this access has come and to the universal life wherein it is made complete. The Faith of the Bible therefore leads straight to the Catholic Church, but this gets its meaning only from the Gospel of God. Thus the general trend of our earlier chapters is corroborated by the specific study of the phrase *he aletheia tou theou*.

Thus interpreted, Catholicism is not a burden upon the mind of the thoughtful Christian but rather the means whereby he can be free. For it frees him from partial rationalisms, such as have identified Christianity with the Bible or with some scholastic system or with some humanistic shibboleth; and it delivers him into an orthodoxy which no individual and no group can possess, since it belongs only to the building up of the one Body in love. As he receives the Catholic sacrament and recites the Catholic creed, the Christian is learning that no single movement nor partial experience within Christendom can claim his final obedience, and that a local Church can claim his loyalty only by leading him beyond itself to the universal family which it represents. Hence the Catholic order is not a hierarchical tyranny, but the means of deliverance into the Gospel of God and the timeless Church.

So far, therefore, from foreclosing the activities of the human mind the Catholicism of the Gospel bids men to think as freely and as fearlessly as they can, and by saving them from rationalisms it enables them to use their reason to the full. For 'all things were made by Him', and all honest endeavour in science, in philosophy, in art, in history, manifests the Spirit of God. But the key to these mysteries of nature and of man is the Word-made-flesh. Hither alone the Church shall point; and here men shall know the Truth, and the Truth shall make them free.

Bibliography

Pre-Reformation

Anselm of Canterbury, *Proslogion*.
Augustine of Hippo, *On Christian Doctrine*.
Bonaventure, *The Mind's Road to God*.

Gregory of Nazianzus, *Theological Orations*.
Origen, *On First Principles*.
Thomas Aquinas, *Summa Theologiae*, Part I, Ch. 1 'Sacred Doctrine', Ch. 16 'Truth', and Ch. 26 'The Beatitude of God'.
G. R. Evans (ed.), *The Medieval Theologians*, Oxford: Wiley-Blackwell, 2001.
G. R. Evans (ed.), *The First Christian Theologians*, Oxford: Wiley-Blackwell, 2004.

Post-Reformation

Hans Urs von Balthasar, *The Glory of the Lord: A Theological Aesthetics*, Vol. 1, Seeing The Form, second edition, San Francisco: Ignatius Press, 2009.
Karl Barth, *The Göttingen Dogmatics*, Grand Rapids, MI: Eerdmans, 1991.
Yves Congar, *A History of Theology*, New York: Doubleday and Company, Inc., 1968.
Hans Frei, *Types of Christian Theology*, New Haven, CT: Yale University Press, 1992.
David Ford, *The Modern Theologians*, third edition, Oxford: Wiley-Blackwell, 2005.
Robert Jenson, *Systematic Theology*, Vol. I, Oxford: Oxford University Press, 2001.
Andrew Louth, *Discerning the Mystery*, Oxford: Oxford University Press, 1990.
Wolfhart Pannenberg, *Systematic Theology*, Vol. I, Grand Rapids, MI: Eerdmans, 1991.
John Webster, Kathryn Tanner and Iain Torrance (eds), *The Oxford Handbook of Systematic Theology*, Oxford: Oxford University Press, 2009.

2

The Trinity

RICHARD NORRIS

'What is the Trinity?', asks the Catechism in the American *Book of Common Prayer*. It then answers its own question, as catechisms do: 'The Trinity is one God, Father, Son, and Holy Spirit.'[1] This brisk statement is perhaps not very helpful to enquirers, any more than is the fuller affirmation in the Thirty-Nine Articles of Religion: 'There is but one living and true God and in the unity of this Godhead there be three Persons, of one substance, power, and eternity; the Father, the Son, and the Holy Ghost.'[2] But if these statements are not very helpful, because they assert something puzzling without explaining it, they are very clear on one basic point. The word 'Trinity' as they understand it refers to – is simply another word for – God. In other words, the Trinity[3] is not a doctrine. It is the 'who' that Christians worship, as the ancient confession Te Deum asserts:

> Throughout the world the holy Church acclaims you; Father, of majesty unbounded, your true and only Son, worthy of all worship, and the Holy Spirit, advocate and guide.[4]

But further still, Christians do not 'worship' the Trinity in the sense that they stand off from it and gawk reverently from a safe distance. On the contrary, their worship is a kind of participation in the relations among the members of the Trinity. Otherwise, what is to be made of the words of one reasonably representative Eucharistic Prayer, which has believers ascribe 'all honor and glory' to God the Father 'through Christ and with Christ and in Christ' and 'in the unity of the Holy Spirit'?[5] It is no surprise, then, that there is a dogma regarding the Trinity: that is to say, a teaching that is both traditional and official. For how should an historical community like the Church not be clear about who and how it worships? One of the plainer formulations of this dogma, if not the most familiar, is contained in a decree (380 AD) of the Emperors Gratian, Valentinian and Theodosius:

> We command that all churches be forthwith delivered up to the bishops who confess the Father, the Son, and the Holy Spirit to be of one majesty and

---

1 *Book of Common Prayer* (USA), p. 852.
2 Article I, in *Book of Common Prayer* (USA), p. 867.
3 The word 'Trinity' is from the Latin *trinitas*, itself a rendering of the Greek term *trios*. The last two words mean (in order) 'threefoldness' and 'threesome'.
4 *Book of Common Prayer* (USA), p. 95.
5 *Book of Common Prayer* (USA), p. 375.

power, of the same glory and of one splendor; making no distinction by any profane division, but rather harmony by the assertion of the trinity of the persons and the unity of the Godhead ...[6]

That, if read carefully, states the dogma of the Trinity without wasting words; and one can go on to consult the so-called 'Athanasian' Creed,[7] or even the Niceno-Constantinopolitan Creed, which speaks of God, of God's unique Son who is 'true God from true God' and finally of the Holy Spirit, who 'proceeds from the Father' and is 'worshiped and glorified together with the Father and the Son'.

To be sure, it would be silly to suggest, at this juncture, that there is nothing more to be said about the Trinity. Dogma – what Christian tradition has defined as essentially belonging to the faith – is always something rather terse and downright. A dogma tends to say as little as possible, but to assert it very definitely. Hence a dogma is not an explication. It is a determination of a particular issue, like certain judicial verdicts. It may raise all sorts of questions. It may, and probably will, require interpretation. Once the move is made from formula to interpretation, however, one leaves the realm of dogma and enters that of catechetical doctrine and ultimately of theology, whose typical product is not a terse assertion but a two-volume treatise. One thus crosses into a realm in which people differ, because they expound the dogma from different points of view and on the basis of different insights. There is no necessary harm in this: as Richard Hooker once said, we should 'take comfort in this variety'; for as long as the explications in question are honest efforts to be true to the dogma, what emerges is the richness and depth of the reality that the dogma engages.

What will be undertaken here, therefore, is not a full-blown, much less authoritative, elaboration of the doctrine of the Trinity, but an arguable, perhaps illuminating, but in any case relatively brief, interpretation of its classical formulation. To be specific, we shall ask where the idea of God as Trinity is rooted, and answer this question by allusion to a passage in Irenaeus of Lyons (d. c.195) which itself looks back to the New Testament. Then, as we explore this formulation, we will comment on it in the light of the settlement that emerged out of the fourth-century Arian controversy – namely, the doctrine as classically set forth by the Cappadocian fathers;[8] and at the same time, weigh some of the problems under discussion in contemporary talk about the Trinity.

Roots of the Doctrine of the Trinity

It would be wrong to begin this enterprise without acknowledging that the doctrine of the Trinity strikes most people as a difficult, speculative and superfluous

---

6 *Codex Theodosianus* 16.1.3 (addressed to Auxonius, Proconsul of Asia).
7 *Book of Common Prayer* (USA), pp. 864f.
8 This expression ordinarily refers to Basil of Caesarea, called 'the Great' (d.379); his friend and ally Gregory of Nazianzus (d.389) called 'the Theologian' because of his eloquent defence of the Nicene faith in a series of addresses given in Constantinople in 380; and Basil's younger brother, Gregory of Nyssa (d. c.395).

afterthought. The very terms it employs – 'substance', for example, or '*hypostasis*' – present themselves as abstractions from abstractions; and to many folk, the whole affair seems to be no more than a bit of bad arithmetic or a ghostly metaphysical speculation whose connection with, or relevance to, human life and experience is difficult to specify. Moreover, to the Enlightenment tradition, which still shapes Western culture where questions of religion are concerned, the doctrine of the Trinity represents the acme of religious particularism and obscurantism; and this perception of it is by now a part of the cultural air that Christians breathe. To see one effect of this tradition, one has only to consider Friedrich Schleiermacher's influential work titled *The Christian Faith* (1821). That work treated the dogma of the Trinity as material for a mildly disparaging appendix, thus marking it as a near irrelevance if not an embarrassment in any serious account of Christian life and belief.

It was around a century later that, at least in Protestant circles, a revival of interest in the doctrine of the Trinity got under way. To correct the prevalent depreciation of that doctrine, the Swiss theologian Karl Barth, abruptly and without warning, repositioned it. He plucked it out of Schleiermacher's appendix and set it right at the opening of the work he called *Church Dogmatics*. Barth expounded the doctrine of the Trinity in the introductory volume (1932) of this monumental opus; and he expounded it not as an 'item' in a list of Christian doctrines, but as an immediate implication of the foundational reality of Christian faith: the self-revelation through which God is made known to human persons as one whom they may deeply trust, gladly obey and joyfully thank. This self-revelation in which 'God reveals Himself as the Lord' shows itself, Barth said, to be the revelation of a threefold Deity; for God is manifested as the One who reveals, as the One who is revealed and as the One who is the givenness of this revelation for us: in Barth's words, as Revealer, Revelation and Revealedness – Father, Son, and Spirit. These are the same God reiterated three times; for on any other hypothesis it would be impossible to say that a revelation of God has in truth occurred. Thus a form of the doctrine of the Trinity is presupposed in the very relationship that God, in the act of self-revelation – the act of speaking God's Word and making it heard – establishes with human persons.

In developing this line of thought, Barth alluded to some words of Irenaeus of Lyons – a Greek Christian writer of the late second century AD – in the latter's work *Against Heresies*.[9] On closer examination, these words indicate, better perhaps than Barth saw, the historical roots of the position he himself develops; for Irenaeus is arguably the earliest Christian author to evolve a reflective, though certainly not a perfectly self-consistent or fully developed, account of the Trinity.

In the passage Barth cited, Irenaeus urges that whenever Paul employs the title 'Christ' ('anointed one', 'messiah'), he is referring to 'Emmanuel', to 'God-with-us' (Matt. 1.23: cf. Isa. 7.14) or, as Irenaeus then rephrases his thought, to 'the Son of God made son of man'. Further, he argues that this is what the

---

9 For the quotations that follow, see *Against Heresies* (hereafter *AH*) 3.18.3; cf. 3.6.1; 3.17.1 in *Ante-Nicene Fathers*, Vol. 1, Alexander Roberts and James Donaldson (eds), Peabody, MA: Hendrickson Publishers, 1996, pp. 315–567.

title 'Christ' properly signifies. For, says Irenaeus, 'in the name "Christ", there is understood by implication the Anointer, the Anointed, and the Ointment itself with which he is anointed: but the Anointer is the Father, while the Son is anointed with the Spirit who is the Ointment, as the Word says through Isaiah: The Spirit of the Lord is upon me, for he has anointed me' (Isa. 61.1; cf. Ps. 45.7). Two centuries later, Basil of Caesarea repeated Irenaeus. Basil explained that to describe baptism as 'into Christ' is to say everything: 'For the naming of Christ is the confession of the whole [Trinity], manifesting as it does the God who gave, the Son who received, and the Spirit who is, the Ointment.'[10]

Barth's interest in this passage lay in its intimation that the focal point of the doctrine of the Trinity is 'the question of the divinity of Christ'. For present purposes, however, it is more relevant to note that what lay in the back of Irenaeus's mind was the Gospel portrayal of Jesus' baptism at the hand of John. This story, told in all four Gospels, marks the first occasion on which Jesus was manifested as 'Christ', a manifestation that in effect intimates the character of his coming ministry. Thus it seeks to set before readers the very sort of thing Barth was talking about, namely, an event of revelation, the revelation of the Anointed One.

If this is the case, however, it is worthwhile to weigh the manner of this revelation. If we ignore John and the onlookers whose presence the story presupposes, there are three participants in this scene. There is God, whose word from on high presents him as Father of this Son. There is the Son himself, Jesus, who has God as his Father. And finally there is that descending dove, the symbol of the invisible Breath or Spirit of God who comes down upon Jesus as the divine 'ointment' that marks him as the Christ.[11] It requires little or no ingenuity, then, to see that this scene of Jesus' revelation as God's Christ is also a manifestation of the Trinity, and indeed of the Trinity caught in the very act of 'doing its thing'.[12] What is more, if any ingenuity is required, Irenaeus has already supplied it. The 'Son' in this scene, he insisted, is one individual, yet at the same time one in whom two realities are somehow wedded, so that a person who contemplates this 'Son' experiences a form of double vision. There is on the one hand, the eternal Son or Word of God and, on the other, the human, finite Son of God, Jesus, in whom other human beings can easily recognize one of themselves; and yet these two somehow stand in together, as the shared title 'son' indicates.

Here, then, is an intimation of the nature of the relationship that is established through God's self-revelation and self-giving to human persons in baptism. A full account of it would require an explication of the whole 'work' of Christ, and therefore, in the end, of the whole credal and scriptural narrative whose meaning Christian baptism recapitulates. What Irenaeus says about the baptism of Jesus, however, indicates what is to be the fruit of Christ's work.

---

10   *On the Holy Spirit* 28, in *Nicene and Post-Nicene Fathers*, Second Series (hereafter *NPNF* 2), Vol. 8, Philip Schaff and Henry Wace (eds), Blomfield Jackson (trans.), Peabody, MA: Hendrickson Publishers, 1996, p. 18.

11   Cf. *AH* 3,9.3; 3.12.7; 3.17.1.

12   See Origen, *Homilies on Genesis* 2.5, in *Sources Chrétiennes*, Vol. 7, H. de Lubac and J. Daniélou (eds), Paris: Les Editions du Cerf, 1976, p. 102: Origen speaks of the Marcan account of the baptism of Jesus, 'ubi et primum coepit sacramentum patescere Trinitatis' ('where the mystery of the Trinity first began to become manifest').

It is the elevation of human beings into the life of God, their 'sharing th
grace' – not merely or even primarily as individuals but as a common body – in
the identity and the destiny of Christ. Needless to say, the basis of such a possibility – the reality that grounds it – is, as Irenaeus saw, twofold. First, there
is the union of God and humanity in Christ, or, to employ the language of the
Fourth Gospel, the becoming flesh of the Word of God. If the Word and Son of
God truly takes on and shares the conditions of a particular human existence,
that action implies, conversely, that human beings can in their own way, though
no doubt in a new way, live their life, individual and common, in the power
of God's life and in union with the eternal Word of God. This very statement,
however, points to a second 'moment' in this relationship with God: the gift
of the Spirit, by which humanity is empowered to live out the Christ-life as its
own.

Furthermore, it is essential to insist that Jesus' baptism in 'water and the
Spirit' (cf. John 3.5; Acts 2.38) does not stand alone in early Christianity. Others – disciples of the first and later generations – marked their solidarity with
him by accepting just such a baptism as their own, though only (as far as one
can tell) after his resurrection. Paul explains what this means: 'For as many of
you as were baptized into Christ have put on Christ. There is neither Jew nor
Greek, there is neither slave nor free, there is neither male nor female; for you
are all one in Christ Jesus' (Gal. 3.27–28; cf. 1 Cor. 12.12–13). In other words,
the baptism with which disciples are graced dresses them up, collectively and
individually, as Christ. It so identifies them with him that other identities, ethnic
identities, for example, or gender identities, tend to have their importance discounted. Baptism even occasions believers to share Christ's death to sin, so that
they may further share his resurrection (cf. Rom. 6.3–4). And all this Paul sums
up in the words: 'God has sent the Spirit of his Son into your hearts, crying,
"Abba! Father!"' (Gal. 4.6).[13] The Spirit of his Son – that is, the same Spirit that
anointed Jesus at his baptism[14] – here manifests the disciples of Jesus as God's
adoptive children, as siblings by grace of the Son of God, and even, according
to Irenaeus, as 'gods'.[15] The baptism of Christians, then, is a reiteration of, and
a sharing in, the baptism of Christ; and indeed Irenaeus asserts that the Spirit
descended on the Christ precisely in order that he in turn might share it with
believers.[16] Active in this baptism are the same God and Father, the same Son
and Word, the same Spirit of holiness – taking human beings into their company

---

13 Note that allusions to baptism in Paul – and not Paul alone – regularly characterize its
effect by reference to the members of the Christian Triad: e.g. 'It is God who establishes us
with you in Christ . . . he has put his seal upon us and given us his Spirit in our hearts as a
guarantee' (2 Cor. 1.2–11); 'You were washed, you were justified, you were sanctified in the
name of our Lord Jesus Christ and in the Spirit of our God' (1 Cor. 6.11); 'To the exiles of the
dispersion . . . chosen and destined by God the Father and sanctified by the Spirit for obedience
to Jesus Christ and for sprinkling with his blood' (1 Pet. 1.1f.). These are references, moreover,
to the effects of baptism, to what happens in baptism, and not merely to the words of a baptismal 'formula' or confession. Matthew 28.19 is no doubt merely another, and somewhat less
interesting, example of this sort of text.
14 See, e.g. Tertullian, *On Baptism* 8.
15 *AH* 3.6.1; cf. Ps. 82.6.
16 *AH* 3.17.1–2; and cf. *AH* 3.9.3 ad fin.

on the ground of the identification of the eternal Word of God as Jesus, who somehow is, and represents, 'us', and whose identity 'we' can share.[17]

It was thus Irenaeus's belief that from the beginning of creation, and throughout the long and chequered history of humanity with God, the Son and the Spirit are, in one way or another, under one set of circumstances or another, the constant companions of the human race: in other words, that the picture of God's relationship to humanity conveyed by the story of Jesus' baptism supplies, as we have said, the paradigm for the structure of that relationship not only in baptism and in creation, but in every time and circumstance.[18] Let us, then, be more specific than Barth. Let us agree that the occurrence of revelation presupposes, generally and in principle, a threefoldness in the manner of God's self-giving to faith, and therefore, if that self-giving is to be real, in the God who is thus conveyed; but let us add that this general truth is concretely instantiated in New Testament accounts of the baptism of Jesus as well as in the baptisms of those who have set out to follow him. Then it becomes clear, as Barth wanted to insist, that the doctrine of the Trinity is anything but an airy and derivative speculation. It is in the first instance a statement of the structure of humanity's relation to God in Christ: that is, a statement that articulates and specifies both the other term of this relation (God the Trinity) and the pattern and logic of the relationship itself. The ultimate 'root' of Christian Trinitarianism, then, is baptismal; for it is in baptism that this relationship is established and sealed.

On the Meaning of 'God' in this Account

The first and most central question that must be raised in connection with this account of the Trinity has nothing to do with 'threes' and 'ones', but rather with the very connotation of the word 'God'. In this context it of course refers, together and severally, to the Father, the Word whom the Father speaks and the Spirit whom the Father breathes. But both Irenaeus in his conflict with Christian Gnostics and the Cappadocians in their later conflict with Arianism dealt with opponents whom they took to work with a false understanding of God – or, as the Cappadocians would put it in what was to become a technical term in the vocabulary of the doctrine of the Trinity, a false understanding of God's *ousia*.[19]

First, then, Irenaeus's Christian Gnostics had raised a question about the identity of God. They had little respect for the one they called the 'artisan' –

---

17 On this fundamental point it is useful to notice the words of Basil (*On the Holy Spirit* 61, in *NPNF* 2 8.38): It is the work of the Spirit that a person 'who no longer "lives after the flesh" but, being "led by the Spirit" is called a Son of God, and is "conformed to the image of the Son of God"'.

18 On this point, see Colin Gunton, *The One, the Three, and the Many*, Cambridge: Cambridge University Press, 1998, pp. 158–60, with its discussion of Irenaeus and the idea of 'economy'.

19 This word has been variously translated as 'substance', 'stuff', 'being', 'subject', 'essence' and 'nature'. Any of these is acceptable; which is correct must be determined contextually. The word is commonly thought of as a technical philosophical term; but it was in common use in a wide range of senses, and was in fact technical in about the same sense and to about the same degree as English words like 'real' or 'reality'.

God – the Deity whose doings are recounted in the creation story of Genesis 1–2. Indeed the very term 'artisan' (*demiourgos*) was, on their lips, a put-down. They contended that this creator-figure could not be the same as the good Father known and proclaimed by Jesus, but was a being of a much lower grade. For this reason, Irenaeus had to insist – at length and with much tiresome repetition – (a) that the Creator God of Genesis 1 is indeed the one and only God; and (b) that this God is, therefore, the very 'Father' alluded to in the stories of Jesus' baptism – the one who sent his own Son and Word as his self-revelation, and who at the same time sent the Holy Spirit to 'adapt' humanity-in-Christ to its new life with God as thus revealed.

Irenaeus's criticism of his opponents' view amounted, then, to an attack on their separation of the Creator (and the created cosmos) from the ultimate, good, transcendent Deity (and the spiritual cosmos that Gnostics called 'the Fullness'). If, he argued, this ultimate God bears no responsibility for the visible cosmos that the artisan-Creator has formed, if the creation of that material cosmos really was an unfortunate, even malignant, act, then not only does the Creator figure fail to qualify as God, but so does the (allegedly) ultimate and hidden Deity who is the Source of the spiritual cosmos. They are like two artists who share the same studio, each of whom spends all his or her time defacing the work of the other. He thinks, in other words, that the two Gnostic God-figures limit each other, with the consequence that neither one can satisfy the conditions for being called 'God' in the proper sense.

Thus when Irenaeus speaks of God, he wants to speak of one unenclosed, illimitable, incomprehensible God, who is the sole author of everything there is, spirit and matter alike: that is the connotation of 'God', as he understands the word. His opponents, to be sure, had employed the same sort of apophatic (i.e. 'negative') language about their ultimate Father; but there were things – anything material, for example – that they sought in the end to exclude from the scope of this ultimate Deity's responsibility. Irenaeus therefore argues in effect that they did not understand the implications of the language they were using. Their two divine figures, since they were pictured as strictly contrary to each other, might perhaps, supposing they were real, be conceived as important cosmic 'powers'; but cosmic powers are not God. The true Deity, says Irenaeus, is strictly unlimited, infinite and immeasurable, because God 'contains all things without being contained by any'.[20] This formula, derived from Hellenistic Jewish sources, implies for him (a) that 'in his greatness, God is unknown to all his creatures' but is known by them through his love;[21] and (b) that God is not 'in' the world (or for that matter 'outside' it).[22] On the contrary, the world is 'in' God, who is the 'place' in which the finite order is set, and is therefore non-mediately

---

20   E.g. *AH* 4.20.2; but see also, in particular, the opening chapters of *AH* 2.
21   *AH* 4.20.4.
22   It also implied for Irenaeus that God does not stand in want of anything: the world is not God's need-fulfiller, as some Gnostics had argued with regard to the Artisan-Creator, maintaining that he as it were 'uses' or milks the material creation for his own purposes. On the contrary, says Irenaeus, God created humanity 'in order to have someone upon whom to confer benefits' (*AH* 4.14.1), and therefore creation is a purely positive act of love. Further, God does not 'need' any helpers to carry through the business of creation, being quite capable of doing the whole job alone.

present to it: and that, oddly enough, explains why 'no one has seen God at any time' (John 1.18). As the world's medium and context, its ground, God does not belong in the same file-folder with created things – or, for that matter, in any file-folder at all. God is everything's holder and upholder.

This account of the reference and meaning of the word 'God' was not, in any of its components, new with Irenaeus; and much later it was reiterated by the Cappadocian fathers as an essential premise of any Christian account of the Trinity. Indeed it was as important to them as to Irenaeus, though for slightly different reasons. The notorious fourth-century Arian or 'Trinitarian' controversy was originally focused on the 'location' or status of the *Logos* or Word of God in the relation between God and the created order. In other words, the turf over which the controversy moved was, roughly speaking, the field defined by the picture of creation conveyed (e.g. in 1 Cor. 8.6 or John 1.3 or Prov. 8.22). These texts were normally taken, at the beginning of the fourth century, to assert that the divine Word or Wisdom or Son, the one through whom God creates, is a derivative and mediatorial figure, one that played the role of a buffer-state between the ultimate Deity and the created order. Arius, starting in about 318, had in effect protested this picture. The title 'God', he insisted, had no business being applied to a secondary figure of this sort – as though there could be such a thing as a descending hierarchy of degrees or 'grades' of divinity. He preferred, Arius said, to acknowledge what must be the true case – that the *Logos* was not God in any sense, but was instead the highest and noblest of created beings.

This teaching, as we know, was repudiated in no uncertain terms by the Council of Nicaea (325). Many years, however – years that were to be filled with misunderstanding, argument, and political conflict – had to pass before the old-fashioned 'conservative' view that there are descending 'grades' of Deity, just as there are grades, say, of beef or of motor oil, could lose its status as the sole alternative to Arianism. It was the task of Athanasius of Alexandria and, later, of the Cappadocian fathers, to defend a third position: (a) that the *Logos* is neither a creature nor a secondary, slightly watered-down Deity, but God in the same sense as the ultimate God; and (b) that the same is true of the Holy Spirit (who had scarcely been mentioned at all in the first stages of the controversy, no doubt because the scriptural 'creation' texts that shaped its agenda did not mention the Spirit).

The opponents that Basil and the two Gregories faced, however, were a different breed, whose position has been labelled 'Neo-Arianism'. This movement did not simply reproduce Arius's views or even those of the conservatives (who have often, and wrongly, been called 'Semi-Arians'). On the contrary, the deacon Aetius of Antioch and his disciple Eunomius, who were rough contemporaries of the Cappadocians, argued not only that the *Logos* and the Spirit are creatures, but that they have to be understood as strictly unlike God, not in the old-fashioned sense that they represent different degrees of Deity, but in the radical sense that they are different sorts of things entirely. Father, Son and Spirit on this view would be like an apple, an alligator and an acid: three quite different kinds of beings (*ousiai*). So much for Nicaea's famous formula, 'of one being': *homoousios*. And indeed, so much for Arius's view that God is so grand – so transcendent – as to be beyond the comprehension even of the *Logos*. For the Neo-Arian argument presupposed that 'God' – the 'nature' or 'being' of God – can be defined. Eunomius in fact insisted that anyone who has clearly grasped the concept of the 'non-generate' (or 'non-begotten') has grasped the essence of what it is to be God: and that since Son and Spirit are not described as non-generate, they are not and cannot be, even in some vague sense, 'the same sort of thing' as God. Hence the Neo-Arian use of the epithet 'unlike'.[23]

Oddly enough, though no one noticed it, this position had something in common with that of Irenaeus's Gnostics. The Neo-Arian argument assumed that the negative – 'apophatic' – terms traditionally employed of God in theological discourse – terms like 'non-mutable', 'non-corporeal' or 'timeless', but above all, in their particular case, 'non-begotten' – imply that a strict contrariety obtains between God and any finite being. In a word, they pictured their definable Deity as the opposite of everything creaturely and therefore as inconsistent, and by nature incompatible, with it[24] – just as the earlier Gnostics had postulated a divorce of sorts between the spiritual (divine and light-filled) world and the material (dark and empty) world and the different God-figures that ruled them. What the Neo-Arians apparently did not notice was that this understanding of God's transcendence is not only open to Irenaeus's criticism of his Gnostics' teaching, in that it would render God limited or finite, but also that it renders God supremely lonely and isolated – untouching and untouchable.

The Cappadocians sensed the futility of this Neo-Arian position. Because (a) it pretended to define the nature of God, and (b) did so on the assumption that the differences between Creator and creature make them out to be contraries, it really succeeded only in 'finitizing' God by suggesting that God can be limited just as created 'natures' are mutually limiting.

Moreover, the alternatives the Neo-Arian vision presupposed – inconsistency or consistency, to put the matter as crisply as possible – had consequences that are echoed in much modern thought, and consequences that illustrate, if nothing else, the annoying persistence of this issue. On the one hand, if one sets about trying to express the transcendence of God in negatives understood as the Neo-Arians had understood them, what one ends up with is not so much a transcendent God as a merely isolated God. On the other hand, if, frustrated by this outcome, one demands that the negatives, implicit or explicit, be dropped, so that God can be 'closer' to human beings and their affairs, a God so conceived will no doubt cease to appear isolated (at least to some degree), but will nonetheless continue to function as one thing among others, differing only by being bigger, more powerful, better intentioned and so on. In other words, both of these models of God, if actualized, would result in a finite Deity; and that, whatever else it might be, would not be God. Yet this paradoxical situation seems to be the one in which much current theology finds itself, as it forever trades in a false transcendence on a reductionist immanence or vice versa.

---

23 In the churches of the third century, *Logos* language and Spirit language seem as often as not to have got dissociated from each other to one degree or another, no doubt because they tended to be employed in different connections. The natural 'field' of *Logos*-language was discourse about creation and incarnation. The natural 'field' of Spirit-language was accounts of prophetic and apostolic inspiration on the one hand, and, on the other, discourse about baptism and about the shape of the new life of the people of God created by baptism.

24 See Gregory of Nyssa's discussion in *Against Eunomius* 1.518 (and indeed the whole surrounding passage): *NPNF* 2, Vol. 5, p. 83.

The Cappadocian solution to this issue – a solution whose implications are not frequently enough pondered – was to assert, with Irenaeus (and others), the incomprehensibility and infinity of God and hence of the divine 'nature'. God's perfection as 'the good' consists, argued Gregory of Nyssa, in the strict infinity of God's goodness: one cannot get to the end of it, and it is thus in the strictest sense unfathomable.[25] Hence the first principle of the Cappadocian account of the Trinity was the proposition that the 'nature' or 'being' of God cannot be grasped conceptually by the human mind because – as Gregory of Nyssa added – it has no borders, internal or external. Just as Irenaeus had said bluntly that 'in his greatness, God is unknown to all his creatures', so Gregory of Nazianzus stated: 'What God is in nature and essence, no one has ever yet discovered or can discover.'[26] But then just as Irenaeus had added that God is known through his 'love', so too Nazianzen asserts that God is discerned in 'the glory which is manifested among the creatures', a glory that is 'the back parts of God ... tokens of himself'.[27]

To understand this, it is important to recall that by the fourth century the idea – which Irenaeus may have taken over from Hermas's Shepherd[28] – of God as the one who contains all things without being contained had become something of a commonplace. This way of speaking was employed originally to answer the question of how God could be said to be 'in' the world as in a 'place', or in some particular place in the world, as the Scriptures seemed often to suggest. The answer given, as we have said, was that God is not 'in' the world as one of the items it contained; rather it had to be said that God is the 'place' in which the world exists – a way of speaking that was meant precisely to deny that God is an item within, or a dimension or region of, the created order while at the same time asserting the unbreakable intimacy between Creator and creation. God is always present and 'walking in the Garden in the cool of the day' (Gen. 3.8), yet not in the sense that God is in the Garden, but in the sense that the Garden is in God because God is the Garden's proper 'place', its 'where'.[29] If this is correct, however, then the notion that God is the world's – and therefore humanity's – contrary needs to be entirely rethought; and this remains true even though the Cappadocians and their posterity could on occasion, unaware of the implications of their own teaching, revert, tacitly or explicitly, to the rhetoric of incompatibility.

---

25 See, e.g., *Against Eunomius* 1.291, in *NPNF* 2, Vol. 5, p. 62. 'The primary Good is by nature unlimited' and 'For that reason the participation of the person who joys in that Good will also, of necessity, be unlimited. He will always be receiving more, and forever discovering something more than that which he has already taken in, and he will never be able to measure up to what he has received, since that in which he participates is unlimited, and on account of such participation, it can never stop growing.'

26 Gregory of Nazianzus, *Oration* 28.1, 7.

27 *Oration*, 28.3; cf. Exod. 33.20ff. With this is worth comparing the language of Calvin (*Institutes* 1.5.1): 'His essence is incomprehensible ... But upon his individual works he has engraved unmistakable signs of his glory'; and of Aquinas (*Summa Theologiae* I. a. 2.1): 'But since, where God is concerned, we do not know what he is, he is not known to us just from what he is: rather does this existence require to be demonstrated by reference to things that are more familiar to us which is to say, by his effects.'

28 The 'Shepherd' of Hermas, Mandate 1, in K. Lake (ed.), *The Apostolic Fathers*, Loeb Library, 2 vols, Cambridge, MA: Harvard University Press, 1959, 2.70.

29 See Philo's remarks on Genesis 3.8 in *Allegories of the Laws* III.4–6.

In other words, this picture – for that is what it is – of God as the world's 'place', containing and embracing the world as its Creator and Sustainer, suggests a possible solution to the problem about contraries. It does not rule out the so-called 'negative' – apophatic[30] – theology: quite the contrary. It does, however, demand that such language be understood in a different way. To envisage God and world as contraries is to make a fundamental mistake: it is to speak of the Creator's relation to the creation as if it could reliably and literally be characterized in the very same terms that are employed to characterize the relations of creatures to one another. It is, in a word, to set them on a level. But if we construct the relation between God and creature as if it were another instance of a type of relation – for example, contrariety – 'that can, and often does, obtain between finite beings, then we talk as though God were indeed another item on the list of the things there are'. In other words, we end up, inevitably, engaging in what was once called 'idolatry'. We erect some finite reality as our God, not unlike the Israelites in the wilderness, whose anxiety and impatience once led them to construct an ill-fated golden calf.

But the original aim of the 'negative' theology as used in Jewish and Christian circles was to say that God is not limited by the world or any of its 'contents', in the way that things in the world limit one another, and so has no business being opposed to them in the manner of a logical contrary. In other words, the negative theology spoke of God dialectically, by way of denial (*apophasis*) that depends upon and presupposes an original affirmation. It was intended to school believers away from idolatry. It meant to say that God's being is not another species of the same genus as the created order, but that it is strictly on another level from created being in the sense that it does not belong to any 'kind'; and this in turn implies that God's 'otherness' in relation to creatures must never be construed as inconsistency, but rather as something that goes beyond what we perceive as consistency and inconsistency. The finite cannot contain the infinite; but of the infinite one says both (a) that it is not finite, and (b) that for just that reason it makes room for the finite and is that with which the finite is most deeply at home, even as the doctrine of creation affirms. 'No one has seen God at any time,' says the Fourth Gospel, but the divine Word, the only begotten Son made flesh, 'has made him known' (John 1.18). This sounds like mere paradox – especially if one understands that the presence of the Son is the presence of the Father; but the point of the paradox is to stress that God's self-identification in and with 'flesh' marks a work far beyond what might be possible for either a merely transcendent deity, who cannot come 'downstairs' without losing face, or a merely immanent deity who has no business getting above herself by venturing 'upstairs'. The Trinity is immanent precisely in its transcendence and transcendent precisely in its immanence. Basil of Caesarea captures this strange thought neatly. He writes that what most truly attests God's 'excellency' is the fact that God, being incomprehensible, should be able, impassibly, through flesh, to have come into close conflict with death, to the end that by his own suffering he might give us the boon of freedom from suffering.[31]

---

30 The Greek word *apophasis* means 'denial'; hence an 'apophatic' theology is one that characterizes God by saying what Deity is not.
31 *On the Holy Spirit* 18, in *NPNF* 2, Vol. 8, p. 12.

The incomprehensible God is beyond suffering, and yet – or perhaps therefore – can take on human suffering. Indeed that is in part what is meant by talk of divine incomprehensibility: not that one cannot ever speak of God in a way that gets God right, but that what one has to say in order to do so is something that does not always 'fit' the ordinary rules of our (finite) thinking and speaking. The divine work of creation and redemption can only be the work of one who does not inhabit our time but makes his own time ours, who is himself our 'place', and who is closer to us than we are to each other in virtue of being at every moment (a) the 'Other' that calls us into being, (b) the 'Other' that represents for us the being that is to be ours, and (c) the 'Other' that is communicating this being to us.

The proposition, then, that God contains all things without being contained by any intimates first of all that God's 'difference' from finite beings is a very different kind of difference from the kind to which they are accustomed. But second, it goes hand in hand with insistence upon a 'negative' or 'apophatic' theology whose point is not to pen God up in heaven, but to supply a corrective to the mental fashioning of a limited God – to point faith beyond every finite reality to the 'Other' in whom alone it is at every point grounded, formed and affirmed and in whose being its finite existence is a kind of participation. Thus the Cappadocians followed Irenaeus's lead:[32] they envisaged a God that (1) stands in non-mediated relationship with every created being, but (2) is no part of the finite order nor subject to its conditions. Their 'negative theology', indeed, seems implicitly to presuppose that (2) above is some sort of condition for the truth of (1).

The 'Threefoldness' of God

This unique and unfathomable Deity, then, is nonetheless the One who eternally speaks a self-objectifying Word in an act of self-conferral, and at the same time breathes a life-giving Spirit that carries and so affirms the Word thus spoken and, in doing so, conforms human beings to it. And so we come to the question of the threefoldness of God asserted in the doctrine of the Trinity: or, to use more familiar language, the threesome of 'persons', by each of whom the one illimitable divine being is completely shared.

Irenaeus did not use any settled, technical term to denote the members of the Trinity – certainly not 'person' (for he did not write in Latin), nor even the Greek term whose equivalent it was later taken to be, namely *hypostasis*. Instead, he used the range of definite descriptions that had become traditional in Christian talk: e.g. 'God' or 'Father'; 'Word' or 'Son' or 'Only-begotten'; 'Spirit' – i.e. 'Breath' – or 'Wisdom'.[33] With or without technical terms, however, Irenaeus's account of Word and Spirit is clearly a doctrine of divine threefoldness (and

---

32 See, e.g. Gregory of Nyssa, *Against Eunomius* 1.26.367, in *NPNF* 2, Vol. 5, p. 69.
33 Note that, contrary to what was already customary in the New Testament, Irenaeus identifies the figure of Wisdom (cf. Prov. 8.22ff.; Wisdom 7.22ff.) with the Holy Spirit rather than with the Christ. This is very likely attributable to the influence of Theophilus of Antioch. More oddly still, Irenaeus's account of the Word or Son of God nevertheless continues to endow the latter with the attributes of Wisdom, even though the title is assigned elsewhere.

not of three Gods). This is made plain enough by his image of the 'two hands' of God. Thus he asserts that the 'one God made and ordered everything by his Word and Wisdom',[34] but for him this means the same as 'by God's two hands', which are the Son and the Spirit, 'through whom and in whom he made all things freely and of himself'. Son and Spirit, then, are not helpers hired, as it were, at some cosmic labour exchange. They are simply the one Deity itself in other modes: that is the primary point of the 'hands' metaphor. They are God's own, indeed they are God, and therefore what they do amounts simply to specific forms of God's doing. In the Father, says Irenaeus, is the being of all things; in the Son, their model; and in the Spirit, their form:[35] a transposition, this, of the picture of God that emerges in the story of Jesus' baptism into the key of a discourse about creation. The members of the Trinity are here identified by their complementary and reciprocal ways of participating in the single business of creation; and this activity of creation Irenaeus understood to be continued in a new form by the same threefold God, no doubt in the same threefold manner, for the purpose of bringing a now fallen humanity to the end originally intended for it – the new creation begun in baptism. For 'God . . . is one and the same. It is he who rolls the heaven up as if it were a book [Isa. 34.4] and renews the face of the earth [Ps. 104.30]. It is he who made the things of time for the sake of humanity, so that, coming to maturity amongst them, it might bring forth the fruit of immortality.'[36]

Hence for Irenaeus, the Son is always the one through whom God brings the created order into being: Irenaeus has read John 1.3 and 1 Corinthians 8.6 and internalized them thoroughly. The Son is the objectification of God – God's self reproduced, the measureless measured, God's mind and purpose rendered articulate – God, one might say, self-expressed with creation in view. It is for this reason that Irenaeus can call the Son or Word – God's image and self-communication – exemplum, 'model'. Not only is the Son the model for humanity, that image of God after which Adam was fashioned, but the Son is for all practical purposes the 'Wisdom' – 'the first-born of all creation' (cf. Col. 1.15–16) – that models God's purpose for the entire created order. Thus the realization of God's will in creation is the actualization in finite form of the Wisdom and Word of God ('God said, and it was so'). Or put it another way: the self-objectification of God in the Son is not only God's eternal self-expression, but also – and for just that reason – the act that eternally grounds the creation of a finite cosmos and, indeed, represents the – logical not chronological – first step of it. It is not possible, save by deliberate abstraction, to talk of God without talking also about what God does with, and holds in, those two 'hands'.

Furthermore, in Irenaeus's scheme – whose baptismal root is evident in the way he supplements John 1.3 and 1 Corinthians 8.6 – the Spirit appears not as next after the Word in a descending series of divine 'persons', but as the Word's divine correlate: like one hand to the other (to use Irenaeus's metaphor), or

---

34 AH 4.20.4; cf. 3.24.2.
35 AH 4.20.1. I follow here the text as reconstructed by A. Rousseau (ed.), *Irénée de Lyon: Contre les hérésies, Livre IV*, Sources chrétiennes 100, Paris: Les Editions du Cerf, 1965, p. 626.
36 AH 4.5.1.

(to alter the metaphor slightly) like a forefinger to the Son's thumb. If God is objectified (for himself and for creatures) in the Word, God is also 'subject-ified' in the Spirit as the divine gift and power by which (a) the Word himself is affirmed as God's self-expression, and (b) believers are conformed to their identity in the Word or Son. Indeed the Spirit is the power by which all the works of God, posited by the Father and given form in God's Word, are affirmed and conformed to their inward identity. Thus Irenaeus writes in his *Proof of the Apostolic Preaching*:

> Paul well says: one God, the Father, who is above all and with all and in us all (cf. Eph. 4:6); for 'above all' is the Father, but 'with all' is the Word, since it is through him that everything was made by the Father, and 'in us all' is the Spirit, who cries, Abba, Father, and has formed man to the likeness of God. So the Spirit manifests the Word, and therefore the prophets announced the Son of God; but the Word articulates the Spirit, and therefore it is himself who gives their message to the prophets, and takes up man and brings him to the Father.[37]

Hence the Spirit is the one that brings about 'increase' in believers, 'preparing humanity for the Son of God' and for the vision of God.[38] If the Word is truly the image of God, and the destiny of humanity is to be conformed to that image, then it is the Spirit who enables human persons to actualize that destiny.

But how was this idea of the equality of the three 'members' of the one God understood and expressed by the Cappadocian fathers? The heart of the Cappadocians' Trinitarianism lay in the way they distinguished between the two Greek terms *ousia* and *hupostasis*: terms which Irenaeus's account of the Trinity did not employ, but which had become central in the fourth-century debate. In ordinary speech the meanings of these two words often overlapped. They could and did, for certain purposes, function as synonyms. Indeed they had been employed as synonyms in one of the propositions condemned by the creed of the Council of Nicaea.[39] This terminological vagueness was one of the sources of misunderstanding among the various parties to the Trinitarian debate; and it was only made worse by the fact that Latin translated both of these Greek words by the one term *substantia*. The Cappadocians, therefore, inherited the task of clarifying the language of the debate, which they did by asserting or assuming that *ousia* was an abstract word that denoted the form of an answer to the question 'What is this?' The *ousia* of something is its 'what', its nature, as we say. To speak of the *ousia* of God, then, is to refer to what God is.

But what of the term *hypostasis*? This was the term that had come to denote the 'three' that were called 'Father', 'Word' and 'Spirit'. What is more, it had for some time been deliberately employed to insist that these words name realities – distinct, objectively existent 'things' with particular identities, and not

---

37 *Proof of the Apostolic Preaching* 5, as translated by J. P. Smith in *Ancient Christian Writers* 16, Westminster, MD: Newman Press, 1952.

38 *AH* 4.20.5, 6.

39 The Council condemned the proposition that the Son is from another *hupostasis* or *ousia*, i.e. other than the Father's.

simply appearances or aspects of God. The Cappadocians, thinking this over, came initially to believe that for the purposes of Trinitarian discourse *hypostasis* should be understood to refer to a concrete instance or exemplification of some nature. Thus, it was argued, Peter, Paul and John are three instances of what it is to be human; and in the same way, the *hypostases* of the Trinity are three instances of what it is to be God.

But there are two difficulties here: and one of them is obvious. On this view, or at least on the most obvious understanding of it, the three *hypostases* of the Trinity would be three Gods and not one, just as Peter, Paul and John are three human beings and not one. Furthermore (and this difficulty is not so obvious), that which distinguishes the three instances or *hypostases* from one another would have to be some individuating attribute – a quality of some sort, like red hair, say, or an acerbic wit – that makes the 'what' of Peter, say, different from that of John or Paul. But by *hypothesis*, the 'what' of God does not differ from one *hypostasis* to another: in other words, Deity is not an abstract 'kind'. It is one given 'thing', one reality – God's self. More than that, the Cappadocians were clear, as we have seen, that the 'what' of God cannot be grasped by any human conceptual apparatus. God is non-finite, non-comprehensible and non-definable; so that when one speaks of the *ousia* of God one is referring (a) to something one cannot grasp in human terms save by indirection – by analogy, negation or metaphor – and (b) to something that cannot be supplemented or diminished.

Hence to the question what differentiates the three *hypostases* or 'persons' from one another (i.e. the characteristic that 'individuates' each of them: *idiotes*), they returned in the end the answer that whatever it is, it could have nothing to do with the category of *ousia*. 'The difference' between Father and Son, says Gregory of Nazianzus, 'is external to the nature [*ousia*]'.[40] The *hypostases* are in the end not to be differentiated – and to that extent constituted – as different species or different particular instances of the genus 'God'. Rather they gradually came to be called, though not explicitly by the Cappadocians, *tropoi hyparxeos* – 'modes of [God's] existence'.[41] Hence what constitutes and differentiates them is not of the order of a 'what', but, as Gregory of Nyssa says, making the same point in his own terminology, of the order of a 'how' (*Os einai*).[42] It is their relations – how they exist in relation to one another – that constitute one as Source, one as Offspring, and one as Gift; but each of them is the same thing, the same identical 'what', namely, God. 'Father is not the name of a nature [*ousia*] or of an activity [*energeia*] . . . But it is the name of the relation in which the Father stands to the Son, and the Son to the Father.'[43]

Further the Cappadocians argued, as we know, that human knowledge of God is not knowledge of the infinite and unutterable *ousia* of God – 'what' God

---

40 Gregory of Nazianzus, *Oration* 29.12, in *NPNF* 2, Vol. 7, p. 306.
41 On this phrase, see G. L. Prestige, *God in Patristic Thought*, London: SPCK, 1952, pp. 245–6, where the author points out the connection of the phrase with modes of origination. Karl Rahner (at least in English translation) rendered it as 'modes of subsisting'.
42 See Gregory of Nyssa, 'To Ablabius, That There Are Not Three Gods', in *Christology of the Later Fathers*, Library of Christian Classics, Vol. 3 (hereafter *LCC* 3), Edward Hardy (ed.), Philadelphia: Westminster Press, 1954, p. 266.
43 Gregory of Nazianzus, *Oration* 29.16.

is. Rather, they thought, it is focused on the *energeia* of God: what God does. Human beings speak of God on the basis of God's activity or working – in creation, in the sustaining of the natural order and in redemption; and the rule of such speech is ultimately the language of the Scriptures.[44] But the Cappadocians asserted that this 'energy' or 'activity' of God is nevertheless the direct expression and revelation of God's 'nature' or 'self': what God does follows upon who and what God is.[45] Therefore just as the three *hypostases* are not three different 'whats', so the divine activity is not three different activities, one for each 'person' of the Trinity. God's doing is a single activity that happens triadically just as God's being happens triadically: a reiteration, this, of a point already made in effect by Irenaeus. This of course does not mean that there is no difference to be observed between the working of the Father, of the Son and of the Spirit. It means that these differences too are of the order of 'how' and not of the order of 'what'. What the three *hypostases* are correctly said to do – for example, create, redeem or sanctify, to allude to a formula now current – is one thing; but the how of their doing it involves three co-ordinate ways of working to accomplish that one thing.[46]

Thus Basil of Caesarea can in principle simply repeat Irenaeus on the score of the 'working' of God in self-revelation: for, reflecting, among other texts, on 1 Corinthians 12.3 ('No one can say, "Jesus is Lord," except by the Holy Spirit'), he writes:

> [T]he way of the knowledge of God lies from the one Spirit, through the one Son, to the one Father; and conversely, the natural goodness and inherent holiness and the royal dignity extend from the Father through the Only-begotten to the Spirit. Thus there is both acknowledgment of the *hypostases*, and the true dogma of the [one God] is not lost.[47]

Questions and Perplexities

This teaching about the *hypostases*, then, performs a twofold function. When it defines the particularity of each member of the Trinity through its relation to the others, it is doing two jobs at the same time. It asserts at once the many-ness of God and the one-ness of God. It discerns the unity of God in the threefoldness of the *hypostases* (because their very differences, being relational, assure their union); and it roots the threefoldness of God in the unity of the divine nature (because the *hypostases* are, in their mutual relations, reiterations of one divine

---

44 On this score, see Basil's account of the *energeiai* of the Holy Spirit: *On the Holy Spirit* 49, in *NPNF* 2, Vol. 8, pp. 30f.

45 This, of course, is merely a paraphrase of Thomas Aquinas's nice Latin aphorism: '*operatio sequitur esse*'.

46 This is a way of stating the principle famously formulated by Augustine in the words, '*Opera trinitatis ad extra sunt indivisa.*' ('The activities of the Trinity are not differentiated in relation to what is outside of God.') He derived this principle from the Cappadocians: see Gregory of Nyssa, 'To Ablabius: That There Are Not Three Gods', in *LCC* 3, p. 261f.

47 'On the Holy Spirit' 47, in *NPNF* 2, Vol. 8, pp. 29f. Cf. Gregory of Nyssa, *Against Eunomius* 1.531, in *NPNF* 2, Vol. 5, p. 84.

reality). The problems commonly faced by Trinitarian theology are therefore problems about maintaining this balance between unity and threefoldness.

The most obvious of these problems, and one that has figured prominently in recent discussions of Trinitarian doctrine, is a distinction between the 'economic' and the 'immanent' (or sometimes 'ontological') Trinity. The phrase 'immanent Trinity' refers to threefoldness as proper to Deity considered simply in and of itself – proper, that is, to God absolute, God abstracted from any relationship to anything other than God. Conversely, 'economic Trinity' refers to threefoldness as discerned or manifested in God's engagement with humanity and its world in the 'economies' of creation and redemption, that is, to God-in-relation. The distinction tacitly presupposes, then, that God's relations to the created order are more or less what, in cinema advertisements, used to be called an 'extra added attraction'. Whence there arises the question whether the divine threefoldness is real apart from those relations – whether, in a word, it may not be a merely secondary quality or phase of Deity and not 'original' to God at all. On that view, God is really a unitary being, and the threefoldness is a cosmetic, and by so much a deceptive, addendum.

There is of course at least one further alternative. This distinction may be one that exists only in the mind of the person who makes it: useful, perhaps, for some purposes, but not corresponding to any real division or separation. After all, the two terms of this distinction cannot coincide either (a) with the difference between essential 'nature' and contingent 'accident',[48] or, for that matter, (b) with the difference between 'being' and 'doing' (*energeia*). The divine unity, after all, is said to be threefold in the sense that God 'happens' in three ways. For that reason – i.e. because they are the modes or the 'hows' of God's being – the *hypostases* cannot be secondary or merely 'accidental', even though they do not define God's 'what' but only embody it in different manners. By the same token, the threefold 'personhood' of God represents not God's 'doing' (*energeia*) as distinct from God's 'being', but the 'hows' of God's doing. That, no doubt, is why the tradition has taught that the ways in which God exists are at the same time the ways in which God acts.

Such being the case, it is easy to see that this distinction between God absolute and God related is a version of the ancient 'Semi-Arian' creed, which set the Son or Word in a mediating position between the ultimate God and the created world, on the hypothesis that the Word is a sufficiently watered-down form of Deity to engage, and even to enter, the visible, created order. Both positions, ancient and modern alike, set real Deity – Deity-in-and-of-itself – off against a lesser type of Deity that is susceptible of relatedness to beings other than itself. The only difference between these two views is that the earlier one seems to trade on the distinction between the uttered 'Word' and the divine 'Speaker', while the more recent version trades on that between God's intrinsic and essential 'being' and God's threefoldness in 'person' or '*hypostasis*'.

The antidote to this intellectual dissection of God is no doubt to assert, in the formula of Karl Rahner – by now a truism in theological circles – that 'The economic Trinity is the immanent Trinity and the immanent Trinity is

---

48 It needs to be observed, of course, that this distinction has ordinarily been declared alien to God, in whose 'being' nothing is contingent or accidental.

the economic Trinity.' This formula, however, correct though it be, does not of itself show the way to overcoming what seems to be a settled disposition on the part of theologians of almost every ilk to suspect that being God and being related are difficult to reconcile.

Ancient and medieval thinkers laid great stress on what one might call the reliability of God. They insisted that God does not change, but simply is, at every moment and in the same way, whatever can properly be meant by 'being God'. These qualities of immutability and timelessness signify that God can be counted on: that, for example, the God whose name is 'love' does not mutate into its opposite – does not have periodic fits of anger or succumb permanently to vengefulness, not even when needled by the perverse behaviour of finite agents. It also entails that God does not 'just happen' – whether by chance or by reaction to the action of an 'other' – to have this or that or any characteristic. God's identity is unchanging, and nothing that you or I do will change that identity (this, I take it, is what is meant by 'impassibility'). It is concerns and ideas like these that underlie, for example, Thomas Aquinas's assertion that while creatures have a real relation to God, God does not have a real relation to the world, but only a relation in thought. The intent of this assertion was of course to affirm that God is not passively reactive to actions or events in the finite world – that God's being is not relative to creaturely actions or attitudes as that of creatures is to God. Certainly Aquinas did not have it in mind to deny God's connectedness to the world or God's active concern for it. Nevertheless his language has a touch of the absurd about it: how can one not affirm that Deity is related to its own creation?

No doubt for this reason as well as for cultural reasons, modern theologians have stressed the Trinity's relatedness to the creation – to nature as well as to human beings in their history and above all in their conscious history with God; and some have insisted that God becomes whatever it is to be God in and through these relations in time to finite beings – thus dispensing with divine immutability. For it is now an axiom that things – and especially 'persons' – are constituted, at least in part, by their relations with others,[49] with the result that where Aquinas subordinated relatedness to 'being' (*substantia*: 'what-ness'), his posterity now subordinates 'being' to relations. In this theological analogue of the debate between nature and nurture, then, stress tends now to be laid not only on the deep involvement of God with creation, but on what one might call the responsiveness of God to finite events and agencies – a quality which must surely qualify as a criterion of moral goodness. The off-chance that the change that this risky involvement brings about in God may be a change for the worse is discounted, perhaps because there lurks somewhere in a corner of theologians' minds a shadow of the classical belief that, at least basically, God does not change very much.

The fact seems to be that these two starkly opposed attitudes terminate in each other, rather like life and death; for each of them, when pressed to its logical conclusion, dissolves into nagging doubt, and it is always the other that

---

49 See the influential and now surely classic study of G. H. Meade, *Mind, Self, and Society*, Chicago: University of Chicago Press, 1967. For Aquinas, of course, 'relation' was the name of a contingent or accidental modification of, or addition to, a creature's given 'being' (*ousia*).

dashes up to occupy the now empty field of conflict. The absolute God cannot be God in any serious sense save as related to the created 'other'; and the related – should one say 'relative'? – God cannot be God in any serious sense save as having a stable identity in relation to the created 'other'. Moreover, in an odd symbolic way this is conveyed by the very story to which this essay has appealed as revealing the root of Trinitarian faith. In the Gospel accounts of Jesus' baptism, the Voice from the opened heavens which says plainly, 'This is my beloved Son', and does this even as 'the Spirit of God' descends 'like a dove' upon the incarnate Word, belongs nevertheless to a Speaker that is not seen. The God who speaks is hidden even in this self-revelation, and remains in some fashion remote and mysterious, 'beyond' human affairs despite intense involvement with them. This God embraces humanity – Adam – as represented in the person of Jesus, and through that humanity, as some would add, the natural order that is its matrix. That embrace, moreover, elevates humanity into the divine life. It is in this act, and not apart from it, then, that God's 'relatedness' is discerned, but discerned precisely as the relatedness of the One who is timelessly 'other' – the 'absolute'. God sees and calls humanity in the Son and blesses and affirms it in that identity by conferring the life-giving Breath, which is the Spirit. This is 'relation' indeed; but it is the relation of the Mystery that creates on its own to the creation that owes it everything – the Mystery that is still shaping its creation as the Word that is God's self-objectification and at the same time bringing it to perfection in the life-giving Spirit that God breathes.

The key to the unity of the 'economic' and the 'immanent' Trinity, then, must lie precisely in the 'apophatic' or 'negative' theology that is, as we have suggested, an essential element in the Irenaean and Cappadocian teaching about God. God is not related to the created order as entities within that order are related to each other. Yet as Creator, God is related to them in a manner that not only makes their mutual relatedness possible but marks it out as an image of, and a participation in, the way that God exists in the relations of 'persons'. By the same token, God is not subject to the successiveness of past, present and future as are the creatures for whose fulfilment God created time; yet for all that, since their time is a dimension of the finite reality that God creates, the Trinity's way of being is not inconsistent with temporality. God is able to embrace time, to act within it and so to be made known to creatures, but always as the ever self-consistent Deity that is time's Alpha and its Omega. As always, then, the presupposition of this pattern of affirmation-and-denial, which is the proper form of what is called 'apophatic' theology, is the idea that the Trinity is the One who contains all things without being contained – or, in the more elegant language of some Greek poet whom Luke perhaps admired, the One in whom 'we live and move and have our being' (Acts 17.28) and therefore One to whom nothing finite is alien, even though nothing finite can fully or properly figure God.

How then is this triadic way of being world-related to be pictured? For if the nature of God on the one hand and the three 'hows' of that nature on the other are in fact not to be classified as two different 'forms' of God, the absolute and the related, but it is the absolute God who is eternally self-related to the finite order as its Origin, as its Model, and as the Empowerment of that Model, something has to be said about the divine 'persons' in their relation to each other;

and in this connection, the first question that arises is that of what 'person' here denotes.

Present-day Christians have to make an effort to recall that 'person' in the language of the fourth and fifth centuries bore none of the engaging, not to say endearing, connotations it has gradually acquired since Boethius defined it, in the sixth century, as meaning 'individual substance of a rational nature'. The Greek word *hypostasis* in its classical usage had many senses, and it could certainly be employed to refer to individuals that we – nowadays – would call 'persons'. Nevertheless none of its connotations conveyed, in and of itself, the notion of being 'personal'. In the Latin-speaking West, as we have seen, *persona*, a rough equivalent of the Greek *prosopon* ('face', 'outwardly manifested identity'; 'role'; 'mask'), was employed instead of *hypostasis*; but the meaning of this term, first used in a Trinitarian context by Tertullian in the third century, had not yet evolved to the point where it connoted a self-conscious centre of thought and action. It meant an identity, or a party (as in 'the party of the first part') – in any case, something one could refer to by a pronoun.

The question, then, whether the word *hypostasis* – and so in the West the word 'person' – can legitimately be employed to denote the members of the Trinity as persons in the modern sense of that term, needs some weighing. They referred, as we have seen, to 'somethings' that were differentiated only by their relations to each other. Hence terms referring to the three members of the Trinity stated, as we have indicated, how God exists and acts (i.e. in three distinct ways), and such a statement is of a different order from any assertion of what God is, i.e. what it is that exists in these three ways. To say, then, 'The Father, the Son and the Spirit are persons' would, in the terms of this classical Trinitarian logic, imply that 'person' is a label for a way of being God, but not a characterization of what God is.

There is, however, an obvious problem here. If 'person' is applied to each of the *hypostases* in the same sense, as, for example, 'God' or 'creator' or 'redeemer' are, the word would stand not for what distinguishes the *hypostases* from each other but for something they have in common. In that case, however, it would seem, 'being personal' would belong to the divine nature rather than to the *hypostases* (this, incidentally, seems to have been Barth's conclusion); for it is the divine *ousia* that the latter have in common. Maybe then it would be better to say that the *hypostases* mark three different ways in which God is personal, just as they mark three different ways in which God exists and acts. In taking this view, however, one would have to remember that the words 'ways' or 'modes' (i.e. of existing or of being), when employed in connection with the Trinity, do not connote mere appearances or aspects of God, but characterize concrete and distinct realities ('somethings' = *hypostases*) that are differentiated from each other not by 'what' they are but by 'how' they are. If to be God is to be personal, then Father, Son and Spirit are indeed personal, but in three different ways.

Given that qualification, there is no reason to think that to speak of the members of the Trinity as 'persons' in the later, modern sense is inconsistent with the traditional language of the doctrine. *Persona* and *hypostasis* could certainly be used, and were used, to refer to what moderns would call persons, even if that was not the going 'dictionary' meaning of the words in the fourth century; and in any case, Jesus and God and the Spirit were addressed and answered and questioned – spoken to, and not just spoken of – in the Church's liturgical and biblical idiom. It is useful to note, moreover, that someone like Gregory of Nyssa ascribes will and self-motion to both the Word and the Spirit as well as to the Father.[50]

How then, to return to our original question, do the relations that mark the persons of the Trinity illuminate the relationship of God to the creation? If one looks closely at the Cappadocian line, one's initial impression is that the persons constitute a series in the order Father —> Son —> Spirit. They are even called, inevitably, 'first', 'second' and 'third' – though of course Basil of Caesarea insisted that such counting be done reverently (i.e. both done and denied) in the best apophatic fashion. Quite apart from Basil, however, this 'serial' account of the Trinity ignores a further crucial element in the Cappadocians' picture of the relations among the persons. The Father generates the Son, to be sure; but it is also the Father who breathes the Spirit. The order, then, is not strictly serial, since the Spirit does not in the first instance proceed from the Son. Rather the two appear, as in Irenaeus, to be in a sense parallel and even co-ordinate; and this impression is reinforced when we discover that Gregory of Nyssa makes two distinctions with regard to the business of origination.[51] There is an initial distinction to be made between 'the cause' and 'that which is out of the cause': in other words, between the Father on the one hand, and Son and Spirit on the other. Then, he adds, there is a further distinction to be made within 'that which is out of the cause': namely, between 'what is immediately out of the original cause' (the Son) and 'what is through that which is immediately out of the original [cause]' (the Spirit). In this form, the doctrine of double procession[52] emphasizes the close connection between the work of the Word and that of the Spirit – their co-ordination. Thus Gregory will say that the Spirit is 'from the Father and of Christ', as the Scriptures teach. The 'thirdness' of the Spirit has to do with his being the one that brings all the works of God to completion.

Moreover the three persons, on this account, are never apart from each other, but always together. One reason for this is that '[t]he Father is never held in mind apart from the Son, nor is the Son grasped separately from the Spirit. For just as it is impossible to mount to the Father unless one has been lifted up by

---

50 See his 'Address on Religious Instruction' 1–2, in *LCC* 3, pp. 271, 273 = J. H. Srawley (ed), *The Catechetical Oration of Gregory of Nyssa*, Cambridge: Cambridge University Press, 1956, pp. 9f., 15.

51 'To Ablabius', in *LCC* 3, 266.

52 See also Athanasius, 'To Serapion' 1.2: 'the Spirit, who proceeds from the Father, and belonging to the Son, is from him given to the disciples and all who believe in him' (C. R. B. Shapland, *The Letters of St Athanasius Concerning the Holy Spirit*, London: Epworth, 1951, pp. 64f.). The doctrine of the 'double procession' of the Spirit is now best known in its embroidered Augustinian form, which is stated in a phrase that was inserted into the Niceno-Constantinopolitan Creed in the West during the late fifth and following centuries. According to this phrase, the Holy Spirit 'proceeds from the Father and the Son' – thus presumably having two simultaneous sources of his being. Gregory's formula – from the Father and 'through the Son' – preserves the role of the First Person of the Trinity as the single source and original of the divine nature reproduced in Son and Spirit; but I am not sure whether the difference between the two formulations amounts to an inconsistency.

the Son's agency, so it is impossible to call Jesus "Lord" save in the Holy Spirit.' Hence Gregory continues:

> For the Father and the Son and the Spirit are acknowledged to be always with one another, in their sequence [*akolouthos*] and in close union, in the full and perfect Trinity. Moreover, from before any creation and before all ages the Father is the Father, and in the Father is the Son, and with the Son is the Holy Spirit. It was not because he stood in need of assistance that the God who rules everything made all things through the Son, nor does the Only-begotten God accomplish everything in the Spirit because his power is inadequate to his project. No: but the wellspring of power is the Father, the power of the Father is the Son, and the spirit of power is the Holy Spirit; and the entire created order, perceptible and incorporeal alike, is the accomplished design of that power.[53]

In these words, one can see the basic principle that, in time, led to many other developments – or refinements – in Trinitarian doctrine. The principle might be stated simply enough by repeating what was said at the beginning of this section: that the Trinity is a unity not only in being one 'thing' but also in and through the relations of the persons. The Word is nothing and does nothing apart from the Father, and the Spirit is nothing and does nothing apart from the Word and the Father; and it follows that the Father is nothing and does nothing apart from Word and Spirit: the three cannot even be thought without being thought together. This point is reinforced by language which speaks of the Son's being eternally in the Father and the Spirit's being ever with the Son: the picture is essentially the Irenaean one and was stated by Athanasius of Alexandria: 'For the holy and blessed Triad is indivisible and one in itself. When mention is made of the Father, there is included also his Word, and the Spirit who is in the Son. If the Son is named, the Father is in the Son and the Spirit is not outside the Word.'[54] The persons of the Trinity take each other in.

Thus that in respect of which God is one is threefold; and that in respect of which God is threefold is one. It is the former point that seems to have been the theme of the controversy that occupied the middle years of the fourth century.

Each of the persons is the one God, though set apart from the others by the relation to them that defines it. The second of these points became central through reflection on the first, and was eventually articulated in the later doctrine of *perichoresis*.[55] This process of reflection began with the Cappadocians, but came to its most stable expression in the work of John of Damascus, who appropriated the ideas – and indeed the words – of the unknown author of

---

53 For these citations, see Gregory of Nyssa, 'On the Holy Spirit', in *NPNF* 2, Vol. 5, pp. 319, 320. Cf. Athanasius, 'To Serapion' 1.9 (ed. Shapland, p. 82): '(the Spirit), in whom the Father, through the Word, perfects and renews all things'.

54 Athanasius, 'To Serapion' 1.14 (ed. Shapland, pp. 93f.).

55 *Perichoresis* is a rare word in Greek. It can mean 'reciprocal alternation' (moving from one thing to another in circular fashion and coming back to the starting-point of the motion): for the Greek verb *choreo* means to go forward or advance and the preposition *peri*- can mean 'around'. The verb, though, can also mean 'contain' or 'make room for'; and *perichoresis* can then connote something like 'interpenetration' or 'permeation'.

a treatise on the Trinity falsely (but usefully) attributed to Cyril of Alexandria (d.444). It was this last-mentioned author who brought to expression the reciprocal indwelling of the three persons by adapting the idea of *perichoresis* to express it. 'Where the Trinity is concerned, the three *hypostases* are and are called one God because of their identity of nature and their *perichoresis* within each other' – a *perichoresis* by which, it was said, they 'hold on' to each other. The persons of the Trinity are so closely involved with each other that they really do constitute one thing without losing their individuality. Conversely, the difference of the persons is sustained by the communication from one to the other of the one nature.

Here then is a picture – sketched partly in a spatial metaphor, partly by way of an analogy with personal relations – of a God whose way of being is sharing and in whom, therefore, one-ness and many-ness, like the lion and the lamb, consent together. The original setting, however, in which this being-that-is-sharing is known and manifested is that of the water- and Spirit-baptism that Jesus shares with his disciples, a setting in which just such a way of being is opened to the participation of creatures – creatures that the God whose nature is inexpressible and whose name is unutterable created for just this purpose. Therefore it has to be said that the Trinity, though needing nothing and no one and being in that sense 'absolute', quite naturally does what it is and for mere love's sake[56] shares being and motion and life with a created order that participates in a multitude of different ways in God's own life – and which, in the case of 'personal' creatures, can image the very manner of God's being by being caught up in the identity of the Word of God through the Father's gift of the Spirit.

Introduction to the Sources

The doctrine of the Trinity was not a prominent issue in the religious agitations of the sixteenth and seventeenth centuries: certainly it was not an issue in the ongoing English debate between Puritans and the defenders of the Elizabethan establishment (commonly called 'Anglicans'). This does not mean that the doctrine of the Trinity was ignored or trivialized, but merely that it was not one of the principal agenda items among the contentions of the time; and, since the period in question was single-mindedly devoted to its contentions, treatises having the Trinity as their explicit subject-matter were not one of its typical products.

Richard Hooker's *magnum opus* entitled *The Ecclesiastical Polity of the English Nation* is a characteristic work of this era in that it is a polemical defence of the foundational principles of the Elizabethan Settlement; and this circumstance makes the appearance of an exposition of the doctrine of the Trinity in Book 5 something striking if not surprising. What renders it unsurprising is Hooker's purpose in introducing it and the manner in which he treats of it. The technicalities of the doctrine he sets out in one dense preliminary paragraph. What

---

56 Creation, then, can indeed be described as an act of God's will; but it is not the fruit of a process of argumentative deliberation – a distinction which, as the age-old critique mounted by Plotinus shows, is an important one.

follows, however, is less interested in those technicalities than in setting forth the way in which 'the union of the soul with God' comes about – that union which is the reality of eternal life, of salvation. The doctrine of the Trinity thus becomes the framework of a lengthy exposition of how 'Life as all other gifts groweth originally from the Father, and cometh not to us but by the Son, nor by the Son to any of us in particular but through the Spirit' (V.56.7) – and all this as the essential preliminary to an account of the manner of Christ's presence for believers in the sacraments. The doctrine of the Trinity as Hooker presents it is therefore not a single 'item' of doctrine alongside others, but is, on the contrary, an account of the structural framework of the Christian life and so the foundation of the gospel itself.

Lancelot Andrewes, a friend and younger contemporary of Hooker's, became, though after Hooker's death, Bishop of Winchester – and a regular preacher before the royal court. He wrote his share of polemical treatises (as who, in his day, did not?); but he presents his teaching on the Trinity not as an apologist or a polemicist, but as a preacher with a uniquely allusive, pedantic and withal artfully learned, style. The occasion for this presentation was the Feast of Whitsunday (Pentecost, in the Greek idiom) in the year 1516, in a sermon that connected the Spirit-baptism of the Apostles and others on that day with John's baptism of Jesus in the Jordan. Here again the doctrine of the Trinity is explicated in connection with an exposition of the divine work of salvation as that is epitomized in the gift of the Spirit by which believers share in the 'sonship' of Christ and so, as members of Christ, become children of God (cf. Gal. 3.26–27; 4.6). Clearly, in Andrewes's view, that is what the doctrine of the Trinity is about – the Father who in baptism brings people into union with his eternal Son through the inwardly bestowed power of the life-giving Spirit. Much the same approach can be observed in some of the sermons of John Donne. But treatments of the Trinity are for all that infrequent, save of course in catechetical materials like Bishop Pearson's *On the Creed*, the paradigmatic work of Anglican 'systematics'.

In truth, the period after 1660 – the later seventeenth and eighteenth centuries – was marked by the emergence and triumph of Enlightenment Deism, one of whose characteristics was a denial of the divinity of Christ and – therefore – of the Trinity: in short, a growing turn in the direction of unitarianism. This movement was initiated both in the theological writings of the empiricist philosopher John Locke (e.g. *The Reasonableness of Christianity* [1695]), and in those of his rationalist critic, Samuel Clarke, whose work titled *The Scripture-Doctrine of the Trinity* (1712), evoked a firm reaction from the High-Church, that is, Tory, interest. The best reply to Clarke came from Daniel Waterland, Master of Magdalene College, Cambridge, and Archdeacon of Middlesex (d.1740). Waterland, whose writings deserve a place among the classics of Anglican tradition, not only wrote a series of treatises defending the divinity of Christ, but also produced a little work, of uncertain date, titled *The Importance of the Doctrine of the Trinity*.

Nevertheless, it was neither the eighteenth century, which saw the rise of Deism and of the Evangelical Movement, nor the days of the Tractarian Movement at Oxford (1830–45), that saw a renewal of theological interest in the doctrine of the Trinity – though, to be sure, the subject was treated homiletically, for example, by J. H. Newman in certain of the addresses published in his *Parochial and Plain Sermons* (and of course, to another end altogether, in his later study of Arianism). The later evidence both of *Essays and Reviews* and of *Lux Mundi*, the collection edited by Charles Gore, suggests that the Trinity was not initially a prominent agenda-item in Anglican reactions to the challenges either of the new science (and especially perhaps Darwinism) or of the new historical criticism of the Bible. Nevertheless, it was the period between, say, 1870 and the opening decades of the twentieth century that saw the appearance of treatments of the doctrine of the Trinity that incorporated themes drawn from philosophical ideas of natural and human reality as in 'process' – that is, as evolving historically. In Britain this was reflected in the neglected work of J. R. Illingworth (one of the contributors to *Lux Mundi*) entitled *The Doctrine of the Trinity, Apologetically Considered* (1907). In the United States, it provided the framework of the treatment of the Trinity by William Porcher DuBose, 'the sage of Sewanee', and perhaps the most original of American Anglican thinkers. It is his reflections on the Trinity that are represented in the third of these selections; and it is notable that, quite apart from his 'process' approach to Christian theology, his Trinitarian teaching is like that of Hooker and Andrewes in being built into an exposition of the way of salvation.

Finally, the so-called 'social' doctrine of the Trinity saw what may have been its earliest exposition in the Croall Lectures of Professor Leonard Hodgson, entitled simply *The Doctrine of the Trinity* (1944); but the final excerpt in this collection comes from a 'popular' work of the late Austin Farrer, which evokes, in a style that combines poetic imagination with logical precision, themes from Augustine's Trinitarian thought, but does so – again – in the style of Hooker and Andrewes (i.e. to provide an account of the divine 'economy' of salvation).

Sources

Richard Hooker, *Of the Laws of Ecclesiastical Polity* Book V, Everyman's Library 202, 2 vols, London: J. M. Dent & Sons, 1954, *passim*.

[50.3] . . . as our natural life consisteth in the union of the body with the soul; so our life supernatural in the union of the soul with God. And forasmuch as there is no union of God with man without that mean between both which is both, it seemeth requisite that we first consider how God is in Christ, then how Christ is in us, and how the Sacraments do serve to make us partakers of Christ.

51.1 'The LORD our God is but one God'[cf. Deut. 6.4]. In which indivisible unity notwithstanding we adore the Father as being altogether of himself, we glorify that consubstantial Word which is the Son, we bless and magnify that co-essential Spirit eternally proceeding from both which is the Holy Ghost. Seeing therefore the Father is of none, the Son is of the Father and the Spirit is of both, they are by these their several properties really distinguishable each from other. For the substance of God with this property to be of none doth make the Person of the Father; the very selfsame substance in number with this property to be of the Father maketh the Person of the Son; the same substance having added unto it the property of proceeding from the other two maketh the Person of the Holy Ghost. So that in every Person there is implied both the substance of God which is one, and also their property which causeth the same person really and truly to differ from the other two. Every person hath his own subsistence, which no other besides hath, although there be others besides that are of the same substance.

51.2 Now when God became man, lest we should err in applying this to the Person of the Father, or of the Spirit, St Peter's confession unto Christ was, 'Thou art the Son of the living God' [Matt. 16.16] and St John's exposition thereof was plain, that it is the Word which was made flesh [John 1.14]. 'The Father and the Holy Ghost (saith Damascen) have no communion with the incarnation of the Word otherwise than only by approbation and assent.' Notwithstanding, forasmuch as the Word and Deity are one subject, we must beware we exclude not the nature of God from incarnation, and so make the Son of God incarnate not to be very God. For undoubtedly even the nature of God itself in the only Person of the Son is incarnate, and hath taken to itself flesh. Wherefore incarnation may neither be granted to any person but only one, nor yet denied to that nature which is common unto all three.

51.3 Concerning the cause of which incomprehensible mystery we may hereby perceive there is cause sufficient, why divine nature should assume human, that so God might be in Christ reconciling to himself the world [cf. 2 Cor. 5.19]. And if some cause be likewise required why rather to this end and purpose the Son than either the Father or the Holy Ghost should be made man, could we which are born the children of wrath be adopted the sons of God through grace, any other than the natural Son of God being Mediator between God and us?

52.3 Christ is a Person both divine and human, howbeit not therefore two persons in one, neither both these in one sense, but a person divine, because he is personally the Son of God, human because he hath really the nature of the children of men. In Christ, therefore, God and man, 'There is (saith Paschasius) a twofold substance, not a twofold person, because one person extinguisheth another, whereas one nature cannot in another become extinct.' For the personal being which the Son of God already had, suffered not the substance to be personal which he took, although together with the nature which he had the nature which he took also continueth. Whereupon it followeth against Nestorius, that no person was born of the Virgin but the Son of God, no person but the Son of God baptized, the Son of God condemned, the Son of God and no other person crucified . . .

These natures from the moment of their first combination have been and are for ever inseparable. For even when his soul forsook the tabernacle of his body, his Deity forsook neither body nor soul, but by personal union his Deity [was] inseparably joined with both.

53.1 The sequel of which conjunction of natures in Christ is no abolishment of natural properties pertaining to either substance, no transmission or transmigration thereof out of one substance into another, finally no such mutual infusion as really causeth the same natural operations or properties to be made common unto both substances; but whatsoever is natural to Deity the same remaineth in Christ uncommunicated unto his manhood, and whatsoever natural to manhood his Deity thereof is incapable.

53.3 Let us therefore set it down as a rule or principle so necessary as nothing more to the plain deciding of all doubt and questions about the union of natures in Christ, that of both natures there is a co-operation often, an association always, but never any mutual participation, whereby the properties of the one are infused into the other.

54.1 If then both natures do remain with their properties in Christ thus distinct as hath been shewed, we are, for our better understanding what either nature receiveth from other, to note that Christ is by three degrees a receiver: first, in that he is the Son of God; secondly, in that his human nature hath had the honour of union with Deity bestowed upon it; thirdly, in that by means thereof sundry eminent graces have flowed as effects from Deity into that nature which is coupled with it. On Christ therefore there is bestowed the gift of eternal generation, the gift of union, and the gift of unction.

54.2 By the gift of eternal generation Christ hath received of the Father one and in number the selfsame substance, which the Father hath of himself unreceived from any other.

54.3 Touching the union of Deity with manhood, it is by grace, because there can be no greater grace shewed towards man, than that God should vouchsafe to unite to man's nature the person of his only begotten Son. Because 'the Father loveth the Son' as man, he hath by uniting Deity with manhood, 'given all things into his hands' [John 3.35]. It hath pleased the Father that in him 'all fulness should dwell' [Eph. 1.5]. The union therefore of the flesh with Deity is to that flesh a gift of principal grace and favour. For by virtue of this grace, man is really made God, a creature is exalted above the dignity of all creatures, and hath all creatures else under it.

54.6 But to come to the grace of unction; did the parts of our nature, the soul and body of Christ, receive by the influence of Deity wherewith they were matched no ability of operation, no virtue of quality above nature? [T]here is no doubt but the Deity of Christ hath enabled that nature which it took of man to do more than man in this world hath power to comprehend; forasmuch as (the bare essential properties of Deity excepted) he hath imparted unto it all things, he hath replenished it with all such perfections as the same is in any way apt to receive . . .

55.1 Having thus far proceeded in speech concerning the Person of Jesus Christ . . . sith God in Christ is generally the medicine that doth cure the world, and Christ in us is the receipt of that same medicine, whereby we are every one particularly cured, inasmuch as Christ's incarnation and passion can be available to no man's good which is not made partaker of Christ, neither can we participate him without his presence, we are briefly to consider how Christ is present, to the end it may thereby better appear how we are made partakers of Christ.

55.3 Impossible it is that God should withdraw his presence from any thing, because the very substance of God is infinite. He filleth heaven and earth, although he take up no room in either, because his substance is immaterial, pure, and of us in this world so incomprehensible, that albeit no part of us be ever absent from him who is present whole unto every particular thing, yet his presence with us we no way discern farther than only that God is present, which partly by reason and more perfectly by faith we know to be firm and certain.

55.4 Seeing therefore that presence every where is the sequel of an infinite and incomprehensible substance (for what can be every where but that which can no where be comprehended?), to inquire whether Christ be every where is to inquire of a natural property, a property that cleaveth to the Deity of Christ. Which Deity being common unto him with none only but the Father and the Holy Ghost, it followeth that nothing of Christ which is limited, that nothing created, that neither the soul nor the body of Christ, and consequently not Christ as man or Christ according to his human nature, can possibly be every where present. Wherefore Christ is essentially present with all things, in that he is very God, but not present with all things as man.

55.7 To conclude, we hold it a most infallible truth that Christ as man is not everywhere present. Yet because this [human] substance is inseparably joined to that personal Word which by his very divine essence is present with all things, the nature which cannot in itself have universal presence hath it after a sort by being no where severed from that which everywhere is present. For the Person of Christ is whole, perfect God and perfect man wheresoever.

55.8 Again . . . the same universality of presence may likewise seem in another respect appliable [to Christ's human nature], namely by co-operation with Deity, and that in all things . . . [T]hat Deity of Christ which before our Lord's incarnation wrought all things without man, doth now work nothing wherein the nature which it hath assumed is either absent from it or idle. Christ as man hath all power both in heaven and earth given him [Matt. 28.18]. After his rising from the dead, then did God set him at his right hand in heavenly places . . . and hath appointed him over all the Head to the Church which is his body, the fulness of him that filleth all in all . . . This government therefore he exerciseth both as God and as man, as God by essential presence with all things, as Man by co-operation with that which essentially is present.

55.9 Which things indifferently every way considered, that gracious promise of our Lord and Saviour Jesus Christ concerning presence with his to the very end of the world . . . he doth perform both as God by essential presence of Deity, and as Man in that order, sense, and meaning, which hath been shewed.

56.1 We have hitherto spoken of the Person and of the presence of Christ. Participation is that mutual inward hold which Christ hath of us and we of him, in such sort that each possesseth other by way of special interest, property, and inherent copulation. For plainer explication whereof we may from that which hath been before sufficiently proved assume to our purpose these two principles, 'That every original cause imparteth itself unto those things which come of it'; and 'whatsoever taketh being from any other, the same is after a sort in that which giveth it being'.

56.2 It followeth hereupon that the Son of God being light of light, must needs be also light in light. The Persons of the Godhead, by reason of the unity of their substance, do as necessarily remain within one another, as they are of necessity to be distinguished one from another, because two are the issue of one, and one the offspring of the other two, only of three one not growing out of any other. And sith they all are but one God in number, one indivisible essence substance, their distinction cannot possibly admit separation. For how should that subsist solitarily by itself which hath no substance but individually the very same whereby other subsist with it; seeing that the Persons of that Trinity are not three particular substances to whom one general nature is common but three that subsist by one substance which itself is particular . . . The Father therefore is in the Son, and the Son in him, and the Spirit in both them.

56.5 All other things that are of God have God in them and he them in himself likewise God hath his influence into the very essence of all things, without which influence of Deity supporting them, their utter annihilation could not choose but follow. Of him all things have both received their first being and their continuance to be that which they are. All things are therefore partakers of God, they are his offspring, his influence is in them.

Whatsoever God doth work, the hands of all three persons are jointly and equally in it according to the order of that connexion whereby they each depend upon other. And therefore albeit in that respect the Father be first, the Son next, the Spirit last, and consequently nearest unto every effect which groweth from all three, nevertheless, they all being of one essence, are likewise all of one efficacy. The Father as Goodness, the Son as Wisdom, the Holy Ghost as Power do all concur in every particular outwardly issuing from the one only glorious Deity which they all are. For that which moveth God to work is Goodness, and that which ordereth his work is Wisdom, and that which perfecteth his work is Power. All things which God in their times and seasons hath brought forth were eternally and before all times in God, as a work unbegun is in the artificer which afterward bringeth it unto effect.

So that all things which God hath made are in that respect the offspring of God, they are in him as effects in their highest cause, he likewise is actually in them, the assistance and influence of his Deity is their life.

56.6 Let hereunto saving efficacy be added, and it bringeth forth a special offspring amongst men, containing them to whom God hath himself given the gracious and amiable name of sons. We are by nature the sons of Adam. When God created Adam he created us, and as many as are descended from Adam have in themselves the root out of which they spring. The sons of God we neither are all nor any one of us otherwise than only by grace and favour. The sons of God have God's own natural Son as a second Adam from heaven, whose race and progeny they are by spiritual and heavenly birth.

56.7 They which thus were in God eternally by their intended admission to life, have by vocation or adoption God actually now in them, as the artificer is in the work which his hand doth presently frame. Life as all other gifts and benefits groweth originally from the Father, and cometh not to us but by the Son, nor by the Son to any of us in particular but through the Spirit. For this cause, the Apostle wisheth to the Church of Corinth 'The grace of our Lord Jesus Christ, and the love of God, and the fellowship of the Holy Ghost' (2 Cor. 13.1-3).

56.10 Thus therefore we see how the Father is in the Son, and the Son in the Father; how they both are in all things, and all things in them; what communion Christ hath with his Church, how his Church and every member thereof is in him by original derivation, and he personally in them by way of the mystical association wrought through the gift of the Holy Ghost, which they that are his receive from him, and together with the same what benefit soever the vital force of his body and blood may yield, yea by steps and degrees they receive the complete measure of all such divine grace, as doth sanctify and save throughout, till the day of their final exaltation to a state of fellowship in glory, with him whose partakers they are now in those things that tend to glory.

J. P. Parkinson (ed.), *Ninety-Six Sermons, By The Right Honorable And Reverend Father In God, Lancelot Andrewes*, Library Of Anglo-Catholic Theology, Vols 1–5. Oxford: B. H. Parker, 1841–43, Vol. 3, pp. 241–60.

'A Sermon Preached Before The King's Majesty At Greenwich On The Twenty-Ninth Day Of May, A.D. MDCXV, Being Whit-Sunday' [excerpted]

Luke 3.21–22

> Now it came to pass, when all the people were baptized, and that Jesus also was baptized, and did pray, the heaven was opened, and the Holy Ghost came down upon him in bodily shape like a dove, and there was a voice from Heaven, saying, Thou art my beloved Son, in whom I am well pleased.

This is the feast of the Holy Ghost. And here we have in the text, a visible descending of the Holy Ghost.

Another there was, besides this; but this hath the vantage of it, three ways: 1. the worthiness of the Person. Here, it descends upon Christ, Who alone is more worth than those there. 2. The priority of time: this here was first, and that other, the Holy Ghost but at second hand. 3. The generality of the good: that other was proper but to one calling, of the Apostles only. All are not Apostles; all are Christians. This of Christ's concerns all Christians; and so the more general by far.

That it is of baptism, is no whit impertinent neither; for this is the feast of baptism. There were 'three thousand' this day baptized by the Apostles [cf. Acts 2.41], the first Christians that ever were. In memory of that baptism, the Church ever after held a solemn custom of baptizing at this feast. And many, all the year, reserved themselves till then; those except, whom necessity did cause to make more haste.

But upon the point, both baptisms fell upon this day. That wherewith the Apostles themselves were baptized, of fire. And that wherewith they baptized the people, of water. So that, even this way, it is pertinent also.

To look into the text, there is no man but at first blush will conceive there is some great matter at hand. 1. First, by the opening of heaven, for that opens not for a small purpose: 2. then, by the solemn presence of so great estates at it; for here is the whole Trinity in person. The Son in the water, the Holy Ghost in the dove; the Father in the voice. This was never so before, but once. Once in the Old Testament, and once in the New. In the Old, at the creation, the beginning of Genesis. There we find God, and the Word with God creating, and 'the Spirit of God moving upon the face of the waters' [Gen. 1.2]. And now here again, at Christ's christening in the New.

The faces of the Cherubims are one toward the other; that is, there is a mutual correspondence between these two. That was at the creation; this, a creation too: 'if any be in Christ, he is a new creature' of this new creation [2 Cor. 5.17]. That was the *genesis*, that is, 'the generation' of the world; this, the *Palingenesias* – the Apostle's word [Titus 3.5] – that is, 'the regeneration', or spiritual new birth, whereby we be born again the sons of God. And better not be born at all, than not so born again.

This, then, being every way as great (indeed, the greater of the twain), meet it was, they all should present themselves at this, no less than at that; and every one have his part in it, as we see they have. All, I say, seeing the commission for baptism was to run in all their names [cf. Matt. 28.19], and itself ever to be ministered accordingly.

'It came to pass that when', &c. Two baptisms we have here: 1. the people's first. 2. Then Christ's. How it should come to pass the people should be baptized, we see good reason. The people, they came 'confessing their sins' [Matt. 3.6] and so needed 'the baptism of repentance' [Acts 19.4] – so was John's baptism.

And not only for their sin: even their righteousness, take it at the best, even that was not so clean but it needs come to baptism; *utpote stillantes quotidie super telam justitiae saniem concupiscentiae.*

Let the people, then, be baptized in God's name: good and bad, men and children and all.

Sed quid facitis baptizantes Jesum? . . . 'What do you, [baptizing] Him' in Whom nothing unclean? What should He do being baptized? . . . Go wash your spotted lambs, and spare not; this Lamb is 'immaculate', hath not the least spot upon Him [1 Peter 1:19].

How came this to pass? Why baptized? Why with the people?

Was it this? Though He needed it not, yet for *exemplum dedi vobis*. He would condescend to it, to give all a good example of humility; as He did at His Maundy, when He washed His disciples' feet?

This sure was great humility, and to it we well might . . . ascribe it, but that Himself will not let us so do. For when the Baptist strained courtesy at it, He bade let be, 'Thus it behoved' *implere omnem justitiam* [Matt. 3:15]. *Justitiam* – mark that, no courtesy, but 'justice'. He makes a matter of justice of it, as if justice should not have been done, at least not 'all justice' if He had not been baptized.

Why, what justice had been broken? What piece of it, if He had not? To shew you how this comes to pass, we are to consider Christ as having two capacities, as they term them. So we are to consider Him – the second Adam; for so do we the first Adam, as a person of Himself, and as the author of a race, or head of a society. And even so do we Christ, either as *totum integrale*, 'a person entire' – they call it a body natural; or as *pars communitatis*, which they call a body politic, in conjunction and with reference to others; which others are His Church, which 'Church is His body' [cf. Eph. 1:22]. They His body and He their head – so told us often by the Apostle. And as by Himself considered, He is *Unigenitus*, 'the Only begotten', hath never a brother; so as together with the people, He is *Primogenitus inter multos*, 'the First begotten among many brethren' [Rom. 8.20].

To apply this to our purpose. Take Christ by Himself, as severed from us, and no reason in the world to baptize Him. He needed it not. Nay, take Him so, Jordan had more need to come to Him, than He to Jordan, to be cleansed. *Lavit aquas Ipse, non aquae Ipsum*, 'The waters were baptized by Him, they baptized Him not.' It is certain; so He received no cleannness, no virtue; but virtue He gave to Jordan, to the waters, to the Sacrament itself.

But then take Him the other way, as in conjunction *cum populo*, they and He one body, and the case is altered. For if he be so cum populo, with them, as He be one of them, as He be part of a body with them, a principal part I grant, yet part though, reason would He do as they do, part and part alike. 'Inasmuch,' saith the Apostle, 'as the children were partakers of flesh and blood, He also took part with them' [Heb. 2.14]. And so, inasmuch as they baptized, He also took such part as they, both went to baptism together . . .

But if we look a little further, then shall we find greater reason yet. A part He is, and parts there be that in some case undertake for the whole . . . And 'it came to pass' that such a part He was; He undertook for us. For in His baptism, He put us on, as we 'put Him on' [Gal. 3.27] in ours. Take Him, then, not only as *cum populo*, but as *pro populo*; not only as *nobiscum* but as *pro nobis*; put Him in the case the Prophet doth . . . 'put upon him the transgressions of us all' [Isa. 53.6]; put him as the Apostle puts him . . . , 'make Him sin for us' [cf. 2 Cor. 5.21], put all our sins upon Him; and then it will come to pass. He will need baptizing, He will need that for me and thee that for Himself he needed not . . .

Only one scruple remains, how Jordan or any water could do this, wash away sin? To clear it shortly, the truth is, it could not. It is no water-work, without somewhat put to it, to help it scour. But nothing on earth: not, if you put to it, 'nitre', 'much soap' [Job 9.30; Jer. 2.22] . . . say the Prophets, all will not do, it will not off so. . . . For after this was past, He spake of another 'baptism He was to be baptized with' [Luke 12.50]. And that was it indeed; that 'the fountain that was opened to the house of Israel, for sin and for uncleanness' [Zech. 13.1]; that was *baptismus sanguinis*. 'For without blood,' without the mixture of that, 'there is no doing away sin.' [Heb. 9.22]

And so he was baptized. And he had *trinam mersionem*; . . . In 'Gethsemane', in His sweat of blood. In 'Gabbatha', in the blood that came from the scourges and thorns; and in 'Golgotha', that which came from the nails and the spear. Specially, the spear. There, met the two streams of 'water and blood' [John 19.34], the true Jordan, the bath or laver, wherein we are purged 'from all our sins' [1 John 1.7]. No sin of so deep a dye but this will command it, and fetch it out . . . And therefore are we baptized into it: not into His water baptism, but into His cross baptism; not into His baptism, but into His death.

Now Christ is baptized. And no sooner is he so, but he falls to his prayers. *Indigentia mater orationis*, we say, 'want begets prayer'. Therefore, yet there wants somewhat. A part, and that a chief part, of baptism is still behind.

There goes more to baptism, if it be as it should be, than *baptismus fluminis*; yea, I may boldly say, there goes more to it, if it be as it should, than *baptismus sanguinis*. Christ 'came in water and blood, not in water only, but in water and blood' [1 John 5.6] – that is not enough, except 'the Spirit also bear witness' [cf. 1 John 5.7]. So *baptismus Flaminis* is to come too. There is to be a Trinity beneath, 1. water, 2. blood, and 3. the Spirit, to answer to that above; but the Spirit's baptism coming too, in the mouth of all three is made sure . . . This is it He prays for as man.

For the baptism of blood that was due to every one of us . . ., that hath Christ quit us of. When He was asked by the Prophet, 'how His robes came so red?' He says, 'He had been in the winepress'. But there He had been, and that He had trod, alone . . . , 'and not one of the people with him', none but he there, in that [cf. Isa. 62.2f.] . . .

But the other two parts, He sets down precisely to Nicodemus, and in him to us all: 1. water, 2. and the Holy Ghost. Now the Holy Ghost we yet lack. So doth St Paul 'baptized in the sea and by the cloud' [1 Cor. 10.2]; by 'the sea' meaning the elementary part, by 'the cloud' the celestial part of baptism. Now that of the cloud we have not yet. And the baptism of the body, is but the body of baptism; the soul of baptism is the baptism of the soul. Of the soul, with the blood of Christ, by the hand of the Holy Ghost, as of the body with water, by the hand of the Baptist . . .

St Paul tells us, that besides the circumcision that was the *manufacture*, there was another, 'made without hands' [Col. 2.11]. There is so, in baptism, besides the hand seen that casts on the water; the virtue of the Holy Ghost is there, working 'without hands' what here was wrought.

And for this, Christ prays; that then it might, might then, and might ever, be joined to that of the water. Not in His baptism only, but in the people's; and as He after enlarges His prayer, in all others' that 'should ever after believe in His name' [John 17.20]. That what in His here was, in theirs might be; what in this first, in all following; what in Christ's, in all Christians'. Heaven might open, the Holy Ghost come down, the Father be pleased to say over the same words . . . so oft as any Christian man's child is brought to his baptism . . .

But first mark. Till the Spirit is come, the voice comes not: all depends on this day's work, the Holy Ghost's coming. He is the *medius terminus*, between Christ in Jordan and the Father in heaven. He it is That makes the Father speak . . . 'Thou', that is, 'Thou on whom the Spirit in this shape comes down, Thou art My Son' . . . So it was in Genesis. 'The Spirit moved upon the face of the waters,' and then *Et dixit Deus*; but no *dixit Deus* before the Spirit be there first.

Then . . . , as Christ elsewhere saith, 'This voice came not for him,' but for us [cf. John 12.30]. Spoken to Him indeed, but to Him, not in His own, but sustaining our persons.

The meaning is, 'Thou', Christ, in their persons, art this. 'Thou art'; and for Thy sake, all that are in Thee, all that by baptism have put Thee on, all and every of them are to Me, as Thou thyself art . . .

William Porcher Dubose, *The Gospel In The Gospels*, New York: Longmans, 1911, pp. 274–89 [excerpted].

The truth takes its own forms and expresses itself in its own ways. Our efforts at defining, proving, or establishing it are all acts after the event. It is what it is, and not what we make it. Christianity prevails in the world in a fact which we have called Trinity, and which is Trinity, however inadequate and unsatisfactory our explanations of the term or our analyses of the thing may be. I would describe Christianity in its largest sense to be the fulfilment of God in the world through the fulfilment of the world in God. This assumes that the world is completed in man, in whom also God is completed in the world. And so, God, the world, and man are at once completed in Jesus Christ – who, as he was the *Logos* or thought of all in the divine foreknowledge of the past, so also is He the telos or end of all in the predestination of the future. That is to say, the perfect psychical, moral, and spiritual manhood of which Jesus Christ is to us the realization and the expression is the end of God in creation, or evolution. I hold that neither science, philosophy, nor religion can come to any higher or other, either conjecture or conclusion, than that. But now, when we come to the actual terms or elements of God's self-realization in us and ours in Him, we cannot think or express the process otherwise than in the threefold form of the divine love, the divine grace, and the divine fellowship, in operation or action. Putting it into scriptural phrase, we speak as exactly as popularly in defining the matter of the Gospel to be, the love of the Father, the grace of the Son, and the fellowship of the Spirit [cf. 2 Cor. 13.14]. As our spiritual life is dependent upon each and all of the three constituents, so we can know God at all only as we know him in the actual threefold relation to us of Father, Son, and Spirit.

The first element is the essential constitution of the Gospel is the fact in itself that God is love. That God is love means that he is so not only in himself but in every activity that proceeds from him. The very phrase The love of the Father expresses the whole principle of the universe. That God is Father means that it is His nature, or His essential activity, to reproduce Himself, to produce in all other that which He Himself is. That God in Himself is love carries with it the truth that from the beginning all things else mean, and are destined to come to, love in the end. The mystery on the way that somehow light must come out of darkness, that love must needs conquer hate, and that in everything good seems to be only the final and far off goal of ill, may puzzle us, but it does not disturb the principle itself. When we come to enter fairly upon the evolution of the future, the higher, not merely psychical or social or moral but spiritual life and destiny of man, all the truth gradually dawns upon us in the following discoveries, which are already established facts of spiritual experience: the truth of all spirit is love; the matter of all law is goodness; God is not creator or cause only, nor lord or lawgiver only, but Father of all things, since all things through man are destined to share His spirit, to be partakers of His nature [cf. 2 Pet. 1.4], and to reproduce Himself as Father in themselves as children. In order to be sons of God through actual participation in divine nature there stands in the way indeed the need of a mighty redemption from sin and an as yet far off completion in holiness; but no matter how unredeemed or incomplete, we know beyond further question that all our salvation lies in redemption and completion, and that we shall be ourselves and the world will come to its meaning only when the self-realization of God as Father shall have accomplished itself in our self-realization as his children. If we knew the fact only that God in Himself is love, it would be to us a gospel indeed of great joy, because it would carry in it the assurance of the highest good, whatever that might be. But it would be but a partial gospel, and in fact only a gospel at all through its certainty of proceeding further.

The phrase Grace of the Son expresses that which perfectly complements and completes all that is meant by the Love of the Father. What is Fatherhood without a correlative Sonship? And what is all love even in God as its subject apart from its actuality and activity as grace in man as its object? The divine propriety of the terms Father and Son as applied to God cannot be too much magnified. The distinction between God as He is in Himself and God as He is in all possible expressions of Himself is one that we cannot think him at all without making. The most perfect expression of love is contained in the statement, that Love loves love. Its nature is to produce, to reproduce, to multiply itself. Love is forever the true object of itself, at the same time that it is going forth from itself into that which is not itself. This essential principle of love or self-reproduction is what makes God eternally Father. But eternal Fatherhood is actualized only in an eternal Sonship. Nothing proceeds from the Father which is not reproduction of the Father, and is not therefore Son. Man sees himself now in nature and destinature son of God. He feels his call and obligation to fulfill God in him as Father by realizing himself in God as Son. His spiritual end and impulse is to know as also he is known, to love in return as he is first loved, to apprehend that for which he is apprehended of God in Christ. In proportion as he finds the meaning and truth of his own being in the reproduction of God, in being Son of God, he finds the meaning and truth of the whole creation realized and expressed in his own sonship as heir of all and end of all. And in proportion again as he thus finds all things meaning and ending in sonship, he comes at last to see God himself as realized in the universal sonship – Himself therein realized as Eternal Father. So it is that in Jesus Christ we see everything expressed, because everything realized or fulfilled. He is all truth, because he is the truth of all things – God, Creation, Man. And because He is thus truth and expression of all, He is *Logos* of all. What else could the *Logos* of all be but Son, or the Son but *Logos*. What could perfectly express God but that which is perfect reproduction of Himself, or what is perfect sonship but perfect likeness?

The Grace of the Son is the divine gift of Sonship. How could we have known God only in himself? How could God have been actually our Father without the actuality of our sonship to Him? And could we have known, could we have wanted . . . , could we have accomplished or attained our sonship without the gift or grace of sonship in Jesus Christ? God, we are told, predestinated us to be conformed to the image of His Son, that he might be the first-born among many brethren [Rom. 8.29]. In bringing many sons to glory, he gave us a Captain of our salvation [Heb. 2.10], an Author and Finisher [Heb. 12.2] of the faith of sonship and so of the sonship of faith, who was Himself perfected through the sufferings that are necessary to the perfecting of sonship in us. We see in Jesus Christ all that is meant, involved, or implied in the fact that He is divine Fatherhood realized and expressed in human sonship.

If that fact, viewed in its totality, signifies not only a human act, but a divine-human act, an act of God in man which is equally an act of man-in-God, – then we say that Jesus Christ is not only as well the humanity as the divinity in that act, but he is the divinity as well as the humanity. He is not only the *gratia gratiata* in it but the *gratia gratians* – not only the manhood infinitely graced but the Godhead infinitely gracing.

Jesus Christ is therefore to us no mere sample or example of divine sonship. He is no mere one man who more successfully than others has grasped and expressed the ideal of a divine sonship. Neither is he a single individual of our race whom God has elected from among equally possible others, in whom as mere revelation or example to all others to manifest the truth of God in man and man in God. On the contrary, Jesus Christ is Himself the reality of all that is manifested or expressed in him. He is as God the grace communicating and as man the grace communicated. He is both Generator and generated with reference to the life incarnate in Him – both the sonship eternally in God to be begotten and the sonship actually begotten in man. As He was in the beginning with God and was God, so is He universally with man and is universal man.

When we have thus adequately conceived Christ as the universal truth and reality of ourselves, and in ourselves of all creation, and in creation and ourselves of God, then we are prepared for the conclusion that we can know God at all, or are sons to him as our Father, or are capable in that relation of partaking of His nature or entering into His Spirit or living His life, only in and through Jesus Christ, because Jesus Christ is the incarnation or human expression to us of the whole *Logos* of God – that is to say, of God Himself as in any way whatever knowable or communicable. We cannot get at God to know or possess Him otherwise than as he reveals and imparts Himself; and He reveals Himself through His own Word and imparts Himself in His own Son. There and there alone is He to be known, and there He is all our own. The *Logos* who is the eternal Self-revelation of God manifests himself as ideal principle, first and final cause, meaning and end, of creation; and the end of the whole creation which manifests God is realized through spiritual humanity in the imparted sonship of the Everlasting Son of the Father.

There is yet one other condition of truly knowing or really possessing God as wholly our God. As God is unknowable and incommunicable but through Christ, so is Christ, however perfectly He is in himself the self-revelation and self-communication of God, not so to us but through the co-equal action of the Holy Ghost. There is no knowledge of God in Himself only, there is no knowledge of God in creation only, or in others, or even in Christ only, without the answering knowledge of God in ourselves also. It is only like that answers to like. The deep that answers to deep must be the same deep [cf. Ps. 42.7]. Jesus Christ expected in every son of man not only the answer of the man in him to Himself as eternal and universal Son of man, but the answer of the God in him to the perfect Godhead in himself. Ye cannot see God in me, he says, because ye have not God in you. No man cometh unto me except the Father draw him. I do not wish to urge the mere conventional language of Christianity, true as I believe it and helpful as I may find it to myself. I would if possible speak in the common language of common experience. When we speak of knowing God, and having God, it must mean knowing him as he is to be known and having him as he is to be had. Now, whatever God is himself, he is knowable to us only in Jesus Christ, and he can be our God only as he is conceived in us by the operation of the Spirit of God and born of the want which he implants and the faith which he generates.

The doctrine of the Trinity is ordinarily thought of as the very extreme of speculative reasoning upon the nature of God. But let us remember that practical faith in the Trinity antedated any speculative thought or doctrine of the Trinity. And behind that faith the fact itself of the Trinity is all that makes God knowable by us or us capable of knowing God. Before there was the word Trinity, the new world of Christianity had come to know God in Christ, and to know Christ in itself. The entire doctrine ... was nothing but a positive affirmation and a determined defence of the fulness of the truth of God in Christ and Christ in us. We can do no better than conclude this entire exposition of the Gospel with an interpretation of it in the only terms in which it is expressible, viz.: in terms of the Trinity.

***

The first condition and constituent of the Gospel is the fact that God in Himself is love. How do we know that God is love? I believe that actually or historically we know it in Christ, in whom the fact of the divine love is consummated and manifested. But in the light now of Christianity I believe that it is also philosophically demonstrable that goodness or love is the essential principle and the ultimate end of the universe. *How* God is love, not only in antecedent nature but in the actuality of self-fulfilment in the world, may be readable too in nature, – after the light thrown upon it by Christianity, – but in fact it is known in its reality only in Christ . . . All the love we know is in concrete relations and the forms of affection determined by the character of those relations . . . The concrete form in which alone we can know God as love is expressed by our designation of Him as eternal Father. That gives shape and definiteness to not only our conception, but the reality itself of His relation to us and ours to Him, and no less of how that relation is to be fulfilled. The full reality of fatherhood comes about only in the full realization of sonship, and that therefore must be God's meaning and end for all that is in the universe of His self-expression. We begin so to anticipate the truth that is to be expressed in such statements as that God has foreordained or predestined us to sonship through Jesus Christ unto Himself, that God has foreordained us to be conformed to the image of His Son, and many others to the same effect. But before we come to these unfoldings of the divine nature and purpose, let us reflect upon the following antecedent truth.

The beginning of all distinction between a pantheistic and a theistic conception of the world lies in recognizing the world as the expression, not of God himself – or, as we say, 'of His substance' – but of his *Logos*, His Thought, Will, Word. Moreover, when once we have conceived and accepted God as eternal Father, we are in position to assume that the *Logos*, not merely as the principle of divine self-expression but as God Himself self-expressed, must manifest Himself universally as Son or in sonship; since universal and everlasting Sonship is the only self-expression of eternal and essential Fatherhood.

The first constituent, therefore, of the Gospel is the fact in itself of the divine love in Fatherhood. The second is, the equal fact in itself of the actualization of the divine Fatherhood in creature – or, definitely, in human – Sonship. The love of the Father fulfills and manifests itself in the grace of the Son. Love is grace *potentia*; Grace is love *actu*, – just as Fatherhood itself is Sonship potential, and Sonship is Fatherhood actualized. When we have once seen all humanity perfected as son in Jesus Christ, it is not hard to see in Him the whole creation so perfected as man as its head and as heir of its destiny. And then still less hard is it to see how we could never have known God as Father if he He had not so fulfilled and manifested Himself as Son.

***

The third constituent of the Gospel is the fact in itself of the fellowship of the Spirit. Truly, our fellowship is with the Father and with his Son Jesus Christ [1 John 1.3]. The possibility or potentiality of such a real unity and community with God must exist somehow beforehand in our nature as spirit, or in the natural relation of our finite spirits to the Father of spirits. But the actuality spiritual . . . intercommunication which we call fellowship is no fact of nature but an act or interaction of spirits. It is not for us to say how . . . spirit can act upon spirit; all that we can do is to understand how, practically and actually, spirit does act upon spirit. The most perfect expression of the actual action of the divine upon the human spirit is contained in the words, The Spirit beareth witness with our spirit that we are the sons of God [cf. Rom. 8.16]. Let us assume the objectivity or truth in itself of the eternal Fatherhood . . . of God in himself. Let us also assume the objective reality of all that we have claimed to have happened in Jesus Christ viz., that in him as *Logos* God revealed himself in the universe, and that in him as Son God fulfilled himself in humanity. When we have assumed all that body of objective truth – the truth in itself of the Father and the Son – what remains still to make it the Gospel to ourselves? Undoubtedly something remains. All the reality in the universe can be no Gospel to us so long as it remains objective, or until it enters into living relation with ourselves. Of course it can never so enter unless there is in us the natural potentiality of entering into relation with it. But equally certainly that potentiality can only be actualized by ourselves. What is necessary within ourselves to give effect to all that is true without us is a corresponding response, or a response of correspondence, on our part When the Spirit bears witness with our spirit, that we are sons of god, it is not only God who communicates the gracious fact, but it is God who awakens the humable and grateful response, and puts it into our heart to say, Abba, Father [Gal. 4.6]. If we cannot thus know God subjectively in ourselves, we cannot know God objectively in Jesus Christ. And if we cannot know him in His Word and by His Spirit, we cannot know him at all.

***

All life is defined as an internal correspondence with external environment. We saw, I think, long ago that as it is the function of the divine Word *aptare Deum homini*, so it is that of the divine Spirit *aptare hominem Deo*. The Spirit . . . brings us first to a perfect correspondence of faith with the fact of our life of God in Christ. But just because faith means life, that is, knows, desires, and intends it – therefore it is it. God already imputes, as he will impart, and faith already appropriates, as it will possess, the life which is so believed in. Attuned to Christ by the anticipatory spell of faith, hope, and love, we shall be by a natural process of spiritual assimilation transformed into his likeness in act, character, and life, until coming to see him perfectly as he is we shall be wholly what he is [cf. 1 John 3.2] . . .

'. . . it is the function of the divine Word to adjust [or "adapt"] God to man,' and 'it is that of the divine Spirit to adjust [or "adapt"] man to God.'

Austin M. Farrer, *Lord, I Believe*, second edition, London: SPCK, 1962, pp. 17ff. [excerpted]

The Trinity cannot be explored except from the centre. And what is the centre? It is the Love of God. The name of Love has been fearfully profaned, yet no other name will do. If, for example, we were content to contemplate the benevolence of God, we should not open up the region in which the Trinity is revealed, but only if we go beyond benevolence into love. Benevolence may be no more than a general and diffused well-wishing; love requires that a person should be infinitely prized. The welfare state is a moral possibility if its officials are predominantly benevolent, but we do not expect them to love us.

In mentioning the welfare state we have hit upon a point of some religious importance, for the influence of political organization on religious feeling has at all times been profound. When we had absolute monarchy we had a theology of divine sovereignty; now we have welfare politics our religion is divine benevolence. It is instinctive in us to think of God's power as taking over where human power leaves off, as caring for the intimate distresses which no public officer relieves, controlling dangers no police can master . . . But God's Kingdom is not paternal government. Paternal government is only a bastard sort of fatherliness, and God is a true father so far as loving his children goes.

And that is easily said. It is easy to tell ourselves a tale about God's love for us, another thing to receive his love and reciprocate it, as it was Moses' privilege to do, when God is said to have spoken with him as a man speaks with his friend, face to face and without disguises. A man's face lights up the face of his friend, and Moses' face shone [Exod. 34.29–30; cf. 34.35], reflecting that countenance which is the Light of the world.

And . . . let us . . . recall another antique personage. If God is said to have spoken with Moses as a man speaks to his friend, he is said to have honored Abraham with the actual title: 'Abraham, my friend,' says the divine voice: his friend because he was admitted to his confidence. 'Shall I hide from Abraham,' said the LORD God, 'the thing that I do, seeing that I know him' [Gen. 18.17]?

What Genesis sets forth in the vividness of the picture is to be enjoyed by every Christian in the reality of spirit. God makes every one of us his friend, he sets us at his table, he shares his thought with us, he shows us his kindness, he puts an infinite price upon our love. God holds our love for him incomparably more dear than we hold the love of those who are dearest to us.

Nothing moves our penitence more than to recognize that we have withheld what God desires, and . . . despised what he prizes most; nothing calls out our adoration more than a love which, knowing us to the bottom, continues to care for us under all our self-obsession and frivolity.

It would be a great thing if we could love any single person as we love ourselves, but we cannot love even ourselves as our Creator loves us. Friendship involves some kind of an equality, or, if not an equality, then an equalization. God equalizes us with himself in the same sense that he makes us party to a friendship with himself, but the equalization equalizes sheer inequalities. A man may make a friend of a child . . . , and such an affection may be stronger than friendship; but friendship it is not, in the strict sense of the word. By making a friend of a child, we extend to him what belongs properly to our equal, and by making friends of us our Father and our God extends to us by a stretch incomparably wider what belongs uniquely to his co-equal Son. If God's love for us were all the love there was, then divine love would never have been. It is only because divine love has a natural object that it overflows to embrace an adopted object. We are the children of God by adoption, the eternal Son of God is Son by nature.

The love whereby our divine Father loves us is an actual part of the one love with which he loves his eternal Son, for God is love and his love is one piece. So all the gifts of the Father's love to Christ are in a manner extended to Christians. 'Thou art my beloved Son, in thee I am well pleased' is an oracle of love that speaks to sinners, because they are among the number of whom Christ says: 'I and the children whom God has given me'.

'To know Christ is to know the benefits we derive from him,' says an old theologian. What benefit do we chiefly derive from him? The heavenly sonship which overflows from him to us. And how do we know him from that benefit? We see that what we have in part and by adoption he has by nature and in fullness, the pure and simple sonship is his. We do not best understand the Divine Father and the Divine Son by drawing analogies from human sons and human fathers, but by a method more real and more direct – that is, from experiencing divine sonship extended to ourselves.

But having grasped this similarity, we must go on to seize the difference: the Son of God differs infinitely from us, his Sonship from ours. It is usual to say that, whereas God made us, he begot his Son, but that is little better than a textbook formula. It draws a distinction, it does nothing to explain it. For we were not made, as we understand making, nor was he begotten as we understand begetting. He was not begotten, for he was begotten in no womb, and we were not made, for we were made of no material. Both the only-begotten Son and we, the many spirits created, depend and derive wholly from the Father of all. The Eternal Son is utterly derived, utterly dependent, but he is the full expression of his Father's nature and being, and, therefore, not less in nature or glory than the Father who begets him. The Son also is eternal God, for otherwise the Father's act of begetting would be imperfect, he would not beget what is best or worthiest of himself. The Son has nothing that he does not derive from the Father, but he derives from the Father all the Father has to give. Were he not equal with the Father, he would lack the capacity to receive all that the Father has the bounty to bestow. His love, like ours, is a response and a reciprocation; and no spirit lower than God can reciprocate all the love of God. He depends on the Father not for less than we do, but for infinitely more. We receive from the Father all that we are, he alone receives from the Father all that the Father is.

We were thinking just now of Moses, and the shining of his face by reflection of the divine radiance. But what a narrow glass is the up-turned face of Moses to reflect the glory of the Light that warms the world! Only the face of God reflects the face of God, there alone is converse in true equality . . . S. Paul, interpreting for us the shining of Moses' face, says that the God who inflows as light on Moses is the Holy Ghost [cf. 2 Cor. 3.12–17]. The apostle's interpretation is true to our experience: if we answer divine love, it is by divine inspiration. But how little there is in us for the divine Spirit to inspire! The Holy Ghost is measured in us by the narrowness of our vessel, to the eternal Son he gives himself without measure. The Son does not measure the Spirit by limiting him, he perfectly expresses him by perfectly receiving him. Holy Ghost means the divine life communicated or bestowed. Holy Ghost has no being except in another; the first and proper being of the Holy Ghost is in the eternal Son.

So there are two acts of God the Father, neither conceivable without the other: to beget and to bestow: to beget the Son, to bestow on him the Holy Ghost. Both acts are perfect: what is begotten is God, and what is bestowed is equally God. The divine persons do not lack perfection by needing one another, for what they require they eternally possess. The Father does not lack for the expression of his Fatherhood, he expresses it perpetually in his Son. The Spirit is not imperfectly real through being the completion of another's life; he enjoys perfection in being perfectly bestowed on a perfect recipient by a perfect giver. Here are not three Gods; here is one Godhead which can be what it essentially is, a society of Love, only through distribution in three persons.

In the pursuit of such high mysteries our thought is lost; and yet the Trinity is no mere conjecture about the heart of Heaven. The Trinity is both the meaning and the setting of that love which the Father has actually bestowed upon us. We need have nothing to do with the Trinity as a cool speculation about the necessary nature of the Godhead; it would be idiocy to place such confidence in theological reasonings as to evolve it by rational argument. The Trinity is revealed to Christians because they are taken into the Trinity, because the threefold love of God wraps them round, because it is in the Trinity they have their Christian being. Every time I worship or pray or make the least motion of heart towards God, I stand with the divine Son in face of the divine Father, the mantle of his Sonship spread around me, and the love of the Father overflowing from him to me in the grace of the Holy Ghost.

Bibliography

Pre-Reformation Materials

Athanasius of Alexandria, 'On the Decrees of the Nicene Synod'.
Athanasius of Alexandria, 'Letter 1 To Serapion'.
Augustine of Hippo, *On the Trinity* VIII–XV.
Basil of Caesarea, *On the Holy Spirit*.
Gregory of Nazianzus, *Orations* 27–32.
Gregory of Nyssa, 'To Ablabius That There Are Not Three Gods'.
Gregory of Nyssa, *Against Eunomius*, Book 1 and Book 12b ('Answer to Eunomius' Second Book').
Richard of St Victor, *On the Trinity*.
Thomas Aquinas, *Summa Theologiae*, Part I, Questions 27–43.

Modern Works

Karl Barth, *Church Dogmatics I.1: The Doctrine of the Word of God*, tr. G. T. Thomson, Edinburgh: T. & T. Clark, 1955.
Leonardo Boff, *Trinity and Society*, tr. Paul Burns, Maryknoll, NY: Orbis Books, 1981.
Leonard Hodgson, *The Doctrine of the Trinity: The Croall Lectures for 1942/3*, New York: Scribner's, 1944.
J. R. Illingworth, *The Doctrine of the Trinity, Apologetically Considered*, London: Macmillan, 1907.
Robert W. Jenson, *Systematic Theology, Vol. 1: The Triune God*, New York and Oxford: Oxford University Press, 1997.
Catherine M. LaCugna, *God for Us: The Trinity and Christian Life*, San Francisco: Harper, 1991.

Jürgen Moltmann, *The Trinity and the Kingdom of God*, San Francisco: Harper and Row, 1981.
Karl Rahner, *The Trinity*, New York: Crossroad, 1997.
A. E. J. Rawlinson (ed.), *Essays on the Trinity and the Incarnation*, London and New York: Longmans, 1928.
Dorothy L. Sayers, *The Mind of the Maker*, London: Religious Books Club, 1942.
Daniel Friedrich Ernst Schleiermacher, *The Christian Faith*, ed. H. R. Macintosh and J. S. Stewart, Philadelphia: Fortress Press, 1928.
Daniel Waterland, *The Importance of the Doctrine of the Holy Trinity Asserted in Reply to Some Late Pamphlets*, 3rd edn, Cambridge: J. Burges, 1800.
Claude Welch, *In This Name: The Doctrine of the Trinity in Contemporary Theology*, New York: Scribner's, 1952.

3

Christology

ROWAN WILLIAMS

Origins and Biblical Sources

Probably the most commonly used words in Christian practice are 'through Jesus Christ Our Lord'. For pretty well the entire history of the Christian Church, this formula, or something very close to it, has been the mark of distinctively Christian prayer; when Christians these days are asked about the possibilities of shared prayer with adherents of other faiths, the biggest difficulty they have to face is how they are to pray without being able to use this formula (a question we shall come back to later). It is important to realize at the outset that the enterprise of Christology does not begin with attempts to solve some sort of theoretical problem about Jesus; it grows out of reflection on the implications of Christian prayer. And in this connection, it is clear that Christology gives us a key to understanding something about the entire enterprise of theology. It is not a 'self-starting' intellectual business, not even an attempt to solve abstract conceptual problems; it is the search to find ways of talking about God that make rough and sustainable sense of how we pray, and thus too of how we imagine what we are finding ourselves to be as human beings relating to God in this kind of prayer. When people become indifferent about Christology or unclear as to why it matters or why it has developed as it has, you might well suspect that something has changed about the way they pray, whether they quite realize it or not. If the governing lines of the classical doctrinal formulations are becoming unrecognizable or unattractive to us, we should not instantly be asking how we adjust them. We should be thinking about whether we have lost something of the corporate experience out of which they came, whether we have lost some sense of the radical character of the newness of human understanding and possibility that was associated with Jesus from the first.

How was that newness initially sensed and spoken of? For St Paul, the community of believers in Jesus Christ, the 'convocation' (*ekklesia*) drawn together by the message concerning Jesus, was the place where the Spirit of God was most fully at work – at work in a way that gave a foretaste of what things would be like on the far side of the end of the world, when God's presence would fill everything and shape everything according to God's purpose (1 Cor. 15.20–28). And one of the most clear and obvious marks of the Spirit's life in the life of this community was that women and men could confidently address God in the same way that Jesus had done: 'Abba, Father'. Praying 'through Jesus Christ' meant praying in a way that would have been impossible without Jesus Christ, depending on what Jesus said and did for the liberty to speak in this particular way to God. As Mark's Gospel suggests, this prayer which signalled the presence of the Spirit was linked in the tradition very specifically to at least one crucial moment in Jesus' life: it is quoted in the record of Jesus' intense and agonizing supplication in the Garden of Gethsemane – as if calling God 'Abba' could best be understood in a situation where God was demanding the most selfless and risky action we could imagine. It is not a cosy word that does no more than tell us that God is there for us in trouble; it is rather that the closer and more intimate relation with God is known to be, the more our own concern to hold on to a secure and untransfigured selfhood comes under pressure. Truly to live and stand where Jesus lives and stands, in the place where God is called 'Abba', is to live by a 'dark' faith in which we must lose ourselves to be ourselves. The Spirit who fills us with Pentecostal joy and exuberant expectation is also the Spirit who hollows out our comfortable identities so that the living energy of God's own love comes alive there. To be praying in and through Jesus is to live in the heart of the reality of crucifixion and resurrection.

In the record of Jesus' ministry in all four Gospels, the special intimacy with God reflected in the word 'Abba' is evident in other, slightly less obvious ways. Jesus assumes the freedom to act on behalf of the God of Israel, without argument and without self-justification. He calls 12 disciples as judges of the renewed people of God, 12 for the 12 tribes – as if he himself stood apart from or above the 12 tribes, on the side of the God who calls not the human beings who are called; he declares that the status of individuals in the new world, where God's rule prevails, depends not on their allegiance to the Law as defined by the experts of the day but on their willingness to trust his own witness to God's forgiveness and welcome; he claims authority to say whom God has forgiven. In all such ways, he appears before us in the Gospels as assuming the right to say who does and doesn't belong in the company of God's people; he is redefining the boundaries of Israel, and his own acts of hospitality and meal-sharing become signs of divine hospitality. The resurrection stories underline this by showing us Jesus sharing meals once again, and commissioning a proclamation of his summons and offer to the ends of the earth. Jesus on the far side of the resurrection remains the same Jesus who was at work in the Galilean ministry; only now his boundary-breaking activity, his hospitality to the marginal, is deliberately extended without geographical or ethnic limit.

All this is fairly commonplace as a summary of what the actual Jesus of Nazareth was recalled as doing and saying; its radical and many-sided character, and its congruence with what we know about the anxieties in Jesus' day over who the 'real' Israel might be, strongly support the conclusion that this was, in essence, rightly remembered. A Jesus whose acts and sayings focused on these things is a wholly credible figure. But the Christian Scriptures also take it for granted that the people to whom he is, historically, speaking have a particular understanding of what it is to belong to God's people, an understanding that is probably less obvious to us; and if we can keep this in mind, a good deal of the biblical picture of Jesus' identity becomes a lot clearer. For the Jewish world in which Jesus lived, to be part of God's people was to be admitted to God's presence as a *worshipper*; uncleanness, sin, some sorts of disease had the effect of banishing you from the community that met to praise God and to offer sacrifice. To be a true member of Israel was to have the dignity of sharing in the worship that both expressed and sustained the harmony of creation, and that reflected

God's glory back to God. The research of recent decades has stressed as never before the centrality of all this in the world in which the Gospels and Epistles (not to mention John's Revelation) were written. So, when Jesus heals, he sends people to offer the prescribed sacrifice; when he protests at the legal exactitude which cuts off certain categories of people from worship or against the commercial system which made the worship of the Jerusalem Temple a complex and exclusive matter, he is affirming that what his work does is to restore the people of Israel to their proper freedom as worshippers, offerers of thanksgiving sacrifice, a 'priestly' nation.

Thus it is not at all surprising that when the first believers look for language and imagery to clarify who and what Jesus is, they go first to the treasury of images connected with the Temple; and when they try to make sense of his death and its effect, it is again to the language of the cult that they instinctively turn. To pick up just a few examples from the Fourth Gospel, the Letter to the Hebrews and the First Letter of Peter, Jesus is the High Priest who calls Israel together for worship, who goes behind the veil to meet the God of Israel face to face and restore peace between God and God's people; he is himself the Temple, the place where perfect worship is offered for the healing of the cosmos; he is the sacrifice that brings about mercy and reintegration. If we read some passages carefully, there is a hint that he is, like the ram that was slaughtered to save Isaac, an offering prepared and given *by God* for humans to offer so that the people may be spared. And so on; the problem or crisis of Israel is that true worship is not being offered or that there is no sacrifice adequate to bring healing or that the call to *all* Israel is not being heard. But however exactly this is understood, the point is that Jesus 'breaks through' on behalf of Israel so that Israel may become its proper priestly self, proclaiming God's glory and sustaining by its common worship the bond between heaven and earth, making and offering peace.

The First Controversies

As I have said, this is probably not a frame of reference we find obvious; but it casts some light on the first beginnings of Christology. Theological thinking on what needed saying about the true and full identity of Jesus begins with the conviction that because of his life and death God's people are placed where they should be placed – in the earthly image of that heavenly sanctuary where God's glory is manifest and God's praise is unbroken. In making all this possible, Jesus is priest, offering and sanctuary all together. He is the mediator, he is the gift that is offered for reconciliation and he is himself the 'place', the ground on which we stand to see and adore God and return God's love to its source. To be in this place is to be confident of an intimacy with God as *Abba* that is incapable of being destroyed even by the most apparently 'Godless' aspects of human experience; it is precisely in those darkest places that we understand the depth of the union that is between Jesus and the God he addresses as Father. So in the earliest thinking about Jesus, we find two themes recurring: he merges with the various figures, rather loosely defined, who inhabit Jewish apocalyptic and visionary literature of the Second Temple period – the Archangel Michael,

Melchizedek, the angels who carry or manifest the Name of God – and who represent not only the possibility of mediation between God and creation, but who are associated with the worship of the heavenly Temple; and his human vulnerability to suffering is underlined, in relation to the experience of trial, suffering and martyrdom that is being faced by the Christian communities. Jesus' fidelity to God and God's to Jesus in the heart of pain and humiliation becomes a crucial element in how Christians cope with their own exposure to the same experiences.

The point is that, from the beginning, Christians were seeking some way of speaking about Jesus that recognized in him both a freedom or power or capacity of initiative that did not depend at all on earthly and historical factors *and* an unequivocal exposure to ordinary human vulnerability. The doctrinal controversies of the early Church repeatedly turn upon this tension, and we can follow how the pressure recurred again and again to let go of one or the other side of the problem. If we simply think about this tension in terms of a problem about how to hold together two abstractions called 'divinity' and 'humanity', we miss the point. People spoke of his 'divinity', because they had come to associate him with actions characteristic of God – he was the agent of a new creation and the one who called a people to be his own and named them with his name. And they were concerned about his 'humanity', because they were anxious that believers should not lose the overpowering conviction of his solidarity with them in their own sufferings. A 'theology of the cross' was fundamental, in the sense that God was to be perceived at work and involved in the most apparently meaningless and painful areas of human experience; but it was crucial that it was indeed *God* who was so involved. A good deal of theological controversy centred upon the various ways one might devise of weakening one or the other pole of this tension.

Thus on one side, one of the most characteristic temptations in the early Christian generations was to say that, if Jesus was in some way the embodiment of a heavenly power, his human identity, his flesh and blood, must have been something he could assume and discard at will, a matter of mere appearance that did not really constrain him. Those theologies we call 'gnostic' – the ones that most emphasized the acquisition of wisdom and spiritual maturity, and the cultivation of these things in groups of 'advanced' believers – seem to have been particularly prone to this. But stressing the reality of Jesus' sufferings brought with it another difficulty: the eternal and changeless God could not be the subject suffering, in that this would suggest that he was in some sense open to being affected by the accidents, the 'contingency' of this world. And if he was open to being affected like this, didn't this compromise what everyone agreed was an essential aspect of divine life, the absolute freedom of God to act according to his nature in all imaginable circumstances?

So on the other side, the temptation was to suggest that the divine power at work in Jesus was somehow less than fully or truly divine – just a delegated and qualified 'divinity', a heavenly, pre-existent power, yes, but something less than the utterly independent energy at the source of all things. Yet, to say this was seen as weakening precisely that radical sense that Jesus had introduced a wholly new context for human action and suffering, a 'new creation'; surely, as John's Gospel had already pronounced with such clarity, this divine agency had to be seen as continuous with the agency that made the universe.

This was the first thing to be formally and technically clarified, at the first of those meetings that came to be called 'general councils' – Nicaea in 325. It took a good 50 years before the theology of Nicaea had really taken root around the churches of the Mediterranean, but by the end of the fourth century it was the standard of belief for the vast majority of Christians. The official declaration of Nicaea shifted the Church decisively away from the ambiguities of the old language about heavenly high priestly and angelic figures; traces of it remained (and still remain) in the liturgies of East and West, quite understandably, but there was a sense that the Church needed a more austere and less pictorial idiom to say what had to be said. And what had to be said was that whatever was 'made flesh', embodied, in Jesus of Nazareth was nothing less than *God by nature* or God 'in substance' – not an inferior or delegated power, but a personal and eternal form of God's reality, inseparable from the act that made the world. The *Logos*, the eternal product of eternal love, perfectly manifesting the reality of that source of all things which is known to us as the eternal Father, and perfectly responding to that reality in absolute liberty and love – *this* was what was at work in Jesus. And this distinct 'subsisting form' of the divine life, the Word or the Son, was 'of one substance' with the divine Father. Slowly and rather clumsily, the technical vocabulary took shape, with the two initially rather vague and fluid words *hypostasis* and *ousia* gradually taking on the formal meanings they have had ever since – *hypostasis* referring to a particular distinct existing bearer of life, a specific 'subsisting form' of God's life, *ousia* to the life that was made real in the actual and particular *hypostasis*. The language of Trinitarian theology took a massive step forward during the fourth century with the clarification that God should be thought of as a single *ousia*, one indivisible life-in-action, and three *hupostaseis*, three interdependent agencies making that life eternally real.

But of course, once this clarification had been made the issue around Jesus' sufferings became even more of a challenge. Granted that we are bound to say that the renewing power that is in Jesus is nothing less than God, how does this square with the deeply held conviction that God does not change or suffer? Some wanted to resolve this by suggesting that the link between God the Word and the humanity of Jesus was a link between two realities on different planes that were *as a matter of fact* united to each other but essentially unaffected. Others preferred to think of Jesus as representing a sort of fusion or even blending of divine and human nature, so that in him both were altered from their previous status and capacity. In 451, the Council of Chalcedon marked out the territory by refusing to qualify either the real humanity or the real divinity of the incarnate Word and by insisting that the human and the divine natures existed in Jesus without either merging with each other or just existing side by side, separable from each other. It was a magisterial balancing act that failed to settle the question, though it eventually came to command majority support in the Eastern Christian world (despite profound and lasting opposition from a number of national churches, especially Egypt and Armenia, who still resist the formula of Chalcedon as giving too much away to those who want to separate the natures).

The Logic of Conversion

The history of Christology is a complex subject that often comes across as a history of aridly technical debates, issuing in a formula dependent on philosophical categories no one can now accept. But this is to misread the record. The Church borrowed some technical terms, but gave them a radically new sense; and, as I have been trying to suggest, the reasons for the debates were not at all abstract. What drove the developments in the doctrine of the incarnation were considerations that still affect believers today very directly. But we do need to be clear about one thing, already noted above. The entire process of reflecting in this way about Jesus depends on the belief that his life and death and resurrection have made a difference that could not have been made in any other way; that they have resulted in a relationship with God that would not otherwise be possible. If Jesus is first and foremost an inspiration or even a legislator or moralist, most of the questions that were discussed in the early Church would never have arisen. The basic issue for us, then, in setting out on any project to state a constructive Christology is whether the *difference* made by Jesus is indeed something we see as radical enough to justify the sort of questions asked by our fathers and mothers in the faith.

There can, of course, be no scientifically objective answer to such a question. We can't get back to a world before Christ to measure the extent of the difference. But we can do two things. One is to try and understand just why this figure and no one else in the history of the ancient world attracted just this kind of reflection and speculation; the other is to try and understand something of what conversion to Christian faith still entails for those who experience it. And what emerges as we think about both these is in fact connected. Those who associated themselves with Jesus in the first days of the Church were convinced not only that he had created a new way of defining the people of God, but that he had made possible a level of trustful and unafraid intimacy with God that had no precedent, for which, indeed, there was little language available except what he had given – *Abba*, 'Our Father in heaven'. It was not that some new method had been created, which guaranteed exceptional 'mystical' experience; more that the entire climate of Christian prayer and activity took for granted that divine energy itself was sustaining these things, and that its presence depended not upon exemplary and unrelaxing human behaviour but on openness – both in thanksgiving and in repentance – to a God who was absolutely to be trusted; on *faith*, in fact. The praying Christian does not have to carve out a path towards God or to 'create the role' of a friend of God: he or she steps into something already (eternally) there, the place and the role of a person existing so totally in and through God's selfless gift that what flows back to God and out to the world is that same selfless gift. When the modern convert speaks about new powers at work in their life, about the sense of even a small movement towards God revealing an overflow of divine welcome, they are expressing the same discovery that fuelled the new and difficult language of the early Church as it attempted to say, on the basis of this, what needed to be said about Jesus.

Jesus is not simply a human being whose example or teaching is specially potent; he is the phenomenon (the unique phenomenon) in the human world that opens up for everyone the possibility of directly standing before God and so worshipping God that it is God's own glory and love that is alive within the believer. And for this to make any sense at all, Christians are bound to say a number of things. They must say that Jesus is not part of the past, not a dead and distantly remembered human individual; they must say that his identity cannot be exhaustively described in terms of the human individual who walked the roads of Galilee; they must say indeed that his full identity is something more than individuality as we understand it, and that what his human identity 'carries' is capable of being carried over into those associated with him. In the more familiar terms of Christian worship and creed, we must say that Jesus is risen, that Jesus is the incarnation of the eternal Word, and that Jesus is for us the source of that divine agency we call 'Spirit' which communicates to us his own relationship with God as Source, as Father.

The history of doctrinal debates should alert us to the need for one or two cautions. The statement 'Jesus is God' is an understandable one in the light of all we have been saying; but it needs careful handling. It should not be used to turn Jesus into *a* god – a human hero with supernatural gifts – or to turn God, without remainder, into a human subject. The caveats of the early Christian writers about not imagining that God could *literally* suffer and die make most of us feel rather awkward these days. We are wary of a discourse about the divine that emphasizes distance, impassibility and unchangeability, because we associate these things with a kind of *human* psychological or emotional detachment that we tend to think of as undesirable – as a mark of some sort of buried fear or immaturity or inner damage. But the classical language about this has nothing to do with God 'shielding' Godself from unpleasant things; it affirms that, because God is the action that makes and sustains everything, we can say what we like about God's awareness and understanding of every finite experience, even that in some way God is aware of it more deeply than any single finite creature could be. But what we can't say is that God is, like any individual person or thing within the system of created life, *at the mercy of circumstances*, that God as such experiences anything just in the way that would be natural for us. That would be to make God simply another inhabitant of this world, instead of the act and energy that keeps it in being.

Thus the central importance of the cross and of the affirmation that the crucified truly is inseparably united to the eternal Word is not – as some theologies, especially in the twentieth century, have argued – that it allows us to say that God acquires an experience that would otherwise have been missing in the divine consciousness (the experience of suffering). It is that here, in the dereliction, the physical and spiritual darkness of a man being tortured to death as if he were a rebellious slave, we see unity with God, tested in the crucible of unspeakable anguish of body and spirit, and yet unbroken. By a supreme paradox, it is when we see God faithfully and stubbornly abiding in the centre of a human identity that is being abused and torn apart at every level that we can see it is indeed *God* we are talking about – the one who is free that not even the extremes of human pain and darkness can make him go away. If – as we said earlier – God's freedom is his liberty to do in all circumstances what is in accord with what and who he is, the cross becomes the supreme sign of that freedom. The horrors of this world and our own experience within it are not made intelligible or easy or easily bearable by this, but we are assured that the transforming act of God is still at work even when there are few or even no obvious signs. And whether this is applied to the circumstances of a whole community undergoing oppression and trauma or to the individual believer in times of personal crisis, doubt and darkness, the point is the same: these states of body and mind do not and cannot exclude the active presence of God. And the seeds of change – or resurrection – can be seen in the fact of that undefeated presence. Loosen the unity between the human Jesus and the eternal freedom of the divine Word and this affirmation of God's total faithfulness in what appears as total darkness is gravely weakened. We should run the risk of saying that there were after all some areas of human experience that God could not occupy and work with. And the implication of this would be that some human circumstances were incapable of being penetrated by hope, by prayer or by loving presence and action. In this connection, the link between Christology and the practical option in favour of the least potent or successful in human society is clear; so is the link (less often discussed in these terms) between Christology and the Church's historic and continuing difficulties in accepting the legitimacy of suicide or euthanasia. Conversion to the Crucified is a turning to the vision of divine fidelity in the heart of human degradation and pain and thus a conversion to the dignity of the suffering and the degraded; a recognition that God has decided to be for ever there with them, calling us to a reverence that is inseparably both God's and theirs to command.

So the unqualified and unbreakable union between divine and human that is claimed to persist even in the 'Godless' horror of the crucifixion of Jesus is not a way of speaking about some 'education' of God by sharing the experience of pain, as if God's divine awareness were, like ours, a matter of accumulating wisdom through the passage of time. The claim is both that it reveals what is eternally true (that no human experience is inaccessible to divine action and love) and that it seals and effects a new level of solidarity between God and creation – a 'new covenant'. Given that the most intimate possible relationship between God and creation is now real in the human world in the active identity of Jesus of Nazareth with the eternal Word, and that in this relationship the darkness of abandonment and apparent meaninglessness is held together with the divine action in unbroken unity, any *lesser* (i.e. less permanent, less stable) relation between God and a created being must be seen in the same light. The triumph of God's grace is thus affirmed, God's capacity to work through any human situation towards healing. And our own summons to be open to him in every situation, ours or our neighbour's, is likewise affirmed. Christology begins, I have argued, in the conviction that through Jesus we are *called* to a new kind of community, the assembly or convocation of God's people; and that link with God's call is evident here as well, in the call to solidarity with the lost and the hopeless, those who are most easily forgotten. The judgement on our selfish and self-protecting habits that is so devastatingly uttered in the fact of the cross (*this* is where all our refusals of grace and pity lead) is to be met no less in the faces of the lost and the hopeless, the faces we so often, so skilfully, persuade ourselves to forget.

To the Ends of the Earth

I spoke just now of an 'active identity' between God the eternal Word or Son and Jesus of Nazareth; and we need to clarify a bit further quite what this is saying. At the simplest level, it means that what Jesus does is what God does within the historical situation of first-century Palestine. The summoning of the outcasts and forgotten of Israel into full participation in the assembly of God's people, the proclaiming of forgiveness, the conferring upon the poor and the guilty of the dignity of being able to welcome God's representative – all of this is divine action, creating something from nothing, as it were, creating irremovable dignity and freedom from guilt in a world where these things are normally debated and contested, granted and withheld according to the fluctuating fortunes of power. It is new creation, the establishing of new facts on the ground, not because God's character has changed, but because the ministry of Jesus has inaugurated a new set of historical possibilities, bringing a renewed people of God into being. And the resurrection demonstrates the radical presence of God in the identity of Jesus: the action inaugurated in Jesus' ministry is not ended or extinguished by his death, but persists as a limitless process of new creation, new stages in the formation of a people for God's possession, passing beyond the ethnic boundaries of Jewish identity. As we saw earlier, the resurrection breaks a further boundary, in succession to the boundary-breaking practice of Jesus in his Galilean ministry. What he has habitually and consistently done as a human individual on the roads of Galilee, he now does as the resurrected Lord on the roads of a whole empire and beyond. The utter conviction of the first Christians that they had an offer to make that would be relevant to any and every human being, the conviction that energized and still energizes mission, is bound up with the recognition of divine action in Jesus. Christology and mission, like Christology and prayer, are inseparable once you recognize that what is *acting* in the life of Jesus (including the death of Jesus) is an agency that is set upon the re-creation of the entire world as a site where glory may be manifest and creation be restored to its proper purpose of harmony with its maker.

And it is in this context that the connection comes into focus between Christology and sacraments. Jesus utilizes the material of this world both to express and to implement his project of renewal; at the simplest level, his body itself is the transmitter of healing, the spittle and clay make the blind man see (John 9), and the sharing of food becomes a sign of divine mercy and welcome. Thus actions done in his name and material things used in his name become in various ways carriers of his work: supremely the act of giving thanks in his name over bread and wine and sharing them effects a degree of personal presence that is unique. The Church's Eucharist is the place where a whole wide range of theological themes converge, almost dizzyingly. It is the continuing of Jesus' actual sharing of food with the outcasts of Israel; it is the ritual Passover consumption of the sacrificed lamb, the celebration of freedom from slavery; it is where the assembly of believers are again and again reconstituted as Christ's Body, because by sharing the bread and wine in which he has promised to communicate his life and strength they become fleetingly but really the presence in the phenomenal world of Jesus the incarnate Word; and so it is the manifestation on earth of the worship of heaven, the action of the eternal Son in praising and adoring the eternal Father. It is where the Word echoes the self-giving of the Source, with the Spirit creating this life of divine love and exchange here in our midst.

But the raw material for all this is literally *material*: it is our human bodies gathered in one place, sharing the material signs of Christ's offering of himself to God, which have also become the signs of the offering of divine love in its fullness to us. And just as the union of the divine Word with humanity in Jesus effects a potential union between the Word and all human beings and human situations, so this sacramental union effects a potential relationship between the incarnate Word and all the material creation, telling us that all things may become pregnant with divine significance, may be effectual signs of God's self-giving when they are the subject of prayer and thanksgiving in the name and Spirit of Jesus. The Christian vision of the world as sacramental is not a general principle of sacredness inherent in all things – although that is one aspect of understanding the material world as God's creation. It is more: it is the belief that the things of the world can become the tools of shared and reconciling love as perfectly embodied in Jesus, when his word is spoken over them.

In the Face of the Stranger

In the light of the discussion so far, it may be possible to approach the thorny question of the 'uniqueness' of Jesus Christ afresh. Contemporary sensibilities are offended by claims to absolute truth; and the idea that any religion is superior to any other is often assumed without argument to be a prelude to fanatical violence. It is perfectly true that the assertion of uniqueness can be the foundation for bullying intolerance, and the history of Christianity will give us far too many shameful examples of this; nor is this spirit extinct. Yet, we need to be careful not to react by running to the equally problematic opposite extreme, a relativism about religious truth that leaves us with nothing *specific* to say about God or the world and no sense that there might be truths about human nature and human dignity that were of incalculable and non-negotiable weight.

And that is why the language of incarnation cannot, for Christians, be reduced to one helpful option among others. The claim that Christology makes is essentially that human beings are all equally made for one end, all equally frustrated in attaining that end and all equally invited to a set of relationships that will open the way to that end. Christology begins where Jewish Scripture begins, in asserting that the goal of the creation of human beings is that they should be liberated to show God's glory by reflecting to God God's own unqualified love and joy. And Christianity, as much as Judaism, asserts equally that this is not just a peculiarity of the ancient Eastern Mediterranean. More specifically – and this is where Christianity is not wholly at one with its Jewish parent – our liberation to be able to show God's glory is associated with what Jesus of Nazareth makes possible. Starting from here, there are any number of ways in which the idioms and images of various religious traditions can fill out such a definition of the purpose of human existence – any number of ways in which the narrowness or clumsiness of our Christian language can be and should be challenged by what other sorts of believer say. And there are undoubtedly moments when Christianity's arrogant and violent historical adventures must be brought under judgement by the encounter with that in other religious practices which in its own way reflects the mystery of Christ's love. The experience of dialogue between the faiths, conducted as it should be, constantly pushes at these uncomfortable boundary places, enlarging everyone's frame of reference through the conversation.

But, granted all of this, if it is true that our destiny is to stand in relation to God both as children to a self-giving parent and as bound in a mutual flow of gift that affirms the liberty of real and 'adult' difference in the same moment that it affirms a life-giving dependence, we are not going to be able simply to treat the doctrinal picture of Christ's unique position as just a picturesque embellishment to some vaguer programme of spiritual growth about which all human beings of good will can agree. If there is such a thing as a coherent shape for human growth in relation to God, something true for all people of whatever background or race or class, and if this coherent shape has found one definitive form in history by the particular grace of God, then the claim that *this* narrative and *this* person constitute the pivot of human history has to be taken with full seriousness, however potentially troubling it may be and whatever moral shadows overhang its outworkings in so much of the Christian record. Denying this in the name of an uncontroversial aspiration for spiritual harmony is implicitly to allow that there may be quite divergent 'goods' for different sorts of human beings. And that is at least as troubling a conclusion.

This need not mean that for those who do not explicitly confess Jesus as Lord and God there is no hope; or that outside the Church there is no divine activity leading to life. God is free to act where God pleases and to offer the divine life and energy to whomever God wills. The Christian has to say, though, that the kind of share in God's life and energy that is possible for human beings is always going to be 'Jesus-shaped' – always about healing, self-forgetting, relating to God the Source of all as a child to a parent; always a matter of what the medieval theologians called *filiatio*, becoming a son or daughter as Christ is. We may find that aspects of other faiths seem to be shaping people in this direction, even where they don't have the words for it; or even that those who passionately oppose Christian faith may do so because they can't see in the Church the signs of the transformed humanity they themselves long for. The Thirty-Nine Articles of the Church of England warn us against thinking that everyone will be saved just by believing sincerely what they believe; and this is absolutely right. It makes a difference whether or not you believe in something true: beliefs have practical consequences. Sheer human intensity of feeling isn't everything, and we shouldn't let ourselves think that any effort of ours can be guaranteed to get us into relationship with God. But it seems quite consistent with this to say both that God's grace offers possibilities even where we as Christians don't see them easily and that other religious traditions have some dimensions both of divine grace and of human discovery of truth in response to this gift.

It is a point connected to the recognition of Christ in the destitute or forgotten, a point constantly reinforced by the spirituality and the folklore of the Christian centuries: Jesus may come to you in a form you did not expect – the beggar with whom Saint Martin shared his cloak in the fourth century or the leper embraced by Saint Francis in the thirteenth. The incarnation establishes universal and unbreakable *solidarity* between God and humanity. What it does not do is to establish a familiarity that allows us to domesticate Jesus into whatever religious or ethical system we feel most comfortable in. The discipline of the Church insists on two fundamental practices in its common life: *listening* to the scriptural record and *being fed* by the Eucharist. Both tell us very simply that we have not finished yet in our learning about Jesus. The Scripture, read in intelligible course but not reduced only to our favourite bits, is there to recall us to the fact that Christ continually comes to the Church in a word that may be strange and challenging, a word that we have not yet heard. The authority of the Bible in the Church is an essential Christological matter, not the cult of an infallible oracle divorced from the Word made flesh. The Bible is read so that we are obliged to ask the question, 'what is Christ calling me to that I have not yet grasped or that I have allowed myself to forget?' And the Eucharist tells me that I cannot live without returning to fellowship at the table with Jesus, recognizing like the first disciples my own complicity in his betrayal and death (and so in the betrayal and death of my fellow human beings). Bible and Eucharist are the primary ways in which Christ comes again to judge and question his Church – to *call* us afresh as he does his disciples after the resurrection (John 21).

Recent developments in the mission of our own Anglican family have brought to light a quite high level of unclarity and uncertainty about both these things. New mission initiatives, the phenomenon of charismatic worship, the 'emergent church' and the 'Fresh Expressions' movement, all manifestly blessed by God and obvious gifts to the Church, have had to become more and more conscious of the temptation to minimize the difficult or indigestible aspects of worship. Subcultures have been created in which – despite eloquent evangelical rhetoric – the public reading and exposition of the Bible has become rare, or in which the celebration of the Lord's Supper has been treated as either a universal fellowship meal or a speciality interest for the elderly and traditionally minded. It is not difficult to see how these developments arise, given the great gaps between the Church's traditional practice and even the best-disposed of enquirers. There is need of immense patience and flexibility in such a context. But there is equal need to remember that it is in meeting a strange and uncomfortable Christ that the disciple and the congregation actually grow in the likeness of Christ (another central paradox). Bible and sacrament are part of the *askesis*, the self-discipline, self-questioning and self-restraint that the Church has accepted for itself as a means of resisting the temptation to make Jesus in our own current image.

Conclusion

Believing in the incarnation is not believing that an individual in heaven turned into an individual on earth for 30 or so years and then went back to heaven. The language of our hymns and carols may suggest this at times, but ever since the New Testament was written Christians have recognized that this is a form of shorthand at best. The doctrine claims the following essential things:

- God is everlastingly a relation of giving and receiving and giving out again; the three eternal and distinct dimensions of this, the three agencies we recognize as more like *personal* agencies than anything else, we call 'Father,

Son and Holy Spirit'; and we say that the second of these dimensions or agencies is the agency of divine life that *receives* in love and *gives back* to the Source what has been given. In recognizing this, we can come to grasp that in God there is room, so to speak, for created beings, responsive beings, who (as created) are always engaging with something prior to them. If created beings can have a share in God, it must be in this way, echoing the responsive engagement of the Word with the Father: the eternal, uncreated Son or Word is the prototype for the relation of created beings to the Source, the Father; and in the light of the acts and prayers of Jesus, we can say that for us the fullest possible relation to this Source or Father is that of the intimacy of a son or daughter.

- This relation had been made effectively impossible by the unbroken history of human selfishness and fear through the history of humanity, so that our real human destiny was rendered both mostly unknown and unreachable. For the path to be opened, there had to be some initiative from God's side to break through and reconstruct human life.
- This breakthrough has happened in the life of Jesus of Nazareth. The initiative of God takes hold of a human identity and forms it in every respect to be a vehicle, from its very beginning (this is the point of the Creed's affirmation of the virgin birth), of divine agency. There is now in the world a human life that offers no obstacle to God's action, a life in which the perfect response to God as Source is made by God as Word. The perfect relationship of Jesus to the Father, culminating in his refusal to avoid death on the cross and his determination to manifest God's faithfulness in the depths of hellish dereliction, becomes the means by which relation is restored – the sacrifice that makes atonement and peace in the language of the Hebrew Scriptures.
- By breaking out of the hold of death and giving to his associates the creative Spirit that enables them to live in the 'atmosphere' of his own love of the Father, Jesus communicates to humanity the renewed possibility of being what they were made to be – joyful adorers of the eternal beauty of God, by God's own strength. Those who receive this gift and affirm and celebrate it form a community which is in its own way a mirror of the identity of Jesus – humans living out divine agency; though what is always perfect and finished in his life is patchy and vulnerable in ours. In the formulae of some of the Greek Christian teachers of the early centuries, 'God became human so that we might become divine' and 'What Christ has by nature, we are given by grace'.

These are the basic elements of incarnational belief. As we have seen, they are reflected in how we understand our prayer and worship as well as our common moral life; they have implications, which we are still trying to clarify, for how we view other religious faiths, because these elements do make a claim to truth and comprehensiveness. But they do not license arrogance and possessiveness, as if we stood in the place that only God can occupy. They also, quite importantly, do not mean that Jesus of Nazareth was only superficially human. His suffering is absolutely real, and his inner life, emotional and spiritual, is like ours. To believe in Christ's divinity, you don't have to imagine that he was conscious of every true proposition in the history of the world or that he was infallible about matters of mere fact (presumably he was capable of forgetting what time it was or getting someone's name wrong?). Much rather unnecessary anxiety has resulted from a reverential caution about ascribing ignorance to Jesus; yet, his 'infallibility' is primarily a matter of his absolute clarity about the nature of God and his absolute freedom to communicate this without ambiguity. This, of course, does entail what earlier generations called his 'sinlessness', but which is perhaps better seen in a positive way as the unbroken capacity to let God come through his feelings, words and deeds. To say he is sinless is to say that nothing he chooses to do, nothing in which his human freedom is involved, is a deliberate blocking-out of God. So – as the New Testament makes quite plain – he knows what it is that pulls us towards selfish and destructive behaviour, yet never gives himself up to it.

The conclusion of the Council of Chalcedon in 451, that we must see in the life of Jesus a complete and unqualified divine agency and a complete and unqualified human reality, physical and mental, is not an unnecessarily complicated elaboration of simple biblical teaching; it is no more than a statement of the duality and tension that pervade every page of the New Testament and that lie behind the practice of Christian prayer. We began with that universal formula, 'through Jesus Christ Our Lord'; it seems we cannot fully make sense of this without the conviction that Jesus has brought us into a place hitherto inaccessible – into the heavenly sanctuary, in the terms familiar to his own contemporaries. What that means the Christian Church has struggled to formalize – and it is never going to exhaust the dimensions of this gift in anything it says. But at the centre of everything is the entitlement given to human beings to speak to God in the words of Jesus. Christology flows from this. Reflection on it leads to the Trinitarian vision, to the sense of Jesus' human identity as somehow opened up for our sharing by the giving of the Spirit, to the belief that all sorts of aspects of our Christian life, from the Eucharist to contemplative prayer to the care of the helpless and the respect we owe to our created environment, find their logic in this context. One of the insights that Anglican theology has often placed at the heart of its vision is that all Christian theology is in one way or another about the incarnation. This is not to reduce theology to a general affirmation of God's presence with or in creation; it is to say that God's will to be 'in Christ, reconciling the world to himself' is the foundation for our identity as a Church, an assembly of renewed human beings – and that this divine decision to be 'for us', this and nothing less, is the word of challenge and assurance we have to speak to our world, so that all things and persons may find themselves ultimately in Christ. May Christ keep us faithful to that calling.

Introduction to the Sources

The Anglican Church of the sixteenth and seventeenth centuries did not become embroiled in the debates over Christology that divided Lutherans and Calvinists on the Continent of Europe. But it is very characteristic of the most systematic Anglican writer of the age, Richard Hooker, that he should go back to some very basic theological principles about the person of Christ in his defence of the Elizabethan Settlement. Because he wishes to make a consistent distinction between primary and secondary theological issues (in opposition to those who regarded all questions of church order as both primary in importance and settled once and for all by the Bible), he puts in central place a theology of the final end of human creatures as defined by loving contemplation of the Father through the Son. He thus has a direct interest in spelling out how the incarnation of the Son makes a difference to human beings; and he does this with remarkable fidelity to both the Greek fathers and the mature thought of Thomas Aquinas.

The incarnation happens so that God can fulfil his purpose of making creatures his sons and daughters, and can reconcile humanity and divinity in the one person that is Christ. Hooker is careful to explain the full detail of the patristic consensus. There is in Christ no human 'person' – that is, no subsisting subject other than the Word of God. This does not mean that there is no 'personality', or that in any sense the human reality of Jesus is incomplete; only that there is no agent in Jesus alongside the Word of God. God is doing human things directly in human reality, and so remaking human nature and its possibilities.

When in the seventeenth century Jeremy Taylor reflects on the imitation of Christ in one of his most popular works, he picks up one aspect of the classical view outlined by Hooker and gives it extra emphasis. Jesus has shown us what is possible and also *made* it possible. He has touched every area of ordinary human experience (notice how important it is for Taylor that Jesus' holiness is a transfiguration of the everyday), and has thus brought to life every aspect of our humanity (he uses the vivid image of the prophet Elisha stretching out his body over the dead child and breathing life into him). We can imitate him only according to our weaker capacity, and we do not have to clear the path as he does; we always depend on his initiative.

Bishop Butler, a century later, is interested in what is added to our knowledge of God by the revelation of the Son and the Holy Spirit. Part of his concern is to counter the idea that 'natural' religion is all we need, and he defines the new element in revelation as the making clear to us that we already stand in relation, not only to God as Father but to Christ as mediator and saviour. The feel of the language is very different from that of the earlier writers; but what is significant is that he insists on our relatedness to Christ. As for Hooker and Taylor, the focal theme is that we are incorporated into a new humanity.

Only in the nineteenth century, with the rise of historical criticism of Scripture, did the question arise of how we should reconcile the claims of the classical credal definitions with a full acceptance of limitations in Jesus' historical humanity. Hence the 'kenotic' Christology, developed especially by Bishop Charles Gore, arguing that to be incarnate God the Word must 'empty' himself of divine attributes (the process of *kenosis,* so called on the basis of the language used in Phil. 2.7). It is not a problem that the Jesus of the Gospels appears not to know everything; the Word has suspended his 'natural' exercise of all-knowing, all-powerful divinity during his time as a human being.

This scheme had much rhetorical and devotional power, but its conceptual confusions occasioned a lot of criticism. When Austin Farrer, the foremost philosophical theologian of the Church of England in the mid twentieth century, turned his attention to this problem, he produced a typically elegant and witty resolution, in terms of Jesus knowing perfectly *how* to lead the human life that will fully embody divinity – or more specifically that divinity that is appropriate to God the Son. And by living that life – and dying as he does – he opens to us the invitation of living as sons and daughters, learning how to be God's children. What might be said about the conceptual content of Jesus' human mind does not affect our belief in the absolute presence of divine omnipotence and omniscience in the whole of his identity.

In other words, Farrer is still preoccupied with the theme of the new humanity. His contemporaries and associates, Gregory Dix and Eric Mascall, develop in radically different but entirely convergent ways the theme of incorporation into Christ's humanity, so that, by relation with this inclusive human nature we may be put in touch with the divine life that 'saturates' his humanity. In this relationship, we are able to offer with and in Christ his own prayer to God as Abba, to be caught up into his triumphant coming to the Father bearing with him a transformed and healed creation, and to experience in contemplation his intimacy with the Father, beyond all concepts and words.

These diverse texts all insist that we think about Christology strictly in connection with the twofold fact that Christ embodies an eternal relationship with the Father and that the Spirit then gives us a relationship with the risen Christ that allows us to share the same relation with the ultimate source of all. Anglican Christology, as exemplified in these texts, brings together doctrine, sacramental practice and contemplative experience as making up an inseparable unity.

Sources

Richard Hooker, *Of the Laws of Ecclesiastical Polity*, Book V, Everyman's Library 202, 2 vols, London: J. M. Dent & Sons, 1954, Chapters 51–2.

Now when God became man, lest we should err in applying this to the Person of the Father, or of the Spirit, St. Peter's confession unto Christ was, 'Thou art *the Son* of the living God,' and St. John's exposition thereof was plain, that it is *the Word* which was made Flesh. 'The Father and the Holy Ghost (saith Damascen) have no communion with the incarnation of the Word otherwise than only by approbation and assent.'

Notwithstanding, forasmuch as the Word and Deity are one subject, we must beware we exclude not the nature of God from incarnation, and so make the Son of God incarnate not to be very God. For undoubtedly even the nature of God itself in the only person of the Son is incarnate, and hath taken to itself flesh. Wherefore incarnation may neither be granted to any person but only one, nor yet denied to that nature which is common unto all three.

Concerning the cause of which incomprehensible mystery, forasmuch as it seemeth a thing unconsonant that the world should honour any other as the Saviour but him who it honoureth as the Creator of the world, and in the wisdom of God it hath not been thought convenient to admit any way of saving man but by man himself, though nothing should be spoken of the love and mercy of God towards, man, which this way are become such a spectacle as neither men nor angels can behold without a kind of heavenly astonishment, we may hereby perceive there is cause sufficient and why divine nature should assume human, that so God might be in Christ reconciling to himself the world. And if some cause be likewise required why rather to this end and purpose the Son than either the Father or the Holy Ghost should be made man, could we which are born the children of wrath be adopted the sons of God through grace, any other than the natural Son of God being Mediator between God and us? It became therefore him by whom all things are to be the way of salvation to all, that the institution and restitution of the world might be both wrought by one hand. The world's salvation was without the incarnation of the Son of God a thing impossible, not simply impossible, but impossible it being presupposed that the will of God was no otherwise to have it saved than by the death of his own Son. Wherefore taking to himself our flesh, and by his incarnation making it his own flesh, he had now of his own although from us what to offer unto God for us.

And as Christ took manhood that by it he might be capable of death whereunto he humbled himself, so because manhood is the proper subject of compassion and feeling pity, which maketh the sceptre of Christ's regency even in the kingdom of heaven amiable, he which without our nature could not on earth suffer for the sins of the world, doth now also by means thereof both make intercession to God for sinners and exercise dominion over all men with a true, a natural, and a sensible touch of mercy.

Thus in Christ the verity of God and the complete substance of man were with full agreement established throughout the world, till such time as the heresy of Nestorius broached itself, 'dividing Christ into two persons the Son of God and the Son of man, the one a person begotten of God before all worlds, the other also a person born of the Virgin Mary, and in special favour chosen to be made entire to the Son of God above all men, so that whosoever will honour God must together honour Christ, with whose person God hath vouchsafed to join himself in so high a degree of gracious respect and favour'. But that the selfsame person which verily is man should properly be God also, and that, by reason not of two person linked in amity but of two natures human and divine conjoined in one and the same person, the God of glory may be said as well to have suffered death as to have raised the dead from their graves, the Son of man as well to have made as to have redeemed the world, Nestorius in no case would admit.

That which deceived him was want of heed to the first beginning of that admirable combination of God with man. 'The Word (saith St. John) was made flesh and dwelt *in us*.' The Evangelist useth the plural number, men for manhood, *us* for the nature whereof we consist, even as the Apostle denying the assumption of *angelical nature*, saith likewise in the plural number, 'He took not *Angels* but the seed of Abraham.' It pleased not the Word or wisdom of God to take to itself some one person amongst men, for then should that one have been advanced which was assumed and no more, but Wisdom to the end she might save many built her house of that Nature which is common unto all, she made not *this or that man* her habitation, but dwelt *in us*. The seeds of herbs and plants at the first are not in act but in possibility that which they afterwards grow to be. If the Son of God had taken to himself a man now made and already perfected, it would of necessity follow that there are in Christ two persons, the one assuming and the other assumed; whereas the Son of God did not assume a man's person unto his own, but a man's nature to his own Person, and therefore took *semen*, the seed of Abraham, the very first original element of our nature, before it was come to have any personal human subsistence. The flesh and the conjunction of the flesh with God began both at one instant; his making and taking to himself our flesh was but one act, so that in Christ there is no personal subsistence but one, and that from everlasting. By taking only the nature of man he still continueth one person, and changeth but the manner of his subsisting, which was before in the mere glory of the Son of God, and is now in the habit of our flesh.

Forasmuch therefore as Christ hath no personal subsistence but one whereby we acknowledge him to have been eternally the Son of God, we must of necessity apply to the person of the Son of God even that which is spoken of Christ according to his human nature. For example, according to the flesh he was born of the Virgin Mary, baptized of John in the river Jordan, by Pilate adjudged to die, and executed by the Jews. We cannot say properly that the Virgin bore, or John did baptize, or Pilate condemn, or the Jews crucify the Nature of man, because these all are personal attributes; his Person is the subject which receiveth them, his Nature that which maketh his person capable or apt to receive. If we should say that the person of a man in our Saviour Christ was the subject of these things, this were plainly to entrap ourselves in the very snare of the Nestorians' heresy, between whom and the Church of God there was no difference, saving only that Nestorius imagined in Christ as well a personal human subsistence as a divine, the Church acknowledging a substance both divine and human, but no other personal subsistence than divine, because the Son of God took not to himself a man's person, but the nature only of a man.

Christ is a Person both divine and human, howbeit not therefore two persons in one, neither both these in one sense, but a person divine, because he is *personally* the Son of God, human, because *he hath* really *the nature* of the children of men. In Christ therefore God and man 'There is (saith Paschasius) a twofold substance, not a twofold person, because one person extinguisheth another, whereas one nature cannot in another become extinct.' For the personal being which the Son of God already had, suffered not the substance to be personal which he took, although together with the nature which he had the nature also which he took continueth. Whereupon it followeth against Nestorius, that no person was born of the Virgin but the Son of God, no person but the Son of God baptized, the Son of God condemned, the Son of God and no other person crucified; which one only point of Christian belief, *the infinite worth of the Son of God* is the very ground of all things believed concerning life and salvation by that which Christ either did or suffered as man in our behalf.

But forasmuch as St. Cyril, the chiefest of those two hundred bishops assembled in the council of Ephesus, where the heresy of Nestorius was condemned, had in his writings against the Arians avouched that the Word or Wisdom of God hath *but one nature* which is eternal, and whereunto he assumed flesh (for the Arians were of opinion that besides God's own eternal wisdom, there is a wisdom of which God created before all things, to the end he might thereby create all things else, and that this created wisdom was the Word which took flesh:) again, forasmuch as the same Cyril had given instance in the body and the soul of man no farther than only to enforce by example against Nestorius, that a visible and an invisible, a mortal and an immortal substance may untied make *one person*: the words of Cyril were in process of time so taken as though it had been his drift to teach, that even as in us the body and the soul, so in Christ God and man make but *one nature*. Of which error, six hundred and thirty fathers in the council of Chalcedon condemned Eutyches. For as Nestorius teaching rightly that God and man are distinct natures, did thereupon misinfer that in Christ those natures can by no conjunction make one person; so Eutyches of sound belief as touching their true personal copulation became unsound by denying the difference which still continueth between the one and the other Nature. We must therefore keep warily a middle course, shunning both that distraction of Persons wherein Nestorius went awry, and also this later confusion of Natures which deceived Eutyches.

These natures from the moment of their first combination have been and are for ever inseparable. For even when his soul forsook the tabernacle of his body, his Deity forsook neither body nor soul. If it had, then could we not truly hold either that the person of Christ was buried, or that the person of Christ did raise up itself from the dead. For the body separated from the Word can in no true sense be termed the person of Christ; nor is it true to say that the Son of God in raising up that body did raise up himself, if the body were not both with him and of him even during the time it lay in the sepulchre. The like is also to be said of the soul, otherwise we are plainly and inevitably Nestorius. The very person of Christ therefore for ever one and the selfsame was only touching bodily substance concluded within the grave, his soul only from thence severed, but by personal union his Deity still unseparably joined with both.

Jeremy Taylor, *The Life of Our Blessed Lord and Saviour Jesus Christ*, in Vol. 1 of the 1839 edition, London: Longman, pp. 61–7.

In the great council of eternity, when God set down the laws, and knit fast the eternal bands, of predestination, he made it one of his great purposes to make his Son like us, that we also might be like his holy Son; he, by taking our nature; we, by imitating his holiness: 'God hath predestinated us to be conformable to the image of his Son,' saith the apostle. For the first in every kind is in nature propounded as the pattern of the rest; and as the sun, the prince of all the bodies of light, and the fire of all warm substances, is the principle, the rule and the copy, which they in their proportions imitate and transcribe; so is the Word incarnate the great example of all the predestinate; for 'he is the first-born among many brethren.' And therefore it was a precept of the apostle; and by his doctrine we understand its meaning, 'Put ye on the Lord Jesus Christ.' The similitude declares the duty. As a garment is composed and made of the same fashion with the body, and is applied to each part in its true figure and commensuration; so should we put on Christ, and imitate the whole body of his sanctity, conforming to every integral part, and express him in our lives, that God, seeing our impresses, may know whose image and superscription we bear, and we may be acknowledged for sons, when we have the air and features and resemblances of our elder brother.

In the practice of this duty we may be helped by certain considerations, which are like the proportion of so many rewards. For this, according to the nature of all holy exercises, stays not for pay, till its work be quite finished; but, like music in churches, is pleasure and piety, and salary besides. So is every work of grace; full of pleasure in the execution, and is abundantly rewarded, besides the stipend of a glorious eternity.

First: I consider that nothing is more honourable than to be like God; and the heathens, worshippers of false deities, grew vicious upon that stock; and we who have fondness of imitation, counting a deformity full of honour, if by it we may be like our prince, (for pleasures were in their height in Capreæ, because Tiberius there wallowed in them, and a wry neck in Nero's court was the mode of gallantry), might do well to make our imitations prudent and glorious; and, by propounding excellent examples, heighten our faculties to the capacities of an evenness with the best of precedents. He that strives to imitate another, admires him, and confesses his own imperfections; and therefore, that our admirations be not flattering, nor our confessions fantastic and impertinent, it were but reasonable to admire Him, from whom really all perfections do derive, and before whose glories all our imperfections must confess their shame, and needs of reformation. God, by a voice from heaven, and by sixteen generations of miracles and grace, hath attested the holy Jesus to be the fountain of sanctity, and the 'wonderful Counsellor', and 'the Captain of our sufferings', and the Guide of our manners, by being his beloved Son, in whom he took pleasure and complacency to the height of satisfaction and if any thing in the world be motive to our affections, or satisfactory to our understandings, what is there in heaven or earth we can desire or imagine beyond a likeness to God, and participation of the Divine nature and perfections? And therefore, as, when the sun arises, every man goes to his work, and warms himself with his heat, and is refreshed with his influences, and measures his labour with his course; so should we frame all the actions of our life by his light, who hath shined by an excellent righteousness, that we no more walk in darkness, or sleep in lethargies, or run a gazing after the lesser and imperfect beauties of the night. It is the weakness of the organ, that makes us hold our hand between the sun and us, and yet stand staring upon a meteor or an inflamed jelly. And our judgments are as mistaken, and our appetites are as sottish, if we propound to ourselves, in the courses and designs of perfections, any copy but of him, or something like him, who is the most perfect. And lest we think his glories too great to behold.

Secondly, I consider, that the imitation of the life of Jesus is a duty of that excellency and perfection, that we are helped in it, not only by the assistance of a good and a great example, which possibly might be too great, and scare our endeavours and attempts; but also by its easiness, compliance, and proportion to us. For Jesus, in his whole life, conversed with men with a modest virtue, which, like a well-kindled fire fitted with just materials, casts a constant heat; not like an inflamed heap of stubble, glaring with great emissions, and suddenly stooping into the thickness of smoke. His piety was even, constant, unblamable, complying with civil society, without affrightment of precedent, or prodigious instances of actions greater than the imitation of men. For if we, observe our blessed Saviour in the whole story of his life, although he was without sin, yet the instance of his piety were the actions of a very holy, but an ordinary life; and we may observe this difference in the story of Jesus from ecclesiastical writings of certain beatified persons, whose life is told rather to amaze us, and to create scruples, than to lead us in the evenness and serenity of a holy conscience. Such as the prodigious penances of Simeon Stylites, the abstinence of the religious retired into the mountain Nitria; but especially the stories of later saints, in the midst of a declining piety and aged Christendom, where persons are represented holy by way of idea and fancy, if not to promote the interests of a family and institution. But our blessed Saviour, though his eternal union and adherences of love and obedience to his heavenly Father were next to infinite, yet in his external actions, in which only, with the correspondence of the Spirit in those actions, he propounds himself imitable, he did so converse with men, that men, after that example, might for ever converse with him. We find that some saints have had excrescencies and eruptions of holiness in the instance of uncommanded duties, which in the same particulars we find not in the story of the life of Jesus. John Baptist was a greater mortifier than his Lord was; and some princes have given more money than all Christ's family did whilst he was alive: but the difference, which is observable, is, that although some men did some acts of counsel in order to attain that perfection, which in Jesus was essential and unalterable, and was not acquired by degrees, and means of danger and difficulty; yet no man ever did his whole duty, save only the holy Jesus. The best of men did sometimes actions not precisely and strictly requisite, and such as were besides the precept; but yet, in the greatest flames of their shining piety, they prevaricated something of the commandment. They that have done the most things beyond, have also done some things short of their duty; but Jesus, who intended himself the example of piety, did in manners as in the rule of faith, which, because it was propounded to all men, was fitted to every understanding; it was true, necessary, short, easy and intelligible. So was his rule and his copy fitted, not only with excellencies worthy, but with compliances possible, to be imitated; of glories so great, that the most early and constant industry must confess its own imperfections; and yet so sweet and humane, that the greatest infirmity, if pious, shall find comfort and encouragement. Thus God gave his children manna from heaven; and though it was excellent, like the food of angels, yet it conformed to every palate, according to that appetite, which their several fancies and constitutions did produce . . .

Thirdly: Every action of the life of Jesus, as it is imitable by us, is of so excellent merit, that, by making up the treasure of grace, it becomes full of assistances to us, and obtains of God grace to enable us to its imitation, by way of influence and impetration. For, as in the acquisition of habits the very exercise of the addition does produce a facility to the action, and in some proportion becomes the cause of itself; so does every exercise of the life of Christ kindle its own fires, inspires breath into itself, and makes an univocal production of itself in a differing subject. And Jesus becomes the fountain of spiritual life to us, as the prophet Elisha to the dead child; when he stretched his hands upon the child's hands, laid his mouth to his mouth, and formed his posture to the boy, and breathed into him, the spirit returned again into the child at the prayer of Elisha; so when our lives are formed into the imitation of the life of the holiest Jesus, the Spirit of God returns into us, not only by the efficacy of the imitation, but by the merit and impetration of the actions of Jesus. It is reported in the Bohemian story, that

St. Wenceslaus, their king, one winter night going to his devotions, in a remote church, barefooted in the snow and sharpness of unequal and pointed ice, his servant Podavivus, who waited upon his master's piety, and endeavoured to imitate his affections, began to faint through the violence of the snow and cold, till the king commanded him to follow him, and set his feet in the same footsteps, which his feet should mark for him: the servant did so, and either fancied a cure, or found one; for he followed his prince, helped forward with shame and zeal to his imitation, and by the forming footsteps for him in the snow. In the same manner does the blessed Jesus; for, since our way is troublesome, obscure, full of objection and danger, apt to be mistaken and to affright our industry, he commands us to mark his footsteps, to tread where his feet have stood, and not only invites us forward by the argument of his example, but he hath trodden down much of the difficulty, and made the way easier, and fit for our feet. For he knows our infirmities, and himself hath felt their experience in all things but in the neighbourhoods of sin; and therefore he hath proportioned a way and a path to our strengths and capacities, and, like Jacob hath marched softly and in evenness with the children and the cattle, to entertain us by the comforts of his company, and the influences of a perpetual guide.

Fourthly: But we must know, that not every thing which Christ did is imitable by us; neither did he, in the work of our redemption, in all things imitate his heavenly Father. For there are some things which are issues of an absolute power, some are expresses of supreme dominion, some are actions of a judge. And therefore Jesus prayed for his enemies, and wept over Jerusalem, when at the same instant his eternal Father laughed them to scorn; for he knew that their day was coming, and himself had decreed their ruin. But it became the holy Jesus to imitate his Father's mercies; for himself was the great instrument of the eternal compassion, and was the instance of mercy; and therefore, in the operation of his Father's design, every action of his was univocal, and he shewed the power of his divinity in nothing but in miracles of mercy and illustrations of faith, by creating arguments of credibility. In the same proportion we follow Jesus as himself followed his Father: for what he abated by the order to his intendment and design, we abate by the proportions of our nature; for some excellent acts of his were demonstrations of divinity, and an excellent grace poured forth upon him without measure was their instrument; to which proportions if we should extend our infirmities, we should crack our sinews and dissolve the silver cords, before we could entertain the instances and support the burden. Jesus fasted forty days and forty nights; but the manner of our fastings hath been in all ages limited to the term of an artificial day; and in the primitive observations and the Jewish rites, men did eat their meal as soon as the stars shone in the firmament. We never read that Jesus laughed, and but once that he rejoiced in spirit; but the declensions of our natures cannot bear the weight of a perpetual grave deportment without the intervals of refreshment and free alacrity. Our ever blessed Saviour suffered the devotion of Mary Magdalene to transport her to an expensive expression of her religion, and twice to anoint his feet with costly nard: and yet if persons whose conditions were of no greater lustre or resplendency of fortune than was conspicuous in his family and retinue, should suffer the same profusion upon the dressing and perfuming their bodies, possibly it might be truly said, 'It might better be sold, and distributed to the poor.' This Jesus received, as he was the Christ and anointed of the Lord; and by this he suffered himself to be designed to burial, and he received the oblation as eucharistical for the ejection of seven devils; for 'therefore she loved much.'

Joseph Butler, *The Analogy of Religion*, Part II, Chapter 1, London: J. M. Dent and Sons, 1906, pp. 120–31.

Christianity is to be considered in a further view, as containing an account of a dispensation of things not at all discoverable by reason, in consequence of which several distinct precepts are enjoined us: Christianity is not only an external institution of natural religion, and a new promulgation of God's general providence as righteous Governor and Judge of the world, but it contains also a revelation of a particular dispensation of Providence, carrying on by his Son and Spirit for the recovery and salvation of mankind, who are represented in Scripture to be in a state of ruin. And in consequence of this revelation being made, we are commanded *to be baptized*, not only *in the name of the Father*, but also *of the Son, and of the Holy Ghost*: and other obligations of duty, unknown before, to the Son and the Holy Ghost are revealed. Now the importance of these duties may be judged of by observing that they arise, not from positive command merely, but also from the offices which appear from Scripture to belong to those Divine persons in the gospel dispensation, or from the relations which we are there informed they stand in to us. By reason is revealed the relation which God the Father stands in to us. Hence arises the obligation of duty which we are under to him. In Scripture are revealed the relations which the Son and Holy Spirit stand in to us. Hence arise the obligations of duty which we are under to them. The truth of the case, as one may speak, in each of these three respects being admitted: that God is the governor of the world, upon the evidence of reason; that Christ is the mediator between God and man; and the Holy Ghost our guide and sanctifier, upon the evidence of revelation; the truth of the case, I say, in each of these respects being admitted, it is no more a question why it should be commanded that we be baptized in the name of the Son and of the Holy Ghost, than that we be baptized in the name of the Father. This matter seems to require to be more fully stated.

Let it be remembered then that religion comes under the twofold consideration of internal and external; for the latter is as real a part of religion, of true religion, as the former. Now when religion is considered under the first notion, as an inward principle to be exerted in such and such inward acts of the mind and heart, the essence of natural religion may be said to consist in religious regards to *God the Father Almighty*; and the essence of revealed religion, as distinguished from natural, to consist in religious regards to *the Son*, and to *the Holy Ghost*. And the obligation we are under of paying these religious regards to each of these Divine persons respectively, arises from the respective relations which they each stand in to us. How these relations are made known, whether by reason or revelation, makes no alteration in the case; because the duties arise out of the relations themselves, not out of the manner in which we are informed of them. The Son and Spirit have each his proper office in that great dispensation of Providence, the redemption of the world; the one our mediator, the other our sanctifier. Does not then the duty of religious regards to both these Divine persons, as immediately arise, to the view of reason, out of the very nature of these offices and relations; as the inward good-will and kind intention, which we owe to our fellow creatures, arises out of the common relations between us and them? But it will be asked, 'What are the inward religious regards appearing thus obviously due to the Son and Holy Spirit; as arising, not merely from command in Scripture, but from the very nature of the revealed relations which they stand in to us?' I answer, the religious regards of reverence, honour, love, trust, gratitude, fear, hope. In what external manner this inward worship is to be expressed is a matter of pure revealed command; as perhaps the external manner in which God the Father is to be worshipped may be more so than we are ready to think; but the worship, the internal worship itself, to the Son and Holy Ghost, is no further matter of pure revealed command than as the relations they stand in to us are matter of pure revelation; for the relations being known, the obligations to such internal worship are obligations of reason, arising out of those relations themselves. In short, the history of the gospel as immediately shows us the reason of these obligations, as it shows us the meaning of the words Son and Holy Ghost.

If this account of the Christian religion be just, those persons who can speak lightly of it, as of little consequence provided natural religion be kept to, plainly forget that Christianity, even what is peculiarly so called, as distinguished from natural religion, has yet somewhat very important, even of a moral nature. For the office of our Lord being made known, and the relation he stands in to us, the obligation of religious regards to him is plainly moral, as much as charity to mankind is; since this obligation arises, before external command, immediately out of that his office and relation itself. Those persons appear to forget that revelation is to be considered, as informing us of somewhat new in the state of mankind and in the government of the world; as acquainting us with some relations we stand in which could not otherwise have been known. And these relations being real (though before revelation we could be under no obligations from them, yet upon their being revealed), there is no reason to think but that neglect of behaving suitably to them will be attended with the same kind of consequences under God's government, as neglecting to behave suitably to any other relations made known to us by reason. And ignorance, whether unavoidable or voluntary, so far as we can possibly see, will just as much, and just as little, excuse in one case as in the other; the ignorance being supposed equally unavoidable, or equally voluntary, in both cases.

If therefore Christ be indeed the mediator between God and man, *i.e.*, if Christianity be true, if he be indeed our Lord, our Saviour, and our God; no one can say what may follow, not only the obstinate but the careless disregard to him in those high relations. Nay no one can say, what may follow such disregard even in the way of natural consequence. For, as the natural consequences of vice in this life are doubtless to be considered as judicial punishments inflicted by God; so likewise, for aught we know, the judicial punishments of the future life may be, in a like way or a like sense, the natural consequences of vice: of men's violating or disregarding the relations which God has placed them in here, and made known to them.

Again: If mankind are corrupted and depraved in their moral character, and so are unfit for the that state which Christ is gone to prepare for his disciples;

and if the assistance of God's Spirit be necessary to renew their nature in the degree requisite to their being qualified for that state; all which is implied in the express, though figurative declaration, *Except a man be born of the Spirit he cannot enter into the kingdom of God:* supposing this, is it possible any serious person can think it a slight matter whether or no he make use of the means, expressly commanded by God, for obtaining this Divine assistance? especially since the whole analogy of nature shows that we are not to expect any benefits without making use of the appointed means for obtaining or enjoying them. Now reason shows us nothing of the particular immediate means of obtaining either temporal or spiritual benefits. This therefore we must learn, either from experience or revelation. And experience the present case does not admit of.

The conclusion from all this evidently is, that, Christianity being supposed either true or credible, it is unspeakable irreverence, and really the most presumptuous rashness, to treat it as a light matter. It can never justly be esteemed of little consequence till it be positively supposed false. Nor do I know a higher and more important obligation which we are under than that of examining most seriously into the evidence of it, supposing its credibility, and of embracing it upon supposition of its truth.

Hence we may clearly see where lies the distinction between what is positive and what is moral in religion. Moral *precepts* are precepts, the reasons of which we see; positive *precepts* are precepts, the reasons of which we do not see. Moral *duties* arise out of the nature of the case itself, prior to external command. Positive *duties* do not arise out of the nature of the case, but from external command; nor would they be duties at all were it not for such command, received from him whose creatures and subjects we are. But the manner in which the nature of the case, or the fact of the relation, is made known, this doth not denominate any duty either positive or moral. That we be baptized in the name of the Father, is as much a positive duty as that we be baptized in the name of the Son; because both arise equally from revealed command, though the relation which we stand in to God the Father is made known to us by reason; the relation we stand in to Christ by revelation only. On the other hand, the dispensation of the gospel admitted, gratitude as immediately comes due to Christ, from his being the voluntary minister of this dispensation, as it is due to God the Father, from his being the fountain of all good; though the first is made known to us by revelation only, the second by reason. Hence also we may see, and, for distinctness' sake, it may be worth mentioning, that positive institutions come under a twofold consideration. They are either institutions founded on natural religion, as baptism in the name of the Father; though this has also a particular reference to the gospel dispensation, for it is in the name of God, as the Father of our Lord Jesus Christ; or they are external institutions founded on revealed religion, as baptism in the name of the Son and of the Holy Ghost.

Charles Gore, *Belief in Christ*, London: Murray, 1922, pp. 225–6.

The divine Son in becoming man must, we conclude, have accepted, voluntarily and deliberately, the limitations involved in really living as man – even as sinless and perfect man – in feeling as a man, thinking as a man, striving as a man, being anxious and tried as a man. Jesus does not indeed appear in the Gospels as unconscious of his divine nature. He knows he is Son of the Father. He 'remembers' how he came from God and would go back to God. But he appears none the less as accepting the limitations of manhood. And St. Paul, I say, gives us the hint which directs our vision. This was no failure of power. God is love, and love is sympathy and self-sacrifice. The Incarnation is the supreme act of self-sacrificing sympathy, by which one whose nature is divine was enabled to enter into human experience. He emptied himself of divine prerogatives so far as was involved in really becoming man, and growing, feeling, thinking and suffering as man. . . . No doubt such a conception raises questions to which we can find no full answer. Thus – Is the self-emptying to be conceived of as a continual refusal to exercise the free divine consciousness which he possessed, or as something once for all involved in the original act by which he entered into the limiting conditions of manhood? And I think if we were wise we shall not attempt to answer the question. We have not the knowledge of the inner life of Jesus which would make an answer possible. Or again, we are asked how we relate this 'limited' condition of the Son as incarnate with his exercise of all the cosmic functions of the eternal Word – what the New Testament calls 'the sustaining' or 'bearing along of all things' or the holding all the universe of things together – and again I think we had better give no answer.

Charles Gore, *Dissertations on Subjects Connected with the Incarnation*, London: Murray, 1895, pp. 94, 203–4.

The Incarnation of the Son of God was no mere addition of a manhood to his Godhead: it was no mere wrapping around the divine glory of a human nature to veil it and make it tolerable to mortal eyes. It was more than this. The Son of God, without ceasing to be God, the Son of the Father, and without ceasing to be conscious of his divine relation as Son to the Father, yet in assuming human nature, so truly entered into it as really to grow and live as Son of Man under properly human conditions, that is to say also under properly human limitations. Thus, if we are to express this in human language, we are forced to assert that within the *sphere* and *period* of his incarnate and mortal life, he did, and as it would appear did habitually – doubtless by the voluntary action of his own self-limiting and self-restraining love – cease from the exercise of those divine functions and powers, including the divine omniscience, which would have been incompatible with a truly human experience.

It will not suffice to say that the Son was limited in knowledge, etc., *in respect of his manhood*, so long as we so juxta-posit the omniscient Godhead with the limited manhood as to destroy the impression that he, the Christ, the Son of God, was *personally* living, praying, thinking, speaking, and acting – even working miracles – under the limitations of manhood. . . . Within the period and sphere of his incarnate and mortal life, he the eternal Son was, doubtless by his own act and will, submitting himself to the limitations proper to manhood. The real Incarnation involves a real self-impoverishment, a real self-emptying, a real self-limitation on the part of the eternal Word of God.

Austin Farrer, *Interpretation and Belief*, London: SPCK, 1976, pp. 136–7.

God's creative will takes effect in every creature's becoming of its own sort; every creature is, so to speak, handed a limited charter of privileges and a limited set of rules to which it has to work: that's what makes it the creature it is, and in being that creature it can be no other. But God himself, the creator, is not subject to any such limitation or particularity of sphere or of kind: he is the sheer creative energy from which all such limitations proceed. To talk about 'divine nature' and 'human nature' as though God's nature were one of the ways of being alongside the human way is sheer paganism.

Thus 'very God and very man' is not the botching together of two ways of being, the divine way and the human way. No: it says something more like this. The infinite energy who creates the human Jesus fortifies and redoubles his creative act in living, or being, that man by personal identification. And God, infinite God, no more ceases to be God by thus being Jesus than he ceases to be God by making Jesus. But neither, on its side, is the humanity of Jesus forced, altered, or overborne. For God's incarnation consists precisely in being the man Jesus and not in being anything else. God, becoming incarnate, does not first become a non-human angelic form and then go and force that form on Jesus. Jesus is the form his incarnation takes, and Jesus is a man.

What, then, is the formula? 'Infinite God living the existence of one of his creatures, through self-limitation to a particular created destiny'? There, perhaps, is an acceptable set of words, but does it mean anything?

Suppose I had never heard of Jesus Christ; suppose, for example, I were a little African boy being instructed by a missionary who was so stupid as to begin with the abstract doctrine of incarnation and only afterwards go on to historical fact. Suppose, then, that the missionary says to me, 'Infinite God living the existence of one of his creatures, through self-limitation to a particular created destiny. "Now, my boy, what sort of a person would you expect this incarnation of Godhead to be?"' We will suppose that the boy is as phenomenally intelligent as the missionary is phenomenally stupid, and furthermore that he has been fortified with all sorts of philosophical techniques and cautions – in fact, he is a surprisingly mature, sophisticated, and learned child, except in the one particular of Jewish history, on which his mind is a perfect blank. What, then will the boy reply? 'Father,' he says, 'I do not think it will be a baboon or a crocodile, I think it will be a man. It will be a good man, a wise man; a man full of the power of Spirit. But not like you, Father. You are full of the power of the Spirit: you get him by going into the prayer hut and asking. He will not do that. Who would he pray to? He is God. He will not pray to himself. He will say to the others, Come and pray to me. I give you what is good for you. I tell you all the answers.'

'Oh dear', says the missionary to himself, 'this instruction isn't going at all as I intended. This was the point when I was going to whip the Gospel out of my cassock-pocket and say, "Exactly! Here is the man. Go away and read about him." But as it is, that would never do. He will say: "That is not God. He prays to the Father in Heaven; and says: 'One only is God. Keep his commandments and thou shalt live.' He says: 'of that day and that hour none knows, not the angels in heaven, nor the Son, but the Father alone.'"'

'I have muffed it again', says the stupid missionary to himself. 'I know what it is: I left out the piece about the Trinity – or anyhow, about the Binity; the doctrine of the third person will keep for another day.'

So the missionary clears his throat, and starts again like this: 'My child, I have put you on the wrong track. It is not just Godhead that becomes incarnate, it is Godhead in the special form or person of Sonship. Divine Son becomes incarnate: and since Divine Son draws his whole person and being from the divine fatherhood anyhow, quite apart from his incarnation, when he becomes incarnate he does not cease to do so. He goes into the prayer hut, he goes out into the hills, he talks with his Father, he draws the Spirit of the Father into him, he opens himself to receive the power and the will. But, you will say, what is this about Divine Son? Are there two Gods? My child, I know . . . But he [the Son] doesn't know who he is himself, he has to find out. He is thirty years old and he still doesn't know. He comes to a man called John who is baptizing the people to make them clean and ready for someone called Messiah, someone very great, to come. Jesus is baptized too, and then bang! The sky splits, down comes the dove, down comes the voice, You are that Messiah, you are my beloved Son. He goes away into the bush to think. The bad spirit comes to him and bothers him plenty, "*If* you really are the Son of God": he keeps saying to Jesus in his mind. And even to the very end he never says just like you told me, "I am the Son of God who is God too." It is a funny thing if Divine Son has to find out that he is Divine Son and never quite manages it. He comes as a man: – all right; that is, he hides himself from the others. But does he hide himself from himself? I mean like this. Divine Son is divine Son because of his thought, not because of his hands, feet, lungs, heart; for those are just like anyone's. But if divine Son doesn't think he is divine Son, how can he be divine Son because of his thought?'

'My boy,' said the missionary, 'did you ever see a picture of President Eisenhower?'

'Yes, plenty . . . with a grin from ear to ear.'

'Yes, I know: they teach them to do that in America. But did you ever see a picture without a grin?'

'Yes, once. Him taking the oath.'

'Good. Well, there is a man rather like that in my native country: he is not top man in politics like Eisenhower, he's top man at thinking. He's called Gilbert Ryle. And he says . . .'

At this moment there was a blood-curdling roar. In jumped a lion, and ate the missionary. The boy ran screaming out, and was eaten by a leopard. So now we have got rid of these tiresome characters and can proceed in our own way.

I want to apply Ryle's famous distinction between *knowing how* and *knowing that* to the mystery of the incarnate consciousness. The little African rightly said that the divine Son could not be in Jesus otherwise than as mind; and rightly, too, that mind must be expressed in knowing, or what is it? But the little African, like so many victims of Ryle's criticism, assumes that 'knowing' means *knowing that*, knowing clear factual truths; for example, in this case, that the thinker is very God of very God, begotten not made, consubstantial with the Father, and mediator of the whole creative process. But such a supposition not only conflicts (as the little African objects) with the evidence in the Gospels, it conflicts no less with the very possibility of genuine incarnation. Christ is very God, indeed, but also very man; and an omniscient being who knows all the answers before he thinks and all the future before he thinks and all the future before he acts is not a man at all, he has escaped the human predicament. And (not to speak of omniscience in general, but to restrict ourselves to the single point of self-knowledge) how can a person who knows his unique metaphysical status with more than Aristotelian exactitude be a largely self-taught Galilean village boy whose store of ideas derived from the Synagogue? How, moreover, can he be tempted at all times like as we are, or fight a lifelong battle of faith, and suffer seeming dereliction on the cross?

On the other hand, he *knows how* to be Son of God in the several situations of his gradually unfolding destiny, and in the way appropriate to each. He is tempted to depart from that knowledge, but he resists the temptation. And that suffices for the incarnation to be real. For 'being the Son of God' is the exercise of a sort of life; and in order to exercise it he must know how to exercise that life: it is a question of practical knowledge. A theoretical knowledge about the nature of the life he lives is unnecessary, it suffices that he should live it. 'I would rather know how to repent than know the definition of repentance' is an ancient saying; and it was enough for Jesus to exercise the personal existence of the Second Person in the Trinity: he might leave to schoolmen the definition of the Trinity, especially in view of the fact that it cannot be verbally defined. There is, indeed, something shocking and absurd about the thought of the divine person talking divinity, as Alexander Pope says in criticizing the bathos of Milton's heavenly scenes: 'And God the Father turns a school-divine.'

God is that lie which schoolmen falter to express, and which an eternity of exploration will not exhaust; but it will be ever new to those deemed worthy of that blessedness.

And God the Son on earth is a fullness of holy life within the limit of mortality; it is for him to be, and for theologians endlessly and never sufficiently, to define.

There are many questions concerning the powers and acts of God incarnate besides the question of his knowledge on which alone I have touched. But I must bring this desultory paper to an end and, since desultory it has been, I will conclude with a summary of the points I have made.

1. Why we should say 'very God and very man' of Christ is not a matter of mere historical inquiry because Christians do not pretend to know about the divine Christ by mere history but through testimony, faith, and life. So what we are asking is whether the formula properly describes the reality with which Christians believe themselves to have to do.
2. The combination of God and Man in Christ is not the combination of two determinate sorts of being, the divine and the human, either compatible with one another or incompatible. It is the act of the Infinite Godhead finitizing his personal action in a unique way, and so that he is purely divine in being purely human.
3. We cannot understand the incarnation without the Trinity. What becomes incarnate is not just the Godhead but the divine Sonship in the Godhead. That is what is translated into human terms, for that is what we are adopted into by association: the sonship is spread to embrace us.

4. The incarnation is not just an accepting of the formal conditions of humanity in general, it is the becoming an actual, particular man in the limitation of his circumstances and his knowledge. The divine infallibility of Christ's knowledge as Son of God is concerned with knowing how to play his divine part rather than with knowing that his part was, in a metaphysical sense, divine.
5. It is an apparent corollary of this that his sense of his uniqueness would be arrived at negatively by the discovery that other men lacked what he was. It was, indeed, a function of his divine compassion for us sinners.

There: that is all I have said. I have really done no more than define and explain a few of the things which the Christian Church teaches and believes. I have proved nothing.

Dom Gregory Dix, *The Shape of the Liturgy*, London: A. & C. Black, 1945, pp. 258–63.

The peculiar turn which primitive jewish christianity gave to this conception was the idea that in the life, death and resurrection of Jesus this 'purpose' of all history had *already been* manifested, and the Kingship of God conclusively vindicated. When the Messiah had in solid historical fact – 'under Pontius Pilate' – offered Himself in sacrifice that the whole will of God might be done, the supreme crisis of history had occurred. When He passed through death to life and so by His ascension into the 'glory' (*shechinah*) of God, in His Person the 'Age to come' has been inaugurated, in which the Kingship of God is unquestionable and unchallenged. In Him – in His human life and death – the rule of God in all human life had been proclaimed absolute and perfectly realized.

'In Christ!' The phrase is perpetually upon the pen of S. Paul. This is the meaning of the church, the Body of Christ. The redeemed, the New Israel of the New Covenant, are those who have been made 'members' of Him by baptism, incorporated (*symphytoi*) thus into Him, they have been transferred 'in Christ' into that Kingdom of God into which He entered at His ascension. 'God *has* resurrected us together with Christ and made us ascend along with Him and enthroned us along with Him in heavenly places in Christ Jesus.'

'The Spirit' and Eschatology

The medium, as it were, by which Christians within time are already thus within the Kingdom of God in eternity is 'the Spirit'. We should beware of understanding the N.T. authors too rigidly in terms of developed Trinitarian theology, even though their writings laid down the lines upon which the fourth century theologians would one day rightly interpret the revelation of God to the apostolic church. In reality the thought of the jews who wrote most of the New Testament is often more akin to that of the Old Testament than it is to that, say, of S. Augustine's *de Trinitate*. As S. Peter explained the coming of 'the Spirit' at Pentecost: 'This is that which was spoken by the prophet Joel: "And it shall come to pass in the last days (*eschatais hēmerais* – this reference to the *eschaton* is a significant Christian addition to Joel's actual words) – saith God, I will pour out My spirit upon all flesh"'. It is the old semitic notion of the 'the Spirit of God' as 'the Presence of God with power', of which we have already spoken. Jesus, 'being by the right hand of God exalted has received of the Father the fulfilment of the promise about the Holy Spirit and has shed forth this which you now see and hear'. This 'pouring forth' of 'the Spirit' is an indication of the *impersonal* view still taken of 'the Spirit'. And in fact the idea of the Spirit as it is developed in the earlier *strata* of the N.T. documents is that of the 'power' or 'presence' of the Ascended Jesus in the eternal Kingdom of God energising within time in His Body the church, so that its members, or rather *His* members, 'walk no more after the flesh but after the Spirit', or as S. Paul puts it elsewhere, 'I have been crucified with Christ yet I am alive; yet no longer I live but (the risen and ascended) Christ liveth in me; and the life which I live in the flesh I live by the faith of the Son of God'. To 'walk after the Spirit' and for 'Christ to live through me' mean for S. Paul the same thing. 'As many as are led by the Spirit of God, these are sons of God' – as Jesus, 'in' Whom they are by 'the Spirit', is the Son . . . 'The Spirit' is the power of presence of the Ascended Christ which incarnates His glorified Body of heaven in the 'Body of Christ', the church on earth. Baptism incorporates a man into that body from the eternal point of view, but the gift of 'the Spirit' in confirmation is what makes him a living member of that Body *within time*. Thus only the confirmed may take part in the eucharist, which is the vital act of the Body in time.

The accident that so much of our New Testament material comes to us from Pauline sources and thus represents a process of translation from Hebrew to Greek modes of thought, makes it a delicate and hazardous matter to discern the exact bearing of Christian ideas before that inevitably distorting process began. But speaking tentatively and with a due sense of the difficulties of the matter, it looks as though for the *original* Christian eschatology we have to get behind the teaching of S. Paul, for whom the *parousia* or 'coming' of our Lord is always in the future, at a 'last judgement' at the end of time. This is an adaptation for the benefit of gentiles. There are traces of a non-Pauline usage of the term *parousia* = 'the coming', to describe what we should call the '*first coming*' of the incarnation only, as something which *has already happened*. It is well known that the fourth gospel regards the last judgement as both a present fact and a future event. So too, the 'coming of the Spirit' is for this evangelist both an historic event and a perpetual 'coming' of Jesus to His own. Such an attitude may well represent not so much a 'development' of Paulinism as the re-emergence of an older and more fully jewish eschatology. The original jewish church had preserved the tradition that our Lord Himself had said that in the sense of the conclusion of history, 'The *eschaton* is not yet'. But it believed with all its heart that in Him the purpose of history had been revealed and the Kingdom of God had been completely manifested and demonstrated. Down to the time of Justin, who is the first to distinguish between the 'first coming' in humiliation and the 'second' to judgement, in our fashion, the word *parousia* is never used in the plural.

There is but *one* 'coming', in the incarnation, in the Spirit, in the eucharist and in the judgement. And that is the 'coming' of 'One like unto the Son of Man' (who is 'the people of the saints of the Most High', *i.e.*, Christ and the church) *to the Father.* This is the end and meaning of human history, the bringing of man, the creature of time, to the Ancient of Days, in eternity. The same eternal fact can touch the process of history at more than one point, and if there is an apparent difference in the effects of such contacts, that difference is entirely on the side of the temporal process, for eternity knows no 'difference', and no 'before' or 'after'. This view of eschatology as manifesting the purpose of history already within time does not deny a 'last judgement'; rather it demands a total judgement of all history in the light of that purpose.

Eric Mascall, *Christ, the Christian, and the Church*, London: Longmans, 1946, pp. 94–7.

'A member of Christ.' I have already said as much about this as we need at the moment. By baptism, without loss of personal identity, we are incorporated into Christ, that is to say, established *in corpora Christi*, given an ontological union with, and participation in, his glorified human nature, so that all that he possesses in it becomes ours. In him we are new creatures; he is the vine, we are the branches; the glory which the Father gave to him, he has given to us.

'The child of God.' Christ is the Son of the Father, by nature, in essential union; in his human nature dwells all the fullness of the Godhead bodily, in hypostatic union; we are one with him in his human nature, by adoptive union. Therefore, since all that he has he communicates to us, we are the sons of God by adoption and grace, as he is the Son of God by nature. This is not just theological theorizing; it is the teaching of the New Testament.

> 'When the fullness of the time came,' wrote St. Paul to the Galatians, 'God sent forth his son, born of a woman, born under the law, that he might redeem them which were under the law, that we might receive the adoption of sons. And because ye are sons, God sent forth the Spirit of his Son into our hearts, crying, Abba, Father. So that thou art no longer a bondservant, but a son; and if a son, then an heir through God.'

Again he writes to the Romans:

> 'Ye received not the spirit of bondage again unto fear, but ye received the Spirit of adoption, whereby we cry, Abba, Father. The Spirit himself beareth witness with our spirit, that we are children of God: and if children, then heirs.'

This Biblical doctrine, we must notice, is not that we are all sons of God by mere fact of our natural birth; or if we are, we are sons who have fallen away from sonship into servitude, we have left the Father's house and gone into a far country and have been reduced to living with the swine. True sonship is restored to us only in Christ; but in him it is a far more wonderful sonship than that which we had lost. Adam, says the Lucan genealogy of Christ, was the son of God; he was made, Genesis tells us, in God's image, after God's likeness; he was God's son by nature, by creation. We who are restored in Christ have a far greater privilege, for our sonship is an adoption by grace into the sonship of him who is not *made in* God's image but *is* that image itself, 'the image of the invisible God, the heir of all creation', 'the impress of his substance'. Wonderfully as God created the dignity of man's substance, he has yet more wonderfully renewed it. In the mystery of his foreknowledge 'he chose us in [Christ] before the foundation of the world . . . having foreordained us unto adoption as sons through Jesus Christ unto himself.' It is in Christ alone that we can cry, 'Abba, Father.' The Lord's Prayer, the *Pater noster*, is the Church's prayer, the prayer of those who dare to approach God with the name 'Father' upon their lips only because the sonship which they had forfeited has been restored to them in Christ. It is of the highest significance that, in the great Christian liturgies, it is only when the divine Victim has been brought mystically before the Father as the unique mediator between God and man, and in his sacramental presence, that the Church dares to offer the prayer which Christ taught it to say. 'Vouchsafe, O Lord, that we may dare with boldness and without condemnation to call on thee, the heavenly God, as Father and say –'

In other words, this adoption as sons of God is not just the concession of certain rights by a legal fiction, a mere imputation, as is done in the process of adoption in English law; it is a real communication of the sonship of Jesus Christ. 'Beloved, now are we children of God.'

'An inheritor of the kingdom of heaven.' This is a direct consequence of our sonship, as our sonship was of our incorporation. 'If a son, then an heir through God', writes the Apostle, or, as another reading has it, 'an heir of God through Christ'. 'If children, then heirs; heirs of God and joint heirs with Christ.' That is to say, everything that is Christ's in virtue of his sonship is ours by our adoption into him. We receive – of course in a way adapted to our mode of existence as creatures, for *quidquid recipitur recipitur ad modum recipientis* – a real participation in the life of the Holy Trinity; through our union with Christ. We are caught up into the act whereby he eternally adores the heavenly Father. We are made, in the New-Testament phrase, 'partakers of the divine nature'. As St. Paul told the Ephesians, God 'raised us up with [Christ] and made us to sit with him in the heavenly places, in Christ Jesus'. This does not, of course, remove us from the conditions of earthly existence; it makes us, on the contrary, members of two worlds at once. We are to '*seek* the things that are above, where Christ is, seated on the right hand of God'; nevertheless, St. Paul says to us in the same context, 'your life is *hid* with Christ in God.'

It is this participation in the life of God, this sharing in the response which the eternal Son makes to the Father's love, that is the basis of the teaching of both the fathers and the mystical theologians about the 'divinization' or 'deification' of man in Christ. It is absolutely essential to remember the conditions under which it takes place if we are to avoid serious heresy. It is a result of the threefold bridge of union which, we have seen, spans the gulf between us and the Father. It is through our adoptive union with Christ and the hypostatic union of his human nature with his divine Person that we are caught up into the life of union which he essentially shares with God the Father. And we saw that one of the characteristics of our adoptive union with Christ is that our personal identity is preserved. Even if, in a strictly guarded sense, we can say, with some of the mystics, that Christ and God are *what* we become, we can never say that they are *who* we become. In describing the supreme stage of mystical union in which 'all the desires of the soul and its faculties . . . are changed into divine operations' and in which 'the soul, having its operations in God, through the union that it has with God, lives in the life of God', St. John of the Cross, while he asserts that 'the understanding of this soul is now the understanding of God, and its will is the will of God, and its memory is the memory of God, and its delight is the delight of God' and will even go so far as to say that 'it is thus God by participation in God', insists that 'the substance of this soul . . . is not the substance of God, for into this it cannot be substantially changed'.

Bibliography

Pre-Reformation sources

Athanasius of Alexandria, *On the Incarnation*.
Athanasius of Alexandria, *Orations Against the Arians*.
Cyril of Alexandria, *Letters*.
A Definition of Faith (the Council of Chalcedon, 451).
Irenaeus of Lyons, *Against the Heresies*.
John of Damascus, *Exposition of the Orthodox Faith*.
Leo the Great, *Letter to Flavian* (The 'Tome of Leo').
Maximus the Confessor, *Ambigua*.
Thomas Aquinas, *Summa Theologiae III*.

Post-Reformation

Hans Urs von Balthasar, *Theo-Drama: Theological Dramatic Theory III. Dramatis Personae: Persons in Christ*, San Francisco: Ignatius Press, 1992.
Karl Barth, *Church Dogmatics* I.2, Edinburgh: T. & T. Clark, 1956.
Dietrich Bonhoeffer, *Christology*, London, Collins, 1966.
John Calvin, *Institutes of the Christian Religion* II.
Walter Kasper, *Jesus the Christ*, London: Burns & Oates, 1976.
John Macquarrie, *Jesus Christ in Modern Thought*, London: SCM Press, 1990.
Jürgen Moltmann, *The Crucified God*, London: SCM Press, 1974.
Gerald O'Collins, *Christology: A Biblical, Historical and Systematic Study of Jesus*, Oxford: Oxford University Press, 1995.
Wolfhart Pannenberg, *Jesus, God and Man*, London: SCM Press, 1968.
Edward Schillebeeckx, *Jesus: An Experiment in Christology*, London: Collins, 1979.

4

Theological Anthropology

KATHRYN TANNER

In a significant strand of the Anglican theological tradition since the sixteenth century, the primary thing to say about human beings is that they are made for a relationship of great intimacy with God.[1] God is the natural desire of our hearts. We are only properly ourselves, happy and fulfilled as the people God meant us to be, when love for God is our life.

These Anglican theologians discuss the state of humans in theological terms – human life as created, fallen and saved – accordingly: in terms of the quality of that relationship between humans and God. Human beings were created to have a close relationship with God, a relationship essential for that reason to the proper exercise of their natural human capacities. We think, feel, will, act and, in general, simply live well – as we should, according to God's intentions in creating us – only insofar as we enjoy such a close relationship, in other words. We do not as a matter of fact, however, live that way. All our own efforts amount to a turning away, an attempt to separate ourselves from God, a fall from the true character of human life that therefore works only to our detriment, bringing inevitably in its train corruption, misery and death. Christ saves us by restoring the human to its lost intimacy with God but now in a higher form that addresses the problem of sin. In Christ we find not simply the fragile communion between human and divine of creation that our fallible and sinful human impulses can and do corrupt, but a re-creation of the human in unbreakable union with the divine, a union achieved in an inimitable way in Christ's person and to be ours through him. All our hopes for a relationship of intimacy with God – our hope of having an uncorrupted one at all, as well as our highest hope for a relationship of total love and devotion in worshipful service to God – lie in our relationship with him.

The story of the human naturally points to Christ, and therefore in this strand of the Anglican tradition the human forms no independent locus for theological discussion. An account of the human is woven, instead, throughout a discussion of God's saving intentions for us in which Christology is foregrounded. Any enquiry about human life is referred as a matter of course to Christ, to the character of his person and life, since in him one finds the ideal of the human. In his person, the relationship of intimacy between the human and the divine that we were created to enjoy is accomplished to an unsurpassable degree. He is the person he is, because in him the human is not just related to the divine but one with it; in him the divine Word is incarnate, so united to the human that the human

---

[1] For examples of this strand see the selections from Anglican writings under 'theological anthropology'. A more comprehensive description of its character is found in A. M. Allchin, *Participation in God: A Forgotten Strand in Anglican Tradition*, Wilton, CT: Morehouse-Barlow, 1988.

becomes the Word's very own. The result is a human life lived throughout its course in perfect and unassailable union with God, a human life lived, that is, in absolute conformity to the Father's saving intentions for a sin-filled world, despite all the trials, tribulations and temptations suffered at the hands of it.

Because it is Christological, this account of the human is also Trinitarian. The Word is in Christ, and therefore his human life is shaped by the relationships that the Word has with the other members of the Trinity, Father and Spirit. Incarnate as a human being, the Word does the work of the Father through the power of the Spirit. And what goes for Christ goes for us: the relationships that the members of the Trinity have with one another figure in our new life of relationship with Christ. The Holy Spirit makes us sharers in Christ's life by binding us to his human body. And by drawing on the power of the Spirit for our own reformation, nourishment and renewal we gain the ability to live according to Christ's own pattern of worship and service to the Father and his saving intentions for the world.

In keeping with the importance of the liturgy for Anglicanism, the Christological, pneumatological and Trinitarian reflections like these in which an account of the human surfaces have, moreover, a highly sacramental cast. In our baptism, we are joined to Christ by the Spirit and become the recipients of Christ's Spirit as the power of new life in the Father's service. By the Spirit's making the bread and wine of the Eucharist into the humanity of Christ for our nourishment, we are able to draw continually upon the divine Spirit of Christ's own human life in ongoing efforts to put sin behind us and lead the life of Christ in obedience to the Father's loving will for the world's good.

In what follows I will try to develop this strand of Anglican reflection on the human in my own way, not by building directly upon it in the course of a more detailed analysis and explication of the writings in that corpus, but by following the direction or trajectory of its own way of thinking on the general themes mentioned. The theologians in this strand of the Anglican tradition develop their individual treatments of these shared themes, not by reference to one another as authorities or sources, but in primary conversation with patristic writings and early ecumenical creeds that shape their reading of Scripture on the Christological and Trinitarian issues so central to their general approach to the human.[2] And I shall do the same. In keeping with the primarily Christological focus of theological anthropology in this strand of Anglicanism, I begin with a Christ-centred account of the image of God, which Scripture says human beings were created in accordance with. If Christ is the primary image of God – the perfect image of the Father – what does this imply about the character of human life, its theologically interesting features? I then draw out the Trinitarian ramifications of the same line of thought for an account of human life, for understanding human life well lived in worship and service to God.

The Image of God

Prompted by the Genesis verses that tell of their creation in the image of God, theological discussion of humans often focuses on their nature in and of itself,

---

2 See in particular the patristic authors mentioned under 'theological anthropology' in the Bibliography at the end of this chapter.

discrete qualities or capacities that reflect the divine nature and distinguish the human character from that of any other creature. Following this very common line of thought in the history of Christianity, humans are created in the image of God, because, unlike other creatures, they have reason or free will or the ability to rule over others as God does.

This preoccupation with characteristics proper to human nature in and of itself can be disrupted, however, if one reads the Genesis passages about humans being created in the image of God through the lens of New Testament, mostly Pauline ones, in which the image of God is identified with Christ (e.g. Rom. 8.29; 2 Cor. 4.4; Col. 1.15). Reading the Genesis verses in that light and in accord with what the ecumenical councils affirm of Christ's person as the Word made flesh, it is possible for the image of God to take on a primarily intra-Trinitarian sense. The image of God is not primarily identified with something human, in other words. The express or perfect image of God (Heb. 1.3) is, instead, a properly divine one, the second person of the Trinity, the Son who is the spitting image, so to speak, of the Father. Jesus Christ is a human image of God, therefore, because he is the incarnation of the second person of the Trinity, the perfect divine image of the Father. And if we are to image God, we have to be formed according to God's own image – the second person of the Trinity – in something like the way Jesus was (Gal. 4.19; Eph. 4.24; Col. 3.10).

The Genesis discussion of human beings' creation in the image of God can be viewed then in Christologically focused Trinitarian terms. Humans are not simply said to be the image but to be created 'in' or 'after' it, because the image referred to here is a divine one: either the second person of the Trinity or the Word incarnate. Which one makes little difference since in the latter case the primary image is still the second person of the Trinity, and the second person of the Trinity becomes an image both broadly applicable to humans and of the most perfect sort, by becoming incarnate.

The Holy Spirit, following the New Testament witness (e.g. Rom. 8.9; 1 Cor. 2.10–16), unites us to Christ and allows us thereby to be made over in his image. Attention is therefore directed to passages in the Genesis story of creation that could be taken to refer to the Holy Spirit – the spirit hovering over the waters (Gen. 1.2), or the living soul breathed into Adam (2.7). The Holy Spirit itself was given to humans when they were created, in order to form them according to the image of God that is the second person of the Trinity; they thereby became a human image of that divine image like (but not exactly like) the Word incarnate to come, Jesus Christ. The theology of Cyril of Alexandria sees the full and explicit development of such a view: 'in the beginning ... the Creator of all, taking dust of the ground and having formed man, breathed upon his face the breath of life. And what is the breath of life, save surely the Spirit of Christ ... ? But since ... the Spirit which is able to gather us and form us unto the Divine Impress [fled away from human nature], the Saviour gives us this anew bringing us again into that ancient Dignity and reforming us unto His own Image.'[3]

An odd refocusing of what is of interest about human beings, both when they actually image God in Christ and when considering their 'capacities' for

---

3 Cyril of Alexandria, *Commentary on the Gospel According to John*, Book V, Chapter II, E. B. Pusey (trans.), Oxford: James Parker, 1874, vol. I, p. 550 (on John 7.39).

it, results. First of all, it is not what humans are in and of themselves that is of interest, but their relationship with God, its character and consequences for human life. Human nature's imaging of God becomes an essentially relational affair. Humans image God in virtue of an actual relationship with God, a relationship that brings with it some sort of correspondence between human and divine life and action. The closer the relationship, the better the correspondence. If humans were originally created in the image of God they must have had, then, a close relationship with God by grace, one lost through sin and to be restored through Christ. The fact that humans in the Garden of Eden enjoyed goodness, wisdom and happiness can only mean, as Augustine for example argues, that they participated in the very goodness, wisdom, and blessedness of God at their creation; like the angels making up the heaven of heavens (the 'light' in 'let there be light'), at their creation they were turned by God to God's own light, and gained thereby their human perfection.[4]

Second, if one should look at human nature per se, what comes to the fore is no well-delimited set of easily encapsulated characteristics but, to the contrary, the fact of our being a mystery to ourselves. If one follows the ecumenical councils and denies the possibly subordinationist import of talking about the second person of the Trinity as the image of the first – i.e. 'image' does not mean any lesser degree of divinity – the second person we are to image is as incomprehensible as the first; and therefore we come to image it not by having some well-defined nature ourselves but through some form of our very own incomprehensibility. There must be something incomprehensible about human nature as it is shaped by a relationship with God, which makes it like God, and, secondarily, even something incomprehensible about it from the very start, one might say, which renders it capable of being worked over into a divine form.

The second person of the Trinity is not comprehensible while the first is incomprehensible, but images it in its very incomprehensibility, and this holds for the incarnation of the second person of the Trinity too. Jesus is not the comprehensible stand-in or substitute for an incomprehensible divinity but the very exhibition of the incomprehensible divinity of the Word in a human form or medium. Jesus displays in his life what it means to be an incomprehensible image in the flesh of an incomprehensible God. If humans are the image of God, they are then an incomprehensible image of the incomprehensible as well: 'If, while the archetype transcends comprehension, the nature of the image were comprehended, the contrary character of the attributes ... would prove the defect of the image ... [S]ince the nature of our mind ... evades our knowledge, it has an accurate resemblance to the superior nature, figuring by its unknowableness the incomprehensible Nature.'[5]

Like God who is incomprehensible because unlimited, humans might have a nature that imitates God only by not having a clearly delimited nature. Every

---

4 Saint Augustine, *The Literal Meaning of Genesis*, Book 8, ch. 12, J. H. Taylor (trans.), New York: Newman Press, 1982, vol. II, pp. 50–2.

5 Gregory of Nyssa, 'On the Making of Man', XI. 4, in H. Wace (ed.), W. Moore and H. A. Austin (trans.), *Gregory of Nyssa: Dogmatic Treatises, etc.*, A Select Library of Nicene and Post-Nicene Fathers of the Christian Church, Second Series, Peabody, MA: Hendrickson, 1994, vol. V, pp. 396–7; sections 2–3 are also relevant.

other creature imitates God by expressing the goodness that God is in a limited form; they are good by being a definite something – a pig or a rock – indeed the best pig or rock they can be. While humans are a definite sort of creature distinct from others and in that sense of course still have a particular nature (they are not God who alone is different from others by not being a kind of thing), humans still stand out by their failure to be clearly limited by a particular nature as other creatures are. Failure of definition by remaining ill-defined is not so much the point; what is primarily at issue here is a failure of definition through excessive love. Humans seem to have an underlying concern for what is absolutely good per se – for God – for what is not merely good in certain respects but fully good in a perfectly unlimited way. They want in some sense to be that absolute good, rather than any particular sort of thing, rather than the specific sort of creature they are, by being formed in and through a relationship with it – for example, by knowing the absolute truth that is God, the absolute good for human cognition, that comes by way of God's very presence to the mind. The weirdly unlimited character of human nature and drives would then be the fundamental reason for traditional theological preoccupation with human intelligence and will when discussing the way humans are the image of God. These 'faculties' are of interest because of their excessive openness, one might say, because of their attraction to formation through what exceeds their own or any limited nature.

Otherwise expressed, if humans are to be made over in God's image – so radically reworked as to take on a divine shape or form in the way Jesus' humanity did – then what is of interest about human nature is its plasticity, its openness to formation through outside influences and the unusually wide range of possible effects of such a process of formation in the human case. For humans to come to be in the image of God is an extreme case of coming to be oneself in relation to what one is not – God, what is most unlike creatures generally. All creatures are formed in relation to what they are not but humans do this in an exaggerated way that opens them to a radical sort of reformation from without in the divine image.

All living creatures become themselves, for example, by taking in things from outside themselves; seeds, for example, require food from without in order to germinate. Humans, because they are made to be in the image of God, require God for their nourishment. In heaven, indeed, God will be our only food and drink: 'while our present life is active amongst a variety of multiform conditions, and the things which we have relations with are numerous, for instance, time, air, locality, food and drink, clothing, sunlight, lamplight and other necessities of life, none of which, many though they be, are God – that blessed state which we hope for is in need of none of these things, but the Divine Being will become all [1 Cor. 15.28], and instead of all, to us, distributing Himself proportionately to every need of that existence . . . . God [will] become . . . locality, and home, and clothing, and food, and drink, and light, and riches, and dominion, and everything thinkable and nameable that goes to make our life happy.'[6]

---

6 Gregory of Nyssa, 'On the Soul and the Resurrection', in H. Wace (ed.), W. Moore and H. A. Austin (trans.), *Gregory of Nyssa: Dogmatic Treatises, etc.*, A Select Library of Nicene and Post-Nicene Fathers of the Christian Church, Second Series, Peabody, MA: Hendrickson, 1994, vol. V, p. 452.

In the case of all other living things, whatever they take in is formed according to the limits of their pre-established nature. For example, light, water, nutrients from the soil – whatever a particular sort of plant takes in – always comes out of the process of transformation as the self-same plant – in the form at best of an increasingly bigger and better one, where there was genuine nourishment for the plant's good. When human beings take in God as their proper nourishment, they come out, to the contrary, as God. They are turned thereby into the matter, so to speak, for a new divine organization of what they are. They become God's image, rather than God's becoming theirs; humans are reworked according to God's pattern of living, rather than God being reworked according to a human one. Humans when they are formed in the image of God take on Christ's identity, in short. Like what happens to light, water and soil in the case of a plant – but now with a peculiar reversal of the usual consequences – men, women, children, Greek and Jew, free and slave – all go into the process of reformation and come out as Christ.[7]

To generalize from this, one might say human beings are unusually impressionable, in a way that the language of image often unpacks in a quite concrete way: they are like soft wax that a vast variety of seals might indent to their image; they are the mirror of whatever they turn towards. They take their identities from the uses to which they put themselves, like vessels that gain their character from whatever they take in and are made to carry.[8]

Using a more contemporary idiom, one could say that human life takes a variety of forms depending on what it is that people care most about.[9] Human beings exercise self-reflective powers; they are able to make an object of themselves in projects of self-fashioning and re-fashioning, following changeable judgements about what it is that is most important to them – fancy cars, the respect of their peers, wisdom and so on. They attach themselves to these objects of desire and draw them into themselves, so to speak, as variable organizing principles of their lives. 'Such is the strength of love, that the mind draws in with itself those things which it has long thought of with love, and has grown into them by the close adherence.'[10] 'Human nature adapts itself to the direction of thought and it changes according to whatever form it is inclined to by the impulse of free choice.'[11] 'Human nature is such that whatever it may wish to be', it 'becomes

---

[7] See Gregory Nazianzen, 'Select Orations', *Oration* VII, section 23, in P. Schaff and H. Wace (eds), C. G. Browne and J. E. Swallow (trans.), *Cyril of Jerusalem, Gregory Nazianzen*, A Select Library of Nicene and Post-Nicene Fathers of the Christian Church, Second Series, Grand Rapids, MI: Eerdmans, 1983, vol. VII, p. 237.

[8] See Basil the Great, *On the Human Condition*, Nona Verna Harrison (trans.), Crestwood, NY: St Vladimir's Seminary Press, 2005, p. 72.

[9] See Harry G. Frankfort, *The Reasons of Love*, Princeton and Oxford: Princeton University Press, 2004.

[10] Augustine, *De Trinitate*, Book X, Chapter 5 [section 7], in P. Schaff (ed.), *St. Augustine*, A Select Library of Nicene and Post-Nicene Fathers of the Christian Church, Second Series, Grand Rapids, MI: Eerdmans, 1976, Vol. III, p. 138.

[11] Gregory of Nyssa, 'Fourth Homily on the Song of Songs', quoted by Verna Harrison, *Grace and Freedom According to St. Gregory of Nyssa*, Lewiston, NY: Edwin Mellen, 1992, p. 181.

that very thing'.[12] This means – to return to a previous metaphor – that 'human nature is very much like a mirror in its ability to change in accordance with the different impressions of its free will. When you put gold in front of a mirror, the mirror takes on the appearance of gold and . . . shines with the same gleam . . . So too, if it catches the reflection of something loathsome, it imitates this ugliness by means of a likeness, as for example of a frog, a toad, a millipede, or anything else that is disgusting to look at, thus reproducing in its own substance whatever is placed in front of it.'[13]

Reflective capacities of self-judgement mean humans can try to reshape in a self-critical fashion even those desires they cannot help having by nature. I may have the natural desire to eat, but that does not mean I have to shape my life around the importance of that for me – asceticism is a case in point. Humans have the capacity to use the passions of their animal natures (as Nyssa would term them) – their natural attraction, for example, to what benefits them – as instruments of either virtue or vice.[14] That attraction may be the energy propelling them towards, say, profligacy – or God. Humans have the power to cultivate or discourage those natural drives and tendencies that they start out with whether they like it or not, making efforts, for example, to alter their intensities through stimulation or neglect, or efforts to rework the way they figure in one's life as a whole. Indeed, these self-reflexive powers account for why human lives can become so horrible, much more horrible than those of other animals; the anger, for example, that an animal might fleetingly feel when faced with an opponent can be husbanded by the human mind – dwelt upon – so as to pervade all one's dealings with others, in a host of variable forms – envy, malice, conspiracy, deceit – with the result that one's whole nature is traced anew after that design.[15]

Human beings have plastic powers, self-formative capacities, and it is the fact that those capacities are not determined to one thing as natural desires are – the fact that those capacities need not incline in a predetermined direction according to the givens of one's nature or essential definition (following a Thomistic understanding, for example, of natural desires) – that accounts for the heightened variability of their effects in operation. People come out in wildly different ways, for better or for worse. Or, one might say the self-formative capacities of humans do have a nature but the particular nature of rational volition is just to have no definite nature to be true to, in the way that animals are true to their natures when acting properly, for their own good. Humans can think of a variety of things that it would be good to do in certain respects or for certain purposes, and what they decide about what is most important to them in the course of such deliberations decides in great part the character of their lives, the identity they come to exhibit in their acts – that is just their nature.

---

12 Gregory of Nyssa, 'Soul and Resurrection', p. 457.
13 Gregory of Nyssa, *Commentary on the Canticle*, sermon 4, in H. Musurillo (trans. and ed.), *From Glory to Glory: Texts from Gregory of Nyssa's Mystical Writings*, Crestwood, NY: St Vladimir's Seminary Press, 1995, p. 171.
14 Gregory of Nyssa, 'Soul and Resurrection', p. 442.
15 Gregory of Nyssa, 'Making of Man', Chapter XVIII, sections 3–4, p. 408.

The early Eastern Church's stress on free will as the image – or often secondarily, rule in the sense of self-rule – could now be taken in a new light, not as the promotion of some vaunted power in a positive sense, an imitation of divine omnipotence, but as an interest in the unusual plasticity of human lives absent any predetermined direction by nature. Free will is an indication of variability. Their unusual powers of self-determination mean humans can become anything along the continuum of ontological ranks, from the bottom to the top. Humans, it is true, are determined to God – being formed in the image of God is their good, by nature. But that is just not to be determined in any particular direction as other things are, since God is the absolute good and not a limited one.

If these early Eastern theologians never said explicitly that what interested them about human nature was its open-ended plasticity – or later Christian theologians have had a hard time understanding them to be saying that – perhaps contemporary cultural trends prove more illuminating in this respect, as templates for a fresh interpretation. We are less inclined to assume, for example, that humans have given, self-enclosed and well-encapsulated natures now that biotechnologies, particularly interspecies gene transfers, have called into question the fixed boundaries of natural kinds. And we are less inclined to consider the having of given natures with well-defined borders an unambiguous good. Violence bred of ethnic and religious division in our world familiarizes us all too well with the bellicose potential of narrowly drawn, closely guarded identities in our sociopolitical lives. Feminists remind us of the way appeals to given, already determined natures solidify unjust social arrangements and disguise their contingency. Postmodernists of various stripes caution more broadly against the insistence on a self-identical, coherent character, rigidly predicated on the exclusion of others so as to promote protective postures that degrade and sever human connection with them. And they lead us to question the ethical priority of self-discovery, as if the truth about oneself – who one originally was, one's given nature or identity – could determine all by itself what one might become, one's place within the world and the character of one's responsibilities, in sovereign independence of any unpredictable entanglements with human and non-human others beyond one's control.

The less dualistic division between matter and mind in contemporary thought might also prove an interpretative help. All the qualities of humans typically highlighted by the early theologians upon which I have drawn have something to do with human rational capacities, and there is probably a good reason for this even from a more contemporary point of view (as I have implied) if indefinite plasticity, the nature that is no nature, is what these theologians are trying to get at. But it is important to see that plastic or non-natured bodies are the ultimate issue even for these early church theologians. At the end of the day it is our bodies that are to be remade into Christ's body.

Human materiality is essential to the image of God so as to take the whole of existence, irrespective of any division between spirit and matter, to God. (This is why angels or disembodied pure intelligences are not the image.) Only in virtue of the fact that they have bodies can the whole world hope in humans. Humans demonstrate that, appearances to the contrary (especially in the cultural and philosophical milieu of the early Church), the material world itself is plastic – by extension just as plastic to divine influence, one might hope, as human lives. God formed humans out of the dust of the earth so that when formed in the image of God humans might show that the earth too can be made over in God's image: both matter and mind are made for a single grace.[16]

A final odd consequence of identifying the image of God primarily with a divine image appropriately closes this section: if the image of God is most properly speaking a divine one, there is a sense in which humans, considered in and of themselves, never become a proper image of God at all, even when formed according to it. The image of God in a proper sense is just God, the second person of the Trinity. Not being God, humans can therefore never simply become that image in and of themselves through any process of transformation. There is no ontological continuum spanning the difference between God and creatures. For that reason, humans cannot hope to become the divine image, this perfect or proper image, through any process of approximation – for example, by improving their mental capacities in some gradual approach to God's own perfect rationality.

And yet, without abolishing or mitigating the difference between God and humans, humans do become the divine image – by attaching themselves to it. It is by being identified with what they are not that the divine image becomes most properly their own. Humans become the image of God in the strongest sense (not imaging the image but simply identified with it) when they are not trying to be it at all, not trying to image the divine image in a human way, but are brought near to it, so near as to be one with it.

Humans, one might say, are never sufficiently fluid or flexible simply to be the image in and of themselves, to be made over into some good approximation of it; they cannot hope, therefore, to achieve a simple reproduction of the divine image in some perfect human imitation considered on its own terms. Humans, instead, have the image of God only by clinging to what they are not – that divine image itself – in love. There is only one perfect or express image of God – the second person of the Trinity – and that perfect image becomes humans' own only through their exceedingly close relationship with it – for example, by its own actual presence within them, made their own by the first person of the Trinity through the power of the Holy Spirit on the basis of the second person's incarnation in human flesh. Humans show off, so to speak, the light that is the divine image itself – and are in that sense good images of God themselves – by exterior illumination, by glowing with a light that remains another's and not by some phosphorescent assimilation of that light into their own natures as some now human property.

All creatures can do this same showing off or shining back of the divine glory. Plasticity is not a prerequisite for it. Even now creatures can glorify God, glow with a kind of divine penumbra by pointing to, and in that sense making manifest, the goodness of the God who made them: the wonders of the world speak of the wonders of God. In the reformation of the world to come, when, for example, death will be no more, all creatures and not just humans can image the divine in the way we have just been talking about by living off, for example, the

---

16 Gregory of Nyssa, 'Address on Religious Instruction', section 6, in E. Hardy (ed.), C. Richardson (trans.), *Christology of the Later Fathers*, Philadelphia: Westminster, 1954, p. 279.

very eternal life of God, by drawing themselves on powers that remain divine, in virtue of a close relationship or oneness with God, that makes those powers their own.

Because of its fluid character, human nature or identity is itself remoulded in the process – that is its peculiarity. Something, in other words, happens to human nature itself when it reflects the image of God. The nature of the human is just not to be inflexibly itself, like other creatures, when feeling the power, brought into the presence of God. Human nature is not made for resistance but for formation through divine presence and power. Being reworked in the image of God is, in other words, what makes human nature itself, what brings it to its own properly human perfections – for example, to be perfectly virtuous or perfectly pious. This refashioning to perfection remains nonetheless specifically human perfection, not the divine image per se, and as such amounts only to a dim, distant analogue of divinity. Human perfection, which follows from union with the divine image, is always an image of an image (Christ) of an image (the second person of the Trinity), in a radically inferior medium – indeed, before the eschaton in which human perfection is achieved, an image of an image of an image in a thoroughly corrupted medium (e.g. one hard and unimpressionable to divine imprint).

Creatures can be more or less the image of God in virtue of their particular created characteristics. We have seen this in the case of human beings – the way they are more the image of God than animals, and more the image of God in certain respects than others – in virtue primarily of the peculiarly plastic capabilities that open them to reformation according to an absolute rather than merely partial or relative good. But this is still imaging at the lowest level – imaging in virtue of the character of created qualities themselves, imaging as imitation in an ontologically inferior, because non-divine, medium. Even what we are to become by being formed in Christ's image is a low-level image of God of this sort – in so far as the end product, so to speak, is a human state – a most excellent state indeed, but still a human one. The reflection of God in us, when the Spirit conforms us to Christ, is in this sense like the reflection of the sun in a mirror: the reflection is not at all like the sun itself in most respects – for example, it is extremely small, relatively cool, quite dim so that we can look at it without being blinded, and so on.

We are the image of God in a much stronger sense, through identification with it, when the divine image that remains so different from us becomes part of us, an ingredient in our constitution. We are the image of God in this sense not by way of a human imitation of God, not by way of what we are ourselves, but in virtue of some sort of incorporation of what remains alien to us, the very perfection of God that we are not. Cyril, for example, and Augustine, too, distinguish between our existence and our well-being and claim that the latter is a function of God's own entrance within us. We are rational creatures, say, and that is a sort of image of God – the low-flying kind by way of imitation – but when we know well, then we are the image of God in a stronger sense in virtue of the fact that the truth itself, God, has entered within us to give us the truth. The excellent functioning of our native capacities is not a self-sufficient operation, then, in the sense of simply unrolling from our own capabilities, but requires a strong dependence on the very powers of God which have become ours for the taking – in some extraordinary gift of God to us of what is not ours by nature. The perfection of human living that is Christ's and (to a lesser degree) ours in him would be the supreme case of this sort of thing – of human powers elevated through the entrance of God's own powers, through the gift of the Holy Spirit itself forming humanity according to the image of the second person of the Trinity.

Here we image God by living off God, so to speak, in the way a foetus lives off the life of its mother, living in and through or with her very life. This is the mirror that is bright not by anything that is its own but only through the presence of the sun's own light. This – to use the more common biblical imagery perhaps – is the branch that lives on the alien sap of the vine to which it has been engrafted.

These two senses of image – weaker and stronger – are obviously bound up with one another. A weak sense of imaging by imitation is the presupposition of the second, stronger sense. The created capacities that make humans the image God in a weak sense provide the openings through which they become an image of God in the strong sense. Those created capacities one might even say are the prerequisites for being an image in the strong sense. God's gift of God's own self can become a true constituent of only certain sorts of created natures – ones whose functions are not limited by nature, those that inherently have room for God internal to them. The strong sense of image in virtue of incorporation and union with the divine is, conversely, what enables the strongest version of the weak way humans image God by imitation. By having the one whom we are not, Christ, the very incarnation of God, for our own, we should one day be able to live a human life that imitates God's own life in the most perfect way possible for mere humans – a Trinitarian form of life.

Trinitarian Life

Discussion of human beings as the image of God leads immediately into a discussion of the Trinitarian character of human life in Christ. If the image in which human beings are created is the second person of the Trinity, that divine image forms us according to the shape or pattern of its relations with the other two. The life of the Word is its dynamic relationships with the other members of the Trinity in virtue of the inseparability of the three; the Word has no life apart from the other two. When human life is in the divine image of the second person of the Trinity, it is, then, the Word's relations to the other members of the Trinity that human life comes to reflect.

If we are created in its image, the second person of the Trinity is our place in Trinitarian life, the position with which we are to be identified in our relations with the Father and Spirit. But the second person of the Trinity is not just the prototype for our relations with the first and third persons of the Trinity, a divine exemplification of the sort of position that we are to take up vis-à-vis the others. The second person of the Trinity is as well our entryway, our point of access into those relations. We are to take up the very position of the second person of the Trinity as that person joins our life to its own through the incarnation.

In Christ one finds the Word's own existence in relation to the other two members of the Trinity translated into a human form for the purpose of making over human life into the form of the Word. Incarnation is for the sake of human redemption, in other words. The ultimate point of the incarnation is not to give the second person of the Trinity a human shape but to bring about an altered manner of human existence, one realizing on a human plane the very mode of existence of that divine person. Here in Christ human life is to be given shape by the second person of the Trinity, to find its organizing principle there, through unity with it; here humanity is to take on the very manner of existence of the second person of the Trinity as that is displayed in its relations with the other two.

The New Testament witness narrates the Trinitarian shape of Jesus' own human life, a human life that comes to include us as we become one with the humanity of Christ through the power of the Spirit. The persons of the Trinity are related in Jesus' life in the following most general way: the Father sends the Son on a mission, which involves his incarnation and earthly mission for our good, a mission that culminates with the Son's sending the Spirit to us upon his death, resurrection, and ascension back to the Father.

More particularly, the Son is from the Father, coming down or sent out to us into the world (e.g. John 3.13, 16–17, 34; 5.36; 6.29, 33, 38–39, 57; 7.28–29; 8.42; 12.44–45, 49; 17.7–8 and so on), in sympathy with our plight (Heb. 4.15; Phil. 2.6–7), as the mediator of the Father's beneficent will to us (James 1.17), thereby reconciling us to the Father (2 Cor. 5.18–19), offering the Father's own mercy and forgiveness (e.g. Matt. 9.2; 20.30; Mark 10.47–48; Luke 5.20–24; 7.47–48), healing us of our infirmities and bringing us into conformity with the Father's own good intentions for human life. The Son is completely of the Father, receiving everything that is the Father's own (e.g. John 3.35; 17.10; Matt. 11.27; Luke 10.22), granting access to the Father (John 1.18; 6.45–46; 14.6–7, 9; Matt. 11.25; Luke 10.23; see also Eph. 2.18; Heb. 7.25), making the very workings of the Father himself present in his own life and mission (e.g. John 5.19–30; 6.37–39; 10.37–38; 12.49), his whole life the doing of the Father's will for us (e.g. John 5.30; 6.38, 57), with complete dedication to and prayerful trust in the Father's will despite all the struggles and hardships such commitment brings. This mission seems to involve the granting of the Spirit to us, the Spirit is one of the gifts that the Son is giving us from the Father (see Luke 11.11–13), and in granting it the life-giving mission of the Father continues through the Son's mediation (John 14.26; 15.26). With that gift of the Spirit coming out to us, the Son returns to the Father (John 6.62; 7.33; 13.1, 3; 20.17 and so on), the mission upon which he was sent on its way to completion through his own Spirit.

Prior to the Son's granting of the Spirit to us, the Spirit is active in all these narrated relations between Son and Father, making them thereby at every moment properly Trinitarian. Son and Spirit are on this mission from the Father together; they accompany one another on the mission, working distinctively as Son and Spirit in and through what the other does. By the Son's becoming incarnate, the power of the Spirit is manifest on earth, working with power wherever Jesus, the Son incarnate, works to heal and save. And as the power by which the Son incarnate works – the power that initiates, sustains and accomplishes the mission that the Son undertakes – the Spirit always makes its appearance in the form of the Son; the Son is the shape such power takes.

Thus, the Son is sent by the Father to become incarnate through the power of the Spirit. The Word takes on human flesh at the behest of the Father through the power of the Spirit. The birth of Jesus is in and through the Spirit, as the Nicene Creed says, following Matthew 1.20–22 and Luke 1.35.

By the power of the same Spirit, moreover, the Son undertakes the mission of the Father over the course of his human life and death. At the baptism in the Jordan, which begins his public ministry, the Spirit of the Father comes down (Luke 3.22; Mark 1.10–11) and rests or remains upon him (John 1.32). The incarnate Son, Jesus, is indeed full of the Spirit: God gives the anointed one, Christ, the Spirit without measure (John 3.34). And it is as this one especially anointed with the Spirit that he ministers to the sick, the blind and the captive (Luke 4.18; Matt. 12.18, following Isaiah 61.1). 'You know . . . how God anointed Jesus of Nazareth with the Holy Spirit and with power; how he went about doing good and healing all who were oppressed by the devil' (Acts 10.38).

The Spirit leads (Matt. 4.1) or drives (Mark 1.12) the Son into the wilderness where his trust in the Father and the nature of his commitment to the mission is subjected to an early testing. Christ enters and returns successfully from there full of the power of the Spirit (Luke 4.1, 14). In and through the power of the Holy Spirit, the close relation that the Son incarnate has with the Father is maintained under trial.

Indeed, the total Godward orientation of Christ's life and death, constituting a kind of return to the Father for the Spirit bestowed upon him, is sustained through the Spirit that abides in him. Thus, he prays to the Father in the Spirit: Jesus 'rejoiced in the power of the Spirit and said, "I thank thee, Father, Lord of heaven and earth"' (Luke 10.21; see John 11.33, 41). He petitions the Father for us through his Spirit – to send that Spirit upon us (John 17.17, 24). He does the Father's will completely – his very food is to do the will of the one who sent him and to accomplish his work (John 4.34) – as someone empowered by it. 'It is in the Spirit that Jesus speaks, acts, teaches, prays, heals and exorcises demons [e.g. Matt. 12.18–21, 28]. It is also in the Spirit that He offers Himself as a sacrifice, consecrates himself [to the Father, John 17.19], and that this sacrifice is accepted by the Father [Heb. 9.14]. The gift of his life by Jesus [in accordance with the Father's mission] is the gift of the Spirit Himself who is in him (John 19:30–34).'[17]

The Son makes a perfect return to the Father of the Spirit given him, by accomplishing the Father's mission that he was sent to us to perform through that Spirit's power. At the death that finishes his earthly mission the incarnate Son returns the Spirit given him: 'Father, into your hands, I commend my Spirit' (Luke 23.46). He is raised by the Spirit (Rom. 8.11), and with the power of the Spirit more fully manifest in his flesh thereby than ever before in his earthly life, he is able to send the Spirit to us through his flesh (John 7.39). The humanity of Jesus must itself, it seems, feel the effects of the Spirit's power fully, if that humanity is to give the Spirit to us (see Matt. 3.11; Mark 1.8; Luke 3.16); Christ's humanity is full of the Spirit in that sense, so as to be a life-giving Spirit for us, post-resurrection and not before (1 Cor. 15.45). Full manifestation of the

---

17 Boris Bobrinskoy, *The Mystery of the Trinity*, A. Gythiel (trans.), Crestwood, NY: St Vladimir's Seminary Press, 1999, p. 88.

Spirit's power is achieved at the end of Jesus' life and not in the struggles leading up to it; only with sin and death defeated through his own death and resurrection is his humanity fully transparent to the Spirit. The Spirit's power cannot be on full display in the humanity of the Son from the first, as a consequence of the very mission upon which the Son has been sent: Jesus does not appear in his earthly life in the form of God but in the form of a servant (see Phil. 2.6–7) – that is, someone undertaking a mission that requires taking up the very position of those burdened by sin and death.

The Spirit having been sent out to us, the narrated story of the way relations among persons of the Trinity enter human life in Christ continues, with a focus now on what happens to us. Receiving the Spirit of Christ we become like Christ in his relations with the Father (see especially Eph. 2.18; Rom. 8.14–17; Gal. 4.6–7). More particularly, the Spirit unites us to Christ in a way that gives us access to the Father and the Father's gifts (Eph. 2.18). The Spirit connects us to Christ – by testifying to Christ (John 15.26; 16.13–14), being the one in whom we see and confess Christ (1 Cor. 12.3), and by making Christ present within us (1 John 3.24) and conforming us to Christ's own mind and pattern of living (1 Cor. 2.10–16). Our connection with the Father is thereby established. Bound to Christ through his Spirit we gain the Father's favour and become recipients of the Father's gifts as Christ was; for example, we become with him the inheritors of eternal life (Rom. 8.17; Gal. 6.8). Empowered by the Spirit, Christ's gift to us from the Father, we are now able to pray to God as our Father (Gal. 4.6–7; Rom. 8.14–17) and participate in the Father's mission in imitation of Christ's own life (Rom. 7.4–6; 2 Cor. 5.17–18).

Through the Spirit the sort of relations among the persons of the Trinity that we traced in Jesus' life reappear in us. Thus, an effective agency of the Spirit joins us to Christ, just as the effective agency of the Spirit joined the humanity of Christ to the Word in the incarnation. The Spirit makes us Christ's – makes us belong to him (Rom. 8.9) – and turns us thereby into adopted sons by grace, brethren of that true Son of God by nature, and therefore joint heirs with him of all the good things of the Father (Gal. 4.5–7; Rom. 8.14–17). Just as the Spirit made humanity the Son of God in the incarnation, the Spirit makes us adopted sons by joining us to Christ.

Joined to Christ by the Spirit, we receive from Christ the Spirit of new life. Made adopted sons by the Spirit we come to act like ones, through the very presence of Christ's Spirit within us as an interior power for action: 'everyone *moved* by the Spirit is a son of God' (Rom. 8.14; italics mine). Jesus is the beloved Son of the Father in this respect too: because he acts like one, faithfully performing the mission upon which he has been sent, by the power of the Spirit that descends upon his humanity at his baptism in the Jordan. The Spirit of God will rest on us (1 Peter 4.14) to transform our lives, because the Spirit first rested on Christ to do the same.[18] When we receive the Spirit we therefore receive Christ to be the new shape of our lives, dying to ourselves and rising with him as participants in the Father's mission of love for the world. Like the

---

18 Dumitru Stăniloae, 'The Procession of the Holy Spirit from the Father and his Relation to the Son, as the Basis of our Deification and Adoption', in L. Vischer (ed.), *Spirit of God, Spirit of Christ*, London: SPCK, 1981, p. 179.

conformity with the loving will of the Father that the power of the Spirit brings about in Jesus' own life, a conformity of life and purpose between ourselves and the Father through the Spirit of Christ within us is to result from the unity between ourselves and Christ that the Spirit effects.

The general pattern of Trinitarian relationships we have traced across the whole story of Christ's life and our relationship with him might be summarized in terms of the biblical motifs of sending and returning. The general pattern begins and ends with the Father: the Father initiates a movement towards us, sends out the Son and Spirit to accomplish it, and in accomplishing it the two return, so as eventually to bring us along with them. This initiative is for our good – it is a work of caring beneficence, like that of a good father or, one might add mother, for a beloved child – and involves the gifts of both Son and Spirit to us. The Son is the laying out of what that good for us is to involve – what is to be achieved in us is first achieved in him, the character of that good is materially exhibited in his life, death and resurrection. And the Spirit is the one who prepares, enables and completes the giving of that good to us. The work of Christ is completed in us, for example, as we are introduced into and maintained within the Son's own relations with the Father by the Spirit.

The movement in short seems circular. There is a going out or down to us (the three persons' initiative towards us in which goods are bestowed on us) and then a return or ascending with us (which involves the accomplishment of that initiative for us, the working out of the consequences of those gifts' bestowal, as well as a crucial means of their continuance in our case). The fulcrum or hinge between the two is formed by the intertwined gifts of Son and Spirit: the Son brings the Spirit to us; the Spirit conforms us to the Son. With the two of them – Spirit and Son – all the goods of the Father are ours, from the Father.

The Spirit sent out to us by Christ upon his return to the Father makes it possible for us to enter into the Trinitarian movements and follow along their own circuit – enabling us first to ascend or return to the Father with him and then to descend or return from the Father in power. The Spirit joins us to Christ in his own movement of return borne by the Spirit – we are carried up to the Father – and thereby we receive from the Father what Jesus has, the abiding or resting of the Spirit in us, so as to be made sons in power like him (in the usual Trinitarian movement of descent, in which all the goods of the Father flow out from him in the form of the intertwined gifts of Son and Spirit). In short, the Spirit inaugurates our ascent with Christ to the Father; and from the Father we then descend with the Father's gifts of Son and Spirit, for our own.[19]

What are we talking about more concretely here? What forms do such movements take in Christian lives? Our initial ascent to the Father requires us to be joined to Christ, to become Christ's own, through the power of the Spirit; and is therefore associated with baptism, with our repentance for sin and conversion to new life. The ascent also involves our being brought back as sinners into the very presence of the Father, just as we are with all our faults, to be found favourable in the Father's sight because of the company we keep. Justification, in other words, is another aspect of this ascending movement; the sense of God's forgiveness and free favour in our lives. We can now approach God

---

19 Bobrinskoy, *Mystery*, pp. 153, 165.

with boldness or confidence despite our sin, because in and through Christ our relationship with God has become one of reconciliation, peace and free access (e.g. Eph. 3.12; Heb. 4.16; Rom. 5.2).

The descending movement of the gifts of Son and Spirit flowing out of the Father to us is our sanctification: we are not just joined to Christ but made over into him by the power of the Spirit; the Spirit does not merely come to us to join us to Christ but enters into us as the power for new life. Baptism is associated with the reception of the Spirit as a power of transformed living: being joined to Christ means the reception of the Spirit for our own, a reception that is to transform our lives into Christ's image. But the Eucharist is clearly the main place where the gifts of God continually stream down to us in and through Christ for our sustenance, as energizing food for new lives. Here the humanity of Christ, his very flesh and blood, show off the life-giving powers of the Spirit that rest within them, for the enhancement and nourishment of our own lives, as they were for his.

The whole of the ascent might indeed be associated specifically with worship. We ascend to the Father by turning to him in confession of sin and petition for the gifts of Son and Spirit we therefore lack as sinners, in praise and thanksgiving for the reception of those gifts and what they bring with them, and in glorification of the one who is all three. Descent would then be the service to the world that follows the ascent of service to God. At the end of worship comes the benediction and we are then sent out like Christ into the world to do the Father's business in the power of the Spirit. But just as the two coincided in Jesus' own life of worship and service to the Father, they should coincide in ours: worship – Godwardness – is an essential dimension of all the tasks we are given for the world, and in serving the world we also turn ourselves to God – our whole lives are to be, in short, God-service (see Rom. 12.1).

Introduction to the Sources

The following selections represent a particular strand of Anglican theological reflection on the human. As the breadth of the selections nevertheless makes clear, it is a strand that spans historical periods (here, the sixteenth through nineteenth centuries), genres of writing (treatises, sermons and hymns), modes of address (apologetic and kerygmatic, analytic and heart-felt), and theological movements (e.g. Cambridge Platonism, evangelicalism, the Oxford Movement and Christian Socialism).

The main thread of this strand of Anglicanism is the claim that human beings are made for a relationship of great intimacy with God. A relationship of that sort with God is integral to our proper functioning, physically, mentally and spiritually. It was to be our normal or natural state; and in that sense constitutes our created character, part of what makes us the specific kind of creature we are, as God intends us to be. By our own fault, however, we fail to exist in a relationship like that with God. We are estranged from God; we have turned away and tried to separate ourselves from God, in a fall from our own true character that therefore works to our detriment, bringing in its train nothing but corruption, misery and death. Christ restores the human to its lost intimacy with God, but in a higher form: not simply fragile communion between human and divine, but unbreakable union, achieved first in his own person and through him by us.

In Christ we therefore see the true form of the human, one with God, the elevation of the human to its highest pitch in a life perfectly conformed to the will of God for us. That true human life becomes ours through the power of the Spirit. By the workings of the Spirit we are converted, turned to the Father as Christ is, in unity with him. The Spirit makes us share in Christ's life by binding us to Christ's own human body; and, by drawing on the power of the Spirit for our own reformation, nourishment and renewal, we gain the ability to live according to Christ's own pattern of worship and service to the Father. For these reasons, theological anthropology rarely forms an independent locus in Anglicanism; the account of the human, as these selections show, is commonly part of Christological, pneumatological and Trinitarian reflections, of an often highly sacramental cast.

Richard Hooker, perhaps the premier authority in Anglican theology, in the course of his magisterial defence of a more catholic-leaning and liturgically fulsome church against Puritanism, sets the tone in a way for all the selections by discussing union with God as the fundamental desire of the human heart, and the way that desire comes to unexpected fruition after the fall through God's plan for salvation in Christ.

Lancelot Andrewes, one of the foremost preachers of the sixteenth century, in these excerpts from his nativity sermons evokes the wondrous undeserved love for the human that God displays in the incarnation and the consummation of that love through the gift of the Spirit that deifies us.

Benjamin Whichcote strikes the typical notes of Cambridge Platonism by discussing in this sermon how partaking of the divine nature perfects our natural human capacities in ways that should be made real in our lives now.

Hymns by the Wesley brothers, the major figures in the evangelical reform movement within Anglicanism in the late eighteenth century, invoke the gift of the Spirit in longing for human freedom from sin and as a foretaste of our existence with God in heaven.

The selections from the Oxford Movement – excerpts from a sermon by Pusey along with the kernel of Newman's treatise on justification – tell the story of humanity from creation to salvation, with an emphasis on our reception of the Spirit through Christ.

Finally, F. D. Maurice, the leader of the Christian Socialist movement in the nineteenth century, shows how both our claim to righteousness and our sense of leading a disordered life of pain and moral bankruptcy are illuminated by seeing that our true state is union with Christ.

Sources

Richard Hooker, *Of the Laws of Ecclesiastical Polity*, London: Everyman's Library, Volume 1, 1969, pp. 165–209.

Again, sith there can be no goodness desired which proceedeth not from God himself, as from the supreme cause of all things; and every effect doth after a sort contain, at leastwise resemble, the cause from which it proceedeth: all things in the world are said in some sort to seek the highest, and to covet more or less the participation of God himself. Yet this doth no where so much appear as it doth in man, because there are so many kinds of perfections which man seeketh. The first degree of goodness is that general perfection which all things do seek, in desiring the continuance of their being. All things therefore coveting as much as may be to be like unto God in being ever, that which cannot hereunto attain personally doth seek to continue itself another way, that is by offspring and propagation. The next degree of goodness is that which each thing coveteth by affecting resemblance with God in the constancy and excellency of those operations which belong unto their kind. The immutability of God they strive unto, by working either always or for the most part after one and the same manner; his absolute exactness they imitate, by tending unto that which is most exquisite in every particular. Hence have arisen a number of axioms in philosophy, shewing how 'the works of nature do always aim at that which cannot be bettered.'

Whatsoever such perfection there is which our nature may acquire, the same we properly term our Good; our Sovereign Good or Blessedness, that wherein the highest degree of all our perfection consisteth, that which being once attained unto there can rest nothing further to be desired; and therefore with it our souls are fully content and satisfied, in that they have they rejoice, and thirst for no more. Wherefore of good things desired some are such that for themselves we covet them not, but only because they serve as instruments unto that for which we are to see: Another kind there is, which although we desire for itself, as health, and virtue, and knowledge, nevertheless they are not the last mark whereat we aim, but have their further end where unto they are referred, so as in them we are not satisfied as having attained the utmost we may, but our desires do still proceed. But we must come at length to some pause. For, if every thing were to be desired for some other without any stint, there could be no certain end proposed unto our actions, we should go on we know not whither; yea, whatsoever we do were in vain, or rather nothing at all were possible to be done. For as to take away the first efficient of our being were to annihilate utterly our persons, so we cannot remove the last final cause of our working, but we shall cause whatsoever we work to itself simply and for no other.

Now that which man doth desire with reference to a further end, the same he desireth in such measure as is unto the end convenient; but what he coveteth as good in itself, towards that his desire is ever infinite. So that unless the last good of all, which is desired altogether for itself, be also infinite, we do evil in making it our end. Nothing may be infinitely desired but that good which indeed is infinite: for the better the more desirable; that therefore most desirable wherein there is infinity of goodness: so that if any thing desirable may be infinite, that must needs be the highest of all things that are desires. No good is infinite but only God; therefore He our felicity and bliss. Moreover, desire tendeth unto union with that it desireth. If then in him we be blessed, it is by force of participation and conjunction with Him. Again, it is not the possession of any good thing can make them happy which have it, unless they enjoy the thing wherewith they are possessed. Then are we happy therefore when fully we enjoy God, as an object wherein the powers of our souls are satisfied even with everlasting delight: so that although we be men, yet by being unto God united we live as it were the life of God. Complete union with him must be according unto every power and faculty of our minds apt to receive so glorious an object. Capable we are of God both by understanding and will: by understanding, as He is that sovereign Truth which comprehendeth the rich treasures of all wisdom; by will, as He is that sea of Goodness whereof whoso tasteth shall thirst no more.

Under Man, no creature in the world is capable of felicity and bliss. First, because their chiefest perfection consisteth in that which is simply best for them, but not in that which is simply best, as ours doth. Secondly, because whatsoever external perfection they tend unto, it is not better than themselves, as ours is. How just occasion have we therefore even in this respect with the Prophet to admire the goodness of God? 'Lord, what is man, that thou shouldst exalt him above the works of thy hands,' so far as to make thyself the inheritance of his rest and the substance of his felicity?

Now if men had not naturally this desire to be happy, how were it possible that all men should have it? All men have. Therefore this desire in man is natural. If the soul of man did serve only to give him being in this life, then things appertaining unto this life would content him, as we see they do other creatures; which creatures enjoying what they live by seek no further, but in this contentation do shew a kind of acknowledgement that there is no higher good which doth any way belong unto them. With us it is otherwise. For although the beauties, riches, honours, sciences, virtues, and perfections of all men living, were in the present possession of one; yet somewhat beyond and above all this there would still be sought and earnestly thirsted for. So that Nature even in this life doth plainly claim and call for a more divine perfection.

This last and highest estate of perfection whereof we speak is received of men in the nature of a Reward. Rewards do always presuppose such duties performed as are rewardable. Our natural means therefore unto blessedness are our works; nor is it possible that Nature should ever find any other way to salvation than only this. But examine the works which we do, and since the first foundation of the world what one can say, My ways are pure? Seeing then all flesh is guilty of that for which God hath threatened eternally to punish, what possibility is there this way to be saved? There resteth therefore either no way unto salvation, or if any then surely a way which is supernatural, a way which could never have entered into the heart of man as much as once to conceive or imagine, if God himself had not revealed it extraordinarily.

Behold how the wisdom of God hath revealed a way mystical and supernatural, a way directing unto the same end of life by a course which groundeth itself upon the guiltiness of sin, and through sin desert of condemnation and death. For in this way the first thing is the tender compassion of God respecting us drowned and swallowed up in misery; the next is redemption out of the same by the precious death and merit of a mighty Saviour, which hath witnessed of himself, saying, 'I am the way the way that leadeth us from misery into bliss.'

Lancelot Andrewes, *Sermons on the Nativity*, Grand Rapids, MI: Baker Book House, 1955, pp. 14–149.

Now what is to be commended to us out of this text for us to lay hold of? Verily first, to take us to our meditation, the meditation which the Psalmist hath, and which the Apostle is this chapter voucheth out of him at the sixth verse. 'When I consider,' saith he, 'the Heavens' (Ps. viii.3) – say we, the Angels of Heaven – and see those glorious Spirits passed by, and man taken, even to sigh with him, and say, 'Lord, what is man,' either Adam or Abraham, 'that Thou shouldest be thus mindful of him, or the seed, or sons of either, that Thou shouldest make this do about him!' The case is here far otherwise – far more worth our consideration. There, 'Thou hast made him a little lower'; here, 'Thou hast made him a great deal higher than the Angels.' For they, this day first, and ever since, daily have and do adore our nature in the personal union with the Deity. Look you, saith the Apostle, 'when He brought His only-begotten Son into the world, this He proclaimed before Him, Let all the Angels worship Him,' (Heb i.6); and so they did. And upon this very day's 'taking the see' hath ensued, as the Fathers note, a great alternation. Before, in the Old Testament, they suffered David to sit upon his knees before them, (I Chron. xxi.26); since, in the New, they endure not St. John should fall down to them, (Rev. xxii.9), but acknowledge the case is altered now, and no more superiority, but all fellow-servants. And even in this one part two things present themselves unto us; 1. His *humility, Qui non est confusus*, as in the eleventh verse the Apostle speaketh, 'Who was not confounded' thus to take our nature. 2. And withal, the honour and happiness of Abraham's seed, *ut digni haberentur*, that were 'counted worthy to be taken so near unto Him.' (Luke xx.35)

The next point; that after we have well considered it we be affected with it, and that no otherwise than Abraham was. 'Abraham saw it,' even this day, and but afar off, 'and he rejoiced at it,' (John viii.56); and so shall we on it, if we be his true seed. It brought forth a *Benedictus* and a *Magnificat*, from the true seed of Abraham; if it do not the like from us, certainly it but floats in our brains – we but warble about it; but we believe it not, and therefore neither do we rightly understand it. Sure I am, if the Angels had such a feast to keep, if He had done the like for them, they would hold it with all joy and jubilee. They rejoice of our good, but if they had one of their own, they must needs to it after another manner, far more effectually. If we do not as they would do were the case theirs, it is because we are short in conceiving the excellency of the benefit. It would have surely due observation, if it had this due and serious meditation.

Farther, we are to understand this, that 'to whom much is given, of them will much be required,' (Luke xii.45); and as Gregory well saith, *Cum crescunt dona, crescunt et rationes donorum*, 'As the gifts grow, so grow the accounts too'; therefore, that by this new dignity befallen us, *Necessitas quædam nobis imposita est*, saith St. Augustine, 'there is a certain necessity laid upon us' to become in some measure suitable unto it; in that we are one – one flesh and one blood – with the Son of God. Being thus 'in hounour,' we ought to understand our estate, and not fall into the Psalmist's reproof that we 'become like the beasts that perish.' (Ps. xlix.12) For if we do indeed think our nature is ennobled by this so high a conjunction, we shall henceforth hold ourselves more dear, and at a higher rate, than to prostitute ourselves to sin, for every base, trifling, and transitory pleasure. For tell me, men that are taken to this degree, shall any of them prove a devil, as Christ said of Judas (John vi.70); or ever, as these with us of late, have to do with any devilish or Judasly fact? Shall any man, after this 'assumption', be as 'horse or mule that have no understanding' (Ps. xxxii.9), and in a Christian profession live a brutish life? Nay then, St. Paul tells us farther, that if we henceforth 'walk like men'.

(I Cor. iii.3), like but even carnal or natural men, it is a fault in us. Somewhat must appear in us more than in ordinary men, who are vouchsafed so extraordinary a favour. Somewhat more than common would come from us, if it were but for this day's sake.

To conclude; not only thus to frame meditations and resolutions, but even some practice too, out of this act of 'apprehension.' (Phil. iii.12) It is very agreeable to reason, saith the Apostle, that we endeavour and make a proffer, if we may by any means, to 'apprehend' Him in His, by Whom we are thus in our nature 'apprehended,' or, as He termed it, 'comprehended,' even Christ Jesus; and be united to Him this day, as He was to us this day, by a mutual and reciprocal 'apprehension.' We may so, and we are bound so; *vere dignum et justum est*. And we do so, so oft as we do with St. James lay hold of, 'apprehend,' or receive *insitum verbum*, the 'word which is daily grafted into us.' (James i.21) For 'the Word' He is, and in the word He is received by us. But that is not the proper of this day, unless there be another joined unto it. This day *Verbum caro factum est* (John i.14), and so must be 'apprehended' in both. But specially in His flesh as this day giveth it, as this day would have us. Now 'the bread which we break, is it not the partaking of the body, of the flesh, of Jesus Christ?' (I Cor. x.16) It is surely, and by it and by nothing more are we made partakers of this blessed union. A little before He said, 'Because the children were partakers of flesh and blood, He also would take part with them' (Heb. ii.14) – may not we say the same? Because He hath so done, taken ours of us, we also ensuing His steps will participate with Him and with His flesh which He hath taken of us. It is most kindly to take part with Him in that which He took part in with us, and that to no other end, but that He might make the receiving of it by us a means whereby He might 'dwell in us, and we in Him;' He taking our flesh, and we receiving His Spirit; by His flesh which He took of us receiving His Spirit which He imparteth to us; that, as He by ours became *consors humanæ naturæ*, so we by His might become *consortes Divinæ naturæ*, 'partakers of the Divine nature' (2 Pet. i.4) Verily, it is the most straight and perfect 'taking hold' that is. No union so knitteth as it. Not consanguinity; brethren fall out. Not marriage; man and wife are severed. But that which is nourished, and the nourishment wherewith – they never are, never can be severed, but remain one for ever. With this act then of mutual 'taking,' taking of His flesh as He hath taken ours, let us seal our duty to Him this day, for taking not 'Angels,' but 'the seed of Abraham.'

The thing sent is full; and fully sent, because made; and fully made, because made once and twice over; fully made ours because fully united to us. 'Made of a woman,' as well as we; 'made under the Law,' as deep as we; both *ex muliere* and *sub Lege*. So of our nature 'of a woman,' that of our condition also 'under the Law.' So, fully united to us in nature and condition both.

And so we are come to the full measure of His sending. And that we are come to the full ye shall plainly see by the overflowing, by that which we receive from the fullness (Gal. iv.5); which is the latter part of the verse and is our fullness, even the fullness of all that we can desire. For if we come now to ask, For whom is all this ado, this sending, this making, over and over again? It is for us. So is the conclusion, *ut nos*, that we might from this fullness receive the full of our wish. For in these two behind, 1. Redemption, and 2. Adoption; to be redeemed and to be adopted are the full of all we can wish ourselves.

We are got from under the Law; and that is much. Till a party come to be once under it, he shall never understand this aright; but then he shall. And if any have been under it, he knows what it is, and how great a benefit to be got thence. But is this all? No, He leaves us not here; but to make the measure complete, yea even to flow over, He gives us not over when He had rid us out of this wretched estate, till He have brought us to an estate as good as He Himself is in. After our redemption we stood but as prisoners enlarged; that was all: but still we were as strangers; no part nor portion in God or His Kingdom, nor no reason we should hope for any. He now goeth one step farther, which is the highest and farthest step of all. For farther than it he cannot go.

'That we might receive the adoption,' that is, from the estate of prisoners condemned be translated into the estate of children adopted. Of adopted, for of natural we could not. That is His peculiar alone, and He therein only above us; but else, fully to the joint fruition of all that He hath, which is fully as much as we could desire. And this is our *fieri* out of His *factum ex muliere*. We made the sons of God, as He the Son of man; we made partakers of His divine, as He of our human nature (2 Pet. i.4). To purchase our pardon, to free us from death and the law's sentence, this 'seemed a small thing' (2 Sam. vii.19) to him, yet this is *lex hominis*. Man's goodness goeth no farther, and gracious is the prince that doth but so much. For who ever heard of a condemned man adopted afterward, or that thought it not enough and enough if he did but scape with his life? So far then to exalt His bounty to that fulness as pardon and adopt both, *non est lex hominis hæc* 'no such measure amongst men;' *zelus Domini exercituum*, 'the zeal of the Lord of Hosts' was to perform this (Isa. ix.7); 'the fulness of the Godhead dwelt in Him' that brought this to pass.

For, to speak of adopting, we see it daily; no father adopts unless he be orbe, have no child; or if he have one, for some deep dislike have cast him off. But God had a Son, 'the brightness of His glory, the true character of His substance.' (Heb. i.3) And no displeasure there was; no, *in Quo complacitum est*, 'in Whom He was absolutely well pleased,' (Matt. xvii.5); yet would He by adoption for all that 'bring many sons to glory.' (Heb. ii.10) Is not this full on His part?

We see again no heir will endure to hear of adoption, nay, nor divide his inheritance; no, not with his natural brethren. Then, that 'the Heir of all things' (Heb. i.2) should admit 'joint-heirs' (Rom. viii.18) to the Kingdom He was born to; and that admit them not out of such as were near Him, but from such as were strangers; yea, such as had been condemned men under the law – is not this full on His part? To purchase us, and to purchase for us, both at once? And not to do this for us alone, but to assure it to us. For as His Father in this verse sends Him, so in the next verse 'He sends the Spirit of His Son' to give us *seisin* of this our adoption; whereby we now call Him, the Jews *Abba*, the Gentiles *Pater*, as children all and He our Father, which is the privilege of the adoption we here receive.

This *Immanu* is a compound again; we may take it in sunder into *nobis* and *cum*; and so then have we three pieces. 1. *El*, the mighty God; 2. and *anu*, we, poor we, – poor indeed if we have all the world beside if we have not Him to be with us; 3. and *Im*, which is *cum*, and that *cum* in the midst between *nobis* and *Deus*, God and us – to couple God and us; thereby to convey the things of the one to the other. Ours to God; alas, they be not worth the speaking of. Chiefly, then to convey to us the things of God. For that is worth the while; they are indeed worth the conveying.

This *cum* we shall never conceive to purpose, but *carendo*; the value of 'with' no way so well as by without, by stripping of *cum* from *nobis*. And so let *nobis*, 'us,' stand by ourselves without Him, to see what our case is but for this Immanuel; what, if this virgin's Child had not this day been born us: *nobiscum* after will be the better esteemed. For if this Child be 'Immanuel, God with us,' then without this Child, this Immanuel, we be without God. 'Without Him in this world,' (Eph. ii.12), saith the Apostle; and if without Him in this, without Him in the next; and if without Him there – if it be not *Immanu-el*, it will be *Immanu-hell*; and that and no other place will fall, I fear me, to our share. Without Him, this we are. What with Him? Why, if we have Him, and God by Him, we need no more; *Immanu-el* and *Imanu-all*. All that we can desire is for us to be with Him, with God, and He to be with us; and we from Him, or He from us, never to be parted. We were with Him once before, and we were well; and when we left Him, and He no longer 'with us,' then began all our misery. Whensoever we go from Him, so shall we be in evil case, and never be well till we be back with Him again.

Then, if this be our case that we cannot be without Him, no remedy then but to get a *cum* by whose means *nobis* and *Deus* may come together again. And Christ is that *Cum* to bring it to pass. The parties are God and we; and now this day He is both. God before eternally, and now to-day Man; and so both, and takes hold of both, and brings both together again. For two natures here are in Him. If conceived and born of a woman, then a man; if God with us, then God. So Esay offered his 'sign from the height above, or from the depth beneath,' (Is. vii.11): here it is. 'From above,' *El*; 'from beneath,' *anu*; one of us now. And so, His sign from both. And both theses natures in the unity of one Person, called by one name, even this name Immanuel.

How came God from us? Nay, ask not that; but how we came from Him. For we went from Him, not He from us; we forsook Him first. Jonas tells us how; 'By following lying vanities, we forsook our own mercy.' (Jonah ii.8)

If we went from Him first, then should it be in reason *nos cum Deo*, not *nobiscum Deus*; we to Him, not He to us. Did we so? No indeed. We sought not Him, He was fain to seek us. *Nos cum Deo*, that would not be; it must be *nobiscum Deus* first, or *nos cum Deo* will never be. This second then; that we began the separation – that long of us; but He begins the reconciliation.

Who hath the hurt if God be without us? We, not He. Why then doth He begin, doth He seek to be with us? No reason but *sic dilexit*, and no reason of that.

That being forsaken, yet He forsakes not though. That He Which should be sought to, seeks first, (Isa. vii.14), and seeks us by whom He shall get nothing.

'With us' – to make us that to God that He was this day made to man. And this indeed was the chief end of His being 'with us;' to give us a *posse fieri*, a capacity, 'a power to be made the sons of God,' (John i.12), by being 'born again of water and of the Spirit;' for *Originem quam sumpsit ex utero Virginis posuit in fonte Baptismatis*, 'the same original that Himself took in the womb of the Virgin to usward, the same hath took in the womb of the Virgin to usward, the same hath He placed for us in the fountain of Baptism to God-ward.' Well therefore called the womb of the Church *sustoichon* to the Virgin's womb, with a power given it of *concipiet et pariet filios* to God. So His being conceived and born the Son of man doth conceive and bring forth (*filiatio, filiationem,*) our being born, our being the sons of God. His participation of our human, our participation of His Divine nature.

And shall He be 'with us' thus many ways, and shall not we be with Him – as many I say not, but some, as many as we can? We with Him, as He with us? Specially, since upon this issue the Prophet puts King Asa, 'The Lord is with you, if you be with Him,' (2 Chron. xv.2) – with you to save you, if you with Him to serve Him. It holds *reciproce*, in all duties of love, as here was love if ever. 'Immanuel, God with us,' requires *Immelanu*, 'us with God', again.

He 'with us' now I hope, for 'where two or three are gathered together in His name, there is He with them.' (Matt. xviii.20) But that is in His Godhead. And we are with Him; our prayers, our praises are with Him; but that is in our spirits whence they come.

These are well, but these are not all we can; and none of these, the proper 'with Him' of the day. That hath a special *Cum* of itself, peculiar to it. Namely, that we be so with Him, as He this day was 'with us;' that was in flesh, not in spirit only. That flesh that was conceived and this day born, (*Corpus aptasti Mihi*) (Ps. xl.6 and Heb. x.5), that body that was this day fitted to Him. And if we be not with Him thus, if this His flesh be not 'with us,' if we partake it not, which way soever else we be with Him, we come short of the *Im* of this day. *Im* otherwise it may be, but not that way which is proper to this feast. 'Thy land, O Immanuel,' (Isa. viii.8), saith the Prophet in the next chapter; and may not I say, This Thy feast, O Immanuel? Sure no being with Him so kindly, so pleasing to Him, so fitting this feast, as to grow into one with Him; as upon the same day, so the very same way He did 'with us.'

This, as it is most proper, so it is the most straight and near that can be – the surest being withal that can be. *Nihil tam nobiscum tam nostrum, quam alimentum nostrum*, 'nothing so with us, so ours, as that we eat and drink down,' which goeth, and groweth one with us. For *alimentum et alitum* do *coalescere in unum*, 'grow into an union;' and that union is inseparable ever after. This then I commended to you even the being with Him in the Sacrament of His Body – that Body that was conceived and born, as for other ends so for this specially, to be 'with you;' and this day, as for other intents, so even for this, for the Holy Eucharist. This, as the kindliest for the time, as the surest for the manner of being with.

And this is the farthest; and this is all we can we come to here – here upon earth. But this is not all; there is a farther to come still. For we are not together; we are parted, He and we. He in Heaven, and we in earth. But it shall not always so be. Beside this day Immanuel hath another day, and that day will come; and when it doth come, He will come and take us to Himself. That as He hath been our Immanuel upon earth, so he may be our Immanuel in Heaven; He with us, and we with Him, there for ever.

This of the Sacrament is a preparative to that; will conceive and bring forth the other. For immediately after He had given them the Holy Eucharist, He prayed straight that they that had so been with Him in the blessed Sacrament – 'Father, My will is,' My prayer, My last prayer, 'that where I am they may be also.' (John xvii.24)

Benjamin Whichcote, 'The Manifestation of Christ and the Deification of Man', in C. A. Patrides (ed.), *The Cambridge Platonists,* London: Edward Arnold, 1969, pp. 69–75.

Speak, now, of the great Benefits that Accrue to us, by our Saviour's being in our Nature. He doth acquire the Right of Redeeming us; and makes Satisfaction in the Nature that had transgressed: And, he doth repair the ruined Nature of Man; by dwelling in it, and by working Righteousness in it:

Now, let us look for the Explication of this, *in our selves;* in our *Nativity from above,* in *Mental Transformation,* and DEIFICATION. Do not stumble at the use of *the Word.* For, we have Authority for the use of it, in Scripture. 2 Pet. i.4. *Being made Partakers of the Divine Nature;* which is in effect our *Deification.* Also, let it appear *in our Reconciliation to God,* to *Goodness, Righteousness,* and *Truth;* in our *being created after God, in Righteousness, and true Holiness.* It was a signal Evidence of a Divine Power in the Disciples of Christ, at the first Publication of the Gospel, that it wrought so great an Alteration in all those that did receive it. The Envious, Debauched, and Disobedient; It made Temperate, Sober, and Religious, Humble and *Good-natured.* It converted the Embracers of it, to a Life more suitable to Reason, and Nature and Moral Vertue.

We may observe from this, that nothing of the Natural State is *base* or *vile.* Whatsoever hath Foundation in God's Creation, or whatsoever this Providence of God calls any Man unto, it is not *base.* For, our Saviour himself *took Flesh* and *Blood*: and *that* is the meaner Part of Humane Nature. Whatsoever is *Natural,* hath nothing of Disparagement in it; nothing that exposeth a Man to Contempt, and Scorn. And this may satisfie those that are in the meanest Offices and Employments; that there is nothing base, that hath place in God's Creation. That which is Vile, Base and Filthy, is *unnatural,* and depends upon *unnatural Use,* and *degenerate Practice.*

Also observe here, the great Honour put upon Humane Nature; when *the Son of God* came into it; when Divine Goodness did take into Consideration the Rise and Advance of Created Nature; and to recover and raise It to all possible Perfection: *He did take to himself a peculiar relation to Human Nature.* – Then, let us take Consolation in this. For, it cannot be thought, that God did so great a thing, and of so deep a Consideration, as to unite Humane Nature to his own Existence, and to set it at his own Right hand, to the Admiration of Angels, (for he saith, *let all the Angels of God worship him;*) that he did such a thing as this is, to begat a Notion, or to raise a Talk, and make a Wonder in the World, and put the Creation into a Gaze and Astonishment. God doth nothing, for so light an end; and especially not his great things, such as these, which call for Fear and Reverence on our part. This we may say, is one of the greatest Works of God. This, if possible, doth transcend the very Creation of

God, at first: for, there was nothing there to resist him: but, in the Restoration, there was Malignity and Sin. God did this, therefore, for the great and unconceivable Good of the *Nature* that he hath so highly honoured. Therefore, what Consolation should we have from it! What Declaration should we make of it! What Thanksgiving for it!

Therefore, let this be explicated, verified, and fulfilled in us. For, *this* you must understand; that *Religion* is not satisfied in Notions; but doth indeed, and in reality come to nothing unless it be in us not only Matter of Knowledge and Speculation; but doth establish in us a Frame and Temper of Mind, and is productive of a holy virtuous Life. There fore, let these things take effect in us; in our *Spirituality*, and *Heavenly-mindedness*; in our *Conformity to the Divine Nature*, and *Nativity from above*. For, whatsoever professes that he believes the Truth of these things; and wants the Operation of them upon his Spirit, and Life; he doth, in fact, make void, an frustrate what he doth declare as his Belief: an so he doth *receive the Grace of God in vain*, unless this Principle, and Belief doth descend into his Heart, and establish a good Frame and Temper of Mind; and govern in all the Actions of his Life and Conversation.

RELIGION is not a *particular Good* only; as Meat against Hunger; or Drink against Thirst; or Cloaths against Cold; but it is *Universally Good;* a Good *without Limitation or Restraint.*

RELIGION (which is, in substance, *our Imitation of God in his Moral Perfections, and Excellency of Goodness, Righteousness, and Truth*) is that wherein our Happiness doth consist: And we *then* relish the truest Pleasure and Satisfaction, *when* we find our selves reconciled to God, by *Participation of his Nature*. They who have not this Sence of God, may have a Religion to talk of, and profess; a *Religion*, to give them a Denomination: but, they are not at all in the true State and Spirit of Religion: nor, have they any real Benefit by it: nor, are they any whit enabled by it: nor have they the more Peace and Satisfaction from it. But, when our Minds are transformed by Religion; then, we feel (at least, *at times*) strong and vigorous Inclinations towards God. And, with these Motions our Minds are best pleas'd and satisfied: because these are most suitable to Nature and the highest Use and Employment that Humane Nature is capable of.

All Things in *real Religion* tend either to *conserve*, or *restore* the Soundness and Perfection of our Minds; and to continue God's Creation in the true State of Liberty and Freedom.

First, Man by his Nature and Constitution, as God made him at first, being an intelligent Agent, hath *Sense of Good and Evil, upon a Moral account*. He hath Judgment and Power of Discerning: He is *made* to know the Difference of Things: And he acts as a mad Man, that knowing what is *better,* chuseth *the worse*. This is the Ground and Foundation of Man's being truly *miserable*. *Secondly*, Man being *made* to know God; hat Sense of his own Privation, in the Loss of so great and universal *a Good* as GOD is. For, he is made happy in the Enjoyment, and miserable in the Loss of Him.

Our Souls acting upon God, discover their Vertues; and display their Powers; and show their Mettle and Sprightfulness. Whereas, if a Man be diverted from God; the *Reason of his Mind* is as much without Employment, as the *Eye* which is *in the Dark*: For, it is the Presence of the Object, that puts the Faculty upon acting. So, if *God* be withdrawn; our Minds cannot be drawn forth; for, they are without their *proper Object*: For, other-where, save on *in God*, our Souls are not matched, so as to make Proof of themselves. We know not our Powers and Faculties, but by their *Acts*: And we cannot act, but in the Presence of the *Object*. If a Man be separated from God; his Mind and Understanding are without their proper Object; and, so, are as little to him, as his Sight is to him, when he is in the Dark. I am apt to think, that in the Heavenly State hereafter, when God shall otherwise declare himself to us, than now he doth; thoses Latent Powers which *now* we have, may open, and unfold themselves; and thereby we may be made able to act in a far higher Way, than we are at present. *Now*, we have many Avocations and Diversions: But, *when* we shall come to have nearer Approaches to God; we shall have more *Use of our selves;* and shall find our selves more *able*, than we are at present, in this limited and contracted State. For, this we have present Experience of; that is we give our selves up, to Meditation upon God; and employ our Mind in sincere Intention of Him, and his Service; we do thereby ennoble, and enlarge our Faculties;

John and Charles Wesley, 'Hymns', in J. A. Hodges and A. M. Allchin (eds), *A Rapture of Praise: Hymns of John and Charles Wesley,* **London: Hodder & Stoughton, 1966, pp. 58–9, 74–5, 80–1, 87–8, 88–9, 99, 116–17, 120, 121, 124, 128 and 149.**

[5]

Let earth and heaven combine,
Angels and men agree,
To praise in songs divine
The incarnate Deity,
Our God contracted to a span,
Incomprehensibly made man.

He laid his glory by,
He wrapped him in our clay;
Unmarked by human eye
The latent Godhead lay;
Infant of days he here became,
And bore the mild Immanuel's name.

Unsearchable the love
That hath the Saviour brought;
The grace is far above
Or man or angel's thought:
Suffice for us that God, we know,
Our God is manifest below.

He deigns in flesh to appear,
Widest extremes to join;
To bring our vileness near,

And make us all divine:
And we the life of God shall know,
For God is manifest below.

[27]

Come, Holy Ghost, all-quickening fire,
Come, and in me delight to rest;
Drawn by the lure of strong desire,
O come and consecrate my breast;
The temple of my soul prepare,
And fix thy sacred presence there.

Eager for thee I ask and pant;
So strong, the principle divine
Carries me out, with sweet constraint,
Till all my hallowed soul is thine;
Plunged in the Godhead's deepest sea,
And lost in thine immensity.

My peace, my life, my comfort thou,
My treasure and my all thou art;
True witness of my sonship, now
Engraving pardon on my heart,
Seal of my sins in Christ forgiven,
Earnest of love, and pledge of heaven.

Come then, my God, mark out thine heir,
Of heaven a larger earnest give;
With clearer light thy witness bear,
More sensibly within me live;
Let all my powers thine entrance feel,
And deeper stamp thyself the seal.

[34]

O God, of good the unfathomed sea!
Who would not give his heart to thee?
Who would not love thee with his might?
O Jesu, Lover of mankind,
Who would not his whole soul and mind,
With all his strength, to thee unite?

Thou shin'st with everlasting rays;
Before the insufferable blaze
Angels with both wings veil their eyes:
Yet free as air thy bounty streams
On all thy works; thy mercy's beams
Diffusive as thy sun's arise.

Astonished at thy frowning brow,
Earth, hell, and heaven's strong pillars bow;
 Terrible majesty is thine;
 Who then can that vast love express
 Which bows thee down to me, who less
Than nothing am, till thou art mine?

High throned on heaven's eternal hill,
 In number, weight, and measure still
  Thou sweetly orderest all that is:
 And yet thou deign'st to come to me,
 And guide my steps, that I, with thee
  Enthroned, may reign in endless bliss.

 Fountain of good! All blessing flows
 From thee: no want thy fullness knows:
  What but thyself canst thou desire?
  Yet, self-sufficient as thou art,
  Thou dost desire my worthless heart;
  This, only this, dost thou require.

  Primeval Beauty! In thy sight
  The first-born, fairest sons of light
   See all their brightest glories fade:
 What then to me thine eyes could turn –
   In sin conceived, of woman born –
   A worm, a leaf, a blast, a shade?

  Hell's armies tremble at thy nod,
 And trembling own the Almighty God,
  Sovereign of earth, hell, air, and sky:
  But who is this that comes from far,
 Whose garments rolled in blood appear?
  'Tis God made Man, for man to die!

 O God, of good the unfathomed sea!
 Who would not give his heart to thee?
Who would not love thee with his might?
   O Jesu, Lover of mankind,
Who would not his whole soul and mind,
 With all his strength, to thee unite?

[43]

 Thou great mysterious God unknown,
 Whose love hath gently led me on,
  Even from my infant days,
  Mine inmost soul expose to view,

And tell me, if I ever knew
Thy justifying grace.

If I have only known thy fear,
And followed with a heart sincere
Thy drawings from above,
Now, now the further grace bestow,
And let my sprinkles conscience know
Thy sweet forgiving love.

Sort of thy love I would not stop,
A stranger to the gospel hope,
The sense of sin forgiven;
I would not, Lord, my soul deceive,
Without the inward witness live,
That antepast of heaven.

If now the witness were in me,
Would he not testify of thee
In Jesus reconciled?
And should I not with faith draw nigh,
And boldly Abba, Father! Cry,
And know myself thy child?

Whate'er obstructs thy pardoning love,
Or sin or righteousness, remove,
Thy glory to display;
Mine heart of unbelief convince,
And now absolve me from my sins,
And take them all away.

Father, in me reveal thy Son,
And to my inmost soul make known
How merciful thou art:
The secret of thy love reveal,
And by thine hallowing Spirit dwell
For ever in my heart.

[56]

Thou hidden Source of calm repose,
Thou all-sufficient Love divine,
My help and refuge from my forces,
Secure I am, if thou art mine:
And lo! From sin, and grief, and shame
I hide me, Jesus, in thy name.

Thy mighty name salvation is,
And keeps my happy soul above;
Comfort it brings, and power, and peace,

And joy, and everlasting love:
To me, with thy dear name, are given
Pardon and holiness, and heaven.

Jesus, my all in all thou art;
My rest in toil, my ease in pain,
The medicine of my broken heart,
In war my peace, in loss my gain,
My smile beneath the tyrant's frown,
In shame my glory and my crown:

In want my plentiful supply,
In weakness my almighty power,
In bonds my perfect liberty,
My light in Satan's darkest hour,
In grief my joy unspeakable,
My life in death, my heaven in hell.

[82]

Thou hidden love of God, whose height,
Whose depth unfathomed, no man knows,
I see from far thy beauteous lift,
Inly I sigh for thy repose;
My heart is pained, nor can it be
At rest, till it find rest in thee.

Thy secret voice invites me still
The sweetness of thy yoke to prove;
And fain I would: but though my will
Seems fixed, yet wide my passions rove;
Yet hindrances strew all the way;
I aim at thee, yet from thee stray.

'Tis mercy all, that thou has brought
My mind to seek her peace in thee;
Yet, while I seek but find thee not,
No peace my wandering soul shall see:
O when shall all my wanderings end,
And all my steps to thee-ward tend!

Is there a thing beneath the sun
That strives with thee my heart to share?
Ah, tear it thence, and reign alone,
The Lord of every motion there!
Then shall my heart from earth be free,
When it hath found repose in thee.

O hide this self from me, that I
No more, but Christ in me, may live!
My vile affections crucify,
Nor let one darling lust survive!
In all things nothing may I see,
Nothing desire or seek, but thee!

Each moment draw from earth away
My heart, that lowly waits thy call;
Speak to my inmost soul, and say,
I am thy Love, the God, thy All!
To feel thy power, to hear thy voice,
To taste thy love, be all my choice.

[88]

Love divine, all loves excelling,
Joy of heaven, to earth come down;
Fix in us thy humble dwelling,
All thy faithful mercies crown:
Jesu, thou art all compassion,
Pure unbounded love thou art;
Visit us with thy salvation,
Enter every trembling heart.

Come, almighty to deliver,
Let us all thy grace receive;
Suddenly return, and never,
Never more thy temples leave:
Thee we would be always blessing,
Serve thee as thy hosts above,
Pray, and praise thee, without ceasing,
Glory in thy perfect love.

Finish then thy new creation,
Pure and spotless let us be;
Let us see thy great salvation,
Perfectly restored in thee;
Changed from glory into glory,
Till in heaven we take our place,
Till we cast our crowns before thee,
Lost in wonder, love, and praise.

[90]

Since the Son hath made me free,
Let me taste my liberty;

Thee behold with open face,
Triumph in thy saving grace,
Thy great will delight to prove,
Glory in thy perfect love.

Abba, Father, hear thy child,
Late in Jesus reconciled;
Hear, and all the graces shower,
All the joy, and peace, and power,
All my Saviour asks above,
All the life and heaven of love.

Heavenly Adam, Life divine,
Change my nature into thine;
Move and spread throughout my soul,
Actuate and fill the whole;
Be it I no longer now
Living in the flesh, but thou.

Holy Ghost, no more delay;
Come, and in thy temple stay;
Now thine inward witness bear,
Strong, and permanent, and clear;
Spring of life, thyself impart,
Rise eternal in my heart.

[95]

Lord, I believe a rest remains
To all thy people known,
A rest where pure enjoyment reigns,
And thou art loved alone;

A rest, where all our soul's desire
Is fixed on things above;
Where fear, and sin, and grief expire,
Cast out by perfect love.

O that I now the rest might know,
Believe, and enter in!
Now, Saviour, now the power bestow,
And let me cease from sin.

Remove this hardness from my heart,
This unbelief remove;
To me the rest of faith impart,
The Sabbath of thy love.

I would be thine, thou know'st I would,
And have thee all my own;
Thee, O my all-sufficient Good!
I want, and thee alone.

Thy name to me, thy nature grant;
This, only this be given:
Nothing beside my God I want,
Nothing in earth or heaven.

[101]

Jesus, all-atoning Lamb,
Thine, and only thine, I am:
Take my body, spirit, soul;
Only thou possess the whole.

Thou my one thing needful be;
Let me ever cleave to thee;
Let me choose the better part;
Let me give thee all my heart.

Fairer than the sons of men,
Do not let me turn again,
Leave the fountain-head of bliss,
Stoop to creature-happiness.

Whom have I on earth below?
Thee, and only thee, I know;
Whom have I in heaven but thee?
Thou art all in all to me.

All my treasure is above,
All my riches is thy love:
Who the worth of love can tell?
Infinite, unsearchable.

[131]

How glorious is the life above,
Which in this ordinance we *taste*;
That fulness of celestial love,
That joy which shall for ever last!

That heavenly life in Christ concealed
These earthen vessels could not bear;
The part which now we find revealed
No tongue of angels can declare.

> The light of life eternal darts
> Into our souls a dazzling ray,
> A drop of heaven o'erflows our hearts,
> And deluges the house of clay.
>
> Sure pledge of ecstasies unknown
> Shall this divine communion be;
> The ray shall rise into a sun,
> The drop shall swell into a sea.

E. B. Pusey, Sermon XV, in *A Course of Sermons on Solemn Subjects*, Oxford: Parker, 1845, pp. 255–71.

We shall 'be equal unto the Angels'. And what were not this? For us, who lay on our 'dunghill', sunk in the mire and foulness of our sins, to be 'set with the Princes of His people', the ministers of His Presence, who have ever done His will! for us, who had made ourselves 'like the beasts which perish', to be like the most perfect of His creation, the highest created wisdom and beauty, who ever kept their high estate and their nearness to God, and did His will and never defiled His Image, perfect in their degree, free from all passion, partakers of the immortality of God, ever beholding the Face of the Father. But now the greatness of our bliss and theirs is told us in more solemn overwhelming words, 'We shall be like Him.' Like Whom? Like God. The very gift, which Satan taught Adam by disobedience to seek to gain for himself, not to receive of God, that same surpassing Gift, through the Obedience and Death of Him, Who is God and Man, will God bestow on man, to be like Himself. 'Ye shall be as God,' said the tempter, and man through lust fell. 'I have said ye are gods, saith God, and ye shall all be children of the Most High'; 'that we having escaped the corruption which is in the world through lust, might be partakers of the Divine Nature'; not by Essence, since that belongs only to the Holy Trinity in Itself; not personally, since that belongs only to the Incarnate Word; but still by grace, although not by nature; by His indwelling in us, now in each according to his measure, more perfectly in glory. 'the Word was made flesh,' says a father, 'in order to offer up this body for all, and that we, partaking of His Spirit, might be made gods, a gift which we could not otherwise have gained, than by His clothing Himself with our created body. For hence we derive our name of "men of God", and "men in Christ".' 'For therefore did He assume a human body, that having renewed it, as its Framer, He might make it god in Himself, and thus might introduce all us into the kingdom of heaven after His likeness. – For therefore the union was of this kind that He might unite what is man by nature to Him Who is the Nature of the Godhead, and man's salvation and deifying might be sure.'

'We shall be like Him.' A likeness we had by nature and by grace, ere it was lost by Adam's fall. About us God vouchsafed to consult, and in our creation was the sacred mystery of the Trinity in Unity first revealed, as in our Baptism it is renewed. 'And God said, Let Us make man in Our image, after Our likeness.' Like God we were by nature, in our royal birth, the lords of all the animal world, the end for whom it was made, as God Himself is The End of all things;

ourselves to obey God Alone, and then all beside to obey us. Of Him we were a shadowy likeness, as the created and finite can be of the Uncreated Infinite God, in that we, by His gift, had a soul one and incorporeal as He is; immortal, by grace, as He by nature; possessed of understanding, will, and memory, and these free, as made free and upheld by Him; uniting in a manner, heaven and earth in ourselves, in that we had in part the nature of angels, in part that of the things below us; yea, for us, heaven and earth and time itself are, since when the number of the elect is finished, heaven and earth shall be changed, and time itself shall be no more, and 'God shall be All in all.' And this image of God flowed over upon the body too. In that was formed upright, to gaze upwards to heaven and towards God, its very form shewed that, although of earth, it was not made for this earth, not, like the beasts that perish, to seek the things of earth, but for its home and in God. Our very look bears witness for Whom we were made. Why look to heaven, if thou grovellest on earth? Yea, if any of dare scarce look up to heaven, it is because like the publican, we feel that, but for God's mercy, we have lost it.

We were then an image of God by nature, and this image, in part, we never lost, can never lose. 'The image', says a holy man, 'can be burnt in hell, not burnt away; it can be all on fire, but not destroyed. Whithersoever the soul shall go, there will it also be. Not so the likeness. It either abideth in good, or if the soul sinneth it is miserably changed, being likened to the beasts that perish.' Our truest, fullest, likeness was in that gift above nature, the soul of the soul, Divine grace. By this was man, ere he fell, clad and gifted with original righteousness, from which by nature we are now far gone; by this, was he capable of receiving, not all knowledge only, so as to grasp in himself, and order, and mould, all thoughts of all created things, but he could receive all wisdom virtue, blessedness, the sight of God, the Spirit of God within him; by this was he a likeness of God in His everlasting rest; for no passions were at war within him; his appetite was subdued to his reason, his reason to God; and so his will was one with the Will of God, and his soul, holding converse with God, as He walked in the blissful Garden, reflected his Maker's Will, as clear water gives back the face of Heaven, or a mirror flashes back the brightness of the earthly sun which shines upon it.

This likeness through Adam we lost, through Christ more blessedly regained. For now are we holy, not only by the gift of God, but by Him Who vouchsafes to be called His Gift, because He is given to us, His 'Holy Spirit Which dwelleth in us'. Now have we a likeness of God, not because we were so made only, but because we were more blessedly 're-made, being renewed after the Image of Him Who created us'. And this Divine Image is engraven upon our souls, not in any outward way, nor even by the grace of God alone, but also by the Spirit of God within us, 'else', as saith a father, 'we had been called the image of the grace, rather than the image of God Himself.' And our Lord said to the Apostles, Receive the Holy Ghost, whereby, through the inbreathing of the Saviour, they became partakers not of grace alone, but of the One Holy Spirit. By the Holy Spirit, Scripture saith, we have been sealed; but, says a father again, 'The seal hath the Form of Christ Who sealeth; and of this Form do the sealed partake, being formed after It; as the Apostle saith, "My little children, of whom I travail again until Christ be formed in you." But they who are so sealed, well are they said to be "partakers of the Divine Nature", as Peter said. And through the Spirit are we all said to be partakers of God. "Know ye not, he saith, that ye are the temple of God, and that the Spirit of God dwelleth in you?"' Not through any creature could we be made partakers of God; not Angel or Archangel could dwell in the soul, but God Who made it for Himself. 'So,' says a father, 'have we the rich gift, that He Who is by Nature and truly God, is our Indweller and Inhabitant, in that from Him we receive the Spirit Which is both from Him and in Him, and His Own, being, by Name and in Truth, equally Lord with Himself, and to us replacing the Son, as being by Nature One with Him.' 'He sent to us the Comforter from Heaven, through Whom and with Whom He is with us and dwelleth in us, pouring into us no foreign but His own Spirit, of His own Substance, and of That of the Father.' And so our Blessed Lord says again, 'If any man love Me, he will keep My words, and My Father will love Him, and We will come unto him, and make Our abode with him.' And lest any one think that the Father and the Son only, without the Holy Spirit, make Their abode with those who love Him, let him consider what was said just before of the Holy Spirit; 'Whom the world cannot receive, because it seeth Him not, neither knoweth Him: but ye know Him; for He dwelleth with you, and shall be in you.' 'So,' adds a father, 'cometh the Spirit, as cometh the Father; for where the Father is, there also the Son, and where the Son is, there is the Holy Spirit. But He cometh not be motion from place to place, but from the grace which quickeneth to the grace which sanctifieth, to transfer us from earth to heaven, from decay to glory, from slavery to the Kingdom. The Spirit so cometh, as cometh the Father, – in Whom, when He cometh, is the full Presence of the Father and the Son.' O the depth of the riches of the condescension and love of god, Who hath not only pardoned us and delivered from death, but given us righteousness and sanctification; not given them us only, but as Scripture says, Himself made His Son such to us, by taking our nature into God, and in our nature dying for us; and not only so, but imparting His grace; and not grace only, but making us sons; and not sons only, but members of His Only-begotten Son; not heirs only, but co-heirs with Christ; to have in our measure what He has, the everlasting Love of the Everlasting Father; and of this He hath given us the earnest, His Holy Spirit, Who with Him is One God, to dwell in us, in His Own Holy Person, and unite us with Him.

My brethren, if such be the first fruits, what shall the harvest be? If such the earnest, what shall the full gift be whereof it is the earnest? 'We shall be like him.'

But we should not be like Him, if we had not, after our measure, and as far as creatures can contain them, the qualities (so to speak) of Almighty God. Such is the love of God, so does His Goodness love to bestow Itself, that He would withhold nothing of Himself. God is love. And when faith is turned into sight, and hope into its substance, then shall 'charity abide' and be perfected; then shall we love with the love of God, shall love God as God loveth Himself, ever through His love cleaving unto His love, ever borne to God, uplifted, filled, overflowing, receiving, giving back so as again to receive, the unutterable love of God, and by His love changed into His own unchangeableness. If we would be 'like Him' in glory, we must in our degree be 'like Him' here by grace. If we would have His Image for ever, we must bear even now the Image of the

Heavenly, after which by His mercy we have been renewed; if we would behold Him in bliss, our heart must be made pure here, that by faith it may here see, Whom by the eye of the body it sees not.

That likeness here is renewed, in proportion as is our love; since God is love. It is begun, when we are wearied and sickened at ourselves that we are so unlike Him, so far removed from Him. It is enlarged, when with penitent love we return from the far country whither we had strayed, to confess our unworthiness in our Father's Presence. It is carried on by His Grace, through every act of self-denial, or virtue, or love, or penitent suffering, for love of Him; every groan that we are unlike Him; every longing to be like Him; every fervent momentary prayer we breathe for His love; for fervent prayer is not our own, but the unutterable groaning of His Spirit Which dwelleth in us. It is renewed by that Heavenly Feast, the Food of Angels, wherein (in the words of our Church) 'our sinful bodies are made clean by His Body, and our souls washed through His most Precious Blood', yea 'we dwell in Christ and Christ in us, are made one with Christ and Christ with us'. It shall be perfected, in those who by His grace, persevere to the end, in that blessed everlasting Sight, when our vile body shall be made like unto the glorious Body of our Redeemer, our soul shall see the Ever-Blessed Trinity, and in that sight receive of the ineffable Beauty and Glory and Majesty and Love which it sees.

O defile we then no more that Royal Image, in which He formed us; which, when sunk in the mire of sin, He came to cleanse anew by His own Precious Blood; which He sought out so diligently, by toil and suffering; which He longs to shew on high rejoicing, to His friends and neighbours in the Heavenly courts. Come we to Him, desiring that His Divine Features be, one by one, retraced on our souls. Long we to be cleansed, and He will cleanse us; long we for His Indwelling, and He will come to us; treasure we His Sacred Presence, when we have received It, and He will cleanse us more and more; hide we no part of our sinful heart from Him, and He will by His light brighten the dark corners over which we grieve, and all, sorrow or joy dryness or refreshment, the light of His Presence of His seeming absence, shall but the more kindle our longing and cleanse our souls for that unvarying, unceasing, unspeakable Presence in bliss. 'We shall be like Him, for we shall see Him as He is.'

John Henry Newman, 'Lecture VI', in *Lectures on the Doctrine of Justification [1874]*, London: Longmans, Green, & Co., 1914, pp. 136–7, 139, 143, 144 and 154.

When Faith is said to be the inward principle of acceptance, the question rises, what gives to faith its acceptableness? Faith is acceptable as having a something in it, which unbelief has not; that something what is it? It must be God's grace, if God's grace act *in* the soul, and not merely externally, as in the way of Providence. If it acts in us, and has a presence in us, when we have faith, then the having that grace or that presence, and not faith, which is its result, must be the real token, the real state of a justified man.

Again: if we say that justification consists in a supernatural quality imparted to the soul by God's grace, as Roman writers say, then in like manner, the question arises, is this quality all that is in us of heaven? Does not the grace itself, as in immediate divine power or presence, dwell in the hearts which are gifted with this renovating principle? It may or it may not; but if it does, then surely the possession of that grace is really our justification, and not renewal, or the principle of renewal.

And thus, by tracing farther back the lines of thought on which these apparently discordant views are placed, they are made to converge; they converge, that is, supposing there to be vouchsafed to us, an inward divine presence or grace (of which both faith and spiritual renovation are fruits). If such a presence be not vouchsafed, then certainly faith on the one hand, renovation on the other, are the ultimate elements to which our state of righteousness can be respectively referred in the two theologies. But if it be vouchsafed, neither Protestant nor Romanist ought to refuse to admit, and in admitting to agree with each other, that the presence of the Holy Ghost shed abroad in our hearts, the Author both of faith and of renewal, this is really that which makes us righteous, and that our righteousness is the possession of that presence.

But further, Scripture expressly declares that righteousness is a definite inward gift . . . this gift, whatever it is, is not any moral excellence or grace, such as faith or a renewed state. Though *within* us, as it must be, if it is to separate us from the world, yet is not properly speaking *of* us, not any quality or act of our minds, not faith, not renovation, not obedience, not anything cognizable by man, but a certain divine gift in which all these qualifications are included. A gift which must of necessity be at once our justification and our sanctification, for it is nothing short of the indwelling in us of God the Father and the Word, Incarnate, through the Holy Ghost.

We now may see that the connection really is between justification and renewal. They are both included in that one great gift of God, the indwelling of Christ in the Christian soul. That indwelling is *ipso facto* our justification and sanctification, as its necessary results. It is the Divine Presence that justifies us, not faith, as say the Protestant schools, not renewal, as say the Roman. The word justification is the substantive living Word of God, entering the soul, illuminating and cleansing it, as fire brightens and purifies material substances. He who justifies also sanctifies, because it is He. The first blessing runs into the second as its necessary limit; and the second being rejected, carries away with it the first.

F. D. Maurice, *Theological Essays*, Chapters IV, VI, XIV, XVI, Third Edition, London and New York: Macmillan, 1871, pp. 66–7, 74–5, 116–17, 367 and 410–11.

The facts I have tried to present in the light in which Scripture exhibits them to us, – Scripture abundantly confirmed by daily observation. We apply the principle to those facts, when we say boldly to the man who declares that he has a righteousness which no one shall remove from him – 'That is true. You have such a righteousness. It is deeper than all the iniquity which is in you. It lies at the very ground of our existence. And this righteousness dwells not merely in a law which is condemning you, it dwells in a Person in whom you may trust.

The righteous Lord of man is with you – not in some heaven to which you must ascend that you may bring Him down, in some hell to which you must dive that you may raise Him up, but nigh you, at your heart.'

The principle is expressed again when we say, 'You maintain that the pain you are suffering is not good, but ill, – a sign of wrong and disorder. You say that it is a bondage, from which you must seek deliverance. You say that you cannot stop to settle in what part of you it is, that it is throughout you, that it affects you altogether, that you want a complete emancipation from it. Even so. Hold fast that conviction. Let no man, divine or layman, rob you of it. (Pain is a sign and witness of disorder, the consequence of disorder.) It is mockery to say otherwise. You describe it rightly; it is a bondage, the sign that a tyrant has in some way intruded himself into this earth of ours. But you are permitted to suffer the consequence of that intrusion, just that you may attain to the knowledge of another fact, – that there is a Redeemer, that He lives, that He is the stronger. That righteous King of your heart whom you have felt to be so near you, so one with you, that you could hardly help identifying Him with yourself, even while you confessed that you were so evil, He is the Redeemer as well as the Lord of you and of man.

While I am exploring these rich mines in myself, I am brought to a stand-still by the discovery that *I* am the worker of them; that I have worked them: that I am bankrupt, and guilty; – then it becomes a necessity – not of my traditional faith, or of my fears, but – of my inmost spirit, that I should find some One whom I did not create, some One who is not subject to my accidents and changes, some One in whom I may rest for life and death. Who is this? What name have you for Him? I say it is the Christ, whose name I was taught to pronounce in my childhood; the Righteous one, the Redeemer in whom Job, and David, and the Prophets trusted, the ground of all that is true, in you, and me and every man; the Source of the good acts, – which are therefore not splendid sins, – of you, and me and every man; the Light that lighteth every man who cometh into the world. Apart from Him, I feel that there dwells in me no good thing; but I am sure that I am not apart from Him, nor are you, nor is any man.

'There is a light within you, close to you. Do you know it? Are you coming to it? Are you desiring that it should penetrate you through and through? Oh, turn to it! Turn from these idols that are surrounding you, – from the confused, dark world of thought within you! It will reveal yourself to you! It will reveal the world to you!' 'What do you mean?' asks the well-instructed, formally, habitually religious man: 'my conscience, I suppose.' 'Call it that, or what you please; but in God's name, my friend, do not cheat yourself with a phrase. I mean a reality; I mean that which has to do with your innermost being; I mean something which does not proceed from you or belong to you; but which is there, searching you and judging you. Nay! Stay a moment. I mean that this light comes from a Person, – from the King and Lord of your heart and spirit, – from the Word, – the Son of God. When I say, Repent; I say, Turn and confess His presence. You have always had it with you. You have been unmindful of it.'

It is good for a man thus to know what is going on within him; thus to see himself stript bare of appearances and plausibilities; thus to be prevented from transferring to accidents, which he cannot remedy, what may be cured when he sees it and confesses it as his own. For there is another set of facts, as we have seen, in the history of Christendom to which, also, there is only a most imperfect parallel in the ancient world. We find men emerging out of darkness into a marvelous light, coming to understand what that strife in themselves meant, and how and why they had fallen into it, coming to see that their true state is that of union with One higher than themselves, their King and their Deliverer, in whom they were created, apart from whom they cannot subsist, in trusting whom they lose that feverish self-consciousness which has been their death, and acquire a pure, and true, and common life.

Charity was needed to make this earth what it ought to be, and human hearts have a profound sense of its necessity for them, an infinite craving to possess it, and be filled with it. Something stood in the way of the good which the earth sighs for, and which man sighs for. A vision of *Sin* rose up before us. It was portentous, for it seemed part of the very creature who had the dream of a perfect good. But he disclaimed it, he tried to account for it by some accidents of his position, or by some essential error in his constitution; at last he said, I have yielded to an oppressor; an *Evil Spirit* has withdrawn me from my true Lord. Then arose the question, Who is this true Lord? Where is He to be found? *Righteousness* was felt to be even more closely intertwined with the being of the man than Evil; for awhile he was disposed to claim it as his own; suffering, and the sense of an infinite contradiction, did not deliver him from that belief. But some one there was who led him to cry for a *Redeemer,* to be sure that He lived, to be sure that Righteousness was in Him, and therefore was Man's.

Was this Redeemer, so near to man, so inseparable from man, of earthly race? The vision of a *Son of God* rose upon us; a thousand different traditions pointed to it; it took the most various forms; but the heart of man said, 'There must be One in whom all these meet; there must be One who did not rise from manhood into Godhead, but who can exhibit the perfection of manhood, because He has the perfection of Godhead.'

Bibliography

Patristic

Athanasius, *On the Incarnation of the Word*, sections 1–19, 41–57.
Augustine, *On the Trinity*, Book XIV.
Basil the Great, *On the Human Condition.*
Cyril of Alexandria, *Commentary on the Gospel According to S. John*, Book IX (In John 14.20).
Gregory of Nyssa, 'On the Making of Man'.
Irenaeus, *Against Heresies*, Book IV, Chapters 37–41, and Book V.

Medieval

Bernard of Clairvaux, *On the Song of Songs* IV, Sermons 80–6.
Julian of Norwich, *Showings (The Long Text).*
Thomas Aquinas, *Summa Theologica*, First Part of the Second Part, Questions 1–5.

Reformation

John Calvin, *Institutes of the Christian Religion*, Book I, ch. XV, and Book II, chs II and VI.

Martin Luther, *Bondage of the Will*, 'II: Review of Erasmus' Preface', sections iii–ix.

Modern Sources

A.M. Allchin, *Participation in God: A Forgotten Strand in Anglican Tradition*, Wilton, CT: Morehouse-Barlow, 1988.

Karl Barth, 'The Being of Man in Jesus Christ', in G. W. Bromiley and T. F. Torrance (eds), *Church Dogmatics IV.1: The Doctrine of Reconciliation*, Edinburgh: T. & T. Clark, 1956, paragraph 58.2, pp. 92–122.

Charles Gore, 'On the Christian Doctrine of Sin', in *Lux Mundi*, New York: Lovell, Coryell, and Company, 1890, Appendix II, pp. 442–52.

Wentzel van Huyssteen, *Alone in the World? Human Uniqueness in Science and Theology*, Grand Rapids, MI: Eerdmans, 2006.

Vladimir Lossky, *In the Image and Likeness of God*, J. Erickson and T. Bird (eds), Crestwood, NY: St Vladimir's Seminary Press, 1985, Chapters 5–7.

Henri De Lubac, *Augustinianism and Modern Theology*, L. Shephard (trans.), New York: Crossroad, 2000.

Jürgen Moltmann, 'God's Image in Creation: Human Beings', in *God in Creation: A New Theology of Creation and the Spirit of God*, M. Kohl (trans.), New York: HarperCollins, 1991, Chapter IX, pp. 215–43.

Panayiotis Nellas, *Deification in Christ: The Nature of the Human Person*, Norman Russell (trans.), Crestwood, NY: St Vladimir's Seminary Press, 1987.

Reinhold Niebuhr, *The Nature and Destiny of Man*, 2 vols, New York: Charles Scribner's Sons, 1941.

Wolfhart Pannenberg, *Anthropology in Theological Perspective*, M. O'Connell (trans.), Philadelphia: Westminster, 1985.

Karl Rahner, *Hearers of the Word*, J. Donceel (trans.), New York: Continuum, 1994.

Friedrich Schleiermacher, *The Christian Faith*, H. R. Mackintosh and J. S. Stewart (eds), Philadelphia: Fortress Press, 1976, paragraphs 60–78, 86–90, pp. 244–324, 355–70.

William Temple, *Nature, Man and God*, London: Macmillan, 1951.

Paul Tillich, *Systematic Theology*, Volume 2, Part III: 'Existence and the Christ', Chicago: University of Chicago Press, 1957, pp. 19–96.

John D. Zizioulas, 'Personhood and Being', in *Being as Communion*, Crestwood, NY: St Vladimir's Seminary Press, 1993, Chapter 1, pp. 27–65.

5

The Church

MARK D. CHAPMAN

The Problem of Anglican Systematics

Dan Hardy, one of the more influential Anglican theologians of recent years, once claimed that '[e]cclesiology is the true form of human being'.[1] Despite the many compromises and ambiguities of the Church, Christians have always seen belonging to the Church as constitutive for authentic human identity. Yet precisely how the Church is to be understood is far from straightforward, not least in Anglicanism. There are three principal reasons: first, Anglicanism developed from a concrete, particular church, which was limited to a set of national boundaries and which never claimed 'universality' in the same sense as the Roman Catholic Church. Second, the development of Anglican churches in different parts of the world meant that the social and political context of Anglicanism was often very different from that in which its early theology was forged. Third – and perhaps most importantly – Anglicanism has always had a complex relationship with ecclesial authority and theological norms.

These ecclesiological problems mean that any 'Anglican systematics' is fraught with difficulties: Anglicans have been characterized by a huge diversity in practice and doctrine. Indeed, it has become a commonplace to suggest that Anglicanism has no particular doctrines of its own. Some – including Bishop Stephen Sykes in acerbic mood[2] – have attacked such a view as symptomatic of the sort of woolly-mindedness associated with a kind of 'anything-goes' comprehensiveness characterized by the 1938 *Church of England Doctrine Commission Report*.[3] Others, including the eirenic Irish bishop Henry McAdoo have made a virtue of a theology that seeks to hold together tensions.[4] On such a view, Anglicanism is more of a way of doing theology, a method or practice rather than a distinctive set of teachings.

Some more recent writers have sought to find a more definitive set of agreed formularies as the basis for doctrine.[5] However, as the discussion about an Anglican Covenant following the recent conflicts in the Anglican Communion has demonstrated, there is little agreement about what would count as Anglican sources and norms. While all would acknowledge the supremacy of Scripture,

---

[1] Colin Gunton and Daniel Hardy (eds), *On Being the Church*, Edinburgh: T. & T. Clark, 1989, p. 34.
[2] *The Integrity of Anglicanism*, Oxford: Mowbray, 1978, pp. 8–25.
[3] *Doctrine in the Church of England*, London: SPCK, 1938.
[4] *The Spirit of Anglicanism*, London: A. & C. Black, 1965, pp. 321–2.
[5] Paul Avis, 'Anglican Ecclesiology', in Gerard Mannion and Lewis Mudge (eds), *The Routledge Companion to the Christian Church*, London: Routledge, 2008, pp. 210–12; see also *The Identity of Anglicanism*, London: T. & T. Clark, 2007, esp. Chapter 4.

the methods of interpretation are widely divergent. Furthermore, it is not clear who could define the essential core of Anglicanism. While some might clamour for a teaching office – something like an Anglican magisterium – few are likely to agree on how this might be constituted. Even the word 'Anglican' is problematic: for most of its life, it has meant simply 'English'.[6] Yet, a theology that emerged in the context of an English state church, where authority was exercised by the civil rulers, is very different from the sort of theology that developed in non-English churches, where Anglicanism was one denomination among others and where the civil powers had only a very limited authority in matters ecclesiastical.

An Anglican systematic theology will always relate to a particular context. It will not be like a Lutheran dogmatics based upon exposition of universally accepted texts (such as the Augsburg Confession); similarly, even though the Anglican formularies are closest to those of Reformed churches, an Anglican systematics is highly unlikely to resemble a work of Reformed dogmatics. Rather than being historicized in quasi-canonical texts, Anglican doctrine instead emerges from a strange combination of text, institution and practice, both ecclesiastical and secular. Consequently, although the Church of England adopted most of the Augsburg Confession, coupled with some more Reformed statements, as part of its theological self-definition in the Thirty-Nine Articles of Religion, the authority accorded to the text – even one ratified by an Elizabethan Parliament – was quite unlike that given to the Augsburg Confession by Lutherans. Being Anglican does not mean subscription to a text and its subsequent interpretation (as might be the case, for instance, in the Presbyterian Church of Scotland where the Westminster Confession still functions as the doctrinal norm). Instead being Anglican – at least at the beginning – required obedience to those in authority, and conformity to what they laid down as law. For this reason, Anglican theology is not usually done primarily through exposition of its historic formularies.

Anglican theology was forged in the heat of controversy, which, given the role of the Church of England as the monopoly state church (in theory until 1689), was always political. The practical theology of authority in matters of interpretation and church order (polity) was usually more important than controversy over doctrine (although there are frequent exceptions to this rule, especially over predestination in the late sixteenth and early seventeenth centuries). While Scripture was universally regarded as sufficient and containing all things necessary to salvation (Art. VI), its interpretation was always open to debate. Furthermore precisely what was contained in Scripture was hotly contested. Who decides on these matters, and how one legislates for those things on which Scripture is silent, has been a perennial – perhaps even the perennial – issue in Anglicanism. It is for this reason that the key doctrine for Anglicanism is the doctrine of the Church, or, more accurately, the doctrine of authority and order in the Church.

While other chapters in this volume have tackled doctrinal topics, where it might be difficult to discern a particular Anglican approach, and where the task of theological construction might therefore be paramount, the doctrine of the

---

6 Avis, *Identity*, pp. 19–21.

Church is altogether different. At least in its early years, as it forged its identity as a church separate from Rome, it was its approach to ecclesiology that gave Anglicanism – or at least the Church of England – its distinctiveness. Indeed, some forms of Anglicanism described themselves as 'Episcopalian' in terms of their understanding of church order. Consequently, as this chapter will show, partly because of its lack of an authoritative teaching office and of uncontested doctrinal norms beyond the Scriptures and ecumenical creeds, Anglican ecclesiology was always constructed on the basis of history: it emerged and continues to emerge from the context of church and state politics and power.

The Church

After the Reformation the Church of England continued to express its doctrine in terms of the three Creeds (the Nicene, Apostles' and Athanasian): it regarded itself as part of 'one, holy, catholic, and apostolic Church' (even if Cranmer somewhat inexplicably omitted the word 'holy' from his version of the Niceno-Constantinopolitan Creed included at Holy Communion in the Book of Common Prayer). The title page of the Book of Common Prayer declares an implicit belief that the Church of England is part of something larger. The Prayer Book contains the orders and rites 'of the Church according to the use of the Church of England'. Similarly, in its recent preface to the Declaration of Assent, the Church of England claims to be 'part of the One, Holy, Catholic and Apostolic Church worshipping the one true God, Father, Son and Holy Spirit'. Precisely what it meant – and means – to be part of 'one, holy, catholic, and apostolic' Church, however, is far from clear.

Although the doctrine of the Church is encapsulated in the Creeds, the particular identity of the Church of England emerged through a long period of doctrinal controversy. Its historic formularies – the Thirty-Nine Articles of Religion, the Book of Common Prayer and the Ordering of Bishops, Priests and Deacons – were each forged in a period of unprecedented conflict. Furthermore, the ecclesiastical settlement that emerged during the reigns of the Tudor sovereigns was equally shaped by political controversy. The declaration in the Act in Restraint of Appeals of 1533 that 'This realm of England is an Empire' meant that there could be no source of authority – including in the Church – from beyond the imperial throne: Article XXXVII famously asserted that '[t]he Bishop of Rome hath no jurisdiction in this realm of England'. Rome was as liable to error as any other part of the church (Art. XIX) (and so are General Councils, which may only be summoned by the authority of Princes (Art. XXI)). Ecclesiastical authority was part of a wider understanding of authority which flowed down from the king himself. While bishops, priests and deacons might have survived, the source of their authority was the single divine law, and part of the purpose of their ministry – at least beyond the sacramental – was to promote decency, good order and civil peace.[7]

---

7 See Mark D. Chapman, *Bishops, Saints and Politics*, London: T. & T. Clark, 2007, pp. 9–32.

If the Church of England was catholic, then, it was not catholic in the same way as the pre-Reformation Church. Gone were the frequent appeals to Rome for dispensations from canon law as well as payments and taxes to support the curia; no bishop from beyond England had any authority at all over the English Church. The idea of what can be called 'spatial catholicity', that is, that there was a single Church occupying the whole of Christendom, was brought into question at the Reformation. 'Catholic' truth had to be located somewhere outside the visible structures of the universal Church. This led in two directions: on the one hand, as was emphasized by the use of a translation of the seventh article of the Augsburg Confession (Art. XIX) in the Thirty-Nine Articles, 'The visible Church of Christ is a congregation of faithful men, in the which the pure Word of God is preached, and the Sacraments be duly ministered according to Christ's ordinance.' This meant that the fundamental locus of the Church was the local church gathered for worship rather than any international or even national hierarchical structure. On the other hand, however, the particular or national church had authority in controversies of faith (Art. XX) and ceremonies (Art XXXIV). To disobey the national church 'offendeth against the common order of the Church, and hurteth the authority of the Magistrate'. What sort of independent authority was left for the Church was unclear. It became a key focus of debate in the years that followed.

The Church in Anglican Apologetics

Key to formulating an Anglican doctrine of the Church was John Jewel (1522–71), Bishop of Salisbury from 1560. As bishop-elect he preached a sermon at Paul's Cross, the leading London pulpit, where he challenged his Roman Catholic opponents 'to bring any one sufficient sentence out of old Catholicke Doctor, or Father; or out of any old Generell Councell; Or out of the Holy Scriptures of God' to justify their practices.[8] Rather than simply identifying Rome with the Antichrist, as some were wont to do, Jewel instead developed an apologetic method that profoundly influenced the shape of Anglican theology: he justifies the abolition of certain abuses by citing the fathers, as well as Scripture. The themes of this sermon were dealt with at greater length in the *Apologia Ecclesiae Anglicanae*, which gained status as the semi-official theology of the Church of England in the reign of James I. The Church of England was neither one of the 'sundry sects', nor had it fallen into the corruption of the Roman Church. Instead it was that form of church which 'agreeth with Christian Religion'. Jewel thus sought to 'shew it plain, that God's holy Gospel, the ancient bishops, and the primitive Church do make on our side, and that we have not without just cause left these men, and rather have returned to the apostles and old catholic fathers'.[9] The counterbalance was consequently to show that the

---

8 *The Works of Bishop John Jewel*, Cambridge: Cambridge University Press for the Parker Society, 1845–50, 4 vols, vol. 1, p. 20 [hereafter *Jewel*].
9 *Jewel* III, p. 56.

Church of Rome had 'forsaken the fellowship of the Holy Fathers'.[10] Arguing against Roman primacy, Jewel challenged the Pope:

> Tell us, I pray you, good holy Father, seeing ye do crake so much of all antiquity, and boast yourself that all men are bound to you alone, which of all the fathers have at any time called you by the name of the highest prelate, the universal bishop, or the head of the Church? Which of them ever said that both the swords were committed to you?[11]

Here Jewel develops an understanding of 'temporal' catholicity. He uses the writings of the fathers to defend his own church:

> As for our doctrine, which we might rightlier call Christ's catholic doctrine, it is so far off from new, that God, who is above all most ancient, and the Father of our Lord Jesus Christ. . . . So that no man can now think our doctrine to be new, unless the same think either the prophets' faith, or the Gospel, or else Christ himself to be new.[12]

For Jewel, the Church of England was not a new church, but was identical to the 'Church of the Apostles and of the old catholic bishops and fathers'.

Jewel was also aware of the importance in claiming an independent authority to rid the Church of abuses: he develops a form of conciliarism to justify the changes in the Reformation. Nothing had been done, he claimed, without synodical approval: Parliament was understood as a lay synod. Thus he writes 'we do not despise councils, assemblies, and conferences of bishops and learned men; neither have we done that we have done altogether without bishops or without a council. The matter hath been treated in open Parliament, with long consultation, and before a notable synod and convocation.'[13] Criticizing the Council of Trent, he emphasized the sole right of the civil authority to convene a general council (Art. XXI). Besides, he claimed, 'Whatsoever it be, the truth of the gospel of Jesus Christ dependeth not upon the councils.'[14]

Jewel emphasized the importance of determining the legitimate authority in matters of discipline and doctrine on which Scripture – 'the very sure and infallible rule, whereby may be tried whether the church doth stagger or err'[15] – was silent. Such areas, which included forms of worship and ecclesiastical dress, proved to be of central importance in Elizabethan England. They were aspects a wider order and uniformity expressed in both church and state, which found its ultimate authority in the divinely appointed monarch. In distinguishing between things necessary and things indifferent to salvation, Jewel was clear that obedience and conformity was of the utmost importance in both:

---

10 *Jewel* IV, p. 901.
11 *Jewel* I, p. 43.
12 *Jewel* I, p. 39.
13 *Jewel* I, p. 47.
14 *Jewel* III, p. 54.
15 *Jewel* III, p. 62.

Nevertheless we keep still, and esteem, not only those ceremonies which we are sure were delivered us from the Apostles, but some others too besides, which we thought might be suffered without hurt to the Church of God; because that we had a desire that all things in the Holy Congregation might (as St. Paul Commandeth) 'be done with comeliness, and in good order'; but as for all those things which we saw were either very superstitious, or unprofitable, or noisome, or mockeries, or contrary to the Holy Scriptures, or else unseemly for honest or discreet folks, as there be an infinite number nowadays where papistry is used; these I say, we have utterly refused without all manner exception.[16]

Anglicans and Puritans

Similar themes emerged shortly afterwards in the reign of Elizabeth, shaping what was later encapsulated in the phrase *via media*. In many ways, this is a misleading term: there was no sense in which the Church of England in the post-Reformation saw itself as anything other than Protestant. However, Scripture was not regarded as providing for all eventualities, which meant there was a sphere in which other legitimate authorities could legislate: crucially these included church order, the liturgy and ecclesiastical dress. Others begged to differ. In a well-known letter, for instance, Theodore Beza in Geneva, wrote to Bishop Grindal that the persistence of pre-Reformation forms in the Prayer Book made it 'an imperfect book culled and picked out of the popish dunghill the mass book full of abominations'.[17] Similarly, Thomas Cartwright (1535–1603), briefly Lady Margaret Professor in Cambridge and a friend of Beza, sought a theocratic system whereby the Church determined the running of the state using principles drawn from the Old Testament.[18] In response, John Whitgift (1530–1604), who later became Archbishop of Canterbury, claimed that there were large areas on which Scripture was silent, but over which the legitimate sovereign was supreme.

Against the Puritan insistence on one type of church government founded in Scripture, Whitgift asserted that since Scripture was silent on this matter then the best form of government was that which proved most expedient. Church government was not 'of the essence and being' of the Church but had to be adapted to the circumstances:[19] 'we do not take upon (as we are slandered) either to blame or to condemn other churches, for such orders as they have received most fit for their estates'.[20] Similarly, ecclesiastical vestments were understood as matters indifferent:

---

16 *Jewel* III, p. 65.
17 Walter Frere and C. E. Douglas (eds), *Puritan Manifestoes: a study of the origin of the puritan revolt, with a reprint of the 'Admonition to the Parliament', and kindred documents*, 1572, reprint, London: SPCK, 1954, p. 21.
18 *The Works of John Whitgift*, Parker Society, Cambridge: Cambridge University Press, 1851, 3 vols, vol. I, p. 329 (Hereafter *Whitgift*).
19 *Whitgift* I, p. 185.
20 *Whitgift* I, p. 5.

> When they were a sign and a token of the popish priesthood, then they were evil, even as the thing was which they signified: but now they be signs and tokens of the ministers of the word of God, which are good, and therefore also they be good.[21]

It was Saint Paul who provided Whitgift with his justification for the episcopal church order.

> in ceremonies and external discipline he hath not in scripture particularly determined any thing, but left the same to his church, to make or abrogate... as shall be thought from time to time most convenient for the present state of the Church; so that nothing be done against the general rule of St Paul, 1 Cor. xiv.: 'Let all things be done decently and in order'.

It was the duty of the Christian to obey the law: the alternative would be 'the seed of contention and brawling'.[22]

For Whitgift the Presbyterian system maintained by his opponents would become 'the very highway to subversion and confusion',[23] since it provided an alternative source of authority from that exercised by the state. While bishops and archbishops were not 'necessary to salvation', he held, they nevertheless functioned 'to keep [the church] in external peace, discipline and order'.[24] In a very clear differentiation between Scripture, tradition and reason, Whitgift argued against Cartwright:

> The papists make their traditions necessary unto salvation; and therefore they are to be rejected, because the word of God containeth all things necessary to salvation. I make those offices part of decency, order, ecclesiastical government and policy, which admitteth alteration as the times and persons require, and are not particularly expressed in the scriptures, no more than divers other things be in the same kind... You have not yet proved that either the name or office of archbishops is in any respect 'oppugned' in the word of God.[25]

To attack bishops was at the same time to attack the legitimating authority for bishops: the queen herself. What emerges here is a clear differentiation between types of authority. When something was not expressly ruled out by Scripture, it was a matter of prudence for the church to legislate for itself. The best model of government, according to Whitgift, was that which would maintain good order and the rule of law, which was something upheld by the king and the civil magistrate. This meant that 'the prince having the supreme government of the realm, in all causes and over all persons, as she doth exercise the one by the lord chancellor, so doth she the other by the archbishops'.[26]

---

21 *Whitgift* I, p. 72.
22 See *Whitgift* I, pp. 245–7.
23 *Whitgift* II, p. 271.
24 *Whitgift* II, p. 97.
25 *Whitgift* II, pp. 236–7.
26 *Whitgift* II, p. 248.

This had been clearly expressed in Article XX: 'The Church hath power to decree Rites or Ceremonies, and authority in Controversies of Faith: And yet it is not lawful for the church to ordain any thing that is contrary to God's word written.' Similarly, Article XXXIV moved in the same direction:

> It is not necessary that Tradition and Ceremonies be in all places one, and utterly like; for at all times they have been divers, and may be changed according to the diversities of countries, times, and men's manners, so that nothing be ordained against God's word. Whosoever, through his private judgement, willingly and purposely, doth openly break the traditions and ceremonies of the Church, which be not repugnant to the word of God, and be ordained and approved by common authority, ought to be rebuked openly, (that others may fear to do the like,) as he that offendeth against the common order of the Church, and hurteth the authority of the magistrate, and woundeth the consciences of the weak brethren.
>
> Every particular or national Church hath authority to ordain, change, and abolish, ceremonies or rites of the Church ordained only by man's authority, so that all things be done to edifying.

The tension here is obvious: there is a legitimate field of manoeuvre for a church, and yet that is an area which falls under authority. The chief issue in Anglican ecclesiology was thus less over doctrine and more over who had the legitimate authority to decide whether something was a matter indifferent and to legislate in these areas.

If there is one theologian who could claim classic status, it is Richard Hooker (1553–1600): he too engaged in controversies over ecclesiology, writing his eight-volume *magnum opus* on the *Laws of Ecclesiastical Polity*. He met the Puritanism of Walter Travers with a theory of the order of the world. Where Travers claimed that Christ promulgated a perfect law for ruling his Holy Commonwealth, Hooker developed a theology of law and order that allowed for a far wider sphere of divine law, which was established on the doctrine of creation. For Hooker, there are several different types of legal authority that derive from the authority of God himself, which he outlines at great length in Book One. Given that Travers's method restricted laws chiefly, if not completely, to those located in Scripture, there is much polemical force in Hooker's writing. When it comes to legislation, the sphere of reason is central, since it leads men to make laws which govern society. This derives both from the 'natural inclination' to desire sociable life and amiable fellowship, as well as the 'order expressly or secretly agreed upon touching the manner of their union of living together'. This is the 'Law of a commonweal'[27] deduced by reason and constrained by the conditions of human depravity. Such laws demand obedience if we are to live together in harmony and good order. Even though 'principal intent of Scripture is to deliver the laws of duties supernatural', it nevertheless contains other sorts of laws.[28]

---

27 Richard Hooker, *The Laws of Ecclesiastical Polity*, John Keble, R. W. Church and F. Paget (eds), Oxford: Clarendon, 1888, Book I.x.5.
28 Hooker, *Laws*, I.xii.1.

This lengthy introduction leads Hooker to differentiate between laws derived from reason and those derived from Scripture, both of which have their origin in the divine order:

> The law of reason doth somewhat direct men how to honour God as their Creator; but how to glorify God in such sort as is required, to the end that he may be an everlasting saviour, this we are taught by divine law, which law both ascertaineth the truth and supplieth unto us the want of that other law.[29]

Human beings thus have a natural inclination to honour God, although the precise form is to be filled out by Scripture. Scripture itself, however, has to be understood using the principle of rational 'collection', as is required for the belief in the Trinity, 'the necessity whereof is by none denied', but which is 'nowhere to be found by express literal mention'.[30] The polarization of God's law and human law; of God's authority and human authority, is overcome as reason itself is given a divine origin. Reason can therefore deduce many actions which are not explicitly commanded or condemned by Scripture.

The remainder of the *Laws* amounts to an elegant effort to counter the arguments of the Puritans using the methods developed in the first book. In Book Two, which counters the Puritan proposition that 'Scripture is the only rule of all things which in this life may be done by man', Hooker claims that 'Wisdom hath diversely imparted her treasures unto the world. As her ways are of sundry kinds, so her manner of teaching is not merely of one kind.'[31] Similarly, much of what appeared to be of divine foundation in Scripture was simply natural law: 'The truth is they are rules and canons of that law which is written on all men's hearts; the church had for ever no less than now stood bound to observe them, whether the Apostles mentioned them or no.'[32] Church polity, as a matter indifferent, is founded on human reason rather than divine injunction.

Following Whitgift, and echoing the Prayer Book, Hooker claims in Book IV that

> [t]he ceremonies which we have taken from such as were before us, are not things that belong to this or that sect, but they are the ancient rites and customs of the Church of Christ, whereof ourselves being a part, we have the selfsame interest in them which our fathers before us had, from whom the same are descended unto us.[33]

Similarly, he writes in Book V, that the 'church hath authority to establish that for an order at one time which at another time it may abolish, and in both may do well ... Laws touching matter of order are changeable, by the power

---

29 Hooker, *Laws*, I.xvi.5.
30 Hooker, *Laws*, I.xiv.2.
31 Hooker, *Laws*, II.i.4.
32 Hooker, *Laws*, III.vii.3.
33 Hooker, *Laws*, IV.ix.i.

of the church; articles concerning doctrine not so'.[34] While he is conservative, and argues for the importance of the episcopate on the grounds of its antiquity, he nevertheless does not make it of the essence of the Church.[35] In these books there is a subtle interweaving of spiritual and rational authority. For example, the development of bishops was not something derived from divine authority, but was grounded rationally by the desire and compulsion to provide a 'sufficient remedy' for the 'emulations, strifes and contentious authority' that beset more democratic forms of government.[36] Ultimately, then, it was the king, the 'common parent' who had the legitimate power 'to order and dispose of spiritual affairs':[37]

> We are to hold it a thing most consonant with equity and reason, that no ecclesiastical law be made in a Christian commonwealth, without consent of the laity as the clergy, but least of all without consent of the highest power.[38]

The theology of the Church developed in this formative period was based upon the relationship between two different God-given laws: on the one hand, there was the law communicated by God in Scripture and interpreted through the tradition using reason; on the other hand, there was the law which was established in creation through which human beings rationally organized their affairs both for good order and for mitigating the effects of their depravity. For Hooker and the other key thinkers in this early period, church order, the liturgy and much else fell into this second category. Since there was much on which Scripture was silent, it was important to legislate as best one could for the good of the commonwealth; and it was the duty of all people to obey the proper legislating authority in all matters. While such matters were open to change and in that sense provisional, they were nevertheless not unimportant or arbitrary: what was commanded by the legitimate authority – the monarch in Parliament – had the status of an absolute law, even though the same power could in theory change it.

Conciliar Authority

A similar method continued into the seventeenth century. For instance, in a piece of apologetic, addressed to a Roman Catholic, William Laud, Archbishop of Canterbury in the period leading up to the British Civil War, was keen to emphasize that since no one part of the Church was free from error, each church was free to make its own decisions in obedience to the rule of Scripture: 'I admit no ordinary rule left now in the Church, of divine and infallible verity, and so of faith, but the Scripture.'[39] There could be no infallible arbiter save that of

---

34 Hooker, *Laws*, V.vii.2.
35 Hooker, *Laws*, VII.xiv.11.
36 Hooker, *Laws*, VII.v.1.
37 Hooker, *Laws*, VIII.vi.8.
38 Hooker, *Laws*, VIII.i.2.
39 'A Relation of the Conference between William Laud and Mr. Fisher the Jesuit', in *The Works of William Laud*, Oxford: Parker, 1849, Vol. II, p. 366.

Scripture: 'For what need is there of another, since this is most infallible; and the same which the ancient Church of Christ admitted.'[40] Virtually the whole of the Conference with Fisher is concerned with the possibility of error in the application of this rule of faith. All institutions of the Church can err including a general council:[41] 'if a General Council will go out of the Church's way, it may easily go without the Church's truth'.[42] While Laud held to a doctrine on 'indefectibility' in the sense that the Church taken as a whole could not err, the Catholic Church could not be identified with any particular institution: it was always far greater and more expansive.

On this basis, Laud develops a theory of the autonomy of the local church, which he regards as a provisional – yet a necessary stopgap – until such time as wider councils can be convened: when a general council 'cannot be had, the church must pray that it may, and expect till it may; or else reform itself per partes, by national or provincial synods'.[43] Indeed, it was crucial that if the wider Church refused to reform itself, then the particular church had the duty to do so:

> Was it not lawful for Judah to reform herself, when Israel would not join? Sure it was, or else the prophet deceives me? ... Besides, to reform what is amiss in doctrine or manners, is as lawful for a particular Church, as it is to publish and promulgate any thing that is catholic in either. ... If she erred in fact, confess her error.[44]

Sometimes Laud uses rather more graphic language: 'Should we have suffered this gangrene to endanger life and all, rather than be cured in time by a physician of a weaker knowledge and a less able hand?'[45] In short, he went on: 'when the universal church will not, or for the iniquities of the times cannot, obtain and settle a free General Council, it is lawful, nay sometimes necessary, to reform gross abuses by a national, or a provincial'.[46]

To justify his claim about the need for national and provincial reform Laud draws on the schoolman Albertus Magnus,[47] as well as the Parisian Conciliarist Jean Gerson (1363–1429), who 'will not deny but that the Church may be reformed in parts; and that this is necessary, and that to effect it, Provincial Councils may suffice; and in some things, Diocesan'.[48] Provincial councils, Laud claims, have the duty to 'decree in causes of faith, and in cases of reformation, where corruptions have crept into the sacraments of Christ'.[49] Jewel had earlier made much the same point, again against a Roman Catholic opponent:

---

40 'Conference', p. 218.
41 'Conference', p. 247.
42 'Conference', p. 266.
43 'Conference', p. 235.
44 'Conference', pp. 167–8.
45 'Conference', p. 170.
46 'Conference', p. 170.
47 'Conference', p. 168.
48 'Conference', p. 170.
49 'Conference', p. 171.

> Ye say, A provincial council may not repeal a council general: as if the authority of your councils stood only in number, and not in truth. . . . Certainly the truth of God is not bound neither to person nor to place. Wheresoever it be, either in few or in many, it is evermore catholic, even because it is the truth of God.[50]

Laud develops this idea further by claiming that the authority of the 'patriarch' of Rome is essentially the same as that of the other patriarchs, and there is no appeal beyond the patriarch who is 'supreme in his own patriarchate'.[51] Laud understands the authority of the Archbishop of Canterbury as that of a patriarch: 'Now, the Britons having a primate of their own (which is greater than a metropolitan,) yea, a patriarch, if you will, he could not be appealed from to Rome, by S. Gregory's own doctrine'.[52]

While Laud conceded that the Bishop of Rome had authority in Rome, it was impossible for his jurisdiction to be exercised over the whole Church, since this threatened the sovereignty of the local king:

> Suppose [the Church] is a Kingdom; yet the Church militant remaining one, is spread in many earthly kingdoms, and cannot well be ordered like any one particular kingdom. And therefore, though in one particular kingdom there be many visible judges and one supreme, yet it follows not that in the universal militant Church there must be one supreme. For how will he enter to execute his office, if the kings of those kingdoms will not give him leave?[53]

Laud's 'conciliarism' – like its Tudor forebears – emphasizes the unity of Church and state ('for both are but one Jerusalem'):[54] the Church was the spiritual arm of this one commonwealth. While its ultimate authority might rest in Scripture, its temporal sovereign over all matters indifferent was the king. After the restoration in 1660, while some disagreed with Laud over the precise location of absolute temporal sovereignty, most nevertheless continued to maintain that the civil authorities were to exercise rightful authority over the Church.

Alternative Anglican Ecclesiologies

If Anglican ecclesiology, as it developed in England, was upheld by the sense of the unity of Church and state, which found expression in a singular expression of sovereignty, the same cannot be said of most of those other parts of the world, where forms of Anglicanism began to develop from the eighteenth century. On the one hand, the Reformation idea of 'contained catholicity' was retained as a key component of the new churches, which gradually developed institutional

---

50 *Jewel*, IV, pp. 1053-4.
51 Laud, 'Conference', p. 189.
52 'Conference', p. 190.
53 'Conference', p. 225.
54 'Conference', pp. 5-6. On this see Julian Davies, *The Caroline Captivity of the Church*, Oxford: Clarendon Press, 1992.

expression and methods of government. On the other hand, however, there was a crucial difference from the ecclesiology of the Church of England, which gave these other expressions of Anglicanism a quite different emphasis. Although there were obviously many connections with the English Crown in the early years of missionary endeavour,[55] the Anglican churches gradually became completely independent of the Crown, despite the occasional experiment with establishment. The ecclesiastical situation in most colonies was too complex and divided to give one church a monopoly.

The most important example of an independent church outside the British Empire was that of the Protestant Episcopal Church of the United States:[56] the Crown simply could have no authority over a church when it had completely lost its political control over the state. What was rapidly adopted at the General Convention in 1789 was a democratic constitution for the church modelled on the new political arrangements for the USA – the church remained synodically governed by a House of Deputies and a House of Bishops. What they governed was a church that was as equally independent as the Church of England from any other church, but one which was also wholly independent from the state: authority in matters indifferent was no longer part of the state constitution or a matter of political obedience justified by a theory of the divine right of rulers. Instead the Church was a completely voluntary affair. The ministry structures of the English Church were retained to a certain degree, but where in England bishops were ordained state functionaries chosen by the Crown and subordinate to it, in the American Church they were completely independent of any formal connection with the state and were answerable to their synods.

Anglo-Catholicism and Its Opponents

Even within England there were serious threats to the theory of the unity of Church and state. While many writers in the years following the Reformation had seen bishops as of divine foundation, none had seriously questioned those aspects of their authority that derived from the state. However, the religious changes that led to Catholic Emancipation in 1829 and the equality of Nonconformists the previous year, meant that some began to question the divine foundation of the authority of Parliament: crucially the Oxford or Tractarian Movement, which began in 1833 under the leadership of John Keble, John Henry Newman and later Edward Bouverie Pusey, thrust the locus of authority away from the state to the supernaturally ordered visible independent Church. The attempt by the government to abolish a number of Irish bishoprics was seen as virtually equivalent to an attack on God himself. As Newman wrote to a friend in 1833: 'The King . . . has literally betrayed us . . . Our first duty is the defence of the Church. We have stood by Monarchy and Authority till they have refused

---

55 On this, see Rowan Strong, *Anglicanism and the British Empire, c. 1700–1850*, Oxford: Oxford University Press, 2007; W. M. Jacob, *The Making of the Anglican Church Worldwide*, London: SPCK, 1997.

56 Peter Doll, *Revolution, Religion and National Identity*, Madison, WI: Farleigh Dickinson, 2000.

to stand by themselves.'[57] The reason for this was straightforward: the visible order of the Church was itself constituted by God and persisted even in the contemporary Church. Where earlier generations of Anglicans had seen the visible structures of the Church as 'matters indifferent', the novelty of the Oxford Movement was to see the structures as of the very essence of the Church.[58] The authority of bishops came directly from the apostles themselves – and no other authority had the same claim. Thus Newman asked in the very first Tract:[59]

> Should the government and country so far forget their God as to cast off the church, to deprive it of its temporal honours and substance, on what will you rest the claim of respect and attention which you make upon your flocks? ... I fear we have neglected the real ground on which our authority is built ... our apostolical descent ... The Lord JESUS CHRIST gave His Spirit to His Apostles; they in turn laid their hands on those who would succeed them; and these again on others ... Exalt our Holy Fathers the Bishops, as the Representatives of the Apostles, and the Angels of the Churches; and magnify your office, as being ordained by them to take part in their ministry.

On such a theory the Church was quite independent of the state and had an authority which no prince could match. The ministry of the Church embodied in the 'representatives of the apostles', became the only real authority in the Church. 'Temporal catholicity' – the identification of the contemporary Church with the Church of the fathers – was stressed in a manner not dissimilar to Jewel, but with the embodiment of that early Church itself in the ministry of the visible Church (rather than just in the dead documents of the tradition).

The discussion of the Church in the latter part of the nineteenth century resembles that of the earlier period but with a crucial difference: the prince's divine right was removed. The independent authority of the Church thereby became increasingly important. This can be illustrated by debates between Charles Gore, the leader of the more liberal school of Anglo-Catholics, and the New Testament scholars, Edwin Hatch and J. B. Lightfoot. In his celebrated dissertation on the ministry appended to his commentary on the Epistle to the Philippians,[60] Lightfoot claimed that any church order was simply a means to an end rather than an end in itself. Orders were 'aids and expedients', which 'a Christian could not afford to hold lightly or to neglect. But they were no part of the essence of God's message to man in the Gospel.'[61] In distinction, Gore affirmed the necessity of the means: 'Christ has instituted a Kingdom of means, a visible channel for His covenanted gifts of grace ... Christianity is as much the establishment of a visible system of means for realizing the end of human life,

---

57 Newman to R. F. Wilson, 8 September 1833, in *The Letters and Diaries of John Henry Newman*, Oxford: Clarendon Press, 1980, vol. 4, p. 44.
58 Peter Nockles, *The Oxford Movement in Context*, Cambridge: Cambridge University Press, 1994, Chapter 3.
59 John Henry Newman, *Thoughts on the Ministerial Commission, respectfully addressed to the Clergy*, London: Rivington, 1833.
60 *Philippians* (1865), sixth edition, London: Macmillan, 1881.
61 *Philippians*, p. 184.

as it is the divine announcement of what that end is.'[62] For Gore – and for most Anglo-Catholics – the Church was a matter of acceptance and submission to 'a visible society as the one divinely constituted home of the great salvation, held together not only by the inward spirit but also by certain manifest and external institutions'.[63]

F. D. Maurice

At much the same time as the Oxford Movement an alternative and extremely influential expression of Anglican ecclesiology emerged in the thought of F. D. Maurice (1805–72). Where Anglo-Catholics upheld the Church as a divinely constituted sacred society with its own structures of authority separate from the larger society, Maurice regarded the Church as coterminous with the world, pointing it to its true goals. It was thus part of the natural constitution of humankind rather than simply a supernatural body. Consequently, Maurice wrote: 'Of your relation to this Church you cannot rid yourselves, any more than you can change the law under which your natural bodies and the members of them exist.'[64] Similarly, in a famous passage, Maurice wrote:

> The world contains the elements of which the Church is composed. In the Church, these elements are penetrated by a uniting, reconciling power. The Church is, therefore, human society in its normal state; the World, that same society irregular and abnormal. The world is the Church without God; the Church is the world restored to its relation with God, taken back by him into the state for which he created it.[65]

Maurice's conception of the Church was of something akin to the family and the nation, but expressing the most universal expression of the filial and fraternal principles which were found only in part in these other social forms: the Church was 'that spiritual constitution of which the nation and the family are the lower and subordinate parts'.[66]

The Church, Maurice claimed, was 'the witness for the true constitution of man as man, a child of God, an heir of heaven'.[67] Instead of original sin, Maurice claimed an original unity rooted in the unity of the Triune God: 'unity among men rests upon a yet more powerful and perfect unity'.[68]

---

62 *The Church and the Ministry* (1888), third edition, London: Longmans, 1893, p. 355.
63 *Catholicism and Roman Catholicism*, London: Mowbray, 1923, p. 1.
64 F. D. Maurice, *Lincoln's Inn Sermons*, London: Longmans, 1891, 6 vols, V, p. 241.
65 F. D. Maurice, *Theological Essays* (1853), London: James Clarke, 1957, p. 403.
66 Frederick Maurice, *Life of Frederick Denison Maurice*, London: Macmillan, 1885, 2 vols, I, pp. 306–7.
67 *Life*, I, p. 166.
68 F. D. Maurice, *The Kingdom of Christ or Hints on the Principles, Ordinances and Constitution of the Catholic Church. In Letters to a Member of the Society of Friends* (first edition, 1837–8), new edition based on second edition of 1842, Cambridge: James Clarke, 1958, 2 vols, I, p. 279.

The idea of the unity of the Father and the Son in the Holy Spirit, as the basis of all unity amongst men, as the groundwork of all human society and of all thought, as belonging to little children, and as the highest fruition of the saints in glory, has been haunting me for a longer time than I can easily look back to.[69]

Since all people found their identity under a common Father, they were ultimately members of the Church: it was the Church's duty to educate them in this knowledge. The Church existed to provide an integrating centre for all people against the tendencies to fragmentation in the modern world:

> The Universal Church, constituted in its Universal Head, exists to protest against a world which supposes itself to be a collection of incoherent fragments without a centre, which, where it reduces its practice to a maxim, treats every man as his own centre. The Church exists to tell the world of its true Centre, of the law of mutual sacrifice by which its parts are bound together. The Church exists to maintain the order of the nation and the order of the family, which this selfish practice and selfish maxim are constantly threatening.[70]

Maurice here stands in continuity with the earlier stress on decency and good order which had characterized so much of the ecclesiological thought after the Reformation.

In *The Kingdom of Christ* Maurice outlines the different 'Signs of a Spiritual Society', which characterized the Church, and which were rooted in 'the idea of a Church Universal, not built upon human inventions or human faith, but upon the very nature of God Himself'.[71] The sign of baptism, for instance, was about interpreting human existence under the headship of Christ, about telling ourselves 'that I am God's child, and may live as if I were'.[72] Baptism was the sign of permanent communion with the Father: it aimed at drawing a man

> continually out of himself, to teach him to disclaim all independent virtue, to bring him into the knowledge and image of the Father and the Son ... The sin of a baptized man consists in acting as if he were not in union with Christ, in setting up his own nature and his own will, and in obeying them.[73]

Baptism is thus about drawing a person from a life lived in partiality and self-reliance to a life lived in reliance on God. It involved incorporation into a society rather than merely individual regeneration. Similarly, the Creeds affirmed that all members of the Church are part of God's family and are united to him. By the act of saying the Creed, Maurice affirmed, 'we claim our spiritual position, we assert our union with that Being. The name into which we are adopted

---

69 *Kingdom of Christ*, I, p. 414.
70 *Lincoln's Inn Sermons*, I, p. 251.
71 *Kingdom of Christ*, II, p. 363.
72 *Life*, II, p. 242.
73 *Kingdom of Christ*, I, p. 284.

[in baptism], is the name we confess here.'[74] It was wrong to consider the Creed as a digest of doctrines; instead of a 'certain scheme of divinity' it affirmed the name of the Triune God.

A further sign was common prayer, which functioned to ensure there is no selfishness in prayer and that true fellowship is expressed:

> If the meaning of baptism be that we are brought into God's family, and that we become therefore capable, with one mind and one mouth, of glorifying his name; if the Creed be teaching us, as children of that one family, severally and unitedly to acknowledge that name, and how it is related to us; we must feel that acts of worship should be, of all acts, those which most belong to our position, and in which our fellowship is most entirely realized.[75]

Corporate prayer served the purpose of drawing 'us out of the individuality which is our curse and ruin' and leading us 'one and all, to take up our position on the same ground of being justified and redeemed in Christ'.[76] Similarly, the Eucharist served as a living and perpetual communion with God, who was present with his universal family. It transcended divisions, becoming the great wedding feast to celebrate the union of the Son of God with the human race. The Eucharist is a sign of unity and of the pledge that Christ offers to us: it 'keeps doctrines from perpetual clashing with each other', drawing us from 'narrow notions and dividing tendencies'.[77]

Maurice claimed that the Church's ministry offered a sign of continuity and order: the Church was neither a crowd nor an anarchy but required a structure. The episcopate was important as a symbol of unity; bishops were 'Fathers in God', who had the 'character of the great flying eagle, overseeing all things – diffusing itself everywhere'.[78] Nevertheless, Maurice did not locate this concept of oversight solely in the doctrine of the apostolic succession. Unlike the Tractarians, Maurice refused to unchurch those churches without the episcopate and left the exact delineation of the extent of the Church to God. Finally, these other signs were all rooted in the Bible, which served as the source of all unity.

Maurice's vision of unity led him to oppose what he called 'systems' or anything that limited truth within its own boundaries: he was deeply opposed to the barriers erected by church parties as well as any form of sectarianism. The sect he defined as something which claims a totality and a unity, but which is not identical to a greater whole; it acts as a world unto itself rather than being identical with the wider world. He detected sectarian tendencies at work in the Church of England: Evangelicalism, he claimed, had become little more than a propaganda agency which existed to attack other parties.[79] The Catholic Party, on the other hand, consisted of 'men who live in closets, and keep lonely

---

74 *Kingdom of Christ*, II, p. 20.
75 *Kingdom of Christ*, II, p. 36.
76 *Kingdom of Christ*, II, p. 231.
77 *Kingdom of Christ*, II, p. 69.
78 *Kingdom of Christ*, II, p. 289.
79 *Reasons for not Joining a Party in the Church*, London: Rivington, 1841, p. 19.

vigils'.[80] Against such sectarianism, the most important feature of the Church of England was its universality and its sense of unity:

> Our church has no right to call herself better than other churches in any respect, in many she must acknowledge herself to be worse. But our position, we may fairly affirm, for it is not a boast but a confession, is one of singular advantage.... Our faith is not formed by a union of Protestant systems with the Romish system, nor of certain elements taken from the one and of certain elements taken from the others. So far as it is represented in our liturgy and our articles, it is the faith of a church and has nothing to do with any system at all. That peculiar character which God had given us, enables us, if we do not slight the mercy, to understand the difference between a church and a system better perhaps than any of our neighbours can, and, therefore, our position, rightly used, gives us a power of assisting them in realizing the blessings of their own.[81]

The nation and the family could function in a similar way to the sect, since by their very nature they were exclusive and limited.[82] In Christ, however, the universal made contact with the human world in the figure of the God–man, which meant that Jesus became the invisible head of all nations and all families. The sectarian tendencies of the world, which were based on the 'natural tendencies and inclinations of men',[83] were thereby relativized by the principle of union founded on Christ. Christ became both the goal and the centre, which limited the claims of all visible churches and institutions.

Ecclesiology after Maurice

Similar themes continued into the twentieth century: in his contribution to the collection, *Foundations*, for instance, William Temple emphasized that apostolic unity was not dependent on the structures of the visible Church, but on the proclamation of the life, death and resurrection of Christ,[84] who 'is the whole life of the Church ... Our function is to receive life from him, and express his one truth, realize his one purpose, according to our capacities.'[85] Visible unity sacramentally represented the unity of Christ. This did not imply uniformity, but was what Temple called a 'socialist' unity, 'where the single life of the whole absolutely depends on the diversity of the parts alike in form and function'.[86] Unity depended on a shared faith, which implied that shared order was 'not

---

80 *Reasons for not Joining a Party*, p. 21.
81 *Kingdom of Christ*, II, p. 343.
82 *Kingdom of Christ*, I, p. 244.
83 *Kingdom of Christ*, I, p. 258.
84 'The Church', in B. H. Streeter (ed.), *Foundations: A Statement of Christian Belief in Terms of Modern Thought*, London: Macmillan, 1912, p. 343.
85 'The Church', p. 343.
86 'The Church', p. 349.

essential at all'.[87] The vision of the ultimate truth, the true Church, served to relativize all partial attempts to give voice to this truth:

> The Church only exists perfectly when all its members are utterly surrendered to Christ and united to him . . . The true church is still coming slowly into historic existence; that process is the meaning of history from the incarnation onwards; it consists both in the drawing of men and nations into the fellowship of the Holy Spirit, and in the completion of his work upon them in perfecting their surrender to Christ and their union with him.[88]

For Temple, the Church was not based on any visible expression in the unity of the episcopate, but was focused on something higher.

In *The Gospel and the Catholic Church*, Michael Ramsey develops a similar understanding. It was wrong, he claimed, to see the episcopate as bearing the whole weight of the unity of the Church: the first fact ought instead to be the 'Church's corporate family life'.[89] While elevating episcopacy to the essence of the Church,[90] he nevertheless emphasizes the role of the Anglican Church in the worldwide fellowship of churches as that of pointing to the provisionality and fragmentary character of any visible church. He identifies this provisionality with catholicism itself, as the

> means of deliverance into the Gospel of God and the timeless Church . . . For it frees [the thoughtful Christian] from partial rationalisms . . . and it delivers him into an orthodoxy which no individual and no group can possess . . . Hither alone the church shall point; and here men shall know the Truth and the Truth shall make them free.

Since all churches pointed forwards, no church could ever be complete:

> As he receives the Catholic Sacrament and recites the Catholic creed, the Christian is learning that no single movement nor partial experience within Christendom can claim his final obedience, and that a local Church can claim his loyalty only by leading him beyond itself to the universal family which it represents.[91]

The most important credentials of the Anglican Church were 'its incompleteness, with the tension and the travail in its soul. It is clumsy and untidy, it baffles neatness and logic.'[92] It was not a 'vague position wherein Evangelical and Catholic are alternatives', but instead was 'founded on the Scriptural faith wherein both elements are one'. Within this church, bishops served not as mediators between the different schools, 'but, without any consciousness of party', were 'the servants

---

87 In 1913, Temple wrote to Ronald Knox: 'I don't believe in the ideal of a Church with sharply defined boundaries'. Cited in F. A. Iremonger, *William Temple*, London: Oxford University Press, 1948, p. 162.
88 *Christus Veritas*, London: Macmillan, 1924, pp. 167–8.
89 *The Gospel and the Catholic Church*, London: Longmans, 1936, p. 152.
90 *Gospel and the Catholic Church*, p. 84.
91 *Gospel and the Catholic Church*, p. 135.
92 *Gospel and the Catholic Church*, p. 220.

of the Gospel of God and of the universal Church'.[93] The ecumenical vocation of Anglicanism was thus to prepare 'the way for reunion not by indifference to the historic order, but by restoring a truer presentation of it in the context of the Gospel and of the universal Church. It does this as it preaches the Gospel.'[94] There could be no infallible authority of any kind, and neither could the usages of one little bit of Christendom be necessarily right.

What emerges is an understanding of the Church as something humble and provisional ever hoping to express something of the gospel of Christ, always looking for its authority from beyond history, but at the same time it was forced to compromise with time and place. The Church is always one, because Christ is one, and yet, it is diverse and manifold, because it is always historical. The oneness of the gospel of Christ, so clearly recognized by Ramsey, stands over and against any visible church. As he put it graphically, 'Catholicism always stands before the Church door at Wittenberg to read the truth by which she is created and by which she is to be judged.'[95]

William Reed Huntington

Even though he was aware of the missionary situation, Maurice's concerns were limited mainly to the Church of England: he was still guided by a vision of the unity between Church and world, in many ways adapting the Hookerian model to the nineteenth century. However, Maurice's theology proved influential on one of the most formative theologians on the development of the theology of the Anglican Communion, William Reed Huntington (1838–1909). Huntington worked in a very different context: he was engaged in promoting unity after the enormous social divisions of the American Civil War. In his *The Church-Idea: An Essay Towards Unity*, he spoke against systems, promoting what he called the 'Anglican principle'.

The Anglican principle, he felt, should move the Church beyond any tendency to sectarianism or provincialism by pointing towards a universality. Like Maurice, he too moved through the different stages of family and nation towards the Church. He used the analogy of a 'quadrilateral' derived from the four great fortress cities of Mantua, Verona, Peschiera and Legnano, which had become famous during the Austro-Prussian War of 1866. Thus he asked: 'What are the essential, the absolutely essential features of the Anglican position?' It had to be more than a vague recollection of 'village spires and cathedral towers' and was understood as offering the possibility of 'America's best hope'.[96] It could be summarized under four simple headings:

1 The Holy Scriptures as the Word of God.
2 The Primitive Creeds as the Rule of Faith.

---

93 *Gospel and the Catholic Church*, p. 209.
94 *Gospel and the Catholic Church*, p. 219.
95 *Gospel and the Catholic Church*, p. 180.
96 William Reed Huntington, *The Church-Idea: An Essay Towards Unity*, New York: E. P. Dutton, 1870, fourth edition, Charles Scribner's Sons, 1899, p. 124.

3 The two Sacraments ordained by Christ himself.
4 The Episcopate as the key-stone of Governmental Unity.[97]

In a manner highly reminiscent of Maurice, Huntington sees the Church as an agent of reconciliation founded on four points. In *The Church-Idea* the first three provide a straightforward description of a kind of 'temporal' catholicism, while the fourth stresses the visible unity of the Church founded on the episcopate. Huntington sought to move the Episcopal Church onto a higher level: its denominational identity was to be found not in a vague recollection of Englishness but in the identity of the Catholic Church itself. Even if it might not become the sole national church, it could at least aspire to this ideal. Towards the end of the book he spoke of the problems of becoming little more than a respectable sect denying all claim to catholicity. Instead, he held:

> If we aim at something nobler than this, if we would have our Communion become national in very truth, . . . then let us press our reasonable claims to be the reconciler of a divided household, not in a spirit of arrogance (which ill befits those whose best possessions have come to them by inheritance), but with affectionate earnestness and an intelligent zeal.[98]

Huntington's four points were taken as constitutive of the identity of Anglicanism at the General Convention held at Chicago in 1886: the aim was to promote national unity and reconciliation. However, what was also inserted was the modest word, 'historic' before episcopate, which emphasized the doctrine of apostolic succession: when applied solely to the American Church, however, this simply stressed the temporal nature of catholicity, which was rooted in the tradition handed down from the apostles and guarded by the episcopate in the present day. There was, however, little sense of spatial catholicity contained in the quadrilateral: the point of the quadrilateral was to promote a kind of Maurician national church which the scattered denominations might be invited to join. The episcopate was seen as the best way of representing this unity.

The Anglican Principle was effectively the principle of the national unified church for all people. This is clear from the broader resolution adopted at Chicago, which was addressed 'especially to our fellow-Christians of the different Communions in this land, who, in their several spheres, have contended for the religion of Christ'. The entry requirement into the church was simply baptism, while in 'all things of human ordering or human choice, relating to modes of worship and discipline or to traditional customs, this Church is ready in the spirit of love and humility to forego all preferences of her own'. Unity was to be established by a return to the undivided Church of the past:

> But furthermore, we do hereby affirm that the Christian unity can be restored only by the return of all Christian communions to the principles of unity exemplified by the undivided Catholic Church during the first ages of its existence; which principles we believe to be the substantial deposit of Christian Faith and Order committed by Christ and his Apostles to the Church unto the end of the

---

97 *Church-Idea*, pp. 125–6.
98 *Church-Idea*, p. 169.

world, and therefore incapable of compromise or surrender by those who have been ordained to be its stewards and trustees for the common and equal benefit of all men. As inherent parts of this sacred deposit, and therefore as essential to the restoration of unity among the divided branches of Christendom, we account the following, to wit:

1. The Holy Scriptures of the Old and New Testaments as the revealed Word of God.
2. The Nicene Creed as the sufficient statement of the Christian Faith.
3. The two Sacraments – Baptism and the Supper of the Lord – ministered with unfailing use of Christ's words of institution and of the elements ordained by Him.
4. The Historic Episcopate, locally adapted in the methods of its administration to the varying needs of the nations and peoples called of God into the unity of His Church.

Furthermore, Deeply grieved by the sad divisions which affect the Christian Church in our own land, we hereby declare our desire and readiness, so soon as there shall be any authorized response to this Declaration, to enter into brotherly conference with all or any Christian Bodies seeking the restoration of the organic unity of the Church, with a view to the earnest study of the conditions under which so priceless a blessing might happily be brought to pass.[99]

The Chicago Quadrilateral was aimed principally at reconciliation at home and as an invitation to other denominations to unite, rather than as a mechanism for defining the international Anglican principle.

The Anglican Communion

The rise of the different national churches in different parts of the world created a new set of problems, not least of which was to find a means of adjudicating between churches, when they fell out with one another. Given that the Church of England was established on the basis of complete internal sovereignty, this proved a particularly complex problem for Anglicanism. Indeed the problem of 'spatial' or transnational catholicity has been a constant theme in Anglican ecclesiological discussion since the mid nineteenth century. The Lambeth Conference was summoned by Archbishop Charles Longley in 1867, partly in response to a number of calls, primarily from Canada and New Zealand, to work out how the newly independent churches were to be regulated. Although there was a clamour for firm leadership and strong decision-making powers, what emerged was quite the opposite. Longley and his successors through the early Conferences resisted centralization[100] – they were unsure of their authority to legislate

---

99 *The Anglican Tradition: A Handbook of Sources*, G. R. Evans and J. Robert Wright (eds), London: SPCK, 1991, pp. 345–6.

100 Alan M. G. Stephenson, *The First Lambeth Conference: 1867*, London: SPCK, 1967; Mark D. Chapman, 'Where is it all going? A plea for humility?', in Kenneth Stevenson (ed.), *A Fallible Church*, London: Darton, Longman Todd, 2008, pp. 122–41.

outside their provinces. While resolutions were issued by the assembled bishops, they had no legal authority unless the constituent churches decided to accept them. However, through much of the nineteenth and twentieth centuries the 'bonds of affection' between the churches survived through imperial and colonial links, and there were still enough connections for a strong set of family resemblances. The Anglican Communion was often characterized by a vague sense of Englishness (and to a lesser extent Americanness). English forms of worship and English hymn books continued (and continue) to be used. But this could hardly be said to be an ecclesiology – as Huntington recognized, Anglicanism had to be more than a 'flutter of surplices'.

The pressing question was what sort of unity a church established on the basis of national independence could adopt at a transnational level. Archbishop E. W. Benson (1829–96) maintained that the unity displayed by the Church did not imply uniformity (which, he held, was the failing of what he called 'Roman Unity').[101] Instead, he held, all unity had to be sensitive to its cultural setting:

> If we wish to prepare a future for our people and our children, we must make provision for an active, realized unity in the Church. . . . But we must avoid a common fancy. We cannot recur to the past for unity. External unity has not existed yet, except superficially. Unity is not the first scene, but the last triumph of Christianity and man. Christ himself could not create unity in His Church. He could pray for it, and his prayer most movingly teaches us to work for it. On earth it is not a gift, but a growth. If any vision of it is granted us we must work both in and towards what we have seen that 'although it tarry, it may be for an appointed time,' but rather still that 'it may come and not tarry'.[102]

The unity of the Church, according to Benson, could thus never be a completely undifferentiated unity imposed from above, but had to respond to local circumstances. A failure to be responsive to the cultural conditions and

> to seek to build up a like Church, stone by stone as it were, spiritually, out of the utterly different characters, experiences, sentiments of another race, is to repeat without excuse the error of the great Boniface, in making not a Teutonic but an Italian Church in Germany. It is to contradict the wise axioms with which Gregory tried to save Augustine from the error.[103]

The crucial question for the Anglican Communion was over precisely how it could function as a catholic church without adopting the alternative model of a centrally imposed uniformity. Benson, like Maurice before him, was clear that true unity resided with God and was always a hope rather than a fact.

The question of unity was addressed at the 1888 Lambeth Conference over which Benson presided. The bishops adopted a slightly more modest version

---

101 'Growing Unity', in Edward White Benson, *Living Theology*, London: Sampson Low, Marston, 1893, pp. 131–45, here p. 139.
102 'Growing Unity', p. 133.
103 Visitation Charge of 1885, in *Life*, II, pp. 465–6.

of the Chicago Quadrilateral as the basis 'on which approach may be by God's blessing made towards Home Reunion'. A crucial difference, however, was that instead of simply seeing the four points as inherent parts of the deposit of faith and order, the Lambeth Resolution regarded the four points as 'articles', presumably akin to the Thirty-Nine Articles and therefore as constitutive of both Anglicanism and the Christian faith.[104] The Anglican principle became less of a clamour for reconciliation and more a description of the visible Church. For the first time an international definition of what constituted Anglicanism was given. Furthermore, the basis in Home Reunion was soon forgotten. Thus, instead of serving the project of ecumenical reconciliation and as an invitation to move beyond denomination through applying what was effectively a temporal criterion for catholicity, the Lambeth Quadrilateral[105] served the opposite purpose of creating a definition of worldwide Anglicanism as a particular denomination. Given that most other Protestant denominations would have had little difficulty with the first three articles, this meant that the distinctive identity of Anglicanism was primarily located in 'The Historic Episcopate, locally adapted in the methods of its administration to the varying needs of the nations and peoples called of God into the Unity of His Church'.

Following the adoption of the Lambeth Quadrilateral the episcopate became central to Anglican identity: the Anglo-Catholic theology of the apostolic succession – which is how 'historic episcopate' has been understood[106] – was elevated into an article of faith and as the key identifying feature of authentic reconciled Christianity. This was noted by William Perry, Bishop of Iowa:

> Our longings for union must not lead us to the surrender of the great trust committed to us as an integral part of the Church Catholic of CHRIST. Concessions involving disloyalty to revealed truths, to Apostolic practice, and to primitive belief, are out of the question. It is not to be expected that the great and overwhelming majority of Christians now living on the earth should abandon the form of Church government which has been theirs 'from the Apostles' time,' and which they believe to be jure divino, with a view of comprehending in their Communion a few most excellent and devoted Christian bodies or individuals who practically recognize no visible Church, who deny the existence of the threefold ministry, who refuse to admit the claims of the Historic Episcopate, and who will not concede the grace of Holy Orders. Thus abandoning the Church's vantage ground, we might, indeed, add to our numbers a small gain, but we should lose the greater possibilities which may

---

104 Gillian R. Evans, 'Permanence in the Revealed Truth and Continuous Exploration of its Meaning', in J. Robert Wright (ed.), *Quadrilateral at One Hundred*, London: Mowbray, 1998, pp. 111–25, esp. pp. 114–15.

105 Resolution 11 of the Lambeth Conference of 1888. Cf. Roger Coleman, *Resolutions of the Twelve Lambeth Conferences*, Toronto: Anglican Book Centre, 1992, p. 13; Alan M. G. Stephenson, *Anglicanism and The Lambeth Conferences*, London: SPCK, 1978. Cf. Jonathan Draper (ed.), *Communion and Episcopacy: Essays to Mark the Centenary of the Chicago–Lambeth Quadrilateral*, Oxford: Ripon College Cuddesdon, 1988.

106 See William Croswell Doane, 'The Historic Episcopate', *The Church Review* 59 (1890), pp. 158–64; William Stevens Perry, 'Church Reunion Discussed on the Basis of the Lambeth Propositions of 1888', *The Church Review* 59 (1890), pp. 165–73.

GOD, in His good time, enable us to realize in the reunion of Christendom, the bringing together of all Christian men and peoples in the unity of God's Church.[107]

Episcopacy, which was regarded by most earlier Anglicans as the best means of ensuring good order, but not as an absolutely necessary feature of a true church, was elevated into the criterion for catholic identity. While the Lambeth Conference may not ever have been able to claim legal authority, the fact that its bishops have been invested with a supernatural authority means that it has taken on a quasi-conciliar structure and has sometimes been seen to be teaching 'authoritatively' rather than simply acting as an advisory body.

The Quadrilateral has continued to function as one of the few standards of Anglican identity. In the famous Lambeth 'Appeal to All Christian People' of 1920, the fourth article was adopted as a principle for reunion on the basis of 'a ministry acknowledged by every part of the Church as possessing not only the inward call of the Spirit but also the commission of Christ and the authority of the whole body'.[108] Similarly, the Committee on the Unity of the Church, which was set up in response to various proposals for reunion of the churches, particular those of South India, reported to the 1930 Lambeth Conference that the episcopate 'occupies a position which is, in point of historical development, analogous to that of the canons of scripture and the creeds. . . . The Historic Episcopate as we understand it goes behind the perversions of history to the original conception of the apostolic ministry.'[109] Since then most attempts at reunion have foundered over the question of episcopacy. A good example is the Meissen Agreement of 1988 between the British Anglican churches and the Evangelical Church of Germany (EKD) – while there is a mutual recognition that both are true churches, there is nevertheless a refusal to allow an interchangeability of ministries on the grounds that the German churches lack 'the historic episcopate'.[110]

Contemporary Issues

Problems of ecclesiology continue to present huge problems for the Anglican Communion. Relations between the different churches, as the well as the issue of transnational authority, have led to much theological reflection.[111] There are many complex reasons behind this focus on ecclesiology: among them one might include the end of colonialism and the reaction to the church planted by the

---

107 Perry, 'Church Reunion Discussed', p. 173.

108 Lambeth Conference 1920, 'Appeal to All Christian People', cited in Wright, 'Heritage and Vision', in *Quadrilateral at One Hundred*, pp. 8–45, p. 26.

109 *The Lambeth Conference Report 1930*, London: SPCK, 1930, p. 115. Cf. Resolution 9 of the 1920 Conference: 'An Appeal to All Christian People', in Coleman, *Resolutions*, pp. 45–48, esp. §7: 'we would urge that [the episcopate] is now and will prove to be in the future the best instrument for maintaining the unity and continuity of the Church'.

110 *The Meissen Agreement Texts* § 16. See also Henry Chadwick, 'The Quadrilateral in England', in Wright, *Quadrilateral at One Hundred*, p. 149.

111 See esp. James M. Rosenthal and Nicola Currie, *Being Anglican in the Third Millennium*, Harrisburg, PA: Morehouse, 1997.

former colonizers; the decline of the relative numerical strength of Anglicanism in the developed world; and the indigenization of leadership and its connections to other systems of authority. All of these mean that the different 'contained catholic' churches have developed separately and in sometimes contradictory ways. Without a firm central authority it is sometimes difficult to see precisely what binds Anglican churches together: no longer can they rely for their identity on being against Roman Catholicism (or Puritanism) as in the early days of the independent Church of England. They might still be 'temporally catholic' in the sense that they see themselves in continuity with the Church of the fathers and as guided by Scripture, but it is far more difficult to locate spatial continuity with other 'Anglican' churches, which might appear very different. The old liturgical and doctrinal identities have gradually been eroded through contextualization and adaptation.

It is consequently easy to see Anglicanism as little more than a collection of 'contained catholic' churches, each relating primarily to their own contexts – from Nigeria to Mexico and from Singapore to New Zealand. But it is not so easy to speak of the Anglican Communion as a church. The question that has emerged since the first Lambeth Conference is precisely what sort of wider catholicity can regulate the 'contained catholic churches'. This has become especially pressing after the controversies following the 1998 Lambeth Conference. If the Anglican Communion is itself a type of catholic church, then what does that catholicity look like? How can a collection of 'contained catholic' (if that is what Anglican means outside England) churches be held together in a catholic network, that is, in an Anglican Church worldwide? A variety of answers to these questions is currently being sought in different places. It is possible that the Anglican Communion and its constituent churches may well locate their identity in something other than the Anglican principle of national autonomy. Disaffected groups may well find authentic Anglicanism beyond the confines of their national church. At present, different models of Anglican identity are being sought which would offer a far more rigid form of identity, but which may well destroy the idea of a national church altogether. It is too soon to know whether voluntary commitment to a Covenant will be enough to prevent serious schism. Anglicanism, it seems, is mutating and dismembering.

Introduction to the Sources

These selections present a representative overview of Anglican writings on the nature and authority of the Church. Selection 1, from Bishop Jewel's *Apology*, was first written in Latin in 1562 and rapidly translated into English. In James I's time it became an official statement of Anglican doctrine. As Bishop-elect of Salisbury, Jewel, who had spent much of the Marian years in exile in Strasbourg and Zurich with the Reformer Peter Martyr Vermigli, preached a famous sermon at Paul's Cross, on 26 November 1559. Here he put forward the challenge to his Roman Catholic opponents: 'to bring any one sufficient sentence out of old Catholicke Doctor, or Father; or out of any old Generell Councell; Or out of the Holy Scriptures of God'[112] to prove that the Church of England had erred.

---

112 *Jewel*, I, p. 20.

This challenge was taken up by Henry Cole, Mary's Dean of St Paul's. The letters that were exchanged between the two men provide the background for the *Apologia*. Jewel's method is that of vigorous apologetic. His principal aim is to prove the truth of the Church of England on the basis of Scripture and the Fathers of the Early Church. In turn, the independent authority of the Church of England in matters that do not affect eternal salvation is justified on the basis of the need for decency and good order in the Church and nation.

The second selection illustrates apologetics conducted against the other extreme between which the Church of England steered its course. It comes from John Whitgift, Master of Trinity College, Cambridge, who went on to become Archbishop of Canterbury. Where Jewel had engaged with Roman Catholics, Whitgift, a man of strong Protestant sympathies, tackled those who defended the Presbyterian system of Church government. His sparring partner was Thomas Cartwright, who was appointed to the Lady Margaret Chair in Cambridge in 1569. His inaugural lectures on the early chapters of the Acts of the Apostles sought to prove a Presbyterian constitution for the Church. This challenged the episcopally structured Church of England. Deprived in 1570 Cartwright returned in 1572 to enter the Admonition controversy provoked by a list of complaints presented to Parliament about 'popish abuses' in the Church. Whitgift was entrusted with the task of replying to the Admonition as well as a second Admonition written shortly afterwards by Cartwright. Whitgift's responses were published in November 1572 with an expanded edition in February 1573. The debate continued with Cartwright writing a *Replye to an Answere of Dr Whitgifte* and Whitgift a counterblast in 1574. Whitgift shared much with Cartwright – his works make extensive use of the Continental Reformers, especially Calvin and Zwingli. The crucial difference was in their understanding of the visible Church: where Cartwright regarded it as a body of the elect and as responsible for its own discipline and constitution, Whitgift held it to be composed of both saints and sinners and therefore in need of external discipline. Since the Bible provided no blueprint for ecclesiastical discipline, the civil powers became central in the organization of the Church. This theme was later taken up by Richard Hooker in his magisterial writing on similar themes in the *Laws of Ecclesiastical Polity*.

The third selection develops this theme in the shape of the seventeenth-century polemics between a Jesuit (A. C.) and William Laud, who became Archbishop of Canterbury. The origins of the selection lie in a series of conversations organized shortly after Laud had been appointed to the see of St David's in 1621. The context was the conversion of the mother of the James I's favourite, George Villiers, Duke of Buckingham. After fears of the duke's conversion, the Conference between Laud and John Fisher, the Jesuit, took place on 24 May 1622. Although initially private, the Conference, together with various other responses to Fisher and other Catholics, was published in 1624. The passage selected emphasizes the importance of royal and parliamentary sovereignty over the Church, as well as a justification for 'provincial autonomy', whereby the Church reforms itself in the absence of any wider general council.

The fourth selection illustrates a changed understanding of the Church of England in response to the challenge to its authority in the 1820s and 1830s. Both the repeal of the *Test and Corporation Acts*, which prevented Non-conformists from holding public office, in 1828, and Catholic Emancipation a year later threatened the Anglican monopoly on power: in response, a group of young Oxford scholars under the leadership of John Keble and John Henry Newman published a series of Tracts from 1833, the first of which is included as the selection. It is a bold statement of the independent and supernatural authority of the Church. Bishops and their assistant clergy became the successors to the apostles and thus to Christ himself, which meant that they were unassailable. This high view of the ministry, quite distinct from that of Whitgift and other earlier writers, had enormous repercussions on the Anglican doctrine of the Church, particularly through the emphasis on holiness and seriousness which characterized the Anglo-Catholic revival.

The fifth selection comes from the American churchman, William Reed Huntington, Rector of All Saints' Church, Worcester, Massachusetts, and then of Grace Church, New York. In the *Church-Idea*, which was written in the aftermath of the American Civil War, he identified Anglicanism with the minimum requirements for a church to be catholic: this later led to the formulation of the so-called Chicago–Lambeth Quadrilateral. What is key in Huntington's thought is the desire for reconciliation and breadth: he felt that most churches would be able to join a national church on these principles. From Huntington's ecumenical statement emerged a definition of Anglicanism as a denomination, which has remained important until the present day.

The final selection is taken from Michael Ramsey's seminal work on ecclesiology, *The Gospel and the Catholic Church*, which was first published in January 1936, when he was a young lecturer at Lincoln Theological College. Deeply influenced by the theology of F. D. Maurice, Ramsey was aware of the ambiguities of Anglicanism, most especially its provisionality. While others felt this was a failing, he regarded it as its greatest strength, since it was forced to be humble, always subjecting itself to testing by the Gospel of Christ. The selection chosen comes from Chapter XIII, which emphasizes the importance of order and ministry, while at the same time showing how the different parties can be united in a broad church.

Sources

John Jewel, *An Apology, or Answer, in Defence of the Church of England with a Brief and Plain Declaration of the True Religion Professed and Used in the Same*, London, 1564, from *The Works of John Jewel, Bishop of Salisbury. The Third Portion*, edited for the Parker Society by the Rev. John Ayre, Cambridge, 1848, pp. 55–65, 85.

But we truly, seeing that so many thousands of our brethren in these last twenty years have borne witness unto the truth, in the midst of most painful torments that could be devised; and when princes, desirous to restrain the Gospel, sought many ways, but prevailed nothing; and that now almost the whole world doth begin to open their eyes to behold the light; we take it that our cause hath already been sufficiently declared and defended, and think it not needful to make many words, since the very matter saith enough for itself. For, if the popes would, or else if they could, weigh with their own selves the whole matter, and also the beginning and proceedings of our religion, how in a manner all their travail hath come to nought, nobody driving it forward; and how on the other side, our cause, against the will of emperors from the beginning, against the wills of so many kings, in spite of the popes, and almost maugre the head of all men, hath taken increase, and by little and little spread over into all countries, and is come at length even into kings' courts and palaces; these same things, methinketh, might be tokens great enough to them, that God Himself doth strongly fight in our quarrel, and doth from heaven laugh at their enterprises; and that the force of truth is such, as neither man's power, nor yet hell-gates are able to root it out. For they be not all mad at this day, so many free cities, so many kings, so many princes, which have fallen away from the seat of Rome, and have rather joined themselves to the Gospel of Christ.

And although the popes had never hitherunto leisure to consider diligently and earnestly of these matters, or though some other cares do now let them, and diverse ways pull them, or though they count these to be but common and trifling studies, and nothing to appertain to the Pope's worthiness, this maketh not why our matter ought to seem the worse. Or if they perchance will not see that which they see indeed, but rather will withstand the known truth, ought we therefore by-and-by to be accounted heretics because we obey not their will and pleasure? If so be, that Pope Pius were the man (we say not, which he would so gladly be called), but if he were indeed a man that either would account us for his brethren, or at least would take us to be men, he would first diligently have examined our reasons, and would have seen what might be said with us, what against us; and would not in his bull, whereby he lately pretended a council, so rashly have condemned so great a part of the world, so many learned and godly men, so many commonwealths, so many kings, and so many princes, only upon his own blind prejudices and fore-determinations, and that without hearing of them speak or without showing cause why.

But because he hath already so noted us openly, lest by holding our peace we should seem to grant a fault, and specially because we can by no means have audience in the public assembly of the general council, wherein he would no creature should have power to give his voice or to declare his opinion, except he be sworn, and straitly bound to maintain his authority (for we have had good experience hereof in the last conference at the council at Trident; where the ambassadors and divines of the princes of Germany, and of the free cities, were quite shut out from their company. Neither can we yet forget, how Julius the Third, above ten years past, provided warily by his writ that none of our sort should be suffered to speak in the council, except that there were some, peradventure, that would recant and change his opinion): for this cause chiefly we thought it good to yield up an account of our faith in writing, and truly and openly to make answer to those things wherewith we have been openly charged; to the end the world may see the parts and foundations of that doctrine, in the behalf whereof so many good men have little regarded their own lives; and that all men may understand what manner of people they be, and what opinion they have of God and of religion, whom the Bishop of Rome, before they were called to tell their tale, hath condemned for heretics, without any good consideration, without any example, and utterly without law or right, only because he heard tell that they did dissent from him and his in some point of religion.

And although St. Hierom would have nobody to be patient when he is suspected of heresy, yet we will deal herein neither bitterly nor brablingly; nor yet be carried away with anger and heat; though he ought to be reckoned neither bitter nor brabler that speaketh the truth. We willingly leave this kind of eloquence to our adversaries, who, whatsoever they say against us, be it never so shrewdly or despitefully said, yet think it is said modestly and comely enough, and care nothing whether it be true or false. We need none of these shifts which do maintain the truth.

Further, if we do show it plain that God's holy Gospel, the ancient bishops, and the primitive Church do make on our side, and that we have not without just cause left these men, and rather have returned to the Apostles and old Catholic fathers; and if we shall be found to do the same not colourably or craftily, but in good faith before God, truly, honestly, clearly, and plainly; and if they themselves which fly our doctrine, and would be called Catholics, shall manifestly see how all these titles of antiquity, whereof they boast so much, are quite shaken out of their hands; and that there is more pith in this our cause than they thought for; we then hope and trust that none of them will be so negligent and careless of his own salvation, but he will at length study and bethink himself to whether part he were best to join him. Undoubtedly, except one will altogether harden his heart and refuse to hear, he shall not repent him to give good heed to this our Defence, and to mark well what we say, and how truly and justly it agreeth with Christian religion. . . .

Wherefore, if we be heretics, and they (as they would fain be called) be Catholics, why do they not, as they see the fathers, which were Catholic men, have always done? Why do they not convince and master us by the Divine Scriptures? Why do they not call us again to be tried by them? Why do they not lay before us how we have gone away from Christ, from the Prophets, from the Apostles, and from the holy fathers? Why stick they to do it? Why are they afraid of it? It is God's cause. Why are they doubtful to commit it to the trial of God's word? If we be heretics, which refer all our controversies unto the Holy Scriptures, and report us to the self-same words which we know were sealed by God Himself, and in comparison of them set little by all other things, whatsoever may be devised by men, how shall we say to these folk, I pray you what manner of men be they, and how is it meet to call them, which fear the judgment of the holy scriptures, that is to say, the judgment of God Himself, and do prefer before them their own dreams and full cold inventions; and, to maintain their own traditions, have defaced and corrupted, now these many hundred years, the ordinances of Christ and of the Apostles? . . .

In like manner, because these men take us to be mad, and appeach us for heretics, as men which have nothing to do, neither with Christ, nor with the Church of God, we have judged it should be to good purpose, and not unprofitable, if we do openly and frankly set forth our faith wherein we stand, and show all that confidence which we have in Christ Jesu; to the intent all men may see what is our judgment of every part of Christian religion, and may resolve with themselves, whether the faith which they shall see confirmed by the words of Christ, by the writings of the Apostles, by the testimonies of the Catholic fathers, and by the examples of many ages, be but a certain rage of furious and mad men, and a conspiracy of heretics. This therefore is our belief.

As touching the multitude of vain and superfluous ceremonies, we know that Augustine did grievously complain of them in his own time: and therefore have we cut off a great number of them, because we know that men's consciences were cumbered about them, and the churches of God overladen with them. Nevertheless we keep still, and esteem, not only those ceremonies which we are sure were delivered us from the Apostles, but some others too besides, which we thought might be suffered without hurt to the Church of God: because that we had a desire that all things in the holy congregation might (as St. Paul commandeth) 'be done with comeliness and in good order'; but, as for all those things which we saw were either very superstitious, or unprofitable, or noisome, or mockeries, or contrary to the holy scriptures, or else unseemly for honest or discreet folks, as there be an infinite number nowadays where papistry is used; these, I say, we have utterly refused without all manner exception, because we would not have the right worshipping of God any longer denied with such follies. . . .

Paul likewise, though the Gospel of Jesus Christ be of many counted to be but new, yet hath it (saith he) the testimony most old both of the law and Prophets. As for our doctrine which we may rightly call Christ's catholic doctrine, it is so far off from new that God, who is above all most ancient, and the Father of our Lord Jesus Christ, hath left the same unto us in the Gospel, in the Prophets' and Apostles' works, being monuments of greatest age. So that no man can now think our doctrine to be new, unless the same think either the Prophets' faith, or the Gospel, or else Christ Himself to be new.

And as for their religion, if it be of so long continuance as they would have men ween it is, why do they not prove it so by the examples of the primitive Church, and by the fathers and councils of old times? Why lieth so ancient a cause thus long in the dust destitute of an advocate? Fire and sword they have had always ready at hand, but as for the old councils and the fathers, all mum, not a word. They did surely against all reason to begin first with these so bloody and extreme means, if they could have found other more easy and gentle ways.

John Whitgift, 'The Defence of the Answer to the Admonition, against the reply of Thomas Cartwright', London, 1574, in *The Works of John Whitgift: The First Portion,* **edited for the Parker Society by John Ayre, Cambridge, 1851, pp. 4–184.**

The state of this church of England at this day, God be thanked, is not heathenish, Turkish, or papistical, in which condition many things might be done that otherwise are not to be attempted; but it is the state of a church reformed, and by authority and consent settled, not only in truth of doctrine, as before is noted, but also in order of things external, touching the government of the church and administration of the sacraments. Wherefore the controversy is not, whether many of the things mentioned by the platformers were fitly used in the apostles' time, or may now be well used in some places, yea, or be conveniently used in sundry reformed churches at this day; for none of these branches are denied, neither do we take upon us (as we are slandered) either to blame or to condemn other churches, for such orders as they have received most fit for their estates . . .

Again, when anything is amiss, it must be considered whether the faults be in the things themselves, or in the persons: for we may not with partial and corrupt judgment impute the faults of the persons to the things, whether they be offices or ceremonies; for then should we continually be altering the state, and never stand stedfast in any kind of government: therefore in such cases we must seek to reform abuses in men, we must not pull away the states and offices, or the things themselves, because they are abused by some men.

I think it not amiss to examine that assertion which is the chief and principal ground (so far as I can gather) of their book; that is that 'those things only are to be placed in the church which the Lord himself in his word commandeth.' As though they should say, nothing is to be tolerated in the church of Christ, touching either doctrine, order, ceremonies, discipline, or government, except it be expressed in the word of God. And therefore the most of their arguments in this book be taken *ab auctoritate negative*, which by the rules of logic prove nothing at all....

Whether all things pertaining to the outward form of the church be particularly expressed, or commanded in the scripture, or no, is the question that we have now in controversy: that God could do it, and therefore 'hath done it', is no good reason, no more than it is for the real presence in the sacrament.

Affirmatively the argument is always good of the authority of the scripture; as, God hath there commanded it to be done; therefore it must be done: or, The scripture affirmeth it to be so; ergo, it is so. But negatively it holdeth not, except in matters of salvation and damnation: which is not my opinion only, but the opinion of the best interpreters.

It is most true, that nothing ought to be tolerated in the church as necessary unto salvation, or as an article of faith, except it be expressly contained in the word of God, or may manifestly thereof be gathered; and therefore we utterly condemn and reject transubstantiation, the sacrifice of the mass, the authority of the bishop of Rome, worshipping of images, &c.

And in this case an argument taken *ab auctoritate scripturæ negative* is most strong; as for example: It is not to be found in scripture that the bishop of Rome ought to be the head of the church; and therefore it is not necessary to salvation to believe that he ought to be the head of the church, &c.

It is also true, that nothing in ceremonies, order, discipline, or government in the church, is to be suffered, being against the word of God: and therefore we reject all ceremonies wherein there is any opinion to salvation, worshipping of God, or merit; as creeping to the cross, holy bread, holy water, holy candle, &c.

That 'matters of ceremonies, discipline, and kind of government, be matters necessary unto salvation', is a doctrine strange and unheard of to me; whereof I will by and by speak more at large, after I have in a word or two answered your objections of 'the bishop of Rome', and of 'the sacraments of baptism, and the Lord's supper': for you say, 'The case which' I 'put, whether the bishop of Rome be head of the church, is a matter that concerneth the government, and the kind of government of the church; and the same is a matter that toucheth faith, and that standeth upon salvation.' Whereupon belike you would conclude, that 'matters of government, and kind of government', are 'matters necessary to salvation'. Surely I put no such case; but I put such an example to prove, that we may reason *ab auctoritate scripturæ negative*. For this is a good argument: We find it not in the scripture that the bishop of Rome ought to be the head of the church; ergo, it is not necessary to salvation to believe that the bishop of Rome is the head of the church: the which thing notwithstanding the papists do affirm; for they say thus: 'To be subject to the bishop of Rome is of necessity of salvation to all men.' Now, sir, my reason is framed thus against them: Whatsoever is necessary to salvation is contained in the scriptures: but that the pope should be the head of the church is not contained in the scriptures; therefore it is not necessary to salvation. But you reason clean contrary; for you conclude thus: Whether the pope be the head of the church is a matter of government, and of the kind of government; but the papists say (for that I take to be your meaning) that it is a matter necessary unto salvation, that the pope should be the head of the church; ergo, matters of government, and kind of government, are necessary unto salvation. Thus you see how popishly, with a popish reason, you make a very popish conclusion. Certainly no government is to be brought into the church that is directly against the word of God, as the pope's is, which doth not only usurp the office and authority of kings and princes, but of Christ also, and commandeth things contrary to faith and to the manifest word of God; wherefore his authority is wicked and damnable: but it doth not therefore follow to make this a general rule, that 'the government of the church, or kind of government, is necessary to salvation'.

But now to your paradox: you say that 'matters of discipline and kind of government are matters necessary to government salvation, and of faith'. And you add that 'excommunication, and other censures of the church, which are forerunners unto excommunication, are matters of discipline; and the same are also of faith and of salvation'. There are two kinds of government in the church, the one invisible, the other visible; the one spiritual, the other external. The invisible and spiritual government of the church is, when God by his Spirit, gifts, and ministry of his word, doth govern it, by ruling in the hearts and consciences of men, and directing them in all things necessary to everlasting life: this kind of government indeed is necessary to salvation, and it is in the church of the elect only. The visible and external government is that which is executed by man, and consisteth of external discipline, and visible ceremonies practised in that church, and over that church, that containeth in it both good and evil, which is usually called the visible church of Christ, and compared by Christ to 'a field' wherein both 'good seeds' and 'tares were sown', and to 'a net that gathered of all kind of fishes'. If you mean this kind of government, then must I ask you this question, whether your meaning is that to have a government is necessary to salvation; or to have some one certain form and kind of government, not to be altered in respect of time, persons, or place? Likewise would I know of you what you mean by 'necessary unto salvation'; whether you mean such things without the which we cannot be saved, or such things only as be necessary or ordinary helps unto salvation: for you know that this word 'necessary' signifieth, either that without the which a thing cannot be, or that without the which it cannot so well and conveniently be.

But, forsomuch as you afterward make mention of 'excommunication, and other censures of the church, which are forerunners unto excommunication', I take it that you mean the external 'government' of the church, and that 'kind of government'. And yet must I ask you another question, that is, whether you mean that this 'government' and 'kind of government' is 'necessary' at all times, or then when the church is collected together, and in such place where it may have government. For you know that the church is sometimes by persecution so dispersed that it appeareth not, as we read Apocal. vi., nor hath any certain place to remain in; so that it cannot have any external government, or exercise of any discipline. But to be short, I confess that in a church collected together in one place, and at liberty, government is necessary in the second kind of necessity; but that any one kind of government is so necessary that without it the church cannot be saved, or that it may not be altered into some other kind thought to be more expedient, I utterly deny; and the reasons that move me so to do be these:

The first is, because I find no one certain and perfect kind of government prescribed or commanded in the scriptures to the church of Christ; which no doubt should have been done, if it had been a matter necessary unto the salvation of the church.

William Laud, 'A Relation of the Conference between William Laud and Mr Fisher the Jesuit', in *The Works of the Most Reverend Father in God, William Laud*, Vol. II, Oxford: John Henry Parker, 1849, pp. 234–5.

The Church of England, God be thanked, thrives happily under a gracious prince, and well understands that a parliament cannot be called at all times; and that there are visible judges besides the law-books, and one supreme (long may he be, and be happy!) to settle all temporal differences; which, certainly, he might much better perform, if his kingdoms were well rid of A. C. and his fellows. And she believes too, that our Saviour Christ hath left in His Church, besides His law-book the Scripture, visible magistrates and judges – that is, archbishops and bishops, under a gracious king, to govern both for truth and peace according to the Scripture; and her own canons and constitutions, as also those of the Catholic Church, which cross not the Scripture and the just laws of the realm. But she doth not believe there is any necessity to have one pope or bishop over the whole Christian world, more than to have one emperor over the whole world – which, were it possible, she cannot think fit. Nor are any of these intermediate judges, or that one which you would have supreme, infallible.

But since a 'kingdom' and a 'parliament' please A. C. so well to pattern the Church by, I will follow him in the way he goes, and be bold to put him in mind, that in some kingdoms there are divers businesses of greatest consequence, which cannot be finally and bindingly ordered, but in and by parliament; and particularly the statute laws, which must bind all the subjects, cannot be made and ratified but there. Therefore, according to A. C.'s own argument, there will be some business also found, (Is not the settling of the divisions of Christendom one of them?) which can never be well settled, but in a General Council; and particularly the making of canons, which must bind all particular Christians and Churches, cannot be concluded and established but there. And again, as the supreme magistrate in the state civil may not abrogate the laws made in parliament, though he may dispense with the sanction or penalty of the law, *quoad hic et nunc*, as the lawyers speak, – so in the ecclesiastical body, no bishop, no, not the pope, where his supremacy is admitted, hath power to disannul or violate the true and fundamental decrees of a General Council, though he may perhaps dispense in some cases with some decrees. By all which it appears, though somewhat may be done by the bishops and governors of the Church, to preserve the unity and certainty of faith, and to keep the Church from renting, or for uniting it when it is rent; yet that, in the ordinary way which the Church hath hitherto kept, some things there are, and upon great emergent occasions may be, which can have no other help than a lawful, free, and well composed General Council. And when that cannot be had, the Church must pray that it may, and expect till it may; or else reform itself *per partes*, by national or provincial synods, as hath been said before.

John Henry Newman, *Thoughts on the Ministerial Commission. Respectfully addressed to the clergy*, London: Rivington, 1833.

I am but one of yourselves, – a Presbyter; and therefore I conceal my name, lest I should take too much on myself by speaking in my own person. Yet speak I must; for the times are very evil, yet no one speaks against them.

Is this not so? Do not we 'look one upon another', yet perform nothing? Do we not all confess the peril into which the Church is come, yet sit still each in his own retirement, as if mountains and seas cut off brother from brother? Therefore suffer me, while I try to draw you forth from those pleasant retreats, which it has been our blessedness hitherto to enjoy, to contemplate the condition and prospects of our Holy Mother in a practical way; so that one and all may unlearn that idle habit, which has grown upon us, of owning the state of things to be bad, yet doing nothing to remedy it.

Consider a moment. Is it fair, is it dutiful, to suffer our Bishops to stand the brunt of the battle without doing our part to support them? Upon them comes 'the care of all the Churches'. This cannot be helped: indeed it is their glory. Not one of us would wish in the least to deprive them of the duties, the toils, the responsibilities of their high Office. And, black event as it would be fore the country, yet, (as far as they are concerned,) we could not wish them a more blessed termination of their course, that the spoiling of their goods, and martyrdom.

To them then we willingly and affectionately relinquish their high privileges and honours; we encroach not upon the rights of the SUCCESSORS OF THE APOSTLES; we touch not their sword and crosier. Yet surely we may be their shield-bearers in the battle without offence; and by our voice and deeds be to them what Luke and Timothy were to St. Paul.

Now then let me come at once to the subject which leads me to address you. Should the Government and Country so far forget their GOD as to cast off the Church, to deprive it of its temporal honours and substance, on what will you rest the claim of respect and attention which you make upon your flocks? Hitherto you have been upheld by your birth, your education, your wealth, your connexions; should these secular advantages cease, on what must CHRIST'S Ministers depend? Is not this a serious practical question? We know how miserable is the state of religious bodies not supported by the State. Look at the Dissenters on all sides of you, and you will see at once that their Ministers, depending simply upon the people, become the creatures of the people. Are you content that this should be your case? Alas! can a greater evil befall Christians, than for their teachers to be guided by them, instead of guiding? How can we 'hold fast the form of sound words', and 'keep that which is committed to our trust', if our influence is to depend simply on our popularity? Is it not our very office to oppose the world? can we then allow ourselves to court it? to preach smooth things and prophesy deceits? to make the way of life easy to the rich and indolent, and to bribe the humbler classes by excitements and strong intoxicating doctrine? Surely it must not be so; – and the question recurs, on what are we to rest our authority, when the State deserts us?

CHRIST has not left His Church without claim of its own upon the attention of men. Surely not. Hard Master He cannot be, to bid us oppose the world, yet give us no credentials for so doing. There are some who rest their divine mission on their own unsupported assertion; others, who rest it upon their popularity; others, on their success; and others, who rest it upon their temporal distinctions. This last case has, perhaps, been too much our own; I fear we have neglected the real ground on which our authority is built, – OUR APOSTOLICAL DESCENT.

We have been born, not of blood, nor of the will of the flesh, nor of the will of man, but of GOD. The LORD JESUS CHRIST gave His SPIRIT to His Apostles; they in turn laid their hands on those who should succeed them; and these again on others; and so the sacred gift has been handed down to our present Bishops, who have appointed us as their assistants, and in some sense representatives.

Now every one of us believes this. I know that some will at first deny they do; still they do believe it. Only, it is not sufficiently practically impressed on their minds. They do believe it; for it is the doctrine of the Ordination Service, which they have recognised as truth in the most solemn season of their lives. In order, then, not to prove, but to remind and impress, I entreat your attention to the words when you were made Ministers of CHRIST'S Church.

The office of Deacon was thus committed to you: 'Take thou authority to execute the office of Deacon in the Church of GOD committed unto thee: In the name', &c.

And the priesthood thus:

'Receive the HOLY GHOST, for the office and work of a Priest, in the Church of GOD, now committed unto thee by the imposition of our hands. Whose sins thou dost forgive, they are forgiven; and whose sins thou dost retain, they are retained. And be thou a faithful dispenser of the Word of GOD, and of His Holy Sacraments: In the name', &c.

These, I say, were words spoken to us, and received by us, when we were brought nearer to GOD than at any other time of our lives. I know the grace of ordination is contained in the laying on of hands, not in any form of words; – yet in our own case, (as has ever been usual in the Church,) words of blessing have accompanied the act. Thus we have confessed before GOD our belief, that through the Bishop who ordained us, we received the HOLY GHOST, the power to bind and to loose, to administer the Sacraments, and to preach. Now how is he able to give these great gifts? Whence is his right? Are these words idle, (which would be taking GOD'S name in vain,) or do they express merely a wish, (which surely is very far below their meaning,) or do they not rather indicate that the Speaker is conveying a gift? Surely they can mean nothing short of this. But whence, I ask, his right to do so? Has he any right, except as having received the power from those who consecrated him to be a Bishop? He could not give what he had never received. It is plain then that he but transmits; and that the Christian Ministry is a succession. And if we trace back the power of ordination from hand to hand, of course we shall come to the Apostles at last. We know we do, as a plain historical fact; and therefore all we, who have been ordained Clergy, in the very form of our ordination acknowledged the doctrine of the APOSTOLICAL SUCCESSION.

And for the same reason, we must necessarily consider none to be really ordained who have not thus been ordained. For if ordination is a divine ordinance, how dare we use it? Therefore all who use it, all of us, must consider it necessary. As well might we pretend the Sacraments are not necessary to Salvation, while we make use of the offices of the Liturgy; for when GOD appoints means of grace, they are the means.

I do not see how any one can escape from this plain view of the subject, except, (as I have already hinted,) by declaring, that the words do not mean all that they say. But only reflect what a most unseemly time for random words is that, in which Ministers are set apart for their office. Do we not adopt a Liturgy, in order to hinder inconsiderate idle language, and shall we, in the most sacred of all services, write down, subscribe, and use again and again forms of speech, which have not been weighed, and cannot be taken strictly?

Therefore, my dear Brethren, act up to your professions. Let it not be said that you have neglected a gift; for if you have the Spirit of the Apostles on you, surely this is a great gift. 'Stir up the gift of GOD which is in you.' Make much of it. Show your value of it. Keep it before your minds as an honourable badge, far higher than that secular respectability, or cultivation, or polish, or learning, or rank, which give you a hearing with the many. Tell them of your gift. The times will soon drive you to do this, if you mean to be still any thing. But wait not for the times. Do not be compelled, by the world's forsaking you, to recur as if unwillingly to the high source of your authority. Speak out now, before you are forced, both as glorying in your privilege, and to ensure your rightful honour from your people. A notion has gone abroad, that they can take away your power. They think they have given and can take it away. They think it lies in the Church property, and they know that they have politically the power to confiscate that property. They have been deluded into a notion that present palpable usefulness, produceable results, acceptableness to your flocks, that these and such like are the test of your Divine commission. Enlighten them in this matter. Exalt our Holy Fathers, the Bishops, as the Representatives of the Apostles, and the Angels of the Churches; and magnify your office, as being ordained by them to take part in their Ministry.

But, if you will not adopt my view of the subject, which I offer to you, not doubtingly, yet (I hope) respectfully, at all events, CHOOSE YOUR SIDE. To remain neuter much longer will be itself to take part. Choose your side; since side you shortly must, with one or other party, even though you do nothing. Fear to be of those, whose line is decided for them by chance circumstances, and who may perchance find themselves with the enemies of CHRIST, while they think but to remove themselves from worldly politics. Such abstinence is impossible in troublous times. HE THAT IS NOT WITH ME, IS AGAINST ME, AND HE THAT GATHERETH NOT WITH ME SCATTERETH ABROAD.

William Reed Huntington, *The Church-Idea: an Essay towards Unity*, fourth edition, New York: Charles Scribner's Sons, 1899, pp. 1–2, 124–6.

Dissatisfaction is the one word that best expresses the state of mind in which Christendom finds itself to-day. There is a wide-spread misgiving that we are on the eve of momentous changes. Unrest is everywhere. The party of the Curia and the party of the Reformation, the party of orthodoxy and the party of liberalism, are all alike agitated by the consciousness that a spirit of change is in the air.

No wonder that many imagine themselves listening to the rumbling of the chariot-wheels of the Son of Man. He Himself predicted that 'perplexity' should be one of the signs of his coming, and it is certain that the threads of the social order have seldom been more intricately entangled than they now are.

A calmer and perhaps truer inference is that we are about entering upon a new reach of Church history, and that the dissatisfaction and perplexity are only transient. There is always a tumult of waves at the meeting of the waters; but when the streams have mingled, the flow is smooth and still again. The plash and gurgle that we hear may mean something like this.

At all events the time is opportune for a discussion of the Church-Idea; for it is with this, hidden under a hundred disguises, that the world's thoughts are busy. Men have become possessed with an unwonted longing for unity, and yet they are aware that they do not grapple successfully with the practical problem. Somehow they are grown persuaded that union is God's work, and separation devil's work; but the persuasion only breeds the greater discontent. That is what lies at the root of our unquietness. There is a felt want and a felt inability to meet the want; and where these two things coexist there must be heat of friction.

Catholicity is what we are reaching after. But how is Catholicity to be defined? And when we have got our definition, what are we to do with it? The speculative and the practical sides of the question are about equally difficult to meet. The humanitarian scheme would make the Church conterminous with the race; the ultramontane would bound it by the Papal decrees.

Clearly we have come upon a time for the study of first principles, a time to go down and look after the foundations upon which our customary beliefs are built. The more searching the analysis, the more lasting will the synthesis be sure to be.

The truth is, Anglicanism is the only form of Christianity of which Rome is seriously and thoroughly afraid. In the national Church of the Anglo-Saxon she sees a plant of hardy growth, and one which all her blasts do not suffice to wither.

'We gave the Protestant religion five centuries to run,' once said an ardent Roman Catholic; 'three of the five are over, and before the other two have passed, the whole thing will be reabsorbed.' Yes; three centuries have gone, but the Anglican Communion has not gone, and will not go. It never was more vigorous in a spiritual sense than now. It stands, as Wellington's squares of infantry stood at Waterloo, firm, patient, dogged, if we must call it so, but true, – true as steel.

We have come to a turning-point in the progress of our argument, to a question in which all the lines of thought upon which we have been moving meet. It is this: What are the essential, the absolutely essential features of the Anglican position? When it is proposed to make Anglicanism the basis of a Church of the Reconciliation, it is above all things necessary to determine what Anglicanism pure and simple is. The word brings up before the eyes of some a flutter of surplices, a vision of village spires and cathedral towers, a somewhat stiff and stately company of deans, prebendaries, and choristers, and that is about all. But we greatly mistake if we imagine that the Anglican principle has no substantial existence apart from these accessories. Indeed, it is only when we have stripped Anglicanism of the picturesque costume which English life has thrown around it, that we can fairly study its anatomy, or understand its possibilities of power and adaptation.

The Anglican *principle* and the Anglican *system* are two very different things. The writer does not favor attempting to foist the whole Anglican system upon America; while yet he believes that the Anglican principle is America's best hope.

At no time since the Reformation has the Church of England been in actual fact the spiritual home of the nation. A majority of the people of Great Britain are to-day without her pale. Could a system which has failed to secure comprehensiveness on its native soil, hope for any larger measure of success in a strange land?

But what if it can be shown that the Anglican system has failed in just so far as it has been untrue to the Anglican principle? And what if it can be shown that here in America we have an opportunity to give that principle the only fair trial it has ever had?

The true Anglican position, like the City of God in the Apocalypse, may be said to lie foursquare. Honestly to accept that position is to accept, –

1st. The Holy Scriptures as the Word of God.
2nd. The Primitive Creeds as the Rule of Faith.
3rd. The two Sacraments ordained by Christ himself.
4th. The Episcopate as the key-stone of Governmental Unity.

These four points, like the four famous fortresses of Lombardy, make 'the Quadrilateral' of pure Anglicanism. Within them the Church of the Reconciliation may stand secure. Because the English State-Church has muffled these first principles in a cloud of non-essentials, and has said to the people of the land, 'Take all this or nothing,' she mourns to-day the loss of half her children. Only by avoiding the like fatal error can the American branch of the Anglican Church hope to save herself from becoming in effect, whatever she may be in name, a sect. Only by a wise discrimination between what can and what cannot be conceded for the sake of unity, is unity attainable.

A. Michael Ramsey, *The Gospel and the Catholic Church*, London: Longmans, 1936, pp. 204–20.

Amid the convulsions of religion in Europe in the sixteenth century the English church had a character and a story which are hard to fit into the conventional categories of Continental Christianity. The Anglican was and is a bad Lutheran, a bad Calvinist, and certainly no Papist. His church grew into its distinctive position under the shelter of the supremacy of the English King, and, its story is bound up with the greed and the intrigues of Tudor statesmen. 'Thus saith the Lord' sounds but faintly in the language of the Tudor settlements; while such phrases as 'over all causes and all persons within his dominions, King, supreme, defender of the Faith' and 'the pure and reformed part of it established in this kingdom' sound more loudly. Yet this church of England cannot be explained in terms of politics alone. It bore a spiritual witness, if only by linking together what Christians elsewhere had torn asunder – the Gospel of God, which had made the Reformers what they were, and the old historical structure which the Reformers as a whole had rejected but without which the Gospel itself lacks its full and proper expression. The impact of Luther and Calvin was felt in the Anglicanism of the latter half of the sixteenth century, and is seen not only in the Thirty-nine Articles but in the general return to the scriptures as the ruling element in faith and piety. The Bible was put once more into the hands of the people. Yet the Anglican church appealed to the Bible along lines very different from those of the Lutherans and the Calvinists; for it appealed also to the primitive Church with its structure and tradition, and thus interpreted the Bible in its true context. By refraining from the Lutheran error of giving particular statements in Scripture a domination over the rest, and from the Calvinistic error of pressing the use of Scripture into a self-contained logical system, it saw that Scripture centres simply in the fact of Christ Himself, and that this fact is to be apprehended with the aid of the whole structure and tradition of the Church. Here, therefore, was an appeal to antiquity, coherent and complete, and a faithfulness to lessons of history which the Reformers on the Continent were missing.

Prominent in the old structure which the Anglicans retained was the Episcopate. The reasons given for this ministry varied; for the stress and the strain of controversy were intense, and the Anglican position had to be defended, often self-consciously, against Rome or the Puritans without and the pressure of the more extreme Reformers within. Hence the English church did not always perceive the meaning of its own order in its deepest relation to the Gospel and the universal Church. For some churchmen, Episcopacy was of a divine law found in Scripture; for others, it was the best way of imitating antiquity; for others, it was well suited as a buttress to the doctrine of the Divine Right of Kings; for others, it happened to be the order of the national church, and it was thought legitimate for other Reformed churches to use other orders. But what matters most is not the opinions of English divines about Episcopacy, but the fact of its existence in the English church, just as what mattered in the first century was not the Corinthians' language nor even S. Paul's language about his Apostleship, but the fact that, under God, it existed. For its existence declared the truth that the church in England was not a new foundation nor a local realization of the invisible Church, but the expression on English soil of the one historical and continuous visible Church of God. It meant that, in spite of the pressure of Erastianism and even the frequent acceptance of Erastianism by the church's leaders, the English church was reminded by its own shape and structure that it was not merely an English institution but the utterance in England of the universal Church. ...

This aspect of the English church – its historic order, its sacramental life, its kinship with the pre-Reformation church and with the Catholic elements still existing in Rome – has always appealed specially to one part of the English clergy and laity. Others have been more concerned with the church's kinship with the Reformers, with the preaching of the Gospel, with the conversion of the individual, and have been indifferent to Church order or have regarded it as something valuable only because it is ancient and because it is useful. Both these schools of thought have existed side by side in the English church; both have had their times of poverty and their times of wealth and revival; and it has become customary to rejoice in the church's comprehensiveness and to stress the need for balance and for the due recognition of these two elements, besides the element which has kept alive the humanism of the Renaissance and has been known as Broad or Liberal. But, if our reading of the New Testament and especially of the Pauline Epistles is correct, these two truths – the Evangelical and the Catholic – are utterly one. To understand the Catholic Church and its life and order is to see it as the utterance of the Gospel of God; to understand the Gospel of God is to share with all the saints in the building up of the one Body of Christ. Hence these two aspects of Anglicanism cannot really be separated. It possesses a full Catholicity, only if it is faithful to the Gospel of God; and it is fully Evangelical in so far as it upholds the Church order wherein an important aspect of the Gospel is set forth. To belittle the witness of the Reformers and the English church's debt to the Reformers is to miss something of the meaning of the Church of God; to belittle Church order and to regard it as indifferent is to fail in Evangelical insight since Church order is of the Gospel. Hence 'Catholicism' and 'Evangelicalism' are not two separate things which the church of England must hold together by a great feat of compromise. Rightly understood, they are both facts which lie behind the church of England and, as the New Testament shows, they are one fact. A church's witness to the one Church of the ages is a part of its witness to the Gospel of God.

Varieties of thought and of apprehension of course exist. There are always those to whom certain aspects of truth appeal more than others. There may always be those who dwell chiefly upon the one Body, the Church, as the pillar and ground of the truth; and there may always be those whose minds are more filled with the thought of Christ and the individual, 'He loved me and gave Himself for me.' But there is a true and a false way of thinking of the comprehensiveness of the Anglican church. It can never be rightly expressed in terms of Victorian latitudinarianism or broad-mindedness, or by saying 'Here are two very different conceptions and theologies, but with a broad common-sense humanism we combine them both.' Rather can the meaning of the church of England be stated thus: 'Here is the one Gospel of God; inevitably it includes the scriptures and the salvation of the individual; as inevitably the order and the sacramental life of the Body of Christ, and the freedom of thought wherewith

Christ has made men free.' Translated into practice this means that the parish priest has a heavy responsibility; he must preach the Gospel and expound the scriptures, and he must also proclaim the corporate life of the Church and the spiritual meaning of its order. In every parish the Prayer-Book entitles the laity to hear the Gospel preached, and the scriptures expounded, and also to receive the full sacramental teaching of the historic Church including the ministry of Confession and Absolution for those who desire it. For the Anglican Church is committed not to a vague position wherein the Evangelical and the Catholic views are alternatives, but to the scriptural faith wherein both elements are of one. It is her duty to train all her clergy in both these elements. Her Bishops are called to be not the judicious holders of a balance between two or three schools, but, without any consciousness of party, to be the servants of the Gospel of God and of the universal Church. . . .

For while the Anglican church is vindicated by its place in history, with a strikingly balanced witness to Gospel and Church and sound learning, its greater vindication lies in its pointing through its own history to something of which it is a fragment. Its credentials are its incompleteness, with the tension and the travail in its soul. It is clumsy and untidy, it baffles neatness and logic. For it is sent not to commend itself as 'the best type of Christianity', but by its very brokenness to point to the universal Church wherein all have died. Hence its story can never differ from the story of the Corinth to which the Apostle wrote. Like Corinth, it has those of Paul, of Peter, of Apollos; like Corinth, it has nothing that it has not received; like Corinth, it learns of unity through its nothingness before the Cross of Christ; and, like Corinth, it sees in the Apostolate its dependence upon the one people of God, and the death by which every member and every Church bears witness to the Body which is one.

Bibliography

Sources

Roger Coleman (ed.), *Resolutions of the Twelve Lambeth Conferences*, Toronto: Anglican Book Centre, 1992.

G. R. Evans and J. Robert Wright, *The Anglican Tradition: A Handbook of Sources*, London: SPCK, 1991.

The Library of Anglo-Catholic Theology (Oxford: Parker) for 'high church' theology.

P. E. More and F. L. Cross, *Anglicanism*, London: SPCK, 1935.

The Parker Society volumes published by Cambridge University Press for writings by the English Reformers.

General

Paul Avis, *The Anglican Understanding of the Church: An Introduction*, London: SPCK, 2000.

Paul Avis, *Anglicanism and the Christian Church*, London: T. & T. Clark, 2002.

Ian T. Douglas and Kwok Pui-Lan (eds), *Beyond Colonial Anglicanism*, New York: Church Publishing Inc., 2001.

W. M. Jacob, *The Making of the Anglican Church Worldwide*, London: SPCK, 1997.

Bruce Kaye, *An Introduction to World Anglicanism*, Cambridge: Cambridge University Press, 2008.

Stephen Platten (ed.), *Anglicanism and the Western Christian Tradition*, Norwich: Canterbury Press, 2003.

William L. Sachs, *The Transformation of Anglicanism*, Cambridge: Cambridge University Press, 1993.

Stephen Sykes, *The Integrity of Anglicanism*, London: Darton, Longman & Todd, 1995.

Stephen W. Sykes, John Booty and Jonathan Knight (eds), *The Study of Anglicanism*, London: SPCK, 1998.

Rowan Williams, *Anglican Identities*, London: Darton, Longman & Todd, 2004.

William J. Wolf (ed.), *The Spirit of Anglicanism*, Edinburgh: T. & T. Clark, 1982.

6

The Beauty of Holiness: Practical Divinity

ELLEN T. CHARRY

Anglican theology takes its point of departure from the English temperament that is reasonable, moderate, practical, aesthetically perceptive and committed to both the rule of law and the dedication of the spirit. It is Augustinian and Benedictine and warmly devotional rather than logically scholastic.[1] We can see thoughtful practicality expressed in the selection of the genre by means of which church reform was first carried out in England. Rather than debate points of doctrine among the erudite, the sixteenth-century English Reformers, led by Archbishop Thomas Cranmer, responded to the strong sentiments for reform of the Church in England by going directly to the heart of Christian practice: worship. The Englishmen kept reform efforts concrete and direct by producing a prayer book in the vernacular, unelaborated articles of religion, two books of homilies for the instruction of clergy and, through them, the laity and a simple catechism that gave concrete practical shape to English Christianity. The hope was that this liturgically renewed Church would unify the realm religiously, so that social harmony would be achieved through a single religious norm.

The utter failure of this policy and the political nature of the stimulus for reform in England meant, among other things, that the shape of reformed Christianity remained fluid in Britain until the mid seventeenth century and, in the minds of some, forever incomplete. The second-generation English Reformers were as practical and as concerned for ecclesiastical order as were the first. While Lutheran and Reformed dogmaticians were tidying up what they believed to be the doctrinal implications of their teachers, Richard Hooker in England wrote the *Laws of Ecclesiastical Polity* that focused on ecclesiastical organization and, building on Cranmer's liturgical work, established Anglicanism around a sacramental ecclesiology. Both Cranmer and Hooker knew that worship rather than doctrinal precision shapes a holy life. Anglicanism after Hooker is conflicted yet distinguished by its interest in worship, the moral life, episcopal structure and a mutually supportive relationship between the Church and government.

The Augustinian Heritage and the Lutheran Challenge

To appreciate any discussion of grace, justification and sanctification in the West we must begin with Augustine of Hippo. Here, Alister McGrath's review is

---

[1] This sentence is indebted to Peter Toon's description of the theology of John Henry Newman, Peter Toon, 'A Critical Review of John Henry Newman's Doctrine of Justification', *Churchman*, 94, no. 4 (1980), pp. 335–44, p. 343, but applies more broadly.

succinctly helpful, although we follow it using more accessible vocabulary than is traditional.[2] There is bad news. Disobeying God in Eden has so injured human desire/will that we now only desire the bad and not the good. The good news is that desire can be healed by divine grace. Healing is possible for us, because God created us capable of wanting to be healed and able to cooperate with his healing grace. Wanting to be healed is aroused by preparatory grace that awakens the desire to become just or righteous. The gift of the Holy Spirit at baptism enables one to love God and neighbour, love being the mechanism of real healing. Love is the key virtue here, for it must precede faith and hope. It is the root of good.

Justification makes the individual righteous by cooperating with the gift of grace understood substantively until its goodness becomes characteristic of the person. For this virtue ethic, justification is a process of becoming righteous/holy. It is a process of personal renewal in the course of recovering/rediscovering/discovering being in the divine Trinitarian image. On the classic view, grace is imparted and enriches the soul/self.

Here, grace is substantive. It is about the power of God to heal the soul. We become righteous or holy (healed of sin) as we co-operate with what has been given to us. Sin diminishes as love for God grows, a love planted in the human heart by the Holy Spirit.

Singling out 'justification' as a focus of doctrinal interest begins with scholasticism. In high scholasticism the desire to suppress heresy pressed for doctrinal specificity with the effect that some theological notions that had had a broad range of meaning were narrowed down and separated from one another for purposes of focused discussion. With Thomas Aquinas, salvation is narrowed to justification and justification to remission of sin. However, this remission is also the making righteous of the individual, and that goes beyond simple remission.[3] This already transformed salvation from the Augustinian view, in which salvation is the healing of the soul's sinfulness, not simply the remission of sins, nevertheless holds the two together. This change set the stage for the Reformation crisis, wherein the event of remission would be separated from becoming just by Luther's separation of God's declaring one just from being just. In short, justification is separated from sanctification.

McGrath sums up the characteristic medieval understanding of justification from the later perspective of the Reformation:

> Justification refers not merely to the beginning of the Christian life, but also to its continuation and ultimate perfection, in which the Christian is made righteous in the sight of God and the sight of men through a fundamental change in his nature, and not merely his status. In effect, the distinction between justification (understood as an external pronouncement of God) and sanctification (understood as the subsequent process of inner renewal), characteristic of the Reformation period, is excluded from the outset.[4]

---

2 Alister E. McGrath, *Iustitia Dei: A History of the Christian Doctrine of Justification*, second edition, Cambridge and New York: Cambridge University Press, 1998, p. 343.

3 Thomas Aquinas, *Nature and Grace*, A. M. Fairweather (ed. and trans.), Ichthus edition, Philadelphia: Westminster Press, 1954, p. 386 at *ST* I:2: Q. 113: 1: 84.

4 McGrath, *Iustitia*, p. 41.

Of course, it is anachronistic to suggest that an idea that did not exist was excluded, as if intentionally. The point to keep in mind is that Luther, in good scholastic fashion, introduced a theological distinction into the notion of salvation that had not existed before.

Augustine's empowering love-driven doctrine of grace and goodness was prevalent in England at the time of the Reformation, and English theologians, to the extent that they grasped Luther's ideas, continued to be pulled between what they knew and the new doctrine that Luther created.

With Luther, grace, justification, righteousness and sanctification take on quite fresh meanings. For him, grace is relational or forensic (declarative), not substantive. It is not a gifting of God's spiritual power unto the soul, but a benevolent attitude towards us on God's part that comforts the sin-sick soul. It pulls a part of the work of God from the work of man that had heretofore been seen as co-operating. In both cases, grace is a free gift, but in the classical case, it is an enabling power given by God, while for Luther, it is a divine attitude of acquittal or non-judgementalism towards the individual. An attitude cannot be imparted (although it can be imitated), but we can believe/trust that God imputes/attributes/applies Christ's righteousness to us who do not deserve it out of benevolence/mercy and declaring us forgiven of sin. Here, we are considered righteous by God in a reworking of justice; we escape divine wrath, by God's vicariously imputing the righteousness of Christ to our case. It is an attitude of mercy on God's part by means of which the righteousness or merits of Christ stand in for our own lack. Our identification with Christ's righteousness that has rescued us from divine wrath is undoubtedly personally transformative in its own way, by the power of gratitude to reshape the self, even without benefit of divine power bestowed sacramentally by the Holy Spirit. Still, Luther was chary of the transformational implications of other interpretations, holding firmly to the reality of ongoing sin throughout life. There is, for him, no sacramental grace bestowed but perhaps imputed grace revealed in the real presence of Christ in the Eucharist.

For our purposes, it is important to note where Luther broke with Augustine and the tradition that developed from him. There are two essential points. One, Luther denied that grace is substantive, arguing for a forensic vision of grace as an attitude of God towards humans that is essentially merciful rather than demanding punishment for sin. It is not a gift given that empowers the goodness of the human will in order to heal it, but a looking at the righteousness of Christ that substitutes for the righteousness of which humans are incapable. Consequently, being declared righteous by God, for Luther, is not to become righteous or just, but only to be regarded as if one were so. The second point is as important. Justification is only possible by seizing on the divine mercy in faith; it is not the result of coming to love God better by knowing him well. It is by trusting that God is merciful that one appeals to the righteousness of Christ and his merits, not by any works or merits enacted by the spiritually empowered believer in love. For Luther, grace is declarative (forensic) not substantive; it is grasped by trust, not by love. In elevating faith rather than love, as 1 Corinthians 13.13 did, Luther radically changed the understanding of Christian piety, the spiritual life and the understanding of salvation. It is admittedly difficult for people who have lived a long time with a settled idea to take in a new one according to which everything must be rethought. With this background we face the English situation.

Grace, Justification and Sanctification in First-Generation Anglicanism

Although the English Reformation was sparked by dynastic concerns – 'the King's business' – it took its theological inspiration from the continental Reformation in its Lutheran form. We see this in the work of Thomas Cranmer (Archbishop of Canterbury, 1533–56), who drafted the Book of Common Prayer of 1547, revised in 1552 and again posthumously in 1559, 1604, 1662 and well beyond, as well as a book of 12 official homilies assigned to be preached in the churches, adopted in 1547. This book was followed by a second similar book of 21 additional homilies organized and edited by John Jewel in 1571. Cranmer drafted the Church of England's Articles of Religion, also adopted posthumously by the Convocation of Clergy in 1563, revised and also imposed on clerics and academics in 1571. Cranmer is clearly the father of first-generation Anglicanism.[5] There is little doubt that he was a Protestant martyr. Yet, he was fully Catholic at the same time, as is evident from his retention of so much traditional liturgy and practice made accessible to the laity. In the politically tense climate in which he lived, it was wise to keep one's theology to oneself, and, although he tried to, it did not save him from the wrath of 'Bloody Mary', who was loyal to the Pope. Mary charged the archbishop with both treason and heresy and sent him to be executed at the stake along with other Protestant martyrs, in 1556. There he recanted his previous recantation of Protestantism, giving the reform deep and lasting encouragement.

The theological tone of the mid sixteenth-century English Church on grace, justification and sanctification, that Caroline Stacey has nicely called 'moderate Lutheranism', may be better appreciated against late sixteenth- and early seventeenth-century Anglicanism and beyond.[6] Since Cranmer did not write theological treatises, discerning his teaching on grace, justification and sanctification must be teased out from what he did write. We see his doctrinal theology reflected in the collects of the Prayer Book, the canon of the Mass, the two books of Homilies and the Thirty-Nine Articles of Religion.

Collects

We see Cranmer's forensic (i.e. Lutheran) doctrine of justification in various collects, several original, but most harvested from traditional Catholic sources and modified to free them from a Roman context. Collects are short structured prayers of adoration and petition designed for each occasion of the Christian year. In their recent collection to celebrate the 450th anniversary of the Book of Common Prayer, Frederick Barbee and Paul Zahl presented the Sunday collects of Cranmer with meditations.[7] They explain a collect as beginning with

---

5 Caroline Stacey, 'Justification by Faith in the Two Books of Homilies (1547 and 1571)', *Anglican Theological Review* 83, no. 2 (2001), pp. 255–79.

6 Ibid., p. 261.

7 C. Frederick Barbee and Paul F. M. Zahl, *The Collects of Thomas Cranmer*, Grand Rapids, MI: W. B. Eerdmans, 1998.

an address to God,[8] followed by an identification of the attributes or activities of God being highlighted. Then, based on these characteristics, comes the petition and sometimes what Barbee and Zahl call the aspiration, the hope of the suppliant. Finally, there is a formulaic plea to God from the petitioner through the Son and the Spirit. The pithiness of collects is their strength. They embed themselves in memory and so are powerful catechetical agents. They teach who God is, what it is fitting to ask for and in whose name we ask it. There are no lofty abstractions here. While sitting on the ground, we are carried aloft as our yearnings are fashioned 'upward'.

In our examination of the collects, we will first consider the doctrine of grace therein, and then turn to Cranmer's portrayal of justification by faith, then the other theological virtues and finally the role of good works. All of these are disputed Reformation issues. It is a great tragedy of modern Christian history that the difference between Catholic and Protestant views of justification has been characterized as justification by works on the Catholic side versus justification by grace on the Protestant side. This is wrong. Both sides believed in justification by faith, perhaps even faith alone, the key difference being whether grace enables our good works to please God or not. The Catholic doctrine of grace is substantive. It is a gift given by God to the soul, a power or ability granted or given to the soul by the Holy Spirit that can be used in various ways. Luther's doctrine of grace, by contrast, is not substantive but attitudinal, relational or forensic. It is a non-judgemental or merciful stance on God's part that decrees us acquitted of our sins, even though we actually did commit them and may continue to. It is, in a sense, an intentional miscarriage of justice undertaken out of divine mercy that overpowers divine justice, for justice has been done in the death of Christ, the slaughter of the great innocent. The effect of God's decision not to treat us punitively but mercifully constitutes his graciousness.

On Luther's view, nothing transfers from God to us, but we are comforted nonetheless. Since nothing transfers, grace cannot be a power of the soul actually to become righteous. Righteousness is imputed not imparted. We are acquitted of sin, but do not become capable of holiness, in Luther's view, even though divine mercy spurs us to love of neighbour freely, rather than for expectation of reward. With this in mind, we turn to Cranmer. Cranmer's teachings on grace, faith and holiness are starkly and unselfconsciously revealed in the collects, even though they give us a quite limited view of his thought. Because most of the collects he used were taken from early medieval sacramentaries, they are unselfconscious about these themes, and Cranmer is too. He comes off as utterly undoctrinaire, faithful to the tradition and non-polemical.

How deeply Cranmer grasped the profound change wrought by Luther's doctrines of attitudinal grace and forensic justification is not clear. He espoused justification by grace through faith and not through works, but whether he meant by that what Luther had in mind is unclear. The collects suggest that he did not much tamper with the views that he inherited on this point. For example, the Collect for the first Sunday in Advent begins 'Almighty God, give us grace, that

---

8 Collects often attempt to express the doctrine of the Trinity by their structure. But instead of being addressed to the Father, many are addressed to God, thus undermining the Trinitarian effect.

we may cast away the works of darkness, and put upon us the armor of light'.[9] Clearly this views grace catholically, as a power added to the soul. The Collect for the fourth Sunday of the same season is a bit ambiguous, however, 'that whereas, through our sins and wickedness, we be sore let and hindered, thy bountiful grace and mercy, through the satisfaction of thy son our Lord, may speedily deliver us', implies Luther's doctrine.[10] The Collect for Christmas Day is equally appropriate in a Lutheran mode, 'Grant that we being regenerate, and made thy children by adoption and grace'.[11] The notion of grace in the Collect for the first Sunday after Epiphany, on the other hand, is clearly Catholic: 'grant that [thy people] may ... have grace and power faithfully to fulfill'.[12] The Collect for the fifth Sunday after Epiphany is reasonably Lutheran: 'that they which do lean only upon hope of thy heavenly grace may evermore be defended by thy mighty power'.[13] The Collect for the fourth Sunday in Lent is definitely of a Lutheran cast: 'that we, which for our evil deeds are worthily punished, by the comfort of thy grace may mercifully be relieved'.[14] The Easter Collect does not fit into either of the two categories for understanding grace at all. It reads, 'we humbly beseech thee, that, as by thy special grace, preventing us, though dost put in our minds good desires'.[15] 'Special grace' is a Calvinist usage that suggests that saving grace is extended to the elect alone. Yet, the Collect acknowledges prevenient grace, as well, that grace which prepares the will, preceding any godwardly movement on our part, a teaching that Diarmaid MacCulloch says Cranmer utterly rejected as meaningless![16] And, prevenient grace recurs in the Collect for the seventeenth Sunday after Trinity.[17] Clearly, in Cranmer's day, these terms had not acquired the denominational freight that polemic would later lay on them. Thus, it would be inappropriate to judge him by them.

To be thorough, let us complete our tour of Cranmer's vision of grace as displayed in the collects of the year. The Collect for the second Sunday after Easter suggests the substantive view of grace as an imparted ability in the petition 'Give us the grace that we may always most thankfully receive that his inestimable benefit and also daily endeavor ourselves to follow the blessed steps of his most holy life',[18] as does that for the first Sunday after Trinity Sunday, with 'grant us the help of thy grace, that in keeping of thy commandments we may please thee, both in will and deed'.[19] The Collect for the eleventh Sunday after Trinity is somewhat ambiguous. 'Give unto us abundantly thy grace' suggests impartation, while 'that we, running to thy promises, may be made partakers of thy

---

9 Barbee and Zahl, *Collects*, p. 2.
10 Ibid., p. 8.
11 Ibid., p. 10.
12 Ibid., p. 16.
13 Ibid., p. 24.
14 Ibid., p. 40.
15 Ibid., p. 50.
16 Diarmaid MacCulloch, *Thomas Cranmer: A Life*, New Haven, CT: Yale University Press, 1996, p. 345.
17 Barbee and Zahl, *Collects*, p. 102.
18 Ibid., p. 54.
19 Ibid., p. 70.

heavenly treasures' implies a more forensic or declarative view.[20] And finally, the Collect for the eighteenth Sunday after Trinity sounds more Catholic; it prays for 'grace to avoid the infections of the Devil and with pure heart and mind to follow'.[21]

All of this suggests either that Cranmer did not grasp how dependent Luther's doctrine of justification by faith was on a particular and radically different doctrine of grace from one the liturgy presupposed or that he chose to ignore the new teaching. What is not clear is that he was confused in retaining both teachings on grace. Rather, in territory where later battle-lines would be drawn, he was incorporating what he understood of justification by grace into the tradition to provide continuity for the faithful and avoid confrontation and confusion; that is, he simply did not see imputed righteousness or attitudinal grace as the foundation of a new religion as opposed to traditional religion but as an acceptable interpretation of the Catholic faith.

Having examined grace in the collects, let us now look at their treatment of faith and its relation to good works. Many of them stress faith, and some specifically point to faith alone, for example, two (both taken from the Gregorian Sacramentary from sixth-century Italy, long before Luther) suggest the importance of faith for medieval liturgy. The Collect for the second Sunday before Lent reads, 'Lord God, which seest that we put not our trust in any thing that we do; mercifully grant that by thy power we may be defended against all adversity.'[22] Similarly, the Collect for the second Sunday in Lent reads, 'Almighty God, which dost see that we have no power of ourselves to help ourselves; keep thou us both outwardly in our bodies, and inwardly in our souls.'[23] While these sixth-century texts point towards Luther's doctrine of justification by faith alone, interestingly, the Collect for the last Sunday before Lent, an original composition of Cranmer's, sets the doctrine of justification in the context of love, a note that Luther would not necessarily have approved, for he feared that the medieval emphasis on loving God would become – or had become – a work in the medieval Church. Cranmer retains the classic Pauline triad of theological virtues – faith, hope and love – rather than elevating only one – faith alone – as Luther did. It reads, 'O Lord which dost teach us that all our doings without charity are nothing worth; send thy holy ghost, and pour into our hearts that most excellent gift of charity, the very bond of peace and all virtues, without the which whosoever liveth is counted dead before thee.'[24] Love appears again in the Collect for the sixth Sunday after Trinity (Sunday): 'God, which hast prepared to them that love thee such good things as pass all men's understanding; Pour into our hearts such love toward thee, that we, loving thee in all things, may obtain thy promises.'[25] and again the following week, 'Lord of all power and might, which art the author and giver of all good things; graft into

---

20 Ibid., p. 90.
21 Ibid., p. 104.
22 Ibid., p. 28.
23 Ibid., p. 36.
24 Ibid., p. 30.
25 Ibid., p. 80.

our hearts the love of thy name, increase in us true religion.'[26] And yet again, for the fourteenth Sunday after Trinity, an appeal to all three theological virtues, so central to Thomas Aquinas: 'Almighty and everlasting God, give unto us the increase of faith, hope, and charity; and that we may obtain that which thou does promise; make us to love that which thou dost command.'[27] Further, Cranmer was not averse to including good works in his prayers. The Collect for the twenty-second Sunday after Trinity reads: 'Lord we beseech thee to keep thy household the church in continual godliness; that through thy protection it may be free from all adversities, and devoutly given to serve thee in good works.'[28] The Collect for the last week in Ordinary Time brings 'Stir up we beseech thee, O Lord, the wills of thy faithful people, that they, plenteously bringing forth the fruit of good works, may of thee, be plenteously rewarded.'[29]

It is difficult to draw conclusions from this tiny taste of Cranmer's grasp of the contended theological issues. What we may minimally venture to suggest is that he did not so lock on to a specific construal of grace, righteousness or justification as forensic that all substantive nuances had to be eliminated. While we know that he did seek to abolish what he believed to be egregious church practices, that reforming zeal did not become a surgical scalpel applied to the theological implications of every liturgical phrase. In short, perhaps he was willing to live with some ambiguity or did not polarize what others would. To put it more simply, perhaps he did not press the issue beyond justification by grace through faith, not works. Let us now turn to his treatment of these themes in the first Book of Homilies, which he edited, and the second Book of Homilies, edited by John Jewel after the archbishop's untimely death.

Books of Homilies

In her assessment of the presence of the doctrine of justification by faith (alone) in the two Books of Homilies, Caroline Stacey argues that the Lutheran doctrine of justification by grace through faith 'is also the cornerstone ... of [Cranmer's] entire theological vision'.[30] Cranmer's 'moderate Lutheranism' is evident from the layout of the first Book of Homilies, which he designed, although he was not the sole contributor. It begins with one homily each on Scripture, sin, justification, faith and good works, most written by Cranmer. Of these, the sermon on justification stresses the point that good works play no role in justification but are its fruit. Justification/salvation is purely by faith in the mercy of God, who looks at Christ's sacrifice on our behalf instead of at our sins. However, the inclusion of separate homilies on good works and on Christian charity and exhortations to obedience and against sexual impropriety already suggests the practical bent of the English religious temperament.

---

26 Ibid., p. 82.
27 Ibid., p. 96.
28 Ibid., p. 112.
29 Ibid., p. 118.
30 Stacey, 'Justification by Faith in the Two Books of Homilies (1547 and 1571)', p. 261.

The people were not to be taught Christian doctrine apart from its application to the Christian life. Although Cranmer stresses that works without faith in the justifying merits of Christ's sacrifice on our behalf are in vain, if not to one's condemnation, the inclusion of two homilies on the theme of works obliquely suggests that Luther's teaching that good works are the natural fruit of being freed from the burden of the law would not quite suffice in England, but needed further elaboration, at least for the stimulation of the moral imagination, if not for explicit doctrinal purposes. What was yet lacking was a vocabulary of holiness to mark justification off from the notion of good works that had strangled Luther in his youth.

Although it is not Cranmer's work, we will consider here briefly the second Book of Homilies edited by John Jewel after Cranmer's death.[31] This second book does not swerve from the doctrine of justification by grace through faith but quite deliberately treats issues dealing with the proper practice of the Christian life. Most of the second Book of Homilies treats specific practical matters like keeping the churches clean, controlling the desire for food and drink, times and places for prayer, almsgiving, celebration of Easter and Christmas, receiving the sacrament, marriage and so on. The selection of topics already expresses the English interest in instruction in appropriate religious practice rather than doctrinal specificity. There is, however, no chance that interest in the practice of the Christian life compromised the Lutheran emphasis on justification by faith here, because religious practice is not considered to be soteriologically significant. Rather, good works show obedience to God, witness to prior justification and encourage others to glorify God.

From what we have examined so far, perhaps we may tentatively conclude that the understanding of grace and sanctification of the first generation of practically minded English Protestants held to the doctrine of justification by grace through faith rather than works and was groping towards helping the faithful distinguish idolatrous activities, such as adorning statuary, from commendable practices, like keeping churches clean. A twist on the distinction between justification by grace and a the good life of holiness would later be introduced by Richard Hooker's distinction between the moral sense, knowable by natural reason, and the justifying knowledge of God available by divine grace alone. For now, however, let us consider our theme in the Thirty-Nine Articles of Religion.

Thirty-Nine Articles of Religion

In 1553, Archbishop Cranmer drew up 42 Articles of the Christian religion to consolidate the faith of the Church of England. Protestant in substance, they were suppressed when fortunes changed during the reign of Roman Catholic

---

31 John Jewel and Church of England, 'The Seconde Tome of Homilies of Such Matters as Were Promysed, and Intituled in the Former Part of Homilies, Set out by the Aucthoritie of the Queenes Maiestie. And to Be Read in Euery Paryshe Churche Agreablye', available online at http://gateway.proquest.com/openurl?ctx_ver=Z39.88-2003&res_id=xri:eebo&rft_val_fmt=&rft_id=xri:eebo:image:15643.

'Bloody' Mary Tudor (1553–8), and Cranmer, along with other Protestant sympathizers, was martyred in 1556. After Mary's death, Elizabeth I reinstated 39 Articles as the doctrinal position of the Church of England, in 1563. In 1571, an English translation of the originally Latin articles was imposed on the clergy by an Act of Parliament as a national policy to solidify England religiously.

Articles X–XII of the 39 affirm respectively the high Augustinian view that 'we have no power to do good works pleasant and acceptable to God, without the grace of God by God "preventing" us' (X), as well as the Lutheran doctrine of justification that 'we are accounted righteous before God, only for the merit of our Lord and Saviour Jesus Christ by Faith' (XI), and the Lutheran teaching that good works are the 'fruits of Faith and follow after justification', qualifying this by adding that they are pleasing to God (XII). There are no separate articles on grace, repentance or sanctification, rendering those that are included somewhat ambiguous.

Henry Chadwick also notes their ambiguity in his presentation of justification before the Anglican Roman Catholic International Commission.[32] He noted that Article XI, which reads, 'we are justified by faith alone', does not define faith, and there is no suggestion that it is other than the apostle's 'faith working by love', a trust in the promises of God, which motivates the justified person to do what is good and right. Nor does the article seek to impose the view that salvation is solely by an imputation of Christ's righteousness to us and of our sins to him. He also notes that Article XII would be acceptable at Trent and that Article XVI on post-baptismal sin is directed against Anabaptists and hated by Calvinist Puritans.[33] Further, Article XVII on predestination was fundamentally Thomist and not sympathetic to the Calvinist insistence on limited atonement.

Reflection

As great a liturgist and homilist as Cranmer was, he was not dogmatically engaged. This may have proved a long-term advantage for moderate Anglicanism, for it enabled some doctrinal ambiguity that encouraged unity within diversity. Further, Cranmer perished before Puritanism was powerful and pressed Anglicans to be more doctrinally specific. Recall that Cranmer died three years before the final version of Calvin's *Institutes* appeared. Calvin, not to speak of Calvinism, certainly was not a force to be contended with in Cranmer's lifetime, but became a point of contention in England only with the return of the Marian exiles after Mary Tudor's death from cancer.

Advance warning of the great struggle between Calvinists and liturgical Anglicans to further define Anglicanism, however, was already brewing as early as the reign of Edward VI, the only son of Henry VIII, the short-lived monarch of the realm (reigned 1547–53). The first phase of the vestiarian controversy broke out over John Hooper's objection to the insistence that the cope and surplice are necessary vestments for ordinations and celebration of the Eucharist. He

---

32 Henry Chadwick, 'Justification by Faith: A Perspective', *One in Christ* 20, no. 3 (1984), pp. 191–225.
33 Ibid., p. 213.

was opposed in this by Nicholas Ridley, by the order of the archbishop. Ridley argued that these vestments are not ostentatious frippery but necessary to maintain order and the authority of the clergy. Hooper eventually backed down, but the seeds of conflict among English Protestants were already evident.

Grace, Justification and Sanctification in Elizabethan Anglicanism

Although the travail with Rome, the Book of Common Prayer, the Books of Homilies, the Articles of Religion and a catechism for the instruction of children, drawn up by John More in 1572, set Anglicanism's path, they should not be taken as definitive. Inviting as it may be to look to the mid sixteenth century as the authoritative Reformation moment, after which distortions of the great masters began, the English situation continued to evolve. Anglicanism took clearer theological shape only gradually and unobtrusively from the late sixteenth to the mid seventeenth century. Although the direction of Anglicanism had been irrevocably stamped as liturgical, further theological debate continued as Puritans and Anabaptists pressed for more radical reform on one hand and tradition and a spirit of moderation, in order not to foment confusion among the laity, tugged on the other.

With the crowning of Roman Catholic Mary Tudor (1553), Protestant sympathizers fled to Geneva and there were acculturated into a more radical Calvinist vision of reform of the Church than had yet been known in England. Bringing it with them on their return at her death (1558), there ensued a struggle within the English Church to define Anglicanism. Good Queen Bess's attempt to settle the Reformation debates in 1559 with the Act of Uniformity and the Act of Supremacy was well intended but ill-conceived, for the issues had not yet sorted themselves out.

Richard Hooker (1554–1600) is the most important figure to do that in the Elizabethan age. The fact that his contribution lay more in synthesizing elements of the Elizabethan Protestant project than in innovation may, in hindsight, be a blessing.[34] By his time, Calvinism was taking clear shape and having influence in England. Arguments among Independents, Presbyterians, Episcopalians and Republicans were frequently over issues of polity (church government) rather than doctrine. Hooker rose to the occasion by setting forth Anglican theology and practice in *The Laws of Ecclesiastical Polity*. Contended doctrinal issues also played their part in the continued forging of Anglicanism that, following the lead of the moderate Cranmer, would be doctrinally broad enough to act as a confederated range of theological positions gathered under one liturgical and episcopal umbrella, yet basically Protestant enough to offer refuge to many under that umbrella.

Although raised a Calvinist himself, Hooker, like many of the Anglicans, read the Church fathers, and this apparently moderated any attachment to high Calvinism in his thought. Perhaps under their tutelage, he came to distrust the notion of instant sanctification in the moment of conversion in favour of slow

---

34 Peter Lake, *Anglicans and Puritans? Presbyterianism and English Conformist Thought from Whitgift to Hooker*, London and Boston: Unwin Hyman, 1988, p. 225.

growth in holiness based in baptismal regeneration. For this reason, he had to tackle the touchy doctrinal question of the relationship between justification and sanctification. He treats this theme both in his sermon entitled 'A Learned Discourse of Justification, Works, and how the Foundation of Faith is Overthrown' of 1585, for which he was censured by Puritans for his ecumenical attitude towards Rome, and in Book V of the *Laws*, for which he was censured for endorsing inherent or imparted grace on the Catholic model.

Whereas Cranmer had made justification by grace through faith and not works central, Hooker recognized the importance of justification, but set it in a larger sacramental and therefore ecclesiological context.[35] He took a step beyond Cranmer to elaborate sanctification and holiness sacramentally in opposition to both Roman Catholics and Anabaptists. In the *Discourse*, he adhered to the Lutheran teaching on justification by imputed grace alone that he contrasted with his presentation of the Tridentine position that justifying righteousness is a two-stage process, the first of which is the bestowal of baptismal grace, and the second is the application of that grace through good works that included what he called a 'maze' of religious activities. Good works increase and sins decrease this grace, while mortal sins destroy it. If destroyed, it can be resuscitated by penance, although it is permanently weakened. Thus, the Roman view of justifying righteousness, according to Hooker, is an accordionesque possession of the believer that expands with doing good and contracts with doing bad.

Hooker's point of disagreement with Trent is: 'We disagree about the nature of the very essence of the medicine whereby Christ cureth our disease; about the manner of applying it; about the number and the power of means, which God requireth in us for the effectual applying thereof to our soul's comfort.'[36] His objection is that Rome viewed justifying righteousness as a divine spiritual quality infused into the soul that enables a person to do good works that render him 'amiable in the sight of God'. He opposes this inherent righteousness with the Protestant idea that justification is fully the work of imputed righteousness that is complete in itself and requires no works. It is never our own as Rome claims.

While Rome holds justification and sanctification too closely together, Hooker, like other Protestants, considers them as separate moments in the *ordo salutis*. The righteousness of justification, taught by Paul, is imputed and perfect. It is wrought by faith that incorporates one into Christ. This is quite distinct though not ultimately separate from the righteousness of sanctification that is spoken of by James. It is imparted/inherent and imperfect in this life and is by works. Protestant separation of justification from sanctification, the work of God from the work of human beings, emphasizes that salvation is purely the work of God without human co-operation. The pastoral goal is to stimulate awe and gratitude on the human side of the equation and expunge human pride in salvation.

Luther's doctrine of imputed righteousness may be taken as a rereading of Paul, and he referred to the Epistle of James as an 'epistle of straw'. He by no

---

35 Egil Grislis, 'Hooker among the Giants: The Continuity and Creativity of Richard Hooker's Doctrine of Justification', *Cithara* 43, no. 2 (2004), pp. 3–17.

36 Richard Hooker, *A Learned Discourse of Justification, Works, and How the Foundation of Faith Is Overthrown*, (1585). Available online at http://www.ccel.org/ccel/hooker/just.pdf, p. 5.

means rejected good works, only quite separated them from justification, which he held to be the central Reformation, i.e. Christian doctrine. Luther's view was that a proper understanding of the work of Christ would stimulate gratitude on the part of the believer and that would in turn naturally lead to generosity towards others. The Anglicans, on the other hand, felt called to honour both scriptural texts, and so their struggle to sort out grace, righteousness, justification and sanctification turned on discerning the best way to honour both biblical views. James became associated with the Roman Catholic view, Paul with the Protestant teaching. Through Hooker, Anglicanism embraced both. While imputed righteousness is the formal cause of justification, grace for sanctification is imparted by God the Holy Spirit. The Anglican solution turned on embracing both the Catholic and the Lutheran vision of grace.

Although he advocated Luther's notion of grace as divinely imputed righteousness, Hooker apparently saw the potential danger emanating from a Protestant teaching that completely cut out the Catholic notion of grace as a substantive gift that requires cultivation. Calvin too, seeing the antinomianism sparked by a facile reading of Luther's doctrine, emphasized sanctification based on gratitude for imputed righteousness far more strongly and did not teach his two kingdoms doctrine. Further, Calvin adopted Melanchthon's third use of the law designed to restrain Christians from evildoing.

Hooker perhaps saw the same problem with Luther's unnuanced doctrine of justification. Still, he does not follow Calvin, but rather Cranmer by retaining regenerating or sanctifying grace as infused. In arguing for the necessity of the sacraments in Book V of the *Laws*, he lifts up sacramental grace precisely as sanctifying grace beginning with the bestowal of the Holy Spirit in baptism as a gift. As Egil Grislis has pointed out, 'In Hooker's view, to deny that believers have a responsibility for the preservation of the gift which they have received [sacramentally], would have been to rule out the freedom which grace has established.'[37] We need 'the sensible tokens of the sacraments to realize that God has bestowed upon us the means to lead us to righteousness'.[38] Faith grafts us into the work of Christ, who reveals God's gracious acceptance of us, while baptism effects the dwelling of the Holy Spirit in us that empowers us for newness of life. Still, these never add up to perfection in this life. Peter Lake sums it up this way. For Hooker, sacraments are an object for devotional contemplation. God in Christ is the medicine that cures the world and Christ in us is the means by which that medicine applies to wounded human nature. Grace heals the damage of sin in the soul. Through Christ's presence in the sacrament, God's causative presence in the world was transformed into his saving presence in the Church.[39]

Just as we saw that Cranmer's collects embraced both imputed and imparted righteousness in justification and sanctification, here we see Hooker following suit. This observer sees no contradiction between his position on grace and justification in the Discourse and his position in the *Laws*, because the discussion

---

37 Grislis, 'Hooker among the Giants', p. 10.
38 Richard Hooker and Christopher Morris, *Of the Laws of Ecclesiastical Polity*, 2 vols, London: J. M. Dent & Sons and New York: E. P. Dutton, 1954, p. 244.
39 Lake, *Anglicans and Puritans?*, pp. 175–6.

of regenerating sacramental grace is within the framework of sanctification, not justification. Still, the Puritans suspected Hooker's acceptance of sanctifying righteousness, because they rejected imparted grace altogether or anything that smacked of it.

Reflection

Hooker's Anglicanism, sometimes referred to as the *via media*, is a principled and distinctive religious statement coming from the English temperament, which sought to honour the sacraments as the foundation of the Christian life. What emerged as distinctively Anglican is sometimes seen as a spineless compromise in the interests of pacifying combatants – as if compromise in itself were meritless. Quite apart from the moral ineptness of such a position, it is inaccurate. Such a characterization of Anglicanism misunderstands the theological concerns involved. Anglicanism became a statement of its own about Christianity as a way of life structured through community life, public prayer, sacramental theology and holy living supported doctrinally by embracing both imputed righteousness and sacramental grace, for both are of God. The criticism of Anglicanism as formalism in contrast to Continental doctrinalism reflects a failure to understand Anglican theology's insistence on the shaping power of divine grace gifted through a sacramental ecclesiology. The Anglican distinctive then is the equal embrace of grace as both imputed and imparted, each operative in its own sphere. This may constitute Anglicanism's reproof to both Roman Catholic and Protestant teaching.[40]

Grace, Justification and Sanctification in Seventeenth-Century England

Things began to change in the seventeenth century, as Puritanism gained strength. While the struggle between Anglicans and Puritans was primarily or overtly over the form of church governance and liturgical style, theological issues were not absent. Calvinist Puritanism insisted on a doctrine of election based on double predestination – the efficacy of the atonement only for some. Debate on this issue set the tone for the theological struggles of the century, especially as the thought of Theodore Beza, Calvin's successor, became dominant, and the Puritans sought a more aggressive reform than that created so far.[41]

The limited atonement position has two dangers. First, it suggests that God has a vicious or arbitrary streak in him, since double predestination implies that he may reject us no matter how much we trust, love and obey him. This could lead to despair rather than comfort. Further, if God's decree of our eternal fate is disconnected from our life, it could lead to moral irresponsibility. The moral life, including moral preaching, becomes irrelevant, and this antinomianism

---

40 It may be arguable that Hooker's position is not far from Luther's, since he maintained a high estimation of the sacraments and insisted on the real presence of Christ in the Eucharist. But we cannot entertain that discussion here.

41 McGrath, *Iustitia*, p. 294.

threatens society. This issue, more than divisions about grace, justification and sanctification, took centre stage. The two issues cannot finally be separated, however, because the relation between justification and sanctification is still involved.

As Puritanism gained strength and sought ecclesiastical and civil redress of grievances, more Anglicans found extreme forms of Puritanism (like eliminating Christmas) difficult and limited atonement distasteful, because it would cultivate anxiety and despair and undermine moral responsibility, as would solafideism. With typical English practicality, they turned away from doctrinal argumentation to moral preaching. Horton Davies sums it up well: 'ultimately it was recognized that the Christian gospel was not a matter of theological contention but of the application of the transforming love of God to the souls that were battered by sin, beaten by suffering, and terrified by the approach of death'.[42] The Augustinian insistence on love resurfaced, as did a characteristically Anglican ability to live with doctrinal ambiguity.

George Herbert (1593–1633)

An excellent example of Davies's point is the poetry of George Herbert, one of the Caroline divines. Diogenes Allen points out that Herbert's *The Temple* is an alternative to John Bunyan's Calvinist vision of the Christian pilgrimage, *The Pilgrim's Progress*.[43] Its 165 poems trace the Christian life from imputed justifying righteousness through growth in holiness completed after this life. Rather than argue the finer points of dogmatics, Herbert sets out a vision of the Christian life that transforms stony hearts into hearts that yield to God's love. Allen argues that Herbert returns to an Augustinian vision of sanctification based on the theme that God's love for us defeats our rejection of his love displayed in Christ's sacrifice.[44] Rather than being enraged, God falls to grieving our spurning of his love and painfully endures in that love to win us over to him.

The Temple is typically Anglican. It is organized around churchly life that is liturgical and sacramental. It is also deeply biblical, as John N. Wall points out in his introduction to the work.[45] By avoiding explicit doctrinal discussion, he turns attention to Christian living holding on to both the Lutheran doctrine of imputed grace and the Augustinian doctrine of salvation as union with God through love. His only poem on faith affirms imputed righteousness:

When creatures had no real light
Inherent in them, thou didst make the sun,

---

42 Horton Davies, *Worship and Theology in England*, 5 vols, Princeton, NJ: Princeton University Press, 1961, p. 242.

43 Diogenes Allen, 'The Christian Pilgrimage in George Herbert's *The Temple*', *Anglican Theological Review* 67, no. 4 (1985), pp. 329–47.

44 Ibid., p. 333.

45 George Herbert, *The Country Parson; The Temple*, Classics of Western Spirituality; New York: Paulist Press, 1981, pp. 38ff.

Impute a luster, and allow them bright;
And in this show, what Christ hath done.[46]

His only poem on grace is more ambiguous.[47] The refrain of its six three-line stanzas is a cry that grace may 'drop from above'. This is not determinative of the vision of grace he is working with, although several stanzas suggest a substantive rather than an attitudinal notion of grace. Here are two examples:

My stock lies dead, and no increase
Doth my dull husbandry improve:
O let thy graces without cease
            Drop from above! . . .

Sin is still hammering my heart
Unto a hardness, void of love:
Let suppling grace, to cross his art,
            Drop from above.

Although both Augustinians and Lutherans might claim this view of grace as their own, there is nothing to rule out the Augustinian view of grace as a power of the soul given by God, so that our works may gain favour in his sight, thus softening the heart and rescuing the soul from a sense of spiritual death that pervades the poem.

Williams Forbes (1585–1634)

William Forbes is another Anglican who demurred from doctrinal specificity. This first Bishop of Edinburgh wrote 'the most important contribution of the Caroline divines to the discussion of justification'.[48] His *Considerationes modestae et pacificae* were a response to Cardinal Robert Bellarmine's treatise on justification in order to help him distinguish among Protestant positions. He dismisses controversy on the nature of justifying faith as leading to 'never-ending dissension and an irreconcilable war'. He portrayed the Protestant account of justification by faith alone as assent to redemption wrought by Christ, working through love in order to undercut Catholic objections to the Protestant position.

McGrath presents Forbes as relinquishing the Protestant position, seeing justification by faith alone instrumentally, so that it is a means of justification. Forbes rejects the Lutheran position of faith alone as unscriptural and argues that faith is a work, McGrath quotes, '"whereby we receive or obtain justice". Thus the opinions of St. Paul and St. James are seen not to conflict.'[49] Forbes sees Protestants divided among themselves over the formal cause of justification,

---

46 Ibid., p. 45.
47 Ibid., p. 54.
48 Alister E. McGrath, 'The Emergence of the Anglican Tradition on Justification 1600–1700', *Churchman* 98, no. 1 (1984), pp. 28–43, p. 34.
49 Ibid., p. 35.

some holding that it is obedience to Christ, while others, and most Romanists, '"hold that Christ's justice or obedience imputed or applied to us is not the formal cause, but only the meritorious or impulsive cause . . . of our justification"'.[50]

McGrath completes his presentation of Forbes with the latter's duplex conception of the formal cause of justification that combines the Catholic and Lutheran doctrines. 'Forbes grants that it is undeniable that there are forensic overtones to the term "justify" as used in Scripture, yet insists that the sinner is not merely pardoned but also healed and cleansed of his sins, so that the whole sanctification or renewal of man ought to be understood as comprehended in the expression "forgiveness of sins".'[51] In short, Forbes has reconnected justification and sanctification in a manner than undid the Protestant separation.

Chadwick too considers Forbes's work on justification exemplary. Whereas McGrath sees Forbes as the beginning of the end of Anglican faithfulness to the Reformation, Chadwick sees it a bit differently. *Considerationes* only appeared 24 years after its author's death and then in Latin. Chadwick opines: 'Already the main body of Anglican theology was in reaction against Calvinism, and shared Forbes's regrets at Luther's extravagant love of hyperbole.'

> Seventeenth-century Caroline divinity cordially disliked the indefensible disjunction of justification and sanctification . . . they shuddered to a standstill before the notion that the act of God in justification . . . is unconditional . . . and therefore that justification sola fide is another way of saying that the elect are predestinate by the operation of irresistible grace and do not need to concern themselves too much about moral lapses.[52]

Henry Hammond (1605–60)

By the mid seventeenth century, Anglican divines were mounting an offensive against English Calvinism and the Westminster Assembly. One of the issues continued to be the preoccupation with details of theological orthodoxy at the expense of attention to piety and the moral life. Henry Hammond, began this anti-Puritan foray with *A Practical Catechism* for youngsters. In it he used covenant theology, but turned it on its head.[53]

Covenant or federal theology became the hallmark of Reformed theology. It first takes shape in the sixteenth century with Johannes Oecolampadius and was given classic shape in the seventeenth by Caspar Olevian and Zacharias Ursinus.[54] The basic idea is that God relates to human beings through covenants. There

---

50 Ibid.
51 Ibid., p. 36.
52 Chadwick, 'Justification', pp. 216–17.
53 Neil Lettinga, 'Covenant Theology Turned Upside Down: Henry Hammond and Caroline Anglican Moralism: 1643–1660', *Sixteenth Century Journal* 24, no. 3 (1993), pp. 653–69.
54 The high point of federal theology was with the work of Johannes Cocceius, Francis Turretin, J. H. Heidegger and Herman Witsius. See R. Scott Clark, 'A Brief History of Covenant Theology', available online at http://public.csusm.edu/guests/rsclark/History_Covenant_Theology.htm.

is a covenant of works negotiated with Adam who represents us all, but Adam failed to keep his end of the bargain. This covenant is associated with the Law of God. A separate covenant, the covenant of grace, was brokered through Christ on behalf of the elect who are united to him by grace. This is the covenant of the gospel.[55]

Hammond, and following him, a group that Neil Lettinga calls the Caroline Anglican Moralists, challenged the Calvinist principles of total depravity and the utter separation of the work of God from the work of man. According to Lettinga, Hammond taught that natural law is a covenant of works, obedience to which is possible for us. Although failure on our part broke our end of the bargain, we yet retained the ability to make some good choices.

Hammond retained original sin but distinguished it from actual sin. He distinguished involuntary sin, the result of the withdrawal of assisting grace, caused by original sin, from deliberate sin for which we are directly responsible. Thus, faithful obedience is possible for us, although we do not earn salvation. We are called to sincere repentance that is a free and rational decision assisted by grace. This leads to a willing obedience to divine commands. In contrast to the Westminster Confession, which taught salvation for the elect alone, Hammond, loyal to the episcopal and sacramental tradition, insisted that the covenant of grace is offered to all the baptized, 'but required "renewed, sincere, honest faithful obedience to the whole Gospel" as "consideration" to validate the contract'.[56]

Lettinga points out that Hammond and those who followed his lead, including Peter Gunning, Thomas Pierce, Richard Allestree and Jeremy Taylor, whom we shall examine below, generally agreed to solafideism but insisted that grace is the means to a holy life. Again, we see the reunification of justification and sanctification in their teaching. Grace is the process through which God makes a Christian holy, and that includes one's duty to receive that grace. In short, for the Puritans, the Church is the company of the elect, while for Anglicans it is the Augustinian company of saints and sinners, who are guided to God by sanctifying grace received sacramentally.[57]

For the Caroline Anglican moralists, we must be free to resist grace and able to obey divine commands. In this they echoed the early Church fathers, while the English Puritans, relying on God's acceptance only of Christ's obedience, appeared to undercut personal responsibility and human freedom.

Jeremy Taylor (1613–67)

Jeremy Taylor was a protégé of the intrepid and hated Archbishop William Laud, who staunchly opposed Puritanism.[58] Like him, Taylor was a royalist and waited out the interregnum writing, until the Restoration of the monarchy under Charles (1660). He was a moral theologian, who rejected abstract philosophy

---

55 Lettinga, 'Covenant Theology'.
56 Ibid., p. 658.
57 Ibid., p. 665.
58 For a more sympathetic view of Laud than is usual, see Edward Christopher Eugene Bourne, *The Anglicanism of William Laud*, London: SPCK, 1947.

and theological disputation apart from the Christian life. He envisioned the latter as an imitation of the apostles, who in turn imitated the life of Jesus. This is evident from his treatise *The Great Exemplar* in which he applied the steps and lessons of Jesus' life to the moral life generally.[59] Like Hammond, Taylor was interested in the moral lessons of Jesus' life that pertained to young adults. He did not address speculative questions such as the resurrection, because they did not concern the moral life. Rather, as is evident from his most famous work *The Rule and Exercise of Holy Living and Holy Dying*, he did not think that good works flow naturally from a grateful heart but that we need structure, direction and practices of holiness round which to organize ourselves.[60] His vision was that the Christian life is the moral life in accordance with God's will. The goal of the spiritual life is basically theoconformity.

Like the other Anglicans, Taylor stressed the practicality and simplicity of Christian faith, rather than intricacy of method for theological specificity. He saw reason as a 'box of quicksilver that abides nowhere';[61] faith and obedience are inseparable. He was deeply Augustinian. As a moralist, faith and understanding are to support the moral life; faith can govern desire and love forms faith and understanding as the proper stance before God.

On the specific points of enquiry here, grace, justification and sanctification, McGrath points out that in his three Dublin Sermons, Taylor teaches that we are justified by faith and works and that these are inseparable, thus harmonizing Paul and James. Justification and sanctification cannot be separated, except perhaps logically.[62]

Taylor's *Discourse IX of Repentance* exemplifies his refusal to abide by the doctrinal distinctions being made by the Protestant scholastics of his day.[63] Here baptism is the event by which God freely gives and we freely receive the grace wrought by Christ that justifies, sanctifies, atones and restores us to 'a condition of innocence and favour'. It is a simple doctrine that is faithful to the broad Augustinian heritage, but which precisely for that reason would appear muddled to the scholastic mind. It is a substantive notion of imparted grace freely given by God that adheres to justification by faith and sanctifies (following 1 Cor. 6.11). We receive it freely, but then it functions to call us to Christian duty. Baptismal grace works in two stages, first as a gift and then as an obligation. Taylor puts it this way: the proper work of Christ is 'the first entertainment of a disciple, and manifestation of that state which is first given him as a favour and next intended as a duty'.[64] He clarifies this with, 'The sanctification is integral, the pardon is universal and immediate.' Taylor made a conceptual but not a practical distinction between justification and sanctification as two steps in a

---

59 B. Harvey, I. V. Hill and Allen S. Davidson, 'Literary Art in the Moral Theology of Jeremy Taylor', *Anglican Theological Review* 76, no. 1 (1994), pp. 27–43.
60 Jeremy Taylor, *Holy Living and Dying*, London: George Bell & Sons, 1883.
61 Henry R. McAdoo, *The Spirit of Anglicanism: A Survey of Anglican Theological Method in the Seventeenth Century*, New York: Scribner, 1965, p. 51.
62 McGrath, 'The Emergence of the Anglican Tradition on Justification 1600–1700', pp. 38–9.
63 Jeremy Taylor, 'Discourse 9 of Repentance', in Thomas K. Carroll (ed.), *Jeremy Taylor*, Classics of Western Spirituality, New York: Paulist Press, 1990, pp. 304–34.
64 Taylor, *Holy Living*, p. 307.

long process of growing into baptismal grace. Grace justifies by remission of sin and sanctifies by enabling us to live a holy life. His interest was clearly in the gradual formation of moral character that he followed through the Gospel narratives.[65]

George Bull (1634–1710)

Like Anglicans before him, George Bull sought to harmonize the testimony of Paul and James on justification against solafideism and antinomianism on one hand and Rome on the other. His *Harmonia Apostolica* was an attack on Hugo Grotius who supported justification by faith and that that faith is imputed.[66] He argued that both faith and works are necessary for salvation, not faith alone on scriptural grounds. Solafideism must be checked by 1 Corinthians 13.2, interpreted to the effect that without love faith is nil.[67] Perhaps misreading Luther and thinking that he understood faith as a work, Bull argued that it is not faith alone that justifies unconditionally, but God's mercy. Both justification and faith are by imputation. Further, justification by faith alone is impossible. Obedience in the form of good works is necessary because God commands them.

McGrath cites Bull as follows: "'A man is therefore said to 'be justified by works' because good works are ordered and established by God . . . as the necessary condition for a man's justification.'" He summarizes Bull's teaching this way. '1. Whoever is acquitted by the law of Christ must necessarily fulfill that law. 2. Therefore, by faith alone no one is acquitted by the law of Christ. Therefore no one is justified by faith without works.'[68] He cites Bull: "'good works not only accompany justifying faith, but also are no less required to justification than faith itself . . . and are as much to be regarded as a cause in this matter of faith (that is, that faith and works are jointly prescribed as the only condition of justification in the Gospel Covenant).'"[69]

Reflection

Alister McGrath has noted that Anglican divines took a turn away from the pure Reformation teaching on justification in 'conscious reaction against the teaching of the Westminster Divines'.[70] While this is a reasonable observation, we have seen that the older Augustinian tradition of grace as substantive and love as transformative – two elements removed by the magisterial Reformers – were never eliminated in England. We have seen both at work all along the line. So, it might be more precise to suggest that the Augustinian heritage that lay deep within English theology and sacramental practice was

---

65 Hill and Davidson, 'Literary Art in the Moral Theology of Jeremy Taylor', p. 2.
66 McGrath, 'The Emergence of the Anglican Tradition on Justification 1600–1700', p. 36.
67 Chadwick, 'Justification', p. 217.
68 McGrath, 'The Emergence of the Anglican Tradition on Justification', p. 37.
69 Ibid., p. 38.
70 Ibid., pp. 39–40.

the resource to which Anglican divines turned to combat what they saw as the dangers of extreme forms of Protestantism.

Grace, Justification and Sanctification in Nineteenth-Century Anglicanism

Since the mid seventeenth-century debates, the most important work on our theme by an Anglican is John Henry Newman's *Lectures on the Doctrine of Justification* of 1837.[71] He was well aware that the doctrine had been neglected by Anglicans, and he sought to revitalize it within the context of the sacramental ecclesiology of Anglicanism that the Oxford Movement stood for. He argued for baptismal regeneration as the context of justification, although its formal cause is the gift of Christ present in the soul.[72]

These lectures have of late drawn heavy criticism from many corners and for several reasons, not least of which – universally agreed – is that he misunderstood and misrepresented Luther, the main antagonist in the book, whose position was far closer to his own than Newman grasps.[73] Luther was a foil for Newman's living target, the popular evangelicalism of his own day.

Further, criticism has opened up the old questions of whether Anglicanism is fundamentally Catholic or Protestant and tallying up lists of theologians to count on each side, as if they were bullets in a war of pride. This rather unedifying tack is no longer necessary in light of the public agreements on justification that have been worked out between Roman Catholics and Lutherans and between Roman Catholics and Anglicans.[74] Rather than rehearse old business, we will enquire how Newman's teaching on justification in the *Lectures* fits

---

[71] John Henry Newman, *Lectures on the Doctrine of Justification*, third edition, London: Rivington, 1874.

[72] See Chadwick, 'Justification', p. 219 for a nice review of Newman's theological setting.

[73] Chadwick, 'Justification'; McGrath, 'The Emergence of the Anglican Tradition on Justification'; William Haugaard, 'A Myopic Curiosity: Martin Luther and the English Tractarians', *Explor: A Journal of Theology* 8 (1986), pp. 41–50; Alister E. McGrath, 'John Henry Newman's "Lectures on Justification": The High Church Misrepresentation of Luther', *Churchman* 97, no. 2 (1983), pp. 112–22; Alister E. McGrath, 'Newman on Justification: An Evangelical Anglican Evaluation', in *Newman and the Word*, Terrence Merrigan and Ian T. Ker (eds), Grand Rapids, MI: W. B. Eerdmans, 2000, pp. 91–107; Thomas L. Sheridan, 'Newman and Luther on Justification', *Journal of Ecumenical Studies* 38, nos. 2–3 (2001), pp. 217–45; Toon, 'Review'; Jose Morales, 'Newman and the Problems of Justification', *Newman Today*, Stanley L. Jale: (ed), San Francisco: Ignatius, 1989, pp. 143–61; Scott R. Murray, 'Luther in Newman's "Lectures on Justification"', *Concordia Theological Quarterly* 54 (1990), pp. 155–78; Henry Chadwick, 'The Lectures on Justification', *Newman after a Hundred Years*, Ian Ker and Alan G. Hill (eds), Oxford: Oxford University Press, (1990), pp. 287–308; Joseph S. O'Leary, 'Impeded Witness: Newman against Luther on Justification', *John Henry Newman*, David Nicholls and Fergus Kerr (eds), Bristol: Bristol University Press, 1991, pp. 153–93; Richard John Neuhaus, 'Newman, Luther, and the Unity of Christians', *Pro Ecclesia* 6 (1997), pp. 277–88; John F. Perry, 'Newman's Treatment of Luther in the Lectures on Justification', *Journal of Ecumenical Studies* 36, nos. 3–4 (1999), pp. 303–17.

[74] 'The Joint Declaration on the Doctrine of Justification between the Lutheran World Federation and the Roman Catholic Church', *One in Christ* 36, no. 1 (2000), pp. 56–74; 'Salvation and the Church: An Agreed Statement by the Second Anglican–Roman Catholic International Commission (Arcic II)', *One in Christ* 23, nos. 1–2 (1987), pp. 157–72.

with and is distinguished from the themes and patterns that we have observed in other Anglicans we have examined here and its place in Anglicanism.

Only at the end of this major work does Newman frame the problem he has been wrestling with. Although there have been earlier allusive phrases, in the last lecture Newman says plainly,

> A system of doctrine has risen up during the last three centuries, in which faith or spiritual mindedness is contemplated and rested on as the end of religion instead of Christ. . . . stress is laid rather on the believing than on the object of belief, on the comfort and persuasiveness of the doctrine rather than on the doctrine itself. And in this way religion is made to consist in contemplating ourselves instead of Christ; not simply in looking to Christ, but in ascertaining that we look to Christ, not in His Divinity and Atonement, but in our conversion and our faith in those traits. . . . the fault . . . is the giving to our 'experiences' a more prominent place in our thoughts than to the nature, attributes, and work of Him from whom they profess to come.[75]

He explains the problem another way. Anglicans hold justification by faith to be a principle, and principles are not directly practical. The popular evangelicalism he is opposing mistakes this principle for a rule of conduct so that the point of religion is to have faith and to pay attention to the feelings that they are told should accompany it. Thus, they treat the conversion experience itself as if it were the Christian rule of life rather than recognizing that justifying faith is the gateway to a life that flows from the presence of Christ in the soul.[76] He frequently refers to his opponents, always unnamed, as advocating feelings and experiences over the reality of the doctrine. This calls to mind the English tradition of experimentalist religion in the testimonies of George Fox, John Wesley and George Whitefield as well as his contemporary, Friedrich Schleiermacher. Although, for the most part, Newman uses Luther as a foil, he is addressing the situation in England. David Newsome has filled in the historical gap for us here by situating this text historically.[77] In short, the Oxford Tractarians had been put on the defensive as Pelagian by broadsides from a group of young evangelical enthusiasts in the pages of the *Evangelical Magazine* and the *Morning Watch* and other correspondence that personally attacked Newman for his criticism of what some might call 'heart religion', an extreme form of Protestantism that fell into individualism.[78]

It is helpful to keep in mind that the central doctrine with which Newman struggled throughout his Tractarian stage was ecclesiology. He saw the popular evangelicalism of his day as eschewing the authority and significance of the Church and its administration of the sacrament in favour of a simple emotional subjectivism in which either assent to the fact that Christ justifies or the feeling of being accepted by God were considered to be Christian faithfulness. In the

---

75 Newman, *Lectures on the Doctrine of Justification*, pp. 324–5.
76 Ibid., p. 332.
77 David Newsome, 'Justification and Sanctification: Newman and the Evangelicals', *Journal of Theological Studies* 15 (1964), pp. 32–53.
78 Ibid., p. 34.

one case, Christ remains external to the convert, while in the other, Christ is pushed away by psychological considerations.

In typical Anglican fashion, he was concerned that the moral dimension of justifying righteousness would be lost, as would the power and authority of the sacraments of the Church, to protect against such psychological subjectivism and individualism. At stake, among other things, was the nurturing authority of the Church for the Christian life over the long haul as opposed to conversionist preaching that encouraged people to examine whether their feelings were rightly aligned at the moment. To combat this, Newman turned to the external tokens and symbols of grace to balance the subjective understanding of justifying righteousness. Again we see the English hesitance to separate justification from sanctification as extreme Protestantism had done in order to protect divine sovereignty.

In this brief compass it is impossible to do justice to the development of Newman's deft argument, and so a quick summary of its features will have to suffice. To appreciate the distinction Newman is making between the Anglican and the popular evangelical position he opposes it may be helpful to recall a central distinction that he made in the construction of his most important work, *Grammar of Assent*, written more than 30 years later. At the outset of the *Grammar*, Newman distinguished two ways of apprehending propositions – notionally and really. Notional apprehension is conceptual abstract, and general. Real apprehension is concrete and actual. It is stronger, more vivid and forcible than notional apprehension. It is possible to apprehend a proposition notionally without grasping its import personally or immediately. Notional 'apprehension then is simply an intelligent acceptance of the idea, or of the fact which a proposition enunciates'.[79] This is a grammatical, philosophical or economic apprehension. Real apprehension, by contrast, is 'an experience or information about the concrete [so that] . . . it remains in our minds. . . . When we make use of the proposition which refers to them, it supplies us with objects by which to interpret it.'[80] This distinction between propositions apprehended abstractly and really, I think, is the distinction, albeit only later fully articulated, driving Newman's opposition to what he knew of popular evangelicalism.

The Anglicanism he advanced in the *Lectures on Justification* wrapped around a real apprehension of justifying righteousness, and he argued that the evangelical view remained on the abstract, notional level. It failed to penetrate the soul at the real or concrete level of being assimilated into the personality and so remained at the conceptual level of assent; conversion by notional rather than real assent to the justifying work of the cross became an end in itself, rather than as the primary means to the end of Christian transformation by the work of the Son and the Spirit in the soul. A more systematically technical way of putting the problem Newman addresses would be that justification, now disjoined from sanctification and the moral life, was identified by these evangelicals as the moment of justification. It was an anticipatory criticism of what the next century would call fundamentalism. To it, Newman reacted vociferously.

---

79 John Henry Newman, *An Essay in Aid of a Grammar of Assent*, new edition, London: Longmans, Green & Co., 1892, p. 20.
80 Ibid., p. 23.

Aside from Newman's argument with evangelicals of his day, his *Lectures on Justification* are interesting on their own terms for at least two systematic theological reasons. First, they embedded the doctrine of justification in a fully Trinitarian, not simply a Christological framework, as much Protestant theology did. In Newman, the Son and the Spirit together are the instrument of justification, the Son coming to dwell in the soul by the work of the Spirit. Second and not unrelated, his teaching is thoroughly grounded in a sacramental ecclesiology, thus undercutting the destructive tendency of Protestantism towards isolated individualism long before it was widely realized as problematic. He did this by arguing that justifying faith is necessary but subordinate to the justifying righteousness given in baptism and replenished by the Eucharist, whose agent is the Holy Spirit. Faith in Christ's righteousness sustains the grace of baptism for post-baptismal sins, but faith is supplemented by the works of the gospel, especially sacraments that are not ruled out by Paul's insistence that justification is accomplished by faith, and not also by works.

To cut a worthy discussion off prematurely, Newman elaborated an expansive doctrine of faith that embraces the other two supernatural graces, love and hope, as well as obedience to the works of the gospel, especially the sacraments, as the gospel path of the enduring Law of God for the moral life. He broadened the doctrine of justification so that sanctification could not be excluded against a narrow and strict teaching that, at least in his own day, appeared to exclude both the moral life and the ministrations of the Church as authoritative as constitutive of salvation. The Anglican desire to do justice both to the Pauline and Jamesian teachings on justification is here reenacted.

Grace and Sanctification in the Twentieth Century

One of the most important Anglican theologians of the twentieth century, if not the most important, was Archbishop William Temple. Like most other Anglican theologians, he was not a scholastic theologian, but did keep scholastic categories in mind as he wrote. Like them also he embraced human freedom to accept or reject divine grace. Yet he refused to give up the notion of divine election. His particular insight is that we become aware of divine grace sometimes gradually and sometimes suddenly. It is this awareness or knowledge of divine grace and maturity to respond to it that enable us to experience salvation at its fullest.

Temple does not have a full treatise on grace and sanctification as such, but he does offer an argument for resistible grace in one of his Gifford lectures.[81] Lecture XV entitled 'Divine grace and human freedom', begins from the theological assumption that some forms of freedom are part of God's gift to us in creation. His interest in this treatise is that 'the capacity for fellowship with God is God's gift in creation'.[82] This gift, however, is not available to us for the most past because we are mired in self-centeredness. All that we can contribute to our

---

81 William Temple, *Nature, Man and God; Being the Gifford Lectures Delivered in the University of Glasgow in the Academical Years 1932–1933 and 1933–1934*, London: Macmillan & Co., 1935.
82 Ibid., p. 401.

salvation is the sin (self-centeredness) from which we need redemption. We can partially escape self-centredness by contemplating the truth and beauty of God's world, but that is not adequate to release us entirely. No amount of humanistic enlightenment will help – only divine revelation of God's love is powerful enough to life us from ourselves.

> The one hope, then, of bringing human selves into right relationship to God is that God should declare His love in an act, or acts, of sheer self-sacrifice, thereby winning the freely offered love of the finite selves which he has created.[83]

That all is of grace begins from the fact that human freedom is a gift of grace and ends with our being seduced by the divine love. Each step or moment in the process is both cognitive and experiential. Understanding is not what Newman objected to as purely notional assent but what he called 'real assent', grounded in what Temple referred to as 'the living experience of personal religion'.[84]

Conclusion

On the issues of grace, justification and the relation of the latter to sanctification, Anglicanism from first to last was a moderate Protestantism that consciously sought two ends. First to rid the English Church of practices that could be construable by the people in potentially idolatrous ways. They set about this, as in all things, with moderation. The second was to avoid or reject features of extreme Protestantism that appeared harmful by undermining moral energy, obedience to the law of God and human freedom, all of which are closely related. In this latter task it was guided primarily by the Augustinian doctrines of grace, sacraments and Church, while rejecting the late or high Augustinian doctrine that implied double predestination.

If this is a *via media* it is a highly principled one, not one backed into but carved out as the practical implications of the doctrinal issues being battled over became evident. We may conclude by suggesting that based on this enquiry there are four Anglican distinctives:

1. Human freedom operates within the context of divine grace.
2. Grace is the instrument of justification. It is grasped existentially by individual believers and administered sacramentally, that is, through the church and its ministers.
3. Justification is the healing of the sinner through the indwelling of the Spirit that unites the soul with Christ.
4. Sanctification is the enlivened and vivifying power of justifying righteousness.

---

83 Ibid., p. 400.
84 Ibid., p. 380.

These generalizations do not do justice to the interesting and often intricate arguments mounted by Anglican theologians on these issues. They may, however, serve to suggest that Anglicanism is a theological tradition that is rooted and grounded in the Catholic faith and continues to grapple with that heritage as the need arises.

Introduction to the Sources

The Books of Homilies are authorized sermons issued in two books for use in the Church of England during the reigns of Edward VI and Elizabeth I. They were to provide for the Church a new model of simplified topical preaching as well as a theological understanding of the Reformation that had taken place in England. Thomas Cranmer broached the idea of a Book of Homilies in 1539, but it was not authorized by the Church's Convocation until 1542. Within a year the 12 homilies of the first book were collected and edited by Cranmer, who also wrote at least five of them. They were not published, however, until 1547. The first six homilies present distinctive Protestant theology, namely the authority and sufficiency of Scripture, the radical sinfulness of man, justification by faith alone (entitled 'Of the Salvation of All Mankind'), evangelical faith and sanctification. The Homilies were revoked under Queen Mary but reinstated by Elizabeth.

Richard Hooker is the definitive voice of Anglican theology and governance. His *Laws of Ecclesiastical Polity* established the basis of and structure for the Church of England. He established Anglicanism on the classic scholastic three-legged stool of Scripture, tradition and reason, as opposed to Luther's insistence on Scripture alone, yet was also deemed an apologist for the Continental Reformation in England.

He supported the Lutheran doctrine of justification, but set it more assertively than Luther had in an ecclesial and sacramental context, thus protecting it from the danger of subjective individualism. This put the Anglican emphasis on sanctification rather than justification. Hooker argued for justification by faith yet not without works. Grace is a gift that nurtures the forgiven sinner into further spiritual growth. In short, Hooker, typically Anglican, drew on both the Catholic tradition and the new insights of the magisterial Reformation, refusing to grant their final incompatibility. His *Discourse on Justification* was criticized by more extreme Protestants for admitting that Rome remains a legitimate expression of the Christian Church despite its errors. In this he shows himself to be what later would be called ecumenical and tolerant, another general characteristic of Anglicanism.

Although widely embracing the Protestant teaching on justification, many Anglicans were concerned that it would undermine sanctification and moral energy. Jeremy Taylor, Anglican priest, theologian and mystic, suffered imprisonment and banishment for his loyalty to King Charles I and Archbishop William Laud (1573–1645). In seclusion during the English Civil War of 1642–51, under the protection of the Earl of Carbery Richard Vaughan at Golden Grove, Taylor wrote *The Rule and Exercises of Holy Living and*

Holy Dying, the former being an autobiography of sorts that reflects the religious and political turmoil of the time. He takes refuge in nature, fasting and prayer.

Holy Living, a guide to the Christian life, comprises four chapters. Chapter 1 covers rules for employing our time, for directing our intentions and includes many prayers, hymns and meditations for the 'practice of the presence of God', perhaps overlapping with the conversations with God of the great French Carmelite Brother Lawrence. Chapter 2 is 'Of Christian Sobriety' and provides rules for temperance in daily life, also accompanied by prayers for various occasions requiring divine aid. Chapter 3, 'Of Christian Justice', lays out the reciprocal obligations of social responsibilities, again with prayers for those who hold public office and those under their care. The final chapter, the longest, is 'Of Christian Religion'. In addition to many more prayers, it treats both internal and external religious acts. The former is explicated under the headings of the three classic Pauline or theological virtues, faith, hope and love, while the latter treats reading and hearing the Word of God, fasting, keeping the Lord's Day and other Christian festivals, prayer, almsgiving, repentance and preparation for the Lord's Supper. These rules set a high standard for piety in the Church of England. Our selections are taken from the dedication to his patron, and all four chapters.

John Henry Newman was the leading theological voice in the Oxford Movement's revitalization of the High Church in Anglicanism in the mid nineteenth century. Ecclesiology was the issue that gnawed at him until he joined the Roman Church in an act of ecclesiastical faithfulness. In his *Lectures on Justification* of 1837, while still an Anglican, Newman reintroduced the importance of good works into the Anglican notion of salvation.

Lecture XV of Archbishop Temple's Gifford Lectures treats of predestination, seeking to respond to the objection that the classical Reformed doctrine leads to spiritual torpor. The argument is that abstract doctrinal formulation divorced from religious experience does lead to such torpor, because doctrine is only a means to lively personal experience of religion that enlivens the soul or the mind to be set free to pursue the truth, beauty and especially the goodness of God that liberates it from self-centredness. Spiritual pride is a dastardly temptation that haunts even those who accept the doctrines worked out by theologians. The mind may be shaped by truth and beauty, but goodness is exceedingly evanescent. The Spirit of God for righteousness is saintliness that must repeatedly battle its way through self-centredness. For the self craves deliverance from self-assertion. One's tendency is to enjoy God and thereby glorify him rather than to glorify him and thereby enjoy him forever. Salvation resides not in the interest of whether one is saved or not, but in the simple glorification of God. Only the one who has renounced interest in his own salvation can be saved, for it consists in the deliverance from the desire to be saved.

Moral progress is possible through the expansion of the self through love that carries us beyond those with whom we are directly connected. That larger fellowship, either through patriotic loyalty to several individuals or to a local community, requites a sense of loyalty and obligation that pull the self into a stronger conformity to the divine.

Sources

Homily On Good Works, from *Short-Title Catalogue* 13675. Renaissance Electronic Texts 1.1. Copyright 1994 Ian Lancashire (ed.), University of Toronto. Available online at http://www.library.utoronto.ca/utel/ret/bk1hom5.html.

A SERMON OF GOOD WORKES ANNEXED VNTO FAITH.

<u>No good workes can bee done without faith.</u> IN the last Sermon was declared vnto you, what the liuely and true fayth of a Christian man is, that it causeth not a man to bee idle, but to bee occupied in bringing foorth good workes, as occasion serueth. Now by GOD'S grace shall bee declared the second thing that before was noted of fayth, that without it can no good worke bee done, accepted and pleasant vnto GOD. For as a branch can not beare fruite of it selfe (sayth our Sauiour Christ) except it abide in the Vine: so can not you, except you abide in me. I am the Vine, and you bee the branches, he that abideth in me, and I in him, he bringeth foorth much fruit: for without me, you can doe nothing (John 15.4–5). And S. Paul prouueth that the Eunuch had fayth, because he pleased GOD. For without fayth (sayth he) it is not possible to please GOD (Hebrews 11.6). And againe to the Romans he sayth, whatsoeuer worke is done without fayth, it is sinne (Romans 14.23). Faith giueth life to the soule, and they be as much dead to GOD that lacke fayth, as they be to the world, whose bodies lacke soules. Without fayth all that is done of vs, is but dead before GOD, although the worke seeme neuer so gay and glorious before man. Euen as the picture grauen or painted, is but a dead representation of the thing it selfe, and is without life, or any maner of moouing: so be the workes of all vnfaythfull persons before GOD. They doe appeare to bee liuely workes, and indeed they bee but dead, not auayling to the euerlasting life. They be but shadowes and shewes of liuely and good things, and not good and liuely things indeed. For true fayth, doth giue life to the workes, and out of such fayth come good works, that be very good workes indeed, & without fayth, no worke is good before GOD, as sayth S. Augustine (Enarratio in Psalm. 31 2, 4 [*Patrologia Latina* 36.259]). We must let no good works before fayth, nor think that before fayth a man many doe any good works: for such workes, although they seeme vnto men to be prayse worthy, yet indeed they be but vaine, and not allowed before GOD. They bee as the course of an Horse that runneth out of the way, which taketh great labour, but to no purpose. Let no man therefore (sayth he) reckon vpon his good workes before his fayth: Where as fayth was not, good workes were not. The intent (sayth hee) maketh the good workes, but fayth must guide and order the intent of man. And Christ sayth, If thine eye be naught, thy whole body is full of darkenesse (Matthew 6.23). The eye doeth signifie the intent (sayth S. Augustine) wherewith a man

doeth a thing. So that he which doth not his good works with a godly intent, and a true fayth, that worketh by loue: the whole body beside (that is to say) all the whole number of his workes, is darke, and there is no light in them. For good deedes bee not measured by the facts themselues, and so discerned from vices, but by the ends and intents for the which they were done. If a Heathen man clothe the naked, feed the hungrie, and doe such other like workes: yet because he doeth them not in fayth, for the honour and loue of GOD, they be but dead, vaine, and fruitlesse workes to him. Fayth is it that doeth commend the worke to GOD: for (as S. Augustine saith) whether thou wilt or no, that work that commeth not of faith, is naught: where the fayth of Christ is not the foundation, there is no good worke, what building so euer we make. There is one worke, in the which be all good workes, that is, faith, which worketh by charity: if thou haue it, thou hast the ground of all good workes. For the vertues of strength, wisedome, temperance, and iustice, be all referred vnto this same faith. Without this faith we haue not them, but onely the names and shadowes of them (as Saint Augustine sayth,) All the life of them that lacke the true faith, is sinne, and nothing is good, without him, that is the authour of goodnesse: where hee is not, there is but fained vertue, although it be in the best workes. And S. Augustine, declaring this verse of the Psalme, The turtle hath found a nest where shee may keepe her yong birds, saith, that Iewes, Heretickes, and Pagans doe good workes, they cloath the naked, feede the poore, and doe other good workes of mercy: but because they bee not done in the true faith, therefore the birdes bee lost. But if they remaine in faith, then faith is the nest and safegard of their birdes, that is to say, safegard of their good workes, that the reward of them be not vtterly lost. And this matter (which Saint Augustine at large in many bookes disputeth) (Ambrosiaster, De Vocatione Gentium 1, 3 [*Patrologia Latina* 17.1078]. Saint Ambrose concludeth in few wordes saying, Hee that by nature would withstand vice, either by naturall will, or reason, hee doeth in vaine garnish the time of this life and attaineth not the verie true vertues: for without the worshipping of the true GOD, that which seemeth to bee vertue, is vice. And yet most plainely to this purpose writeth Saint Chrysostome in this wise, (Pseudo-Chrysostom, De Fide et Lege Naturae 1 [*Patrologia Graeca* 48.1081–2]). You shall finde manie which haue not the true faith, and bee not of the flocke of Christ, and yet (as it appeareth) they flourish in good workes of mercy: you shall finde them full of pitie, compassion, and giuen to iustice, and yet for all that they haue no fruit of their workes, because the chiefe worke lacketh. For when the Iewes asked of Christ what they should doe to worke good workes: hee answered, This is the worke of GOD, to beleeue in him whom hee sent (John 6.29): so that hee called faith the worke of GOD. And assoone as a man hath faith, anone hee shall florish in good workes: for faith of it selfe is full of good workes, and nothing is good without faith. And for a similitude, he saith that they which glister and shine in good workes without fayth in GOD, bee like dead men, which haue godly and precious tombes, and yet it auayleth them nothing. Faith may not bee naked without good workes, for then it is no true faith: and when it is adioyned to workes, yet it is aboue the workes. For as men that be verie men indeed, first haue life, and after bee nourished: so must our faith in Christ goe before, and after bee nourished with good workes. And life may bee without nourishment, but nourishment cannot bee without life. A man must needes bee nourished by good workes, but first hee must haue faith.

Hee that doeth good deedes, yet without faith hee hath no life. I can shew a man that by faith without workes liued, and came to heauen: but without faith, neuer man had life. The thiefe that was hanged, when Christ suffered, did beleeue onely, and the most mercifull GOD iustified him. And because no man shall say againe that hee lacked time to doe good workes, for else he would haue done them: trueth it is, and I will not contend therein, but this I will surely affirme, that faith onely saued him. If hee had liued and not regarded faith and the workes thereof, hee should haue lost his saluation againe. But this is the effect that I say, that faith by it selfe saued him, but workes by themselues neuer iustified any man. Here yee haue heard the minde of Saint Chrysostome, whereby you may perceiue, that neither faith is without workes (hauing opportunity thereto) nor workes can auaile to euerlasting life, without faith.

Homily on Christian Love and Charity, *Book of Homilies,* **1547, Short-Title Catalogue 13675. Renaissance Electronic Texts 1.1. Copyright 1994 Ian Lancashire (ed.), University Of Toronto. Available online at http://www.anglicanlibrary.org/homilies/index.htm.**

A SERMON OF CHRISTIAN LOUE AND CHARITY.

OF all things that be good to bee taught vnto Christian people, there is nothing more necessary to be spoken of, and dayly called vpon, then charity: aswell for that all maner of workes of righteousnesse bee contayned in it, as also that the decay thereof is the ruine or fall of the world, the banishment of vertue, and the cause of all vice. And for so much as almost euery man, maketh and frameth to himselfe charity after his own appetite, and how detestable soeuer his life bee, both vnto GOD and man, yet hee perswadeth himselfe still that he hath charity: therfore you shall heare now a true and plaine description or setting foorth of charity, not of mens imagination, but of the very wordes and example of our Sauiour Iesus Christ. In which description or setting foorth, euery man (as it were in a glasse) may consider himselfe, and see plainely without errour, whether hee bee in the true charity, or not.

What charitie is. The loue of God. Charity is, to loue GOD with all our heart, all our soule, and all our powers and strength. With all our heart: That is to say, that our heart, minde, and study be set to beleeue his word, to trust in him, and to loue him aboue all other things that wee loue best in heauen or in earth. With all our life: that is to say, that our chiefe ioy and delight be set vpon him and his honour, and our whole life giuen vnto the seruice of him aboue all things, with him to liue and die, and to forsake all other things, rather then him. For he that loueth his father or mother, sonne or daughter, house, or land, more then me (sayth Christ) is not woorthy to haue me (Matthew 10.37). With all our power, that is to say, that with our hands and feete, with our eyes and eares, our mouthes and tongues, and with all our parts and powers, both of body and soule, we should be giuen to the keeping and fulfilling of his commandements.

<u>The loue of thy neighbor.</u> This is the first and principall part of charity, but it is not the whole: for charity is also to loue euery man, good and euill, friend and foe, and whatsoeuer cause be giuen to the contrary, yet neuerthelesse to beare good will and heart vnto euery man, to vse our selues well vnto them, aswell in wordes and countenances, as in all our outward actes and deedes: for so Christ himselfe taught, and so also hee performed indeed. Of the loue of GOD hee taught in this wise vnto a doctour of the law, that asked him which was the great and chiefe commandement in the Law, Loue thy Lord GOD, (sayd Christ) with all thy heart, with all thy soule, and with all thy mind (Matthew 22.37). And of the loue, that wee ought to haue among our selues each to other, he teacheth vs thus, You haue heard it taught in times past, Thou shalt loue thy friend, and hate thy foe: But I tell you, Loue your enemies, speake well of them that defame and speake euill of you, doe well to them that hate you, pray for them that vexe and persecute you, that you may be the children of your father that is in heauen. For he maketh his Sunne to rise both vpon the euill and good, and sendeth raine to the iust and vniust. For if you loue them that loue you, what reward shall you haue? Doe not the Publicanes likewise? And if you speake well onely of them that be your brethren and deare beloued friends, what great matter is that? Doe not the Heathen the same also (Matthew 5.43–47)? These bee the very wordes of our Sauiour Christ himselfe, touching the loue of our neighbour. And forasmuch as the Pharisees (with their most pestilent traditions, and false interpretations, and glosses) had corrupted, and almost clearly stopped vp this pure Well of GODS liuely word, teaching that this loue and charity pertayned onely to a mans friends, and that it was sufficient for a man to loue them which doe loue him, and hate his foes: therefore Christ opened this Well againe, purged it and scoured it by giuing vnto his godly law of charitie, a true and cleare interpretation, which is this: that we ought to loue euery man, both friend and foe, adding thereto what commodity we shall haue therby, and what incommodity by doing the contrary. What thing can we wish so good for vs, as the eternall heauenly father, to reckon, and take vs for his children? And this shall we be sure of (sayth Christ) if we loue euery man without exception. And if we doe otherwise (sayth he) we be no better then the Pharisees, Publicanes, and Heathen, and shall haue our reward with them, that is, to be shut out from the number of GOD'S chosen children, and from his euerlasting inheritance in heauen.

Thus of true charitie, Christ taught that euery man is bound to loue GOD aboue all things, and to loue euery man, friend and foe. And this likewise hee did vse himselfe, exhorting his aduersaries, rebuking the faults of his aduersaries, and when hee could not amend them, yet hee prayed for them. First hee loued GOD his Father aboue all things, so much that hee sought not his owne glorie and will, but the glorie and will of his Father. I seeke not (sayd hee) mine owne will, but the will of him that sent mee (John 5.30). Nor hee refused not to die, to satisfie his Fathers will, saying, If it may bee, let this cuppe of death passe from mee: if not, thy will bee done, and not mine (Matthew 26.39, 42). Hee loued not onely his friends, but also his enemies, which (in their heartes) bare exceeding great hatred against him, and with their tongues spake all euill of him, and in their actes and deedes pursued him with all their might and power, euen vnto death, yet all this notwithstanding, hee withdrew not his fauour from them, but still loued them, preached vnto them in loue, rebuked their false doctrine, their wicked liuing, and did good vnto them, patiently taking whatsoeuer they spake or did against him. When they gaue him euill wordes, hee gaue none euill againe. When they did strike him, hee did not smite him againe: and when hee suffred death, hee did not slay them, nor threaten them, but prayed for them, and did put all things to his fathers will. And as a sheepe that is lead vnto the shambles to be slaine, and as a lambe that is shorne of his fleece, maketh no noyse nor resistance, euen so hee went to his death, without any repugnance, or opening of his mouth to say any euill. Thus haue I set foorth vnto you what charity is, aswell by the doctrine, as by the examples of Christ himselfe, whereby also euery man may without errour know himselfe, what state and condition hee standeth in, whether he bee in charity, (and so the child of the father in heauen) or not. For although almost euery man perswadeth himselfe to be in charity, yet let him examine none other man, but his owne heart, his life and conuersation, and he shall not be deceiued, but truely discerne and iudge whether hee bee in perfect charity or not. For hee that followeth not his owne appetite and will, but giueth himselfe earnestly to GOD, to doe all his will and commandements, hee may bee sure that hee loueth GOD aboue all things, and else surely hee loueth him not, whatsoeuer hee pretend: as Christ sayd, If yee loue mee, keepe my commandements. For hee that knoweth my commandements, and keepeth them, he it is (sayth Christ) that loueth mee (John 14.15, 21). And againe he sayth, Hee that loueth me, will keepe my word, and my Father will loue him, and we will both come to him, and dwell with him: and hee that loueth mee not, will not keepe my words. And likewise hee that beareth a good heart and minde, and vseth well his tongue and deeds vnto euery man, friend and foe, he may know thereby that he hath charitie. And when hee is sure that Almighty GOD taketh him for his deare beloued sonne, as S. Iohn sayth, Heereby manifestly are knowne the children of GOD, from the children of the Diuell: for whosoeuer doeth not loue his brother, belongeth not vnto GOD (1 John 3.10).

Richard Hooker, *Learned Discourse of Justification, Works, and how the Foundation of Faith is Overthrown* (1585). Available online at http://www.ccel.org/ccel/hooker/just.pdf.

> 'The wicked doth compass about the righteous; therefore perverse judgment doth proceed.' Habakkuk 1:4

Wherein then do we disagree [with Rome]? We disagree about the nature of the very essence of the medicine whereby Christ cureth our disease; about the manner of applying it; about the number and the power of means, which God requireth in us for the effectual applying thereof to our soul's comfort.

When they are required to show what the righteousness is whereby a Christian man is justified, they answer that it is a divine spiritual quality, which quality, received into the soul, doth first make it to be one of them who are born of God; and, secondly, endue it with power to bring forth such works as they do that are born of him; even as the soul of man, being joined unto his body, doth first make him to be in the number of reasonable creatures, and, secondly, enable him to perform the natural functions which are proper to his kind; that it maketh the soul gracious and amiable in the sight of God, in regard whereof it is termed grace; that by it, through the merit of Christ, we are delivered as from sin, so from eternal death and condemnation, the reward of sin. This grace they will have to be applied by infusion, to the end that, as the body is warm by the heat which is in the body, so the soul might be righteous by inherent grace; which grace they make capable of increase; as the body may be more and more warm, so the soul more and more justified, according as grace shall be augmented; the augmentation whereof is merited by good works, as good works are made meritorious by it. [Council of Trent Session VI, chapter 10] Wherefore the first receipt of grace is in their divinity the first justification; the second thereof, the second justification.

As grace may be increased by the merit of good works, so it may be diminished by the demerit of sins venial; it may be lost by mortal sin. [Trent VI, chs 14, 15] Inasmuch, therefore, as it is needful in the one case to repair, in the other to recover, the loss which is made, the infusion of grace hath her sundry aftermeals; for which cause they make many ways to apply the infusion of grace. It is applied unto infants through baptism, without either faith or works, and in them it really taketh away original sin and the punishment due unto it; it is applied unto infidels and wicked men in their first justification through baptism, without works, yet not without faith; and it taketh away both sin actual and original, together with all whatsoever punishment eternal or temporal thereby deserved. Unto such as have attained the first justification, that is to say, the first receipt of grace, it is applied further by good works to the increase of former grace, which is the second justification. If they work more and more, grace doth more and more increase, and they are more and more justified.

To such as have diminished it by venial sins it is applied by holy water, Ave Marias, crossings, papal salutations, and such like, which serve for reparations of grace decayed. To such as have lost it through mortal sin, it is applied by the sacrament (as they term it) of penance; which sacrament hath force to confer grace anew, yet in such sort that, being so conferred, it hath not altogether so much power as at the first. For it only cleanseth out the stain or guilt of sin committed, and changeth the punishment eternal into a temporary satisfactory punishment here, if time do serve, if not, hereafter to be endured, except it be either lightened by masses, works of charity, pilgrimages, fasts, and such like; or else shortened by pardon for term, or by plenary pardon quite removed and taken away. [Trent VI, ch. 14]

This is the mystery of the man of sin. This maze the Church of Rome doth cause her followers to tread when they ask her the way of justification. I cannot stand now to unrip this building and to sift it piece by piece; only I will set up a frame of apostolical erection by it in a few words, that it may befall Babylon, in presence of that which God hath builded, as it happened unto Dagon before the ark.

'Doubtless,' saith the Apostle, 'I have counted all things but loss, and I do judge them to be dung, that I may win Christ, and be found in him, not having mine own righteousness, but that which is through the faith of Christ, the righteousness which is of God through faith.' [Phil. 3.8f.] Whether they speak of the first or second justification, they make the essence of it a divine quality inherent, they make it righteousness which is in us. If it be in us, then it is ours, as our souls are ours, though we have them from God and can hold them no longer than pleaseth him; for if he withdraw the breath of our nostrils we fall to dust; but the righteousness wherein we must be found, if we will be justified, is not our own: therefore we cannot be justified by any inherent quality. Christ hath merited righteousness for as many as are found in him. In him God findeth us, if we be faithful, for by faith we are incorporated into him.

Then, although in ourselves we be altogether sinful and unrighteous, yet even the man who in himself is impious, full of iniquity, full of sin, him being found in Christ through faith, and having his sin in hatred through repentance, him God beholdeth with a gracious eye, putteth away his sin by not imputing it, taketh quite away the punishment due thereunto, by pardoning it, and accepteth him in Jesus Christ as perfectly righteous, as if he had fulfilled all that is commanded him in the law: shall I say more perfectly righteous than if himself had fulfilled the whole law? I must take heed what I say; but the Apostle saith, 'God made him who knew no sin to be sin for us, that we might be made the righteousness of God in him.' [2 Cor. 5.21] Such we are in the sight of God the Father as is the very Son of God himself. Let it be counted folly, or phrensy, or fury, or whatsoever. It is our wisdom and our comfort; we care for no knowledge in the world but this: that man hath sinned and God hath suffered; that God hath made himself the sin of men, and that men are made the righteousness of God. You see therefore that the Church of Rome, in teaching justification by inherent grace, doth pervert the truth of Christ, and that by the hands of his Apostles we have received otherwise than she teacheth.

SANCTIFICATION

Now concerning the righteousness of sanctification, we deny it not to be inherent; we grant that, unless we work, we have it not; only we distinguish it as a thing in nature different from the righteousness of justification: we are righteous the one way by the faith of Abraham, the other way, except we do the works of Abraham, we are not righteous. Of the one, St. Paul, 'To him that worketh not, but believeth, faith is counted for righteousness.' [Rom. 4:5] Of the other, St. John, 'He is righteous who worketh righteousness.' [1 John 3.7] Of the one, St. Paul doth prove by Abraham's example that we have it of faith without works. [Rom. 4] Of the other, St. James by Abraham's example, that by works we have it, and not only by faith. [James 2.18ff.] St. Paul doth plainly sever these two parts of Christian righteousness one from the other; for in the sixth to the Romans he writeth, 'Being freed from sin and made servants of God, ye have your fruit in holiness, and the end everlasting life.' [Rom. 6.22] 'Ye are made free from sin and made servants unto God'; this is the righteousness of justification; 'Ye have your fruit in holiness': this is the righteousness of sanctification. By the one we are interested in the right of inheriting; by the other we are brought to the actual possessing of eternal bliss, and so the end is everlasting life.

The prophet Habakkuk doth here [Hab. 1.4] term the Jews 'righteous men,' not only because being justified by faith they were free from sin, but also because they had their measure of fruit in holiness. According to whose example of charitable judgment, which leaveth it to God to discern what men are, and speaketh of them according to that which they do profess themselves to be, although they be not holy whom men do think, but whom God doth know indeed to be such; yet let every Christian man know that in Christian equity he standeth bound so to think and speak of his brethren as of men that have a measure in the fruit of holiness and a right unto the titles wherewith God, in token of special favour and mercy, vouchsafeth to honour his chosen servants. . . .

THE GROUND OF SALVATION

. . . This is then the foundation whereupon the frame of the Gospel is erected; that very Jesus whom the Virgin conceived of the Holy Ghost, whom Simeon embraced in his arms, [Luke 1.34f.; 2.25ff.] whom Pilate condemned, whom the Jews crucified, whom the Apostles preached, he is Christ, the Lord, the only Saviour of the world: 'other foundation can no man lay.' [1 Cor. 3.11] Thus I have briefly opened that principle in Christianity which we call the foundation of our faith. It followeth now that I declare unto you what it is directly to overthrow it. This will better appear if first we understand what it is to hold the foundation of faith. . . .

The cause of life spiritual in us is Christ, not carnally or corporally inhabiting, but dwelling in the soul of man, as a thing which (when the mind apprehendeth it) is said to inhabit and possess the mind. The mind conceiveth Christ by hearing the doctrine of Christianity. As the light of nature doth cause the mind to apprehend those truths which are merely rational, so that saving truth, which is far above the reach of human reason, cannot otherwise than by the Spirit of the Almighty be conceived. All these are implied wheresoever any one of them is mentioned as the cause of spiritual life. Wherefore when we read that 'the Spirit is our life,' [Rom. 8.10, KJV] or 'the Word our life,' [Phil. 2.16; 1 John 1.1] or 'Christ our life,' [Col. 3.4] we are in every one of these to understand that our life is Christ, by the hearing of the Gospel apprehended as a Saviour, and assented unto by the power of the Holy Ghost. The first intellectual conceit [concept] and comprehension of Christ so embraced St. Peter calleth the seed whereof we be new born. [1 Pet. 1.23] Our first embracing of Christ is our first reviving from the state of death and condemnation. [Eph. 2.1–6] 'He that hath the Son hath life,' saith St. John, 'and he that hath not the Son of God hath not life.' [1 John 5.12] If therefore he who once hath the Son may cease to have the Son, though it be but a moment, he ceaseth for that moment to have life. But the life of them who live by the Son of God is everlasting, not only for that it shall be everlasting in the world to come, but because, as 'Christ being raised from the dead dieth no more, death hath no more power over him,' [Rom. 6.9] so the justified man, being alive to God in Jesus Christ our Lord, by whom he hath life, liveth always. [Rom. 6.11]

Jeremy Taylor, excerpts from Holy Living, London: George Bell, 1883 [1650]. Available online at http://faculty.gordon.edu/hu/bi/ted_hildebrandt/spiritualformation/texts/taylor_holyliving.pdf.

CONSIDERATION OF THE GENERAL INSTRUMENTS AND MEANS TO A HOLY LIFE, BY WAY OF INTRODUCTION.

It is necessary that every man should consider, that since God hath given him an excellent nature, wisdom, and choice, an understanding soul, and an immortal spirit; having made him lord over the beasts, and but a little lower than the angels; he hath also appointed for him a work and a service great enough to employ those abilities, and hath also designed him to a state of life after this, to which he can only arrive by that service and obedience. And therefore, as every man is wholly God's own portion by the title of creation, so all our labours and care, all our powers and faculties, must be wholly employed in the service of God, and even all the days of our life; that this life being ended, we may live with him for ever.

CHAPTER IV. OF CHRISTIAN RELIGION.

Religion, in a large sense, doth signify the whole duty of man, comprehending in it justice, charity, and sobriety; because all these being commanded by God, they become a part of that honour and worship which we are bound to pay to him. And thus the word is used in St. James, Pure religion and undefiled before God and the Father in this, to visit the fatherless and widows in their affliction, and to keep himself unspotted from the world. [James i.27] But, in a more restrained sense, it is taken for that part of duty which particularly relates to God in our worshippings and adoration of him, in confessing his excellencies, loving his person, admiring his goodness, believing his word, and doing all that which may, in a proper and direct manner, do him honour. It contains the duties of the first table only, and so it is called godliness, [Tit. ii.12] and is by St. Paul distinguished from justice and sobriety. In this sense I am now to explicate the parts of it.

Of the internal Actions of Religion

Those I call the internal actions of religion, in which the soul only is employed, and ministers to God in the special actions of faith, hope, and charity. Faith believes the revelations of God, hope expects his promises, and charity loves his excellencies and mercies. Faith gives us understanding to God, hope gives up all the passions and affections to heaven and heavenly things, and charity gives the will to the service of God. Faith is opposed to infidelity, hope to despair, charity to enmity and hostility; and these three sanctify the whole man, and make our duty to God and obedience to his commandments to be chosen, reasonable, and delightful, and therefore to be entire, persevering, and universal.

SECTION I. OF FAITH

The Acts and Offices of Faith are,

1. To believe everything which God hath revealed to us: [Demus, Deum aliquid posse, quod nos fateamur investigare non posse. – St. Aug. 1. xxi. c.7. de Civitat.] and, when once we are convinced that God hath spoken it, to make no further inquiry, but humbly to submit; ever remembering that there are some things which our understanding cannot fathom, nor search out their depth.

2. To believe nothing concerning God but what is honourable and excellent, as knowing that belief to be no honouring of God which entertains of him any dishonourable thoughts. Faith is the parent of charity, and whatsoever faith entertains must be apt to produce love to God; but he that believes God to be cruel or unmerciful, or a rejoice in the unavoidable damnation of the greatest part of mankind, or that he speaks one thing and privately means another, thinks evil thoughts concerning God, and such as for which we should hate a man, and therefore are great enemies of faith, being apt to destroy charity. Our faith concerning God must be as himself hath revealed and described his own excellencies; and, in our discourses; we must remove from him all imperfection, and attribute to him all excellency.

3. To give ourselves wholly up to Christ, in heart and desire, to become disciples of his doctrine with choice, (besides conviction,) being in the presence of God but as idiots, that is, without any principles of our own to hinder the truth of God; but sucking in greedily all that God hath taught us, believing it infinitely, and loving to believe it. For this is an act of love reflected upon faith, or an act of faith leaning upon love.

4. To believe all God's promises, and that whatsoever is promised in Scripture shall, on God's part, be as surely performed as if we had it in possession. This act makes us to rely upon God with the same confidence as we did on our parents when we were children, when we made no doubt but whatsoever we needed we should have it, if it were in their power.

5. To believe, also, the conditions of the promise, or that part of the revelation which concerns our duty. Many are apt to believe the article of remission of sins, but they believe it without the condition of repentance, or the fruits of holy life; and that is to believe the article otherwise than God intended it. For the covenant of the Gospel is the great object of faith, and that supposes our duty to answer his grace; that God will be our God, so long as we are his people. The other is not faith, but flattery.

6. To profess publicly the doctrine of Jesus Christ, openly owning whatsoever he hath revealed and commanded, not being ashamed of the word of God, or of any practices enjoined by it; and this without complying with any man's interest, not regarding favour, nor being moved with good words, not fearing disgrace, or loss, or inconvenience, or death itself.

7. To pray without doubting, without weariness, without faintness; entertaining no jealousies or suspicions of God, but being confident of God's hearing us, and of his returns to us, whatsoever the manner or the instance be, that, if we do our duty, it will be gracious and merciful.

These acts of faith are, in several degrees, in the servants of Jesus; some have it but as a grain of mustard-seed; some grow up to a plant; some have the fullness of faith; but the least faith that is must be a persuasion so strong as to make us undertake the doing of all that duty which Christ built upon the foundation of believing. But we shall best discern the truth of our faith by these following signs. St. Jerome reckons three. [Dial. adver. Lucif.]

Signs of true Faith.

1. An earnest and vehement prayer: for it is impossible we should heartily believe the things of God and the glories of the gospel, and not most importunately desire them. For everything is desired according to our belief of its excellency and possibility.

2. To do nothing for vain-glory, but wholly for the interests of religion and these articles we believe; valuing not at all the rumours of men, but the praise of God, to whom, by faith, we have given up all our intellectual faculties.

3. To be content with God for our judge, for our patron, for our Lord, for our friend; desiring God to be all in all to us, as we are, in our understanding and affections, wholly his.

Add to these:

4. To be a stranger upon earth in our affections, and to have all our thoughts and principal desires fixed upon the matters of faith, the things of heaven. For, if a man were adopted heir to Caesar, he would (if he believed it real and affective) despise the present, and wholly be at court in his father's eye; and his desires would outrun his swiftest speed, and all his thoughts would spend themselves in creating ideas and little fantastic images of his future condition. Now God hath made us heirs of his kingdom, and co-heirs with Jesus: if we believed this, we should think, and affect, and study accordingly. But he that rejoices in gain, and his heart dwells in the world, and is espoused to a fair estate, and transported with a light momentary joy, and is afflicted with losses, and amazed with temporal persecutions, and esteems disgrace or poverty in a good cause to be intolerable – this man either has no inheritance in heaven, or believes none; and believes not that he is adopted to the son of God – the heir of eternal glory.

5. St. James's sign is the best: 'Show me your faith by your works.' Faith makes the merchant diligent and venturous, and that makes him rich. Ferdinando of Arragon believed the story told him by Columbus, and therefore he furnished him with ships, and got the West Indies by his faith in the undertaker. But Henry the Seventh of England believed him not, and therefore trusted him not with shipping, and lost all the purchase of that faith. It is told us by Christ, 'He that forgives shall be forgiven': if we believe this, it is certain we shall forgive our enemies; for none of us all but need and desire to be forgiven. No man can possibly despise, or refuse to desire such excellent glories as are revealed to them that are servants of Christ; and yet we do nothing that is commanded us as a condition to obtain them. No man could work a day's labour without faith; but because he believes he shall

have his wages at the day's or week's end, he does his duty. But he only believes who does that thing which other men, in like cases, do when they do believe. He that believes money gotten with danger is better than poverty with safety, will venture for it in unknown lands or seas; and so will he that believes it better to get to heaven with labour, than to go to hell with pleasure.

6. He that believes does not make haste, but waits patiently till the times of refreshment come, and dares trust God for the morrow, and is no more solicitous for the next year than he is for that which is past; and it is certain that man wants faith who dares be more confident of being supplied, when he hath money in his purse, than when he hath it only in bills of exchange from God; or that relies more upon his own industry than upon God's providence when his own industry fails him. If you dare trust to God when the case, to human reason, seems impossible, and trust to God then also out of choice, not because you have nothing else to trust to, but because he is the only support of a just confidence, then you give a good testimony of your faith.

7. True faith is confident, and will venture all the world upon the strength of its persuasion. Will you lay your life on it, your estate, your reputation, that the doctrine of Jesus Christ is true in every article? Then you have true faith. But he that fears men more than God, believes men more than he believes in God.

8. Faith, if it be true, living, and justifying, cannot be separated from a good life; it works miracles, makes a drunkard become sober, a lascivious person become chaste, a covetous man become liberal; it overcomes the world, it works righteousness, [2 Cor. xiii.5; Rom. viii.10.] and makes us diligently to do, and cheerfully to suffer, whatsoever God hath placed in our way to heaven.

SECTION II. OF THE HOPE OF A CHRISTIAN.

Faith, differs from hope in the extension of its object, and in the intention of degree. St. Austin thus accounts their differences: [Enchirid. c. 8.] Faith is of all things revealed, good and bad, rewards and punishments, of things past, present, and to come, of things that concern us, of things that concern us not; but hope hath for its object things only that are good, and fit to be hoped for, future, and concerning ourselves; and because these things are offered to us upon conditions of which we may so fail as we may change our will, therefore our certainty is less than the adherences of faith; which (because faith relies only upon one proposition, that is, the truth of the word of God,) cannot be made uncertain in themselves, though the object of our hope may become uncertain to us, and to our possession. For it is infallibly certain that there is heaven for all the godly, and for me amongst them all, if I do my duty. But that I shall enter into heaven is the object of my hope, not of my faith; and is so sure as it is certain I shall persevere in the ways of God.

The Acts of Hope are,

1. To rely upon God with a confident expectation of his promises; ever esteeming that every promise of God is a magazine of all that grace and relief which we can need in that instance for which the promise is made. Every degree of hope is a degree of confidence.

2. To esteem all the danger of an action, and the possibilities of miscarriage, and every cross accident that can intervene, to be no defect on God's part, but either a mercy on his part, or a fault on ours; for then we shall be sure to trust in God when we see him to be our confidence, and ourselves the cause of all mischances. The hope of a Christian is prudent and religious.

3. To rejoice in the midst of a misfortune, or seeming sadness, knowing that this may work for good, and will, if we be not wanting to our souls. This is a direct act of hope to look through the cloud, and look for a beam of the light from God; and this is called in Scripture rejoicing in tribulation, when the God of hope fills us with all joy in believing.' Every degree of hope brings a degree of joy.

4. To desire, to pray, and to long for the great object of our hope, the mighty price of our high calling; and to desire the other things of this life as they are promised, that is, so far as they are made necessary and useful to us, in order to God's glory and the great end of souls. Hope and fasting are said to be the two wings of prayer. Fasting is but as the wing of a bird; but hope is like the wing of an angel, soaring up to heaven, and bears our prayers to the throne of grace. Without hope, it is impossible to pray, but hope makes our prayers reasonable, passionate, and religious; for it relies upon God's promise, or experience, or providence, and story. Prayer is always in proportion to our hope, zealous and affectionate.

5. Perseverance is the perfection of the duty of hope, and its last act; and so long as our hope continues, so long we go on in duty and diligence; but he that is to raise a castle in an hour, sits down and does nothing towards it; and Herod, the sophister, left off to teach his son, when he saw that twenty-four pages, appointed to wait on him, and called by the several letters of the alphabet, could never make him to understand his letters perfectly.

SECTION III. OF CHARITY, OR THE LOVE OF GOD.

Love is the greatest thing that God can give us; for himself is love; and it is the greatest thing we can give to God; for it will also give ourselves and carry with it all that is ours. The apostle calls it the band of perfection; it is the old, and it is the new, and it is the great commandment, and it is all the commandments; for it is the fulfilling of the law. It does the work of all other graces without any instrument but its own immediate virtue. For as the love to sin makes a man sin against all his own reason, and all the discourses of wisdom, and all the advices of his friends, and without temptation, and without opportunity, so does the love of God; it makes a man chaste without the laborious arts of fasting and exterior disciplines, temperate in the midst of feasts, and is active enough to choose it without any intermedial appetites, and reaches at glory through the very heart of grace without any other arms but those of love. It is a grace that loves God for himself, and our neighbours for God. The consideration of God's goodness and bounty, the experience of those profitable and excellent emanations from him, may be, and most commonly are, the first motive of our love; but when we are once entered, and have tasted the goodness of God, we love the spring for its own excellency, passing from passion to reason, from thanking to adoring, from sense to spirit, from considering ourselves to an union with God: and this is the image and little representation of heaven; it is beatitude in picture, or rather the infancy and beginnings of glory.

We need no incentives by way of special enumeration to move us to the love of God, for we cannot love anything for any reason real or imaginary, but that excellence is infinitely more eminent in God. There can but two things create love – perfection and usefulness: to which answer on our part, 1. Admiration; and 2. Desire; and both these are centered in love. For the entertainment of the first, there is in God an infinite nature, immensity or vastness without extension or limit, immutability, eternity, omnipotence, omniscience, holiness, dominion, providence, bounty, mercy, justice, perfection in himself, and the end to which all things and all actions must be directed, and will, at last, arrive. The consideration of which may be heightened, if we consider our distance from all these glories, our smallness and limited nature, our nothing, our inconstancy, our age like a span, our weakness and ignorance, our poverty, our inadvertency and inconsideration, our disabilities and disaffections to do good, our harsh natures and unmerciful inclinations, our universal iniquity, and our necessities and dependencies, not only on God originally and essentially, but even our need of the meanest of God's creatures, and our being obnoxious to the weakest and most contemptible. But for the entertainment of the second, we may consider that in him is a torrent of pleasure for the voluptuous; he is the fountain of honour for the ambitious; an inexhaustible treasure for the covetous. Our vices are in love with fantastic pleasures and images of perfection, which are truly and really to be found nowhere but in God. And therefore our virtues have such proper objects that it is but reasonable they should all turn into love; for certain it is that this love will turn all into virtue. For in the scrutinies for righteousness and judgment, when it is inquired whether such a person be a good man or no, the meaning is not, What does he believe? or what does he hope? but what he loves. [St. Aug. I. ii. Confess. c. 6]

The Measures and Rules of Divine Love.

But because this passion is pure as the brightest and smoothest mirror, and, therefore, is apt to be sullied with every impurer breath, we must be careful that our love to God be governed by these measures:

1. That our love to God be sweet, even, and full of tranquillity, having in it no violences or transportations, but going on in a course of holy actions and duties, which are proportionable to our condition and present state; not to satisfy all the desire, but all the probabilities and measures of our strength. A new beginner in religion hath passionate and violent desires; but they must not be the measure of his actions; but he must consider his strength, his late sickness and state of death, the proper temptations of his condition, and stand at first upon defence; not go to storm a strong fort, or attack a potent enemy, or do heroical actions, and fitter for giants in religion. Indiscreet violences and untimely forwardness are the rocks of religion against which tender spirits often suffer shipwreck.

2. Let our love be prudent and without illusion, that is, that it express itself in such instances which God hath chosen or which we choose ourselves by proportion

to his rules and measures. Love turns into doating when religion turns into superstition. No degree of love can be imprudent, but the expressions may: we cannot love God too much, but we may proclaim it in indecent manners.

3. Let our love be firm, constant, and inseparable; not coming and returning like the tide, but descending like a never-failing river, ever running into the ocean of divine excellency, passing on in the channels of duty and a constant obedience, and never ceasing to be what it is till it be turned into sea and vastness, even the immensity of a blessed eternity.

John Henry Newman, (1801–1890), Lectures on the Doctrine of Justification, third edition, London: Rivington, 1874, pp. 304–6.

Note on Lecture 12. On Good Works as the Remedy of Post-Baptismal Sin

FROM what has been said, it would seem that, while works before justification are but conditions and preparations for that gift, works after justification are much more, and that, not only as being intrinsically good and holy, but as being fruits of *faith*. And viewed as one with faith, which is the appointed instrument of justification after Baptism, they are, – (as being connatural with faith and indivisible from it, organs through which it acts and which it hallows), – instruments with faith of the continuance of justification, or, in other words, *of the remission of sin after Baptism*. Since this doctrine sounds strange to the ears of many in this day, and the more so because they have been taught that the Homilies, which our Church has authoritatively sanctioned, are decidedly opposed to it, I make the following extracts from that important work, for the accommodation of the general reader who may not have it at hand. Deeply is it to be regretted that a book, which contains 'doctrine' so 'godly and wholesome and necessary for *these* Times', as well as for the sixteenth century, should popularly be known only by one or two extracts, to the omission of such valuable matter as shall now be quoted:

'Our Saviour Christ in the Gospel teacheth us, that it profiteth a man nothing to have in possession all the riches of the whole world, and the wealth and glory thereof, if in the mean season he lose his soul, or do that thing whereby it should become captive unto death, sin, and hell-fire. By the which saying, he not only instructeth us how much the soul's health is to be preferred before worldly commodities, but it also serveth to stir up our minds and to prick us forwards to seek diligently and learn by *what means* we may preserve and keep our souls ever in safety, that is, *how we may recover our health* if it be lost or impaired, and how it may be defended and maintained if once we have it. Yea, He teacheth us also thereby to esteem that *as a precious medicine* and an inestimable jewel, that *hath such strength and virtue in it*, that can either procure or preserve so incomparable a treasure. For if we greatly regard that medicine or salve that is able to heal sundry and grievous diseases of the body, much more will we esteem that which hath *like power over the soul*. And because we might be better assured both to know and to have in readiness *that so profitable remedy*, He, as a most faithful and loving teacher, showeth Himself both what it is, and where we may find it, and *how we may use and apply it*. For, when both He and His disciples were grievously accused of the Pharisees, to have defiled their soul in breaking the constitutions of the Elders, because they went to meat and washed not their hands before, according to the custom of the Jews, Christ, answering their superstitious complaints, teacheth them *an especial remedy how to keep clean their souls*, notwithstanding the breach of such superstitious orders; "*Give alms,*" saith He, "and behold all things are clean unto you."

'He teacheth, then, that to be merciful and charitable in helping the poor, *is the means* to keep the soul pure and clean *in the sight of God*. We are taught therefore by this, that *merciful almsgiving is profitable to purge the soul from the infection and filthy spots of sin*. The same lesson doth the Holy Ghost also teach in sundry other places of the Scripture, saying, "Mercifulness and almsgiving purgeth from all sins, and delivereth from death, and suffereth not the soul to come into darkness." [Tobit iv.] *A great confidence* may they have *before the high God*, that show mercy and compassion to them that are afflicted. The wise Preacher, the Son of Sirach, confirmeth the same, when he saith, that "as water quencheth burning fire, even so mercy and alms resisteth and reconcileth sins." And sure it is, *that mercifulness quaileth the heat of sin so much*, that they shall not take hold upon man to hurt him; or *if ye have by any infirmity or weakness been touched and annoyed with them, straightways shall mercifulness wipe and wash them away, as salves and remedies to heal their sores* and grievous diseases. And therefore that holy father Cyprian taketh good occasion to exhort earnestly to the merciful work, to giving alms and helping the poor, and then he admonisheth to consider how wholesome and profitable is it to relieve the needy and help the afflicted, *by the which we may purge our sins* and heal our wounded souls.'

Such is the virtue of works, not before justification, but after, as the means of keeping and restoring, not of procuring it, as fruits of faith done in the grace of Christ and by the inspiration of His Spirit, not as dead works done in the flesh, and displeasing to God. Attention should be especially called to a parallelism between one sentence in this extract and what was quoted in Lecture X. (pp. 223, 224) from the Sermon on the Passion, as showing how our Reformers *identified* faith and works, not in idea, but in fact. The one Homily says 'It remaineth that I show unto you how to apply Christ's death and passion to our comfort as a *medicine to our wounds* . . . Here is the mean, whereby we must apply the fruits of Christ's death unto our deadly wound, . . . namely, faith.' The other speaks of alms as 'a precious *medicine*, a profitable *remedy*', which we are to 'use and apply', '*salves* and *remedies* to heal' our 'sores and grievous diseases'.

It must be observed, moreover, that though faith is the appointed means of pleading Christ's merits, and so of cleansing (as it were) works done in faith from their adhering imperfection, yet that after all those works, though mixed with evil, are good in themselves, as being the fruit of the Spirit. Hence, in the passage which follows what has been quoted, very slight mention is made of faith, and the grace of God is made all in all, as 'working in us both to will and to do', and 'giving us power to get wealth'; [Deut. viii. 18.] the contrast lying not between faith and works, but between God's doings and man's doings. Nay, even when the image of the tree and fruit is introduced, it is interpreted of the *grace* of God the Holy Ghost in us, and of the *effects* in us of His gracious Indwelling.

William Temple, Nature, Man and God: Being the Gifford lectures delivered in the University of Glasgow in the academical years 1932–33 and 1933–34, London: Macmillan, 1960, pp. 378–403.

LECTURE XV: DIVINE GRACE AND HUMAN FREEDOM

... Now there are two main ways in which the self is delivered from self-centredness and its resultant antagonisms in those relationships. One is by the activity of genuine and disinterested love within the self; the other is by the widening of the area within which obligation and loyalty are recognised as holding sway. The natural self is capable of disinterested love; indeed it is probable that every child has for its mother a love which is in part disinterested so soon as it is capable of any true emotion as distinct from animal desire. The vitiation of selfhood by self-centredness is never complete, though it is very pervasive and there are few children who come to years of so-called discretion in whom self-interest has not contaminated what elements they once had of disinterested love. Yet the capacity for such love is always there in some degree; it is part of selfhood as God designed and created it. By grace of creation man is made in the image of God, and however much that image may be blurred, it is seldom if ever effaced, and never until the corruption of self-concern has eaten deeply into the very constitution of the self. ...

Disinterested love and devotion are called out chiefly by persons who have some special affinity for the person concerned, or by the society or nation to which he belongs. This love and devotion may attain to very great heights, even beyond the sacrifice of life to that only true self-sacrifice which is the ignoring or forgetting of every self-centred interest. But admittedly this is rare; and even when it occurs two facts are to be noticed which give warning of grave limitations. The first is that this response, so far as it is given to persons, is given only to a few or to one, and so far as it is given to a community is always to a limited community; it is therefore compatible with antagonism and even hatred towards other persons or communities, and sometimes seems, at least, to be deepened and intensified by these. The other fact is closely connected with this, namely, that this devotion, with all its selflessness, is called forth by some affinity to the self, so that the lover not only belongs to the beloved but the beloved to him, the patriot not only belongs to the country but the country to him. ...

Yet it has in it the same essential contradiction. It is a self-devotion resting on appeal to the self in its particularity; it is the devotion of the Englishman to England, of the Frenchman to France and so forth; it is the discovery of himself not only in his other but specifically in his own other. In such devotion the sun of self may be setting behind the horizon, but it never quite disappears; and if it did, it would destroy the occasion of the devotion. This natural love may be truly disinterested; it is its own reward and looks for no return; yet it is in itself a return, and depends for its very existence on being so. A loves B because B is the appropriate object of A's love. A does not love B for the sake of any result, nor even for the enjoyment of the sentiment of love; A loves B for being B. Yet this love is rooted in the special appeal which B has for A, and which neither does B exercise over others, nor does A find exercised over him by others. Consequently the complex unit AB may be exceedingly self-centred.

Similarly with devotion to group or country, the patriot's love for his country depends on its being his. Consequently patriotism may be a genuinely disinterested love, and yet co-exist with antagonism and hatred towards other countries. It does not appear that the way to true emancipation from self-centredness is to be found in this natural capacity for devotion. It is very noble; it is akin to God; but it is, as Nurse Cavell said of Patriotism, 'not enough'.

And yet when all is said, *advance which comes as continuous progress is an expansion of the circle of which self is still the centre. It may theoretically be so expanded as to include all mankind, even all spiritual beings. But self is still the centre, and if God Himself be included in the circle, He is peripheral, not central; He is, for me, my God, not God whose I am.*

At first it may even seem that, in so far as moral growth is only the expansion of the circle of which self is the centre, the greater the growth the greater the evil; to make much centre on the self is worse than to make little, and to include God on the periphery is worse than to exclude Him altogether. But this is to press the spatial metaphor beyond its intention, and it is equally true to say that the self which is centre to a large circle counts for less relatively to that circle than it would relatively to a small circle; and where God comes in at all, He begins to count for what He is even where that is not as yet accepted.

It is, perhaps, idle to speculate whether the purely moral progress, which consists in lengthening the radius of the circle drawn round the self as centre, could bring satisfaction to man in respect of his temporal interests. Probably it could not do this. . . . What is more to our purpose is that the colossal structures of enlightened egoism to which that way of progress leads will never effect the deliverance of the self from self-centredness, but can only seek to make self-centredness compatible with final well-being. And this it can never be, if God exists; for it fixes the self in a false relation to God; it makes self prior and God secondary; at best it makes self and God two entities equal in type and principle, however much one may exceed the other in scale. . . .

With this reflection we pass beyond the morality of areas of loyalty and obligation. The problem now is not the relation of finite selves to one another, in isolation or in groups. The problem now is the relation of the finite spirit to the infinite. . . . *What is quite certain is that the self cannot by any effort of its own lift itself off its own self as centre and resystematise itself about God as its centre. Such radical conversion must be the act of God, and that too by some process other than the gradual self-purification of a self-centred soul assisted by the ever-present influence of God diffused through nature including human nature. It cannot be a process only of enlightenment. Nothing can suffice but a redemptive act. Something impinging upon the self from without must deliver it from the freedom which is perfect bondage to the bondage which is its only perfect freedom.*

So we have the self not only taking itself as centre and thus falsifying its whole scale of values, but confirmed and hardened in self-centredness by both the attraction and the repulsion of the other self-centred selves among which it must live. It is by no means wholly corrupt, if that means that there is no aspiration after good left in it; on the contrary, pursuit of good is its only motive of deliberate action – even of wrong action – though its vision of good is distorted, so that this leads it astray. But it is wholly corrupt if by that is meant that there is no part of it untainted by this corruption. There is much in it that is the very stuff of good, the ineffaceable image of God. But there is nothing that is unadulterated good, and the image of God is blurred.

How can God deliver such a soul? The soul is helpless, fixed in the vicious circle whereby it both determines and is determined by its apparent good. And the ways of escape which we have considered, while they offer a real liberation, never lead to a complete deliverance. The soul or self can contribute nothing except a certain passivity of response. If salvation comes it is the gift of God alone.

In what sense, then, is there spiritual freedom in man before God . . .? It is tempting at first to say that though God gives the call, and the strength of perseverance to him who responds, the response at least is the free act of the human soul. And this is not wholly or merely untrue. For whether or not the soul responds is determined by the moral character of the soul. The divine claim is presented; some refuse it, some respond to it; and so they are judged. Which they do depends on what they are. And that is not wholly determined by past history or present environment, because every self is in part an original contribution to the scheme of reality and is moreover, in the very act of giving or refusing its response, a self-determining system of experience. The fact that the soul or self responds, or refuses to respond, is a result, in part at least, of what comes into being with that self. It is free, because nothing outside the self compels it.

And to that very freedom the divine appeal must be addressed. If God exercised compulsion by forcing obedience or by remaking the character of a self against its will, He would have abandoned omnipotence in the act which should assert it, for the will that was overridden would remain outside His control. The only obedience congruous with the nature of either God or man is an obedience willingly, and therefore freely, offered – a response which is given because the self finds it good to offer it. Our question therefore is this: How can the self find it good to submit willingly to removal from its self-centredness and welcome reconstitution about God as centre? There is in fact one power known to men, and only one, which can effect this, not only for one or another function of the self (as beauty and truth can do) but for the self as a whole in its entirety and integrity. When a man acts to please one whom he loves, doing or bearing what apart from that love he would not choose to do or bear, his action is wholly determined by the other's pleasure, yet in no action is he so utterly free – that is, so utterly determined by his apparent good. And when love is not yet present,

There is one power and only one that can evoke it; that is the power of love expressed in sacrifice, of love (that is to say) doing and bearing what apart from love would not be willingly borne or done. The one hope, then, of bringing human selves into right relationship to God is that God should declare His love in an act, or acts, of sheer self-sacrifice, thereby winning the freely offered love of the finite selves which He has created.

Here the last great problem confronts us. For one great religion at least consists in the conviction that God has so revealed Himself; but not all within whose experience that revelation has been proclaimed have offered their response. What is still lacking? Is the decisive step which is required a step to be taken by man or by God? If we say that God must first act, we seem to be involved in all the difficulties of Predestination: does God then arbitrarily choose to call some with the appeal that will stir their response, leaving others to await in vain the transforming touch? If so, how is He just or even loving? But on the other side, if we say that man's is the decisive step, we make him master of his fate even over against God; if God's grace is a universally bestowed assistance, the use of which depends upon ourselves alone, then we are again in the centre and not God.'

Against this all deep religious experience, and all the authority of reason, loudly protests. . . .

If there is any reality at all in the experience called Religion, we must admit and affirm both the priority and the all-sufficiency of God. For the only idea of God that is possible to the scientific and philosophic reason is such as to claim for Him these qualities. Moreover, religious experience when it is most intense confirms this. All is *of* God; the only thing of my very own which I can contribute to my own redemption is the sin from which I need to be redeemed. My capacity for fellowship with God is God's gift in creation; my partial deliverance from self-centredness by response to truth, beauty and goodness is God's gift through the natural world which He sustains in being and the history of man which He controls. One thing is my own—the self-centredness which leads me to find my apparent good in what is other and less than the true good. This true good is the divine love and what flows from it appreciated as its expression. In response to that good, man finds his only true freedom, for only then does the self act as what it truly is and thus achieve true self-expression.

Bibliography

Background

Anselm of Canterbury, *The Prayers and Meditations of Saint Anselm*.
Augustine of Hippo, *Anti-Pelagian Writings*.
Geoffrey Chaucer, 'Second Nun's Prologue', and 'Second Nun's Tale', *Canterbury Tales*.
Hildegard von Bingen, *Ordo Virtutem, Vox Animae*.
Julian of Norwich, *Showings*.
Thomas à Kempis, *The Imitation of Christ*.
Martin Luther, 'Two Types of Righteousness', in *Martin Luther's Basic Theological Writings*, T. F. Lull (ed.), Minneapolis: Augsburg Fortress, 1989.
Gordon Rupp et al. (eds), *Luther and Erasmus: Free Will and Salvation*, Philadelphia: Westminster Press, 1969.
St Thomas Aquinas, *The Gospel of Grace, Summa Theologiae*.

Modern Works

John Bunyan, *The Doctrine of Law and Grace Unfolded*, Richard L. Greaves (ed.), Oxford: Clarendon, 1976 [1659].

John Bunyan, *A Holy Life with A Treatise of the Fear of God and The Greatness of the Soul*, Richard L. Greaves (ed.), Oxford: Clarendon Press, 1981 [1679], pp. 251–365.

Alban Butler, *Lives of the Saints*, Collegeville, MN: Liturgical Press, 1995.

Joseph Butler, 'Dissertation on the Nature of Virtue', in *Analogy of Religion*, Philadelphia: Lippincott, 1900 [1736], pp. 324–32.

John Calvin, *Institutes of the Christian Religion*, Book III, John T. McNeill (ed.), Philadelphia: Westminster Press, 1960, pp. 542–725.

'Canons of Dort', 'Westminster Confession', 'Westminster Shorter Catechism', in Jaroslav Pelikan and Valerie R. Hotchkiss (eds), *Creeds and Confessions of the Faith in the Christian Tradition*, 4 vols. New Haven: Yale University Press, 2003, pp. 571–662.

Horton Davies, *Worship and Theology in England*, 5 vols, Princeton, NJ: Princeton University Press, 1970–96.

Jonathan Edwards, *Religious Affections*, John E. Smith (ed.), New Haven, CT: Yale University Press, 1959 [1746].

Karlfried Froehlich, 'Justification Language and Grace: the Charge of Pelagianism in the Middle Ages', in *Probing the Reformed Tradition: Historical Studies in Honor of Edward A. Dowey, Jr.*, Elsie McKee and Brian G. Armstrong (eds), Louisville, KY: Westminster/John Knox Press, 1989, pp. 21–47.

Kenneth E. Kirk, *The Vision of God*, Cambridge: James Clarke & Co., 1990 [1928].

William Law, *A Serious Call to a Devout and Holy Life*, New York: Vintage Books, 2002.

John Henry Newman, *Lectures on the Doctrine of Justification*, 3rd edn, New York: Scribner, Welford, & Armstrong, 1874.

Geoffrey Rowell, Kenneth Stevenson and Rowan Williams (eds), *Love's Redeeming Work: The Anglican Quest for Holiness*, Oxford: Oxford University Press, 2001.

Francis De Sales, *Introduction to the Devout Life*, New York: Image Books, Doubleday, 1989 [1609].

Edmund Spenser, *The Faerie Queene*, Book I, New York: Penguin Putnam, 1987.

The Thirty-Nine Articles of the Church of England (1571), in *Confessions and Catechisms of the Reformation*, Mark A. Noll (ed.), Grand Rapids, MI: Baker, 1991.

7

The Sacraments

KENNETH STEVENSON

Introduction

Danube is the name of a book by the Italian literary critic Claudio Magris.[1] The reader is taken on a fascinating journey along Europe's most famous river, starting at possible sources in the springs in Bavaria and travelling through Austria, Hungary, Serbia, Romania and on to the Black Sea. But the story is not just about waterways. It is about the peoples, the civilizations, the ideas that have formed the Danube communities. It is, therefore, a tale of diversity and conflict, social and religious included. But the whole picture is somehow held together by that extraordinary river, at times beautiful, frequently colourful and, on occasion, risky. Applying those images to Anglican sacramental thought and practice, this essay sets out to look at some key trajectories that can help give this particular theological river some shape and coherence, while not ignoring the unresolved issues.

Six tributaries emerge from the Anglican story and form significant trajectories for our discussion: Participation, Covenant and Sacrifice, Consecration, Presence, Contemporaneity and Conversion. These are focused on the six historical figures chosen for the accompanying Readings section – Richard Hooker, Jeremy Taylor, Robert Isaac Wilberforce, Oliver Quick, John Gaden and Colin Buchanan. We shall use these trajectories freely in order to look primarily – but not exclusively – at baptism and the Eucharist. Anglicanism is so profoundly shaped by the way new and old ideas are synthesized that it is impossible to define one single, unitary 'system'.

Background – Origins

First of all, some historical background. It is always tempting to assume that everything that has already happened is a prelude to a grand finale in the present. But every age has its own contributions, faults, challenges and foibles – and this holds true as much for theology as anything else. There is, moreover, something of the maverick about each of these six authors. Like the best theology, none of them is dull, mainstream or easily labelled. That suits well a discussion about sacramental theology, as the whole area can be a slippery one. The word 'sacrament' is derived from the Latin word used of a Roman soldier's oath, and it was taken over to translate the Greek word 'mystery' in the New Testament,

---

1 Claudio Magris, *Danube: A Sentimental Journey from the Source to the Black Sea*, translated from the Italian by Patrick Creagh, London: Collins Harvill, 1989.

when referring to the work of Christ (cf. Col. 1.26f.; Eph. 3.4, 9; 6.19). When words have to be translated, there is often some interpretation in the process. Those two words, with their different resonances, provide the foundation for the way Christians have expressed key aspects of the experience of the life of faith. As the Anglican story will show, the Latin approach can be over-mechanistic, whereas the Greek is more adverbial, all-embracing.

But how many sacraments are there? In Augustine's time, the word had a wide application. It embraced even the Lord's Prayer, highlighting its uniqueness, especially for those preparing for baptism. And in the Eucharist, sacrament embraced both word and altar – something dear to the heart of the Reformation. Moreover, there was no consistent numbering. The Eastern churches have never closed the book on how many 'mysteries' there are: Pseudo-Dionysius (fifth century) has three – baptism, Eucharist and unction. Seven, however, was a favourite symbolic number in the medieval West, for example in the structure of the Lord's Prayer, the Gifts of the Spirit or the Deadly Sins. When Peter Lombard in the twelfth century defined the seven sacraments – baptism, Eucharist, confirmation, marriage, ordination, penance and unction (last rites) – he was probably expressing accepted thinking of his time; and the scheme was refined by Thomas Aquinas a century later. All seven were taken to be derived from the Lord himself, and all were believed necessary for the Church in the work of the gospel.

Background – the Reformation

It was inevitable that this scheme would be challenged at the Reformation, because any sacrament needed a full scriptural base in the Gospels. This had consequences for how the Bible was to be used, including at every act of worship. Luther kept baptism, the Eucharist and penance (initially) as sacraments. Calvin adhered to the first two only as truly 'dominical', instituted by Christ himself. Forms of service were provided for the remaining 'ordinances' (with the exception of confirmation), but there remained the question of their status, in other words, whether they were necessary. The Anglican formularies walk circumspectly. Article XXV singles out baptism and Eucharist as 'the two sacraments ordained of Christ our Lord in the Gospel'. But it immediately goes on to refer to the other five, 'commonly called sacraments', which, however, 'are not to be counted as sacraments of the Gospel . . . but yet not have the like nature of sacraments . . . for that they have not any visible sign or ceremony ordained of God'.

Such an approach expresses both the Reformation protest against the medieval system and the wholeness of Catholic tradition. It is reflected in the provisions in the early English *Prayer Books* and persists in the liturgical books of worldwide Anglicanism today. Baptism and Eucharist are pre-eminent, whereas the other five may be called sacraments, or they are often referred to as sacramental rites or ordinances. Time and experience have shown that they are all needed for the life of the Church and not optional extras, which has meant constant teaching to that effect, for example in Samuel Seabury's exhortation to New Englanders about the importance of coming to Communion. People need to be confirmed, married and visited when sick; and others again need to be ordained in order for these sacraments and rites to be properly carried out, not just on their own behalf, but in the name of the whole Church, the bishop embodying a universal (catholic) and local (diocesan) ministry.

So much for the number of the sacraments – what of their meaning and function? Augustine with his penchant for one-liners referred to a sacrament as a 'visible word', with outward and inward aspects. From that kind of loose definition developed the much more sophisticated approach of the later Middle Ages, where a sacrament requires for its validity both matter (the outward sign) and form (the required words), together with the right intention on the part of the priest. All this meant that the sacrament 'happened', regardless of the priest's worthiness. Such a minimalistic theory the Reformers found unacceptable, because it could drive a wedge between what the Church is doing and what the Christian is receiving.

Hot disputes arose, therefore, about the meaning and function of the sacraments. The Reformers rejected the medieval scheme. That included transubstantiation, defined at the Fourth Lateran Council in 1215 and worked out by Thomas Aquinas, as well as eucharistic sacrifice, much elaborated in the Middle Ages, but defined only at the Council of Trent to answer Reformation criticism. Instead, by generally adopting the term 'Lord's Supper', they all stressed faithful reception. Aquinas did not teach that Christ was 'located' on the altar, nor that he was 're-offered' in the Mass, but subsequent piety and writing often came near to implying this. The Anglican formularies and liturgies therefore respond to this situation – but, as with the number of sacraments, in a circumspect way. While Article XXVI rejects any condemnation of a sacrament performed by an unworthy or wicked man, a fine line is drawn between what the Church 'does', in the set liturgies, and how Christians 'digest' that divine grace, in daily living. Word and Sacrament must go hand in hand, a deeply patristic principle. But so, in some way, must sacrament and experience – a needful response to the medieval inheritance.

Background: Models of Sacramental Theology

Sixteenth-century sacramental disputes, which sometimes seem like a minefield, have been clarified by the Presbyterian scholar Brian Gerrish.[2] Three models are offered in relation to the Eucharist, but they can be applied to baptism as well. 'Symbolic memorialism', approximately the view of Zwingli, locates the eucharistic act in the heart of faithful recipients, with the event commemorated in the past. 'Symbolic parallelism', approximately the view of Zwingli's successor, Bullinger, places the sacramental event in parallel with the work of Christ, but there is still a gap between them; such an approach can be useful, for example, for those trying to justify infant baptism in anticipation of subsequent growth in the Christian faith. 'Symbolic instrumentalism', approximately the view of the later Calvin, sees the sacrament as an 'instrument' of God's grace, using Augustine's distinction between the signs (bread and wine) and the reality (the body and blood of Christ).

---

2 B. A. Gerrish, *Grace and Gratitude: The Eucharistic Theology of John Calvin*, Minneapolis: Fortress Press, 1993, p. 167.

These three views overlap, and they were held in varying degrees by the early English Reformers, particularly as Zwingli, Bullinger and Calvin were all influential – along with others, such as Beza – on the evolving English religious scene, and that included a leading Puritan like William Perkins. Gordon Jeanes's study of Cranmer's sacramental theology adopts Gerrish's terminology, coming down on the side of Cranmer as a symbolic instrumentalist, who often sounds like a symbolic parallelist![3] Throughout the Communion and baptism rites in the 1549, 1552 and 1559 Prayer Books, there is a balance between spiritual eating and drinking and symbolic washing as acts of God in his Church and the faithful recipient's spiritual journey. But there is a noticeable shift in 1662, where the water is explicitly blessed at baptism, and the 'Prayer of Consecration' is the title given to the prayer containing the institution narrative.

Much – obviously – happened in the ensuing centuries. The High Calvinist sacramental pattern based on 'symbolic instrumentalism' was pushed further by Stuart divines such as Lancelot Andrewes into a view of real presence sometimes described as 'effectual instrumentalism'. Such an approach broadly embraces patristic tradition, on the analogy of the two natures co-existing in the person of Christ, a view taken by Martin Chemnitz.[4] Lutheran influence should not be overlooked, whether from Luther himself on Cranmer over baptism, and the overall conservative liturgical provisions of the Prayer Book itself, or later on, in the Elizabethan and Stuart eras, when it was not politic to acknowledge Lutheran sources. This strand develops in the eighteenth century, with the Non-Jurors and in the Scottish and American liturgies. But however variegated the Anglican story, the ascended Christ remains an enduring theme. Cranmer's Ascensiontide prayers draw us more expressly alongside Christ in heaven than the medieval Latin texts, hence the concluding words of his Ascension collect – 'and with him continually dwell'.

We do not, however, have to be signed up to a spatial view of heaven of this kind in order to baptize new Christians as the children of eternity or celebrate the Eucharist as the earthly copy of the heavenly reality. The Sanctus, ancient doxology as it is, joins earth and heaven in a single stream of prayer and praise to the Triune God, without defining where and how. To the question, 'what does Christ do now?' the answer must include 'the outpouring of his heavenly gifts'.

Trajectory 1 – Participation – Hooker

Sharing in the life of God is a fundamental truth for the Christian faith. But how does it find ritual form in the daily business of being a Christian disciple? In this quest, Anglicans share the Protestant concerns about being a fallible community that is capable of self-deceit, the Western Catholic confidence in

---

3 Gordon Jeanes, *Signs of God's Promise: Thomas Cranmer's Sacramental Theology and the Book of Common Prayer*, Edinburgh: T. & T. Clark, 2008; and Diarmaid MacCulloch, *Thomas Cranmer: A Life,* New Haven, CT and London: Yale University Press, 1996.

4 On Chemnitz, and the sometimes 'hidden' Lutheran influence, see Peter McCullough (ed.), *Lancelot Andrewes: Selected Sermons and Lectures*, Oxford: Oxford University Press, 2005, pp. xx, lvii, 380, 382–4, 388–90. I owe the term 'effectual instrumentalism' to Jeffrey Steel.

the long-term effects of a disciplined way of worshipping sacramentally and the Eastern Orthodox tradition of valuing the quest for holiness often referred to as 'spirituality'. So when we approach the concept of participation, what Cranmer signals on Ascension Day is a careful blend of these traditions. Whereas the old Latin proper preface ends with 'sharing in his divinity' (echoing 2 Peter 1.4), Cranmer speaks of Christ 'preparing a place for us, that where he is, thither might we also ascend, and reign with him in glory'.

Those who gather to wash new Christians and to feed at the Lord's Table can still do so with confidence, because the Christian vocation is ultimately about sharing the life of heaven. This is the point Richard Hooker makes when dealing with the sacraments, starting with baptism as the beginning and continuing with the Eucharist as the regular nourishment which follows in consequence. Washing and feeding are human realities, which are blessed by God and turned into sacramental signs of the new and heavenly life given us in Christ.

Like many later Anglican writers as different as Edward Bickersteth, Michael Ramsey and John Macquarrie, Hooker sets sacramental worship in the context of God in Trinity and the work of Christ. Central is the principle of participation: 'God has deified our nature, though not by turning it to himself, yet by making it his own inseparable habitation', and 'participation is that mutual hold which Christ hath of us and we of him'. In these intricate terms, Hooker is not so much striking a self-conscious 'balance', like a trapeze artiste, but boldly affirming the life of faith as vibrant and real and as the work of God and no other. From that starting-point, he distinguishes the functions of the two dominical sacraments. This provides him with the opportunity to meet his Puritan critics, who did not think the Elizabethan Church sufficiently Reformed. And he does the same with the other services, including confirmation, marriage, the visitation of the sick and ordination.

Sacraments, therefore, are part of God's presence: 'presence everywhere is the sequel of an infinite and incomprehensible substance'. While he – like other Anglican writers – stresses the mysterious character of that presence, he equally adheres to the view that sacraments are 'moral instruments', conveying the meaning intended for them by God; and this makes him speak of the Eucharist as a 'transubstantiation within us' – the faithful recipient again, but the recipient truly transformed. Here we have an echo of the Prayer Book Consecration Prayer, 'that we receiving these thy creatures of bread and wine . . . may be partakers of his most blessed body and blood'. That same movement, of the heavenly to the earthly, is replicated in baptism with the washing away of sin, the dying and rising with Christ and the promise of rebirth in the Spirit. And it provides the foundation for the rest of the Christian life, whether in daily living, or in those occasions, such as marriage or private confession (in the visitation of the sick), when the Christian comes for a specific blessing, for a new context of life.

The theme of 'deification' is taken up more overtly by later writers, such as Lancelot Andrewes, Charles Wesley and Edward Pusey.[5] The foundations

---

5 A. M. Allchin, *Participation in the Life of God: A Forgotten Strand in Anglican Tradition*, London: Darton, Longman & Todd, 1988; for a more cautious reading of Hooker, see John E. Booty, in W. Speed Hill (ed.), *The Folger Library of the Works of Richard Hooker*, Vol. 5, Pt 1, Medieval and Renaissance Texts and Studies, New York: Binghampton, 1993, pp. 197ff.

provided by Hooker, borrowed and adapted from Cranmer (and through him from Cyril of Alexandria), give an opportunity to hang a great deal of sacramental devotion onto the theological peg of 'participation'. Whenever the language of 'deification' enters Anglican parlance, the starting-point is usually – as in Hooker – with the work of Christ as it has been accomplished, rather than narrowly applied to the workings of the sacraments. We 'participate' in the life given us, first in baptism, and thereafter at the eucharistic table, as receivers in history of an eternal and heavenly gift. Sacraments are necessary. They are not visual aids – or, as he put it, 'bare resemblances or memorials of things absent, neither for naked signs'. That is why the distinction can be made between what they outwardly resemble and the hidden grace which they convey.

In one of Charles Wesley's eucharistic hymns ('How glorious is the Life above'), the theme of deification is intricately linked not just to the work of Christ in us now, or in the life of the communicant at the time, but in the life of heaven in the hereafter. Eschatology was not at the theological forefront of the Reformation era in relation to sacramental theology, which makes Wesley's concluding verse all the more poignant:

Sure Pledge of Ecstasies unknown,
Shall this Divine Communion be,
The Ray shall rise into a Sun,
The Drop shall swell into a Sea.[6]

If the divine life given to the Christian community in the sacraments of baptism and Eucharist is to be a real 'participation' in the work of redemption, that perspective is only limited if confined to the here and now. 'Participation' rubs up against the relationship between what we are doing now, and the heavenly Christ. We are back – again – to the ascension, perhaps not as statically as it is sometimes portrayed, but active in conferring grace and pardon, forgiveness, mercy and renewal.

But 'participation' on its own has its limitations – the language of memorial, *anamnesis*. Hooker does not tackle directly the manner in which baptism or Eucharist are an *anamnesis* of Christ's baptism in the Jordan, or the meal he shared with his disciples on the night of his arrest. It is as if the language of transubstantiation and eucharistic sacrifice had to be 'excommunicated' from any kind of theological discourse, except in order to refute it. Perhaps Hooker – and others like him in the period since – regards the language of participation as sufficient, a way of blending into one, the way Christ is present, in memory of his death. But, as we shall see, later writers could not fail to look further at these questions, and they often did so with their own blend of two deeply biblical notions – covenant and sacrifice.

---

6 Daniel B. Stevick, *The Altar's Fire: Charles Wesley's Hymns on the Lord's Supper, 1745: Introduction and Exposition*, Peterborough: Epworth, 2004, pp. 135–6 (No. 101).

Trajectory 2 – Covenant and Sacrifice – Taylor

Covenant and sacrifice lie at the heart of the Old Testament experience of the people of God. The two have distinct origins. Covenant is a legal term, used in such contexts as marriage, but taken over in order to express the relationship between God and his people. Sacrifice, on the other hand, is a religious term, which the Israelites used – in company with their neighbours – to describe their offerings in worship. The unsatisfactory nature of how this worked out is signalled in Jeremiah, when he speaks of a 'new covenant' (Jer. 31.31ff.) in the future. The New Testament draws these two notions together – in a new covenant, in the sacrificial death of Christ (Heb. 7.22, 12.24), which is celebrated in the Eucharist (1 Cor. 11.25).

At the Reformation, the two terms were treated differently. Sacrifice was applied exclusively to the work of Christ, in response to which the Church offers her sacrifice of praise, and the self-offering of the Christian community (Rom. 12.1). Cranmer's prayer of oblation after Communion expresses this in one of his finest compositions, which has kept reappearing in different guises in the prayers of worldwide Anglicanism since: 'O Lord and heavenly Father, we thy humble servants entirely desire thy fatherly goodness mercifully to accept this our sacrifice of praise and thanksgiving . . . And here we offer and present unto thee our souls and bodies, to be a reasonable, holy and lively sacrifice unto thee . . .' The sacrifice, therefore, is spiritual, commemorating the one sacrifice offered by Christ – a very patristically inspired notion.

Covenant, however, required no such readjustment, remaining at the centre of how the work of Christ was described and at the heart of the institution narrative in the Eucharist. While Cranmer himself did not use it in relation to baptism (and Hooker only sparingly), Calvin and the other Reformers did. It was almost inevitable, therefore, that it should enter common theological parlance in emerging Anglicanism (it is a prominent feature of Perkins' sacramental theology). One of the reasons was the need to defend infant baptism – on the basis that children of believing parents were part of the covenant with them and therefore could be baptized, even though they were not able to make a public profession of faith. And that argument is still used today.

How should the term 'covenant' be used? There has always been a tension in Anglicanism between restrictive and less restrictive approaches to the nature of the Church, and that applies to questions over who should be baptized and who should be admitted to Communion. It is the gospel balance of love and obedience. By the middle of the seventeenth century, those of a more 'open' disposition, like Jeremy Taylor, adopted covenant as a key hermeneutical tool in relation to the two dominical sacraments, in a way that helped to answer the more restrictive approach adopted by many of the Puritans, such as Richard Baxter.[7] More recently, covenant has been used to embrace marriage, the Apostles' Creed is often described as the baptismal covenant, and (more controversially) it has been adopted in connection with tensions in the Anglican Communion.

---

7 Bryan D. Spinks, 'Two Seventeenth Century Examples of Lex Credendi, Lex Orandi: The Baptismal and Eucharistic Liturgies of Jeremy Taylor and Richard Baxter', *Studia Liturgica* 21 (1991), pp. 165–89.

Taylor's major contribution is to shift the theological emphasis towards discipleship, 'holy living', the daily work of the follower of Christ in prayer and good works. Two consequences follow. One is the need for confirmation to include a public profession of faith (championed by Puritans as well), which was added to the service in the Restoration Prayer Book (1662). The legacy of that move is known all over the Anglican world today where the traditional rite of confirmation is celebrated: baptism, followed by nurture and preparation (catechism), leading into confirmation. But there is an inbuilt tension over exactly what confirmation is and does: the giving of the Holy Spirit, public profession of faith – or both. That tension persists, not least in those areas where Communion is given on the basis of baptism before confirmation, and where – following the example of the American Book of Common Prayer (1979), other rites with the laying-on of hands are included, for receiving from other churches, and providing opportunities for those who wish to reaffirm their faith. Moreover, the growing pattern of the baptism and confirmation of adults is an indication of a Church where by no means everyone is a 'cradle Christian'.

The other consequence concerns original sin, a term not found in the Bible, but coined by Augustine at the end of the fourth century. As with questions of what sacraments are supposed to do, definitions of original sin are many, not without controversy. Article IX is characteristically circumspect, avoiding the negative language of Luther and Calvin, though embracing the view that we inherit original sin from Adam and that baptism washes it away. Taylor tried to move the debate on in a more positive direction, for which he was severely criticized. His teaching here, in effect, prepares the ground for the mainstream twentieth-century consensus, Catholic and Protestant, that original sin belongs to the nature of the human person, rather than results from direct heredity. This can be explained by a figurative rather than literal interpretation of Augustine (just!), although his positive views on sex can in no way be squared with the great North African. To try to lead a holy life means handling our humanity. The redemption wrought by Christ offers us a covenant of grace, which we enter sacramentally in baptism, renew in Holy Communion and experience in daily forgiveness and spiritual growth. That covenant is the source of forgiveness, where baptism and Eucharist are central. This links with Andrewes's conviction that the Eucharist conveys the forgiveness of sins (the Lutheran position condemned at the Council of Trent), which he took from Chemnitz.

Sacrifice, however, has always been a tricky area, and not just for Anglicans. Sacrifice is a powerful metaphor, ensuring as it does the seriousness of the sacraments, which are far more than jolly get-togethers in sometimes suffocating fellowship. Yet, it must not undermine the once-and-for-all sacrifice of Christ. Taylor's particular contribution, elaborated and popularized in his writings, is to link the heavenly and the earthly through the intercession of Christ, which also signals a shift from Hooker's Aristotelian approach to a Neoplatonist one. Developing Calvin's view of the ascended Christ (cf. Heb. 7.25), Taylor provides a model for Christological – and eucharistic – reflection by subsequent Anglican writers, richly portrayed in the hymns of Charles Wesley. H. R. McAdoo, first Anglican Co Chairman of ARCIC, used to summarize Taylor's view as 'pleading Christ's sacrifice'. Although Taylor did not actually use the term, it is an apt (even ecumenical) summary, a fresh way of expressing 'anamnesis' as dynamic memorial. Richard Baxter, the Puritan leader, was the first to adopt it, and he is followed by Simon Patrick, Edward Pusey and Charles Gore; it was also used by the Scots Presbyterian William Milligan in his pioneering study of the ascension and more recently by the Roman Catholic David N. Power.[8]

Uniquely for his time, Taylor expresses the patristic (almost iconographic) view of Jesus at the Jordan as the prototype for baptismal celebration, hallowing the waters and hallowing the faith of those who come for the sacrament. He also speaks of the guardian angel assigned to each new Christian at their baptism. In the baptism rite in the liturgy he compiled for use during the Commonwealth, when the Prayer Book was proscribed, he has the narrative of Christ's baptism (Matt. 3.13–17) read as a lection – common nowadays, but rare in patristic times and unknown in the Reformation era.

In the Eucharist, Taylor draws together the eternal altar of Christ in heaven and the table where his work is graciously celebrated on earth. 'Christ comes to meet us clothed in a mystery', he writes, echoing Hooker's insistence on the mysterious character of the Lord's Supper, but with his own stress on the work of the Holy Spirit. Such an approach propels Taylor (and others like him) into a strong view of eucharistic sacrifice that avoids any hint of 're-offering' Christ – so that 'the virtue of the eternal sacrifice may be salutary and effectual', depicting the ascended Christ not as a static figure but as an active Saviour. It also helped him to emphasize the role of the priest at the earthly altar, recovering part of the medieval heritage that the Reformers were anxious to cast off. The notions of covenant and sacrifice developed here require a powerful pneumatology in order to prevent them from becoming over-mechanical. They have become fruitful ground for ecumenical dialogue, as McAdoo has shown.

Trajectory 3 – Consecration – Wilberforce

In all sacramental worship, some sort of blessing is pronounced, in order to set the person or the thing (or both) apart for a unique use. For example, at baptism, it is about water, at the Eucharist, about bread and wine, and at confirmation, marriage and ordination, the people concerned. The question is, in what sense are they 'set apart'? Is it for the duration of the service concerned, in which case there is a strong implicit or explicit connection with that holy use? Or is it a more objective kind of setting apart, so that, for example, the eucharistic food remains what it is, for the purposes of Communion after the service or for prayer and devotion?

These were the questions which the early Anglican formularies had to wrestle with, and, although much of the heat of theological controversy has toned down in the period since, the same tensions remain. Some of that concern can be detected in the language used in Article XXVIII, when it speaks of the eucharistic presence as 'after an heavenly and spiritual manner'. It was not just the (then) objectionable) doctrine of transubstantiation which lay behind this. It was the

---

[8] H. R. McAdoo, *The Eucharistic Theology of Jeremy Taylor Today*, Norwich: Canterbury Press, 1988; and William Milligan, *The Ascension and Heavenly Priesthood of Our Lord*, London: Macmillan, 1892, p. 142.

proliferation of blessings of inanimate objects – oil, ashes, palm crosses, wedding rings – through the Middle Ages that called into question the traditional rationale of blessing and consecration. The language of instrumentality that we discussed earlier goes a long way to explain why Anglican tradition has tended to draw together the blessing of something with its use by people in that sacred context, to the extent that it may be a blessing of the people as they consume or use those holy things. This, of course, allows for a spectrum of theological approach, hence the language often used in the old Anglican catechisms of 'exhibiting', 'sealing', 'showing', as Ian Green has demonstrated.[9] The liturgical outworking of this tension can be seen if we compare the language of the 1662 Prayer Book, 'that we receiving these thy creatures' with the language of 'be for us' in modern eucharistic prayers.

Liturgical language has to carry a great deal – not just accepted theology, but the devotional practice of the worshipper. The old Roman 'Canon' (Eucharistic Prayer 1 of the 1970 Missal) uses the form *ut nobis fiant* – 'that they may become for us/to us', in words that go back to the early centuries. That sensitivity – antedating later controversy – nonetheless betrays a conviction about consecration that connects the bread and wine with the communicants. As David Kennedy has recently shown,[10] the language of consecration has been – and continues to be – rich and varied. Those on the Catholic wing have long been content with the stronger language of objective change, while evangelicals have been suspicious of it. Kennedy produces a scriptural armoury, from both the Old Testament and the New, to indicate that the blessing of 'inanimate objects' need not be unacceptable at all – particularly if one considers 1 Timothy 4.4–5, about sanctification of things through prayer.

So we are back to outward gift and inward grace – a point made forcibly by Robert Wilberforce, who has been described as the only systematic theologian among the nineteenth century Tractarians.[11] Like other Anglican writers, his starting-point is the institution narrative of Christ at the Last Supper. Cranmer made the narrative the immediate prelude to Communion, whereas liturgical revision in the period since has placed it at the centre of the Eucharistic Prayer, surrounded by thanksgiving and supplication – thanksgiving in the form of praise, supplication in the form of prayer for the Spirit (*epiclesis*) on the eucharistic celebration. Unlike other Anglicans, particularly evangelicals, Wilberforce saw himself as a true heir of the Western Catholic tradition, hence the considerable emphasis placed on the narrative as 'words of consecration'; for the Reformers, on the other hand, those words are primarily there as a scriptural warrant for the Supper. Wilberforce, moreover, takes the word 'is' to a high level, that of identification, not representation, a presence effective not through the laws of nature but by the law of grace. He relates this, moreover, to the need for an ordained minister to perform this act of consecration. Anglicans

---

9 Ian Green, *The Christian's ABC: Catechisms and Catechizing c. 1530–1740*, Oxford: Clarendon Press, 1986, pp. 508–56.

10 David J. Kennedy, *Eucharistic Sacramentality in an Ecumenical Context: The Anglican Epiclesis*, Aldershot: Ashgate, 2008.

11 Alf Hardelin, *The Tractarian Understanding of the Eucharist*, Uppsala: Almqvist and Wiksell, 1965, pp. 141–7, 160–8, 215–19.

may vary in how 'priestly' ordination is, but for them all, the Eucharist is so central to Christian identity that it requires such a person, representing not just the community gathered on a particular occasion, but the whole Church Catholic.

The real liturgical president is, of course, Christ himself – a truth that is easily forgotten. So the human president, properly ordained, represents him – hence the solemnity of those ordination prayers: 'send down the Holy Spirit on your servant N., for the office and work of a priest in your Church'. Wilberforce tries to make a distinction between the Eucharist and baptism on the grounds that the Eucharist has both outward and inward aspects, and the grace of partaking, whereas baptism has only the first two. The weakness of this scheme is that it lacks the dimension of growth in the faith, the follow-on from partaking of baptism by the candidate in question, infant or adult, for that matter. The strength is that the Eucharist receives a real and unique prominence. For Wilberforce, the water does not need to be blessed, but the bread and wine do have to be consecrated – for Communion. We may add here, in general terms, that when rings are blessed at marriage, and oils are hallowed at chrism Eucharists, the prayers used usually link the ring – or the oil – closely with those who are going to use them and benefit from them.

There is – as must be obvious by now – a great deal of movement, both theological and linguistic, around the notions of consecration. Alongside the need to hold inward and outward together (Wilberforce says that they 'make up together a real, but heterogeneous whole'), there is the corresponding need to hold subjective and objective aspects together. Fresh approaches to language do sometimes involve using older words in a new way – like the verb 'show', in the Eastern tradition of the eucharistic prayers attributed to Basil of Caesarea.[12] Anglicans tend nowadays to see the institution narrative as a central part of the Eucharistic Prayer, partly following in the footsteps of their Latin forebears, but they can be equally keen on the invocation of the Holy Spirit, following in the rich traditions of the Christian East. They have yet, however, fully to recover – as Jeremy Taylor did – the sense of the patristic notion of Christ's baptism as that foundational sacrament's narrative of institution. It is – after all – Christ who is the real sacrament.

Trajectory 4 – Christ as Sacrament – Quick

All theology arises out of a context, and so far we have encountered a number of approaches to what sacraments are and what they do. It may, however, be asked, why can we not look at these issues from a wider perspective? After all, the word 'sacramentum' had a wide reference in the early centuries, and definitions only appear to have developed in order to respond to controversy. Wilberforce was writing as the Tractarian Movement gathered momentum and, like a few of their number, left the Church of England in order to become a Roman Catholic. That signals an important part of the story – Anglican theology did not develop in a vacuum, but generally grew not only as a result of internal

---

12 William R. Crockett, *Eucharist: Symbol of Transformation*, New York: Pueblo, 1989, p. 59.

questions but from what other Christian bodies were doing and thinking. One only has to consider the influences on Hooker of patristic, medieval and European Reformed traditions. In some ways, the most creative theology loosens up ideas and provides fresh perspectives. Oliver Quick stands out as an unusual example, at a time of acute tension between Anglo-Catholics and evangelicals – not just in England – in the period between the two World Wars.

Quick brings a philosopher's mind to old questions that were in danger of becoming rather tired, focused – but by no means confined – to such questions as how Christ is present in the Eucharist and in what sense the Eucharist can be described as a sacrifice. In many ways he pioneered the theme of Christ as 'the perfect sacrament', a notion that was not new; William Temple comes near this position, and it becomes central to Roman Catholic writers such as Edward Schillebeeckx. In a way, it is a variant on what the early fathers taught, but the language of the Church as 'the sacrament of human society' is more direct. With his philosophical background, he has a wide starting-point that is far from Wilberforce, who begins with consecration. From that point of origin flows all Christian experience, the radically fresh New Testament notion of the holy (Christ) not just drawing disciples into the life of God, but preventing them from being separate from the rest of the world, which is still the terrain of the work of the gospel, whether it is heeded or not.

So the sacramental scheme moves from the general to the particular. In the process, Quick brings another fresh wind into the picture, by trying to withdraw the wedge between inward and outward that medieval theologians like Aquinas and Reformation theologians like Calvin worked with in their different ways. Aquinas was using Aristotelian language already becoming familiar in his time, whereas Calvin was trying to steer an emerging Christian community through a theological minefield where some of his critics suspected him of being insufficiently Reformed. Quick had no such limitations. He was not using a scheme that was widely accepted, nor was he shackled by a particular group within the Church. That is one of the reasons why he is such a refreshing influence.

Quick builds on the notion of instrumentality that we saw in Hooker. Outward and inward are distinct, but they operate together, as the water is blessed and used by God, and the bread and wine are consecrated through the intention given them by Christ at the Supper. That provided Quick (and Temple) to speak of the elements transformed in terms of 'value' – a word that combines what something is in itself with what it is in relation to how people perceive it. Although it has never gained wide acceptance, it is not far from the notion of 'signification', which Mascall saw in Wilberforce, and which the Roman Catholic Benedictine Anscar Vonier used in providing a critique of his own Church's teaching.[13] We are back to the language of 'being' and 'doing' and the language of presence and sacrifice – and the need to hold these two sets of polarities together.

Among the offshoots of this kind of approach, two stand out with particular prominence. One concerns the widening of our understanding of sacra-

---

13 E. L. Mascall, *Corpus Christi: Essays on the Church and the Eucharist*, second edition, London: Longmans, 1965, p. 133; and William Temple, *Christus Veritas: An Essay*, London: Macmillan, 1924, pp. 229ff.

mentality, which has been explored at length and in depth by David Brown, and which in some ways harks back to Augustine's approach, although he extends it considerably.[14] Combining a genuine love of tradition with a fresh approach to life in its fulness, Brown argues for the sacramentality of deep experience through moments of disclosure, contemplation, and paradox; it is the God who speaks to us 'outside the box', in music of every kind, the impact of buildings on the religious imagination, to say nothing of the theatre and the cinema. For Brown, the whole created order is potentially sacramental, and that embraces fallen human creativity as well; and while he will guard and nurture the formal sacramental system of the Church, in its worship and prayer, he will likewise widen our perspectives, to prevent that worship and prayer from being too churchy, too narrowly focused – and too unimaginative in the process. The two axes need each other – we are back to Quick's view of the radical New Testament idea of the holy, separate from the world, yet intertwined with it. And this includes great works of art – by musicians, painters, dramatists – who may not describe themselves as conventionally Christian, or even religious.

The other offshoot is about widening our understanding of sacrifice. Perhaps this is the doctrine which the violent history of the twentieth century has brought out in a particularly fresh way. More people have been killed in warfare than in all the preceding centuries put together, we are sometimes told. So the notion of sacrifice gains prominence, and yet invites ever greater scrutiny. Dorothy L. Sayers has provided her own critique of the more sentimental glosses on this reality. The noble, worthy, easy-going idea that we give things up for their own worth is contrasted with the harsh reality that sacrifice is actually about pain, suffering, surrender to the unknown, with a great deal of fear, ambivalence and doubt behind it. Love and resignation can find no common ground between them.[15] If the life of baptism and Eucharist are about self-oblation, then it cannot be cosy and ecclesiastical. It must be costly and demanding. And that makes the sacraments startlingly contemporary.

Trajectory 5 – Contemporaneity – Gaden

Every Eucharist is a celebration of an eternal reality in the here and now. Although this is a universal insight, shared by every Christian tradition, there is still, as Rowan Williams has observed, 'something distinctive in the quite single-minded focus of so many Anglican writers on the active Christ',[16] and he goes on to allude to one of George Herbert's poems which refers to the Eucharist as 'The haste of Thy good will'. This is reflected in the language of instrumentality that pervades much Anglican writing, and not just about the Eucharist. There is a strong sense in which God is active – Christ as the true celebrant. That may explain, for example, why during Anglicanism's early centuries, the nor-

---

14 David Brown, *God and Grace of Body*, Oxford: Oxford University Press, 2007; and *God and Mystery in Words*, Oxford: Oxford University Press, 2008.
15 Dorothy L. Sayers, *The Mind of the Maker*, London: Methuen, 1941, pp. 107–9.
16 Rowan Williams, Foreword, McAdoo and Stevenson, *Mystery of the Eucharist*, p. ix.

mal position for the priest was to stand at the north end of the holy table – as if leaving space for Christ himself. The other positions – more universal since – are those commonly used by other Christians: eastward facing implies offering praise and prayer on behalf of the community, awaiting the coming Lord, whereas westward facing expresses presidency over the community gathered around that table. Perverse as it may sound, it is good that all three uses continue to be known and experienced.

These liturgical points are worth making, because Anglicanism is – as we have noted on a number of occasions so far – a Church that values its liturgical formulae in a particular way. That brings us to the wide-sweeping liturgical changes of the twentieth century, with their considerable influence on the piety of ordinary congregations throughout the world. Dom Gregory Dix's monumental study of the Eucharist *The Shape of the Liturgy* appeared as World War Two ended and was a powerful force in helping many Christians – not just Anglicans – to look more deeply and critically at the Eucharist in history. Above all, he encouraged them to look at the actions, and not just at the words. 'Was ever another command so obeyed?', he writes of Jesus' command to 'do this', in a purple passage towards the book's end.[17] Dated as some of his scholarship has become, his emphasis on the whole community (not just the individual) 'doing the Eucharist' has endured, and the same is true of his writings on baptism, confirmation, holy orders and much else. His flair with words and his inbuilt historical perspective saw tradition as something inherently living, and the sacraments not 'said' but 'done', hence the importance of environment and context as theological issues as well.

Dix was also part of a whole movement of liturgical, historical and theological scholarship that looked back to the early centuries for norms and patterns that were seen to be worth restoring in a much-changed world. This held true, for example, of a Paschal theology that sees the Easter Vigil as a focus for the Church's celebration of the passing from death to life, in the sharing of light, the readings of Israel's sacred story, the proclamation of the Easter gospel, the baptism and confirmation of new Christians, culminating in the Easter Eucharist itself. All this – and more – came to fruition in the Roman Catholic Church at the Second Vatican Council. But it was part of a worldwide movement, in which Anglicans had their share as well.

John Gaden offers a picture of the sacraments that captures this changed, corporatist register. Here are sacraments that 'do', that are experienced in the here and now, and in the most vivid and tangible ways. Water is poured lavishly – as I used to do when baptizing new Christians in the large patristically inspired font in Portsmouth Cathedral during my time as bishop there. Moving through a building that expresses the transition from darkness to light is a theological journey of its own, especially with the climax at the altar, the community surrounding the space and making it their own. But Gaden does more. He applies the 'doing' to the other sacraments as well, using anger as a hermeneutical tool – a basic, human instinct that is not often applied in this kind of context. Gaden provides a quintessentially twentieth century approach, encapsulating the fragmented,

---

17 Gregory Dix, *The Shape of the Liturgy*, London: Dacre, 1945, p. 743.

dislocated, damaged aspects of life as people experience it, and in a way that refuses to be in denial over the reality of failure.

What Gaden says about penance and marriage – and the anger that can constantly lie beneath the surface – enables people to let the liturgies and doctrines of the Church 'carry' their experiences and offer them to God for his forgiveness, blessing and mercy. The Light shines in the darkness – and this is where the sacraments can find meaning and real celebration. Such an approach draws out of baptism its three main aspects that are embedded in the New Testament and are what social anthropologists would describe as 'organizing metaphors', washing (1 Cor. 6.11), rebirth (John 3.5) and dying and rising (Rom. 6.3–11).[18] It also links with David Ford's idea of 'the eucharistic self', where the communicant is 'blessed' by an all-embracing God, 'placed once more face to face with Christ', 'timed' in a new world, for all that the distractions of this one persist, and 'commanded' to live more faithfully.[19]

'Now I am washed clean. I have stepped out of the bath', writes Gaden. The immediacy and perceptibility of the sacrament of baptism is not about dramatic words interpreting an attenuated, limp liturgical rite. The words express what has been done, and the newly baptized moves to Eucharist, 'where we are made strong in him'. Herbert's words from the same poem, 'The Holy Communion' spring to mind – 'This gift of all gifts is the best'. The Liturgy has a shape – and at its heart is Christ's movement, which is to reshape us. As John Wesley reminds us all, the Eucharist is a converting ordinance.

Trajectory 6 – Conversion – Buchanan

Conversion is at the centre of the gospel, which is about repentance and new life. How repentance and new life are celebrated is therefore pivotal to the life of the Church. We have seen in a number of ways so far how the sixteenth-century Reformation was formative to the evolution of what we call Anglicanism. Yet, we have also seen how from the very beginning and since there have been undercurrents that sometimes grew into flowing streams of continuity from the medieval and patristic eras. Much of what has happened since then bears testimony to the ebb and flow of different strands within Anglicanism, broadly termed evangelical, Catholic and liberal. If one looks at the renewal of theology and liturgy of the past 60 years, much of it can be seen in terms of the 'retour aux sources', the return to what Charles Gore used to call 'the divine originals'. That continues to fascinate not just scholars but those who are concerned about the renewal of local church life. Stories from the past suddenly unearthed can bring fresh light on what we do in the present.

And yet Reformation questions remain, and they can be felt and believed deeply. Reformation studies, as we have seen, have helped to clarify what were

---

[18] Kenneth Stevenson, *The Mystery of Baptism in the Anglican Tradition*, Norwich: Canterbury Press/Harrisburg, PA: Morehouse, 1998, pp. 175ff.

[19] David F. Ford, *Self and Salvation: Being Transformed*, Cambridge Studies in Christian Doctrine, Cambridge: Cambridge University Press, 1999, pp. 137ff.

the intentions of the Reformers, and not just Cranmer himself.[20] We live in a very different world today. But the Anglican inheritance is one of fidelity to the Reformation as well; Anglican identity in the late Elizabethan era belonged just as much to Perkins as it did to Hooker. Our last trajectory, in Colin Buchanan, takes us back to these roots. A well-known name throughout the Anglican Communion, he has brought evangelical sensibilities to the work of liturgical reconstruction and ecclesiology. He stands in a line with such figures as Charles Simeon, Edward Bickersteth and Nathaniel Dimock – pastoral theologians with an acute eye on gospel-truths as these are known and experienced.

Buchanan's summary of the evangelical stance on sacramental theology takes us back, therefore, to the Articles, the early Catechisms and their insistence on the fundamental relationship between the two dominical sacraments, the importance of faithful reception (hence his stress on 'the administration of water') and the centrality of Christian nurture ('there is no sacrament in the "consecrated" elements independent of proper reception of them'). He thus alerts us to the abiding question of the relationship between sacramental event and spiritual growth. To what extent is it about event and process, divine and human? And as we look again at our teaching and our liturgies, is it enough to look 'behind' the Reformation disputes to a supposed age of patristic innocence, when all was (arguably) more straightforward? Supposed 'primitive' notions of eucharistic offering are unacceptable to many evangelicals on the basis solely of their antiquity.

These are proper questions, and they keep recurring, as theological writers such as Christopher Cocksworth show us, albeit in a more nuanced way, in relation to both history and ecumenical dialogue, and the centrality of seeing the reading and preaching of the Word as inextricably connected to the sacraments.[21] Whatever the answers given to these questions – and there will be many different flavours, Anglicanism being what it is – they are fundamental to the nature of the universal gospel. The Reformation insights about the relationship between baptism and Eucharist hold both together, so that each has a separate but overlapping function, and each is a place of real encounter with the living God.

One of the areas where Buchanan and others have entered troubled waters concerns what it means to renew one's faith, and how this should be ritualized. We mentioned earlier the growing practice in a dislocated world of people with fragmented lives returning to the font, but in the context of an extra kind of confirmation. This is not just a liturgical issue. It is about providing a sacramental theology of human continuity, when there has been personal fracture or deep distance which avoids rebaptism. It takes us back to the sacramental system itself. But the problem posed by 'stretched confirmation' in this way is that, by being repeated – as an extension of baptism – the distinction between baptism and Eucharist becomes blurred.

---

20 Colin Buchanan, *What Did Cranmer Think He Was Doing?* Grove Liturgical Study 7, Bramcote: Grove, 1976.

21 Christopher Cocksworth, *Evangelical Eucharistic Thought in the Church of England*, Cambridge: Cambridge University Press, 1993.

We are face to face once more with the issue that Jeremy Taylor and others answered when they maintained that we enter the covenant of grace sacramentally at the font, and we renew that covenant sacramentally at the Lord's Table. This is one of the arguments for placing the two dominical sacraments 'above' the other five. And it throws fresh light on the sacramental principle of blessing people. The Bible has given us a gesture, the laying on of hands, which is in effect non-negotiable, and a given that is powerfully eloquent in its own right. It is the Church's responsibility to delineate between what kind of blessing is intended, in three ways. Who gives the blessing (bishop or presbyter)? At what stage in life is the blessing given (confirmation, marriage, ordination, reconciliation)? How do the liturgical texts describe the tasks envisaged for the person receiving the blessing (the way the rite is expressed)? And what is the significance of the bishop's ministry in this theological array of interlocking liturgies? These are questions that pervade the 'five' sacramental rites as well as their various pastoral (and often informal) offspring.

When it comes to baptism and Eucharist, however, of the models suggested by Gerrish outlined earlier, Anglicans probably vary from a form of symbolic parallelism, through symbolic instrumentalism, to effectual instrumentalism. There may be a few on the outer edges who opt for symbolic memorialism, on the one hand, and an exaggerated view of transubstantiation, on the other. But the 'doing' of the sacraments, in the context of growing faith, is, at the end of the day, too close to the Anglican DNA for those options to hold the field satisfactorily. Perhaps this is a qualified way of saying that 'going back' to the origins of Christianity, in the early centuries as well as the Bible, is always going to be a critical hermeneutical tool. It has certainly borne fruit in recent ecumenical agreements, with their broader, ecclesial approach to areas of divergence.

Conclusion

So where does all this leave us? We began with the River Danube as an illuminating model for our story, with all its variations of width, depth, strength, creativity and danger. Aquatic language is hardly alien to the Christian vocabulary. In the Bible it is a constant image of the mercy and renewing power of God. The Fourth Gospel, in particular, employs it at several points in connection with Jesus' very public ministry of transformation; to take one example, as the living water springing up to eternal life for the Samaritan woman, as she stands ready to raise stagnant water from a well (John 4.14). It was, therefore, inevitable that it should be used sacramentally and not just in relation to baptism. Lancelot Andrewes describes the eucharistic bread and wine as 'conduit-pipes' of heavenly grace, using imagery taken from the technology – relatively new in his time – of urban water-supply. What, then, are the main features of this Anglican sacramental irrigation-system?

First, Anglicans claim to be only 'part of the one, holy, catholic and apostolic Church, worshipping the one true God, Father, Son and Holy Spirit'. We are only 'part', and our very existence predicates the commitment to worship the Triune God. As part of the Church Universal, our historical roots lie with the Christian West, Catholic, but at the same time Reformed, hence a theological inheritance that goes back through the Reformers to the early centuries, embracing the Christian

East as well, a constant source for Anglican theology. This tradition shares an underlying commitment to viewing the sacraments as 'outward signs' conveying 'invisible grace'. There are variations of emphasis – and we have described some of these – but official formularies tend to be 'instrumentalist' in tone, veering in the direction of 'effectual' rather than 'symbolic'. Even though tensions inevitably centre on the relationship between the individual and the community and between the sacramental event and the growing faith of believers, faithful reception is not invariably synonymous with subjectivity; as Charles Gore puts it, 'we must never distinguish the objective presence from the gift that is communicated to us.'[22]

Second, if there is a weakness in this basic inheritance, it is an intermittent lack of emphasis on pneumatology and eschatology – the work of the Spirit, and the place of the sacraments in the Church as both sign and foretaste of the kingdom of God, to use the language of modern ecumenical agreements.[23] Both these aspects point to the incompleteness of the Church, a favourite theme of Michael Ramsey. It is to the Scottish Episcopal tradition that we owe the first expressions of these truths, in the 1764 Liturgy, with the invocation of the Spirit on the eucharistic gifts, and in the 1928 Prayer Book with the addition at the end of the *anamnesis* of the words, 'and looking again for his coming with power and great glory'.

Many a Eucharistic Prayer since then contains considerable variations and expansions of these two themes, whether one thinks of Anglicans in Brazil or Korea, to say nothing of other Christian churches. They are both, of course, strong in the traditions of the Christian East, with which Anglicanism has long had a theological love-affair. Indeed, the Alexandrian language of 'transelementation', highlighted in recent Roman Catholic–Orthodox dialogue, comes near to some of the stronger uses of instrumentalism in Anglican writing. And in that context, Jeremy Taylor's heavenly–earthly axis with its stress on Christ as the universal prototype of baptism and the dynamic celebration of Christ's sacrifice at the altar should not be overlooked.

Third, distinguishing the two 'dominical' sacraments from the other five (whether they are called sacraments or sacramental rites) has a number of important consequences. The strong relationship between baptism and Eucharist means that for all the rich ecclesial emphasis placed on the Eucharist in such contemporary Roman Catholic writers as Paul McPartlan, Anglicans looking at their own tradition will insist that it is both baptism and Eucharist that 'make' the Church. They are obviously, and inherently, different. Baptism is not for repetition, like a piece of consumer goods; it is done once, as we are commanded (Matt. 28.19). But the Eucharist has to be repeated (1 Cor. 11.23–26), because we continue to need feeding and sustaining. The other 'five' are about those significant stages in life and faith-experience for which the blessing of the Church needs to be invoked, often functioning like 'rites of passage', but as real and living vehicles of God's grace, rather than personal and social markers and no

---

22 Charles Gore, *The Body of Christ: An Enquiry into the Institution and Doctrine of the Holy Communion*, London: Murray, 1901, p. 98.

23 Kennedy, *Eucharistic Sacramentality*; and the ground-breaking work of Geoffrey Wainwright, *Eucharist and Eschatology*, London: Epworth, 1971/New York: Oxford University Press, 1972.

more. Jesus' presence at Cana (John 2.1–11) can be said to sanctify marriage; his breathing the Spirit on the apostles after the resurrection at least suggests commissioning and ordination (John 20.22); and the Letter of James indicates the (surely early) practice of reconciliation, and healing with oil (James 5.14–16).

As we have seen, how they differ from one another is determined by who does the blessing and what the blessing says – both of which criteria are matters that require collective ('catholic') agreement, and are not spur-of-the-moment ('local') whims. Usually the distinctions are clear. We have observed both the needs and the pitfalls of a 'stretched' view of confirmation. This inevitably serves to give greater prominence to baptism, which has been a key development of the self-understanding of all the churches (by no means only Anglican) over the past century, regardless of whether confirmation is observed strictly as the gateway to Communion, or whether Communion starts earlier. We can, too, observe a similar tension of need and risk in services of healing, where the given liturgical gesture (the laying on of hands) is sometimes accompanied by prayer *ad libitum* that can be as much about healing as about forgiveness. Perhaps this is another way of saying that it is not really possible to limit the other sacramental rites to the traditional five. In a *lex orandi–lex credendi* Church, doctrinal critique needs to accompany – not follow – pastoral need.

At the end of the day, none of all this should ever be seen in isolation. Like other Christians, Anglicans bring their history – tensions and all – to the ecumenical enterprise, where together we can understand our own and each other's traditions, as these are studied together from fresh perspectives. Historical theology has made us all far more aware of how and why our traditions have grown, flourished and split apart, and that includes Roman Catholic understandings of issues like transubstantiation as well.

For most people most of the time life is a bit of a mess, and a neat, pre-packaged approach to sacramental living is not in practice achievable this side of eternity. In any case, there is probably no such thing as a specifically Anglican systematic theology of the sacraments. But there is an Anglican way of doing and expressing that theology, a theology that has always been historically and pastorally rooted. Ecumenical dialogue, with Roman Catholics, the Orthodox, Lutherans, the Reformed Churches as well as the 'new' Christian bodies, has produced areas of agreement on sacramental theology and ministry that show time and again how pluriform and yet partial is the nature of the Anglican inheritance. In the world of globalization, multiculturalism and new attitudes to ecology necessitated by climate change, those tangible, costly sacramental signs – water, bread and wine, oil and the laying on of hands – will continue to find ways of being moral instruments of God's love and conduit-pipes of his new life. The gifts of the ascended Christ – with whom we 'continually dwell' – are the fruits of that humanity which he took upon himself, for us and for our salvation.

Introduction to the Sources

The extracts selected to illustrate sacramental theology come from some very varied authors. Anglicans have been used to debate, and these writers are no exception. Each one was writing at a time when important issues needed to be addressed about the meaning and function of the sacraments.

We begin with Richard Hooker, often and rightly regarded as one of our 'founding fathers', Anglicanism's first real systematic theologian. In the famous Fifth Book of his *Laws of Ecclesiastical Polity*, which appeared in 1597, he looks specifically at the Prayer Book, seeing it as embodying the faith of the Church of England, and countering Puritan critics who want a more Reformed polity. He uses the notion of 'law', which pervades his writings, to embrace Christian worship, and in particular the two main sacraments; but his treatment covers the other offices of the Church as well. None of these rites, therefore, is an optional extra – they are necessary, constituent aspects of the Christian life. Key to his somewhat Aristotelian approach, inherited from the Middle Ages, is the idea of participation – the sharing of God's life with humankind, which make the sacraments real and instrumental, and therefore more than mental acts. In a nutshell, baptism begins the Christian life, and Holy Communion sustains it.

In Jeremy Taylor, the language is more devotional in method, and less compressed in style. His first main work was *The Great Exemplar* (1649), the first ever devotional life of Christ in English, and it was an immediate success. The 'Discourse' on baptism, which was added in 1653, makes Christ the prototype, providing an almost iconographic approach to the Christian's journey to the font. In 1660, he produced 'Worthy Communicant', which expounds his understanding of eucharistic doctrine, following up the success of his Rules and Exercises of *Holy Living* and *Holy Dying* which appeared in 1650 and 1651. Like his other writings on the Lord's Supper, 'Worthy Communicant' emphasizes the earthly offering of the eucharistic sacrifice in union with Christ's intercession in heaven. This is expressed in terms that reflect the strong Platonist strand in mid seventeenth-century theology. A key hermeneutic in his writings is the notion of covenant, sacramentally entered at baptism and renewed at the Eucharist.

Robert Isaac Wilberforce, son of William, the anti-slavery campaigner, was probably one of the Oxford Movement's finest theologians. His writings breathe the air of the High Church tradition increasingly conscious of its medieval and patristic roots. Particularly interested in the sacraments, he took a juridical approach in his teaching. Like Hooker, he sharply distinguishes their functions. In baptism, he emphasized regeneration and in the Eucharist the importance and effects of consecration by the priest, the objective nature of Christ's presence, as well as the sacrifice offered by the Church in union with Christ. These themes have their roots in the fathers, but he pushed them further than earlier Tractarians, and his stress on the role of the institution narrative reflects a view that is more Latin than Greek. His 'Doctrine of the Eucharist', his greatest work, appeared in 1853, the year before he became a Roman Catholic.

When we come to Oliver Quick, the register changes once more. This time it is about charting a creative course through the eucharistic controversies between evangelicals and Anglo-Catholics, and the rest of the Church. Quick brings a theological cooling-system to the process, with a philosophical approach (somewhat dated now) that was influenced by idealism, as well as a conviction that some of the terminology used in the past needs proper scrutiny. He walks carefully round the language of outward and inward in relation to sacraments, and tries to show how different modes of Christ's presence in the Eucharist can be expressed without recourse to an (outmoded) spatial view of heaven. Fundamental to his approach is the notion of Christ as the Sacrament, which provides a wider – and outward looking – context in which to view the Christian life. *The Christian Sacraments* (1927), along with *Doctrines of the Creed* (1938), were influential on generations of students.

In John Gaden, the voice changes again, this time with the radical tones of the contemporary Church, whose sacramental practice is much influenced by the liturgical movement. Here the deep structures of ancient liturgies, and a vividly affective way of speaking about how God 'acts' directly in the outward symbols, are both strongly stressed and brought together in a unique way that causes him to write of the sacraments as encountered in the here and now, and of the human condition's way of relating to this encounter, exemplified in the experience of human anger. This is not exactly a traditional approach. But it rings true with the dislocated and fragmented lives of people today, and what they bring to the font and the altar. His writings were edited after his death.

Finally, with Colin Buchanan we are in the world of liturgical renewal, as well as one that cries out for a genuinely evangelical voice that is faithful to the Anglican formularies and the Reformed roots of Anglicanism. His work on Thomas Cranmer stressed the evangelical tenor of the great Archbishop's theological mind. A familiar figure throughout the Anglican Communion, he gave evangelicals a much-needed liturgical focus that is faithful to their tradition. He had the courage to challenge what he saw as the patristic fundamentalism of much mid twentieth-century liturgical and sacramental thought. This has spilt over into such issues as Communion before confirmation, and an inbuilt suspicion of any approach to eucharistic sacrifice that downgrades the centrality of the work of Christ.

Each one of these writers stresses the centrality of baptism and Eucharist. But they also see the other rites (whether they call them sacraments or not) as part of the sacramental system or family of ordinances which revolve around them: confirmation, marriage, ordination, anointing and reconciliation. They do this in different ways, and from different starting-points, reflecting the contexts from which they were writing, and their place in the wider Anglican panorama.

Sources

Colin Buchanan, *Is the Church of England Biblical?* London: Darton, Longman & Todd, 1998, pp. 238–40, 250–1.

The issue of sacraments was central to the Reformation. The Reformers had to grapple, in the light of Scripture, with the definition of sacraments, the related issue of the number of sacraments, the efficacy of sacraments, the doctrinal formulas and liturgical texts for sacraments, and the status to be attributed to those rites which were not now being counted as sacraments. In essence they inherited a mystical scheme of seven sacraments, a scheme derived from Peter Lombard in the thirteenth century, and they had to recreate a whole sacramental theology, and recreate it in relation to both soteriology and ecclesiology. The issues were fought through by stages, and a good indication of a mature restatement comes in Article XXVI of the Forty-Two Articles of 1553:

> Our Lord Jesus Christ hath knit together a company of new people with Sacraments, most few in number, most easy to be kept, most excellent in signification, as is baptism and the Lord's Supper.

This statement delightfully unites the two sacraments with each other in an ecclesially related confession. In a period when a large amount of debate on the sacraments concerned the quantity of benefit to the individual recipient, the ecclesial frame is crucial. But the extract also gives us the following further clues:

1. It traces the concept of a sacrament to the institution of Christ, and from Edward VI's reign onwards it became standard Anglican exposition, thus:

- There are two Sacraments ordained of Christ our Lord in the Gospel, that is to say, baptism and the Supper of the Lord (Article XXV of 1571);
- 'How many Sacraments hath Christ ordained in his Church? *Answer*: Two only, as generally necessary to salvation; that is to say, baptism and the Supper of the Lord' (catechism section added to Book of Common Prayer in 1604).

2. It sets the two in juxtaposition and relationship to each other: as we have seen in the New Testament, baptism is the sacrament of once-and-for-all admissions to the people of God, and the Lord's Supper the sacrament of continuance in them. Both are the Lord's way of knitting together his new people; both are strongly ecclesial. But the Reformers also saw the two as mutually interpretative. Thus baptism gave a major clue about the Eucharist, for no one thinks that there is any sacrament of baptism save in the *administration* of water on the candidate, and this was used as an example from which to understand the Eucharist – that there is no sacrament in the 'consecrated' elements independent of proper reception of them, and all liturgical usage must move towards reception, and all spiritual benefits are to be found in the 'worthy' (i.e. penitent and believing) recipient. Conversely, once it is established from the doctrine of communion that it is worthy reception which conveys the benefits of the sacrament, rather than mere outwardly correct administration (*ex opera operato*), then that becomes the key for understanding baptismal regeneration as well as eucharistic fruitfulness.

3. The phrase 'most excellent in signification' shows that the Reformers intended the sacraments to play a major part in church life. While being driven to protest against the superstitions which the medieval had attached to their sacramental system, they wished to live churchwise by a positive sacramentalism, not be mere denials. Their 'test' or definition of the 'visible church' in Article XIX included the phrase, '[the visible church is a congregation] in the which . . . the Sacraments be duly ministered according to Christ's ordinance'. They saw the sacraments as conveying saving grace, and one of their earliest changes in the liturgical round of the average parish was an attempt not only to have the Lord's supper ministered in both bread and wine, but to bring the people to be regular recipients – ideally,

weekly recipients – of that sacrament. It is a matter of history that the long centuries of the Dark and Middle Ages had so accustomed the people to receiving the elements no more than once a year that the Reformers were unable to change the people's devotional habits by Acts of Parliament.

Baptism

While the Reformers retained and enjoined infant baptism, it is arguable that they were thin in their public pronouncements on the subject. For an Anabaptist to read in Article XXVII that the baptism of infants is to be retained 'as being most agreeable to the institution of Christ' is hardly compelling; and to find in the liturgy for infant baptism of 1549, 1552 and 1662 that Cranmer both thought on the one hand that a kind of apologia for infant baptism could be helpfully provided in a three-minute exhortation on the gospel, and on the other that the chosen gospel passage for this heroic exposition was to be Mark 10.13–16, is almost mind-blowing in its futility. The actual rationale offered ('he favourably alloweth this charitable work of ours in bringing this child to holy baptism') would never convince a Baptist and ought not to convince an Anglican. Yet infant baptism was more than just allowed – it was virtually enforced. The rubrics of the 'private baptism of infants' and the cannons of 1604 required the presbyter to hunt out all infants born in his parish and bring them to baptism. The presupposition, easily forgotten today, is that England was a rural nation, and the incumbent knew all the families, and could not but know all the pregnancies also.

Do we believe in invariable regeneration in baptism? The language of all our baptismal rites has always been categorical – this is, those who are baptized (infant or adult) are, after baptism, declared to be regenerate or born again, or adopted into the family of God. So strong has this categorical language been that evangelicals have at times been tempted into denouncing it, while non-evangelicals, have been tempted into trying to expound it as universally true, at least for infants, at whatever cost that might involve for any doctrine of regeneration. But the categorical language would seem to be true to the New Testament allusions to baptism (as shown in Part I above), and true to the liturgical structure of the baptism service, where a once-for-all passage from darkness to light, or death to life, is being worked through. The presence of such categorical language would not, however, of itself determine that the benefit of regeneration was always (let alone automatically) conferred. The emphasis in Article XXV upon right reception of sacraments, and the particular choice in Article XXVII of the phrase, 'those who receive baptism rightly', suggest that a cautious approach may be advisable.

Revision of the eucharistic rites in the recent decades has always been inspired or led by the Catholic party in the life of the Church of England. The reasons are twofold: firstly, because they have dominated the field of liturgical scholarship; and, secondly, because they have come to believe over the decades that the 1662 eucharistic rite is not after all for them. In addition to this, they have usually known what models – ancient (as Hippolytus) or modern (as Paul VI) – they wished to follow or adapt. In the process there has been thrown up for the Church of England (and also for the whole Anglican Communion) a series of problems in euchartistic theology – the nature of consecration, the content of an anamnesis paragraph, the appropriateness of 'euchartist sacrifice', the position and character of an epiclesis. Evangelicals have had to be defensive, as if playing second on a chessboard where the first player had made a brilliant gambit; but they have produced two minor initiatives of their own – lay presidency and the *agape*.

There have also been explorations in new ways of stating Eucharistic theology without imitating Rome directly. One such has been the recurrent attempt to 'get behind the disputes of the Reformation' and find early Church explanations of the Eucharist. These, however, tend to run towards texts about offering the elements to God, texts which were innocent enough in the second and third centuries, but which can hardly regain their innocence now (just as pre-Nicene statements about the Trinity do not actually get behind fourth-century and fifth-century disputes, but instead land us with material which, however innocent of heresy when first compiled, leads straight into heterodoxy today). 'Getting behind' controversies is almost certainly a methodological mistake.

Richard Hooker, *Of the Laws of Ecclesiastical Polity*, Book V, chs 57.4–58.3, in *The Folger Library Edition of the Works of Richard Hooker* Vol. II, W. Speed Hill (ed.), London: The Belknap Press, 1977, pp. 246–50.

Seeing therefore that grace is a consequent of sacraments, a thing which accompanieth them as their end, a benefit which he that hath receiveth from God himself the author of sacraments, and not from any other natural or supernatural quality in them, it may be hereby both understood that sacraments are necessary, and that the manner of their necessity to life supernatural is not in all respects as food unto natural life, because they contain *in themselves* no vital force or efficacy, they are not physical but *mortal instruments* of salvation, duties of service and worship, which unless we perform as the Author of grace requireth, they are unprofitable. For all receive not the grace of God which receive the sacraments of his grace. Neither is it *ordinarily* his will to bestow the grace of sacraments on any, but by the sacraments; which grace also they that receive by sacraments or with sacraments, receive it from him and not from them. For sacraments the very same is true which Solomon's wisdom observeth in the brazen serpent, 'he that turned towards it was not healed by the thing he saw, but by thee, O Saviour of all'.

This is therefore the necessity of sacraments. That saving grace which Christ originally is or hath for the general good of his whole Church, by sacraments he severally deriveth into every member thereof. Sacraments serve as the instruments of God to that end and purpose, moral instruments, the use whereof is in our hands, the effect in his; for the conditional promise: so that without our obedience to the one, there is of the other no apparent assurance, as contrariwise where the signs and sacraments of his grace are not either through contempt unreceived, or received with contempt, we are not to doubt but that they really give what they promise, and are what they signify. For we take not baptism nor the eucharist for bare *resemblances* or memorials of things absent, neither for *naked signs* and testimonies assuring us of grace received before, but (as they are indeed and in verity) for means effectual whereby God when we take the sacraments delivereth into our hands that grace available unto eternal life, which grace the sacraments represent or signify.

There have grown in the doctrine concerning sacraments many difficulties for want of distinct explication what kind or degree of grace doth belong unto each sacrament. For by this it hath come to pass, that the true immediate cause why Baptism, and why the Supper of our Lord is necessary, few do rightly and distinctly consider. It cannot be denied but sundry the same effects and benefits which grow unto men by the one sacrament may rightly be attributed unto the other. Yet then doth baptism challenge to itself but the inchoation of those graces, the consummation whereof dependeth on mysteries ensuing. We receive Christ Jesus in baptism once as the first beginner, in the eucharist often as being by continual degrees the finisher of our life. By baptism therefore we receive Christ Jesus, and from him that saving grace which is proper unto baptism. By the other sacrament we receive him also, imparting therein himself and that grace which the eucharist properly bestoweth. So that each sacrament having both that which is general or common, and that also which is peculiar unto itself, we may hereby gather that the participation of Christ which properly belongeth to any one sacrament, is not otherwise to be obtained but by the sacrament whereunto it is proper.

Now even as the soul doth organize the body, and give unto every member thereof that substance, quantity, and shape, which nature seeth most expedient, so the inward grace of sacraments may teach what serveth best for their outward form, a thing in no part of Christian religion, much less here to be neglected. Grace intended by sacraments was a cause of the choice, and is a reason of the fitness of the elements themselves. Furthermore, seeing that the grace which here we receive doth no way depend upon the natural force of that which were presently behold, it was of necessity that words of express declaration taken from the very mouth of our Lord himself should be added unto visible elements, that the one might infallibly teach what the other do most assuredly bring to pass.

In writing and speaking of the blessed Sacraments we use for the most part under the name of their Substance not only to comprise that whereof they outwardly and sensibly consist, but also the secret grace which they signify and exhibit. This is the reason wherefore commonly in definitions, whether they be framed larger to augment, or stricter to abridge the number sacraments, we find grace expressly mentioned as their true essential form, elements as the matter whereunto that form doth adjoin itself. But if that be separated which is secret, and that considered alone which is seen, as of necessity it must in all those speeches that make distinction of sacraments from sacramental grace, the name of a sacrament in such speeches can imply no more than what the *outward substance* thereof doth comprehend. And to make complete the outward substance of a sacrament, there is required an outward form, which form sacramental elements receive from sacramental words. Hereupon it growth, that many times there are three things said to make up the substance of a sacrament, namely, the grace which is thereby offered, the element which shadoweth or signifieth grace, and the word which expresseth what is done by the element. So that whether we consider the outward by itself alone, or both the outward and inward substance of any sacrament; there are in the one respect but two essential parts, and in the other but three that concur to give sacraments their full being.

Furthermore, because definitions are to express but the most immediate and nearest parts of nature, whereas other principles father off although not specified in defining, are notwithstanding in nature implied and presupposed, we must note that inasmuch as sacraments are actions religious and mystical, which nature they have not unless they proceed from a serious meaning, and what every man's private mind is, as we cannot know, so neither are we bound to examine, therefore always in these cases the known intent of the Church generally doth suffice, and where the contrary is not manifest, we may presume that he which outwardly doth the work, hath inwardly the purpose of the Church of God.

Jeremy Taylor, *The Great Exemplar*, Pt. I, Sec. IX, 'Discourse on Baptism' (1649), 11, 21, 25, 27, in R. Heber and C. Eden (eds), *The Whole Works of Jeremy Taylor*, Vol. II, London: Longmans, 1864, pp. 232, 240-1, 244-5.

The holy Jesus having found His way ready prepared by the preaching of John, and by his baptism and the Jewish manner of adopting proselytes and disciples into the religion a way chalked out for Him to initiate disciples into His religion, took what was so prepared, and changed it into a perpetual sacrament. He kept the ceremony, that thy who were led only by outward things might be the better called in, and easier enticed into the religion, when they entered by a ceremony which their nation always used in the like cases: and therefore without change of the outward act, He put into it a new spirit, and gave it a new grace, and a proper efficacy; He sublimed it to higher ends, and adorned it with stars of heaven; He made it to signify greater mysteries, to convey greater blessings, to consign the bigger promise to cleanse deeper than the skin, and to carry proselytes farther than the gates of the institution. For so He was pleased to do in the other sacrament: He took the ceremony which He found ready in the custom of the Jews, where the *major domo*, after the paschal supper, gave bread and wine to every person of his family; He changed nothing of it without, but transferred the rite to greater mysteries, and put His own spirit to their sign, and it became a sacrament evangelical. It was so also in the matter of excommunication, where the Jewish practice was made to pass into Christian discipline: without violence and noise 'old things became new', while He fulfilled the law, making it up in full measures of the Spirit.

The holy Ghost descends upon the waters of baptism, and makes them prolifical, apt to produce children unto God: and therefore St. Leo compares the font of baptism to the womb of the blessed Virgin, when it was replenished with the holy Spirit. And this is the baptism of our dearest Lord: His ministers baptize with water; our Lord at the same time verifies their ministry with giving the holy Spirit: they are joined together by St Paul; 'we are by one Spirit baptized into one body,' that is admitted into the church by baptism of water and the Spirit. This is that which our blessed Lord calls 'a being born of water and of the Spirit'; by water we are sacramentally dead and buried, by the Spirit we are made alive. But because these are mysterious expressions, and, according to the style of scripture, high and secret in spiritual significations, therefore that we may understand what these things signify, we must consider it by its real effects, and what it produces upon the soul of a man.

First: It is the suppletory of original righteousness by which Adam was at first gracious with God, and which he lost by his prevarication. It was in him a principle of wisdom and obedience, a relation between God and himself, a title to the extraordinary mercies of God, and a state of friendship. When he fell, he was discomposed in all; the links of the golden chain and blessed relation were broken; and it so continued in the whole life of man, which was stained with the evils of this folly and the consequent mischiefs. And therefore when we began the world again, entering into the articles of a new life, God gave us His Spirit, to be an instrument of our becoming gracious person, and of being in a condition of obtaining that supernatural end which God at first designed to us. And therefore as our baptism is a separation of us from unbelieving people, so the descent of the holy spirit upon us in our baptism is a consigning or marking us for God, as the sheep of his pasture, as the soldiers of His arm, as the servants of His household.

'By baptism we are saved': that is, we are brought from death to life here, and that is 'the first resurrection'; and we are brought form death to life hereafter, by virtue of the covenant of the state of grace into which in baptism we enter, and are preserved from the second death, and receive a glorious and an eternal life. 'He that believeth and is baptized, shall be saved,' said our blessed Saviour; and 'according to His mercy He saved us, by the washing of regeneration and renewing of the holy Ghost.'

It remains now that we enquire what concerns our duty, and in what person, or in what dispositions, baptism produces all these glorious effects: for the sacraments of the church work in the virtue of Christ, but yet only upon such as are servants of Christ, and hinder not the work of the Spirit of grace. For the water of the font, and the Spirit of the sacrament, are indeed to wash away our sins and to purify our souls; but not unless we have a mind to be purified. The sacrament works pardon for them that hate their sin, and procures grace for them that love it.

Jeremy Taylor, *The Worthy Communicant* (1660), in *The Whole Works of Jeremy Taylor*, Vol. VIII, Reginald Heber (ed.), Charles Page Eden (revised), Hildesheim: Georg Olms Verlag, 1969, pp. 3, 4, 36, 37–8.

Faith is the inward applicatory, and if there be any outward at all, it must be the sacraments; and both of them are of remarkable virtue in this particular;

for by baptism we are baptized into the death of Christ; and the Lord's supper is an appointed enunciation and declaration of Christ's death, and it is a sacramental participation of it. Now to partake of it sacramentally, is by sacrament to receive it; that is, so to apply it to us, as that can be applied: it brings it to our spirit, it propounds it to our faith, it represents it as the matter of eucharist, it gives it as meat and rink to our souls, and rejoices in it in that very formality in which it does receive it, viz., as broken for, as shed for the remission of our sins. Now then what can any man suppose a sacrament to be, and what can be meant by sacramental participation? For unless the sacraments do communicate what they relate to, they are no communion or communication at all; for it is true that our mouth eats the material signs; but at the same time, faith eats too; and therefore must eat, that is, must partake of the thing signified. Faith is not maintained by ceremonies: the body receives the body of the mystery; we eat and drink the symbols with our mouths; but faith is not corporeal, but feeds upon the mystery itself; it entertains the grace, and enters into that secret which the Spirit of God conveys under that signature. Now since the mystery is perfectly and openly expressed to be the remission of sins; if the soul does the work of the soul, as the body the work of the body, the soul receives remission of sins, as the body does the symbols of it, and the sacrament.

It is the greatest solemnity of prayer, the most powerful liturgy and means of impetration in this world. For when Christ was consecrated on the cross and became our high-priest, having reconciled us to God by the death of the cross, He became infinitely gracious in the eyes of God, and was admitted to the celestial and eternal priesthood in heaven; where in the virtue of the cross He intercedes for us, and represents an eternal sacrifice in the heavens on our behalf. That He is a priest in heaven, appears in the large discourses and direct affirmatives of St. Paul; that there is no other sacrifice to be offered but that on the cross, it is evident, because 'He hath but once appeared in the end of the world to put away sin by the sacrifice of Himself'; and therefore since it is necessary that He hath something to offer so long as He is a priest, and there is no other sacrifice but that of Himself offered upon the cross; it follows that Christ in heaven perpetually offers and represents that sacrifice to His heavenly Father, and in virtue of that obtains all good things for His church.

Now what Christ does in heaven, He hath commanded us to do on earth, that is, to represent His death, to commemorate this sacrifice, by humble prayer and thankful record; and by faithful manifestation and joyful eucharist to lay it before the eyes of our heavenly Father, so ministering in His priesthood, and doing according to His commandment and His example; the church being the image of heaven, the priest the minister of Christ; the holy table being a copy of the celestial altar, and the eternal sacrifice of the lamb slain from the beginning of the world being always the same; it bleeds no more after the finishing of it on the cross; but it is wonderfully represented in heaven, and graciously represented here; by Christ's action there, by His commandment here. And there event of it is plainly this; that as Christ in virtue of His sacrifice on the cross intercedes for us with His Father, so does the minister of Christ's priesthood here, that the virtue of the eternal sacrifice may be salutary and effectual to all the needs of the church both for things temporal and eternal. And therefore it was not without great mystery and clear signification that our blessed Lord was pleased to command the representation of His death and sacrifice on the cross should be made by breaking bread and effusion of wine; to signify to us the nature and sacredness of the liturgy we are about; and that we minister in the priesthood of Christ, who is 'priest for ever after the order of Melchisedec'.

John Gaden, *The Vision of Wholeness*, Duncan Reid (ed.), Ridgefield, CT: Morehouse, 1995, pp. 60–1, 281–3.

Sacraments of Anger

The sacraments may be understood as sacraments of anger, for they all arise out of the paschal mystery of Christ's death and resurrection. The initiation complex of baptism, confirmation, and eucharist plunge us into Jesus' baptism of blood and fire, to drink the cup of God's wrath and to be filled with the Spirit of God's passionate love (Mark 10.38f.; 1.7f.). To celebrate these sacraments seriously is to take on the anguish of love; to abuse them is to bring judgment on ourselves (cf. 1 Cor. 11.27–32).

Penance, of the sacrament of reconciliation, deals with anger in terms of our personal relationships with God and others, as anointing of the sick does with our suffering the more impersonal consequences of evil. Marriage has been called by one writer, 'the savage sacrament', for marriage produces more anger than any other relationship, but it also provides a context in which it may be processed creatively. This only leaves ordination and there are plenty of angry and frustrated clergy around, which has more to do with the state of the church perhaps than ordination *per se*. However, we may see ordination at one level as setting aside people to become the scapegoats and nagging goads for the community, bearers of our anger and God's, for Christ's sake in the power of the Spirit.

The Experience of the Easter Mystery

Darkness and Light

Night. All is dark. I can see no sense in things. Thousands are dying of starvation, thousands drowned in floods for no reason. Nations promise one thing and do another. Our leaders mislead us. I feel repressed, restricted. All is dark. The darkness is outside, it is inside, too. In myself I see darkness, failure. I hurt those whom I love. I shout and scream at them. Is there any light?

Look! A light, but it is so faint. And there's another, and another. All through the world, and the history of humankind, I see lights. Where does this light come from? Is it a reflection? This man's life, this hero, his life stands out like a light. Or this woman, she reflects a bright spot in the gloom. This man, this woman, Gandhi, Martin Luther King, Mother Teresa, Desmond Tutu, the mother who gives herself to her family, all these and many more, appear to shine with a light that is not their own. As I look now, I can see *the* light behind them, brighter than the rest, which all the others reflect. This Light shines in the darkness, and is not put out. This Light is the life of all human beings. I turn to the Light, the Light of the world. 'Give me your light: let me reflect your light. Light of the world, Light of Christ, shine through my life too. Bright Sun, let me shine with your light, as the full moon now shines in the dark sky.'

Baptism

What is it that obscures the light in me? My failures. Knowing what I should do, the love I should have for people, I just can't rise to it. Other forces seem to tie me down. The darkness is outside and in. But I hate evil. I am against repression, the restrictions that destroy people's lives. I renounce the powers of darkness. I stand looking at the dark, and turn away to face the Light.

The Voice asks, 'What do you believe? On what do you stand against the dark?' In springtime, I have seen a daffodil unfold, the pale yellow petals burst from their green sheaths. At the tips of branches I have seen buds, pregnant with life, ready to spring forth. I put my hand to my heart and listen to the dull, pulsating beat driving the blood of life through me. I am alive, I have life. Again, I've looked up and seen a bird drifting in the wind, or at evening sat and watched the sun, a huge red ball, go down upon the sea. So I affirm, this world is good. Despite all the darkness of evil, I belong here. My life is a gracious gift, given me to live. I will be baptized in the name of the Father, Creator of heaven and earth.

But there is more than the living, physical and world of beauty. I take my stand on love, the depths of love that forgives and accepts me, love that gives itself for others, love that is stronger than death, the love that I see around me in children, women and men, but most clearly in Jesus. I will be baptized in the name of the Son, Jesus Christ or Lord.

As well as love, I believe in a creative spirit, the enthusiasm of the young with their hopes and dreams, the creativity of artists, writers, musicians, poets. There is a spirit, too, which ties together those with a common purpose, families, groups, the spirit of unity, the spirit of humanity. I will be baptized in the Name of the Holy Spirit.

Yet it is not I alone making this stand. I stand with others, all those who have had this same faith and vision, all those who are here with me now. Alone, my voice is small and weak: with ten, twenty, a hundred, thousands more added, it is strong. Together we will shout down the walls that imprison us and all people.

Now I am washed clean. I have stepped out of the bath. I smell with the perfume of fragrant oil. White clothes, clean and fresh, cover me. The dawn is breaking outside, and the first fingers of light spread across the sky. I feel new, made whole. My life has meaning. The darkness has been washed away. I have seen the darkness of death, the gloom of despair. I have seen the darkness of death, the gloom of despair. I have stood on the brink of the void of nothingness, but I am alive. Nothing can terrify me now, neither death nor prison, neither earthquake nor sin. I am Christ's and Christ is mine. Nothing can separate me from his live and love. His Spirit is with us, refreshing, comforting, insistently urging us to live.

The Eucharist

Together we move on to the Eucharist, the Great Thanksgiving for the life, death and resurrection of Jesus. We have passed from death to life. Christ our Passover is sacrificed for us; let us keep the feast. Christ is our life. Taste and see how gracious the Lord is. We feed, and are made strong in Him. Christ is our peace, who makes us one. We receive the Bread and the Wine, and feel his touch. We touch each other and know we are together in Christ. Is not this the Bread of God? Illumined by his Light, strengthened by his Life, in touch with one another, we go our ways to love and serve the world, God's world, material for God's kingdom.

'The mystery of your dispensation, O Christ our God, has been fulfilled so far as in us lies. We have made the memorial of your death, we have seen the type of your resurrection, we have been filled with our eternal life, of which, we pray, make us more worthy hereafter. And now, in the power of your hold and life-giving spirit, let us depart in peace. Amen.'

Oliver Quick, *The Christian Sacraments*, London: Nisbet, 1927, pp. 105–9.

The life of Jesus Christ is seen at once as the perfect sacrament. The manhood of Jesus is severed and differentiated from that of all other men, in order both to represent what all manhood truly is and is meant to be, and also to be the means whereby all manhood may realize its end. But this general mark of sacramental nature applies much more widely, and is instructive in many connexions. Sunday, for instance, may be said to be severed and differentiated from all other days of the week, in order both to represent to us the meaning and purpose of all days, and also to be the means whereby the purpose is fulfilled in all. The Church-building is severed and differentiated from other places with an exactly analogous intention. Again, the Church as an organized society is sacramental, inasmuch as its aim is to represent the ultimate meaning and purpose of all human society and to be the living means whereby all human society is incorporated into the fellowship which it represents.

Sacramental rites, inasmuch as they consist of acts rather than of things or person, demand a slight variation of the definition, which we shall consider presently. But we may say at once, by anticipation, that Baptism both represents and declares a spiritual birth which belongs to all human beings as God's children, and is also the means whereby that spiritual relationship is made effectively real in the baptized. And the Holy Communion, whatever else it may be, is at least an act in which the Godward meaning and purpose of all life are embodies and by which they are realized in the souls of faithful receivers.

Thus we may say that, as Jesus Christ Himself is the perfect sacrament of created being, so in the lift of that one sacrament the Church appears as the sacrament of human society, Baptism as the sacrament of man's spiritual birth to God, Holy Communion as the sacrament of human fellowship in Him, holy days as sacraments of time, and holy places as sacraments of space.

Underlying this conception of the nature of sacraments there is everywhere the same principle of separation for the double purpose both of true representation and of effective inclusion. And this principle gives its most characteristic meaning to the Christian idea of holiness, apart from which Christian sacraments are unintelligible. The Jews, as St. Paul so clearly saw, were separated off from all other nations to be the people of God, in order that they might ultimately draw the whole human race into the circle of their holiness. And as soon as the missionary purpose of their election was fully declared through Christ, the old Israel had to be merged in the new Israel of the Catholic Church. The God of Israel was revealed first as jealous and holy in the negative sense, in order that the claim of His jealousy might ultimately be revealed in Christ as the exacting demand of all-inclusive love, which can only be satisfied by the incorporation of all men and of the whole of every life into the fellowship of His family. Thus in Christian thought holiness always contains within itself a double movement, a movement first of separation away from everything that is 'common' or 'profane', a movement secondly of inclusion, whereby the separate-holy goes forth again to draw into itself everything from which its separation has removed it. This duplicity of movement is exactly represented in the difference between the holiness of Jehovah in the Old Testament and the holiness of the Father of Jesus Christ in the New. The presence of the One was sought by withdrawal into the dreadful emptiness of the Holy of Holies. The Other has sent forth His Son, consubstantial with Himself, to be partaker of common flesh and blood for common man's redemption. Yet there are not two Gods in the Bible but one, manifested in two Testaments. And the same double movement of holiness goes on endlessly repeating itself in relation to everything to which in Christian thought the term holy is specially applied. The life of Jesus himself, as the ministry proceeds towards its climax, manifests an ever increasing tension between the completeness of His spiritual isolation and the perfection of His spiritual sympathy. And we can hardly begin to understand the meaning of such Christian titles as Holy Communion and Holy Catholic Church, until we realise that they involve something like a contradiction in terms. For holiness in its original meaning of mysterious separation is precisely the negation of catholicity and communion – the connexion of 'communion' with 'common' of *koinonia* and *koinos*, is something more than an etymological accident. And indeed the fact that the Christian ideal of holiness points, as it were, in two opposite directions at one, has been one of the commonest sources of controversy in the Christian Church. Should Christians continue to emphasise the awful 'otherness' of God by banishing from their worship all material images of the divine? Or does the Incarnation justify the sensible representation even of Godhead, and perhaps enable us to acknowledge the presence of spiritual truth even in what seems outwardly to be idolatrous? Is the holiness of a Christian Church more honoured by the stillness which promotes awe, or by the sounds of food and voice which tell of common people coming and going unafraid? Is the Christian Sunday best observed by the rigorous forgoing of week-day occupations, or rather by the freedom which may help to redeem what it allows? Is the true type of Christian saintliness to be found in ascetic withdrawal from the world, or rather in that life of family cares and business worries which yet seems to sanctify all by seeking in them the service of the Kingdom? Christians have differed and will continue to differ in their answers to such questions. Yet perhaps the truly Christian mind will be willing to acknowledge that everything which it calls holy is separated and set apart, only in order that it may both represent the whole and in the end effectively include it.

And so we may come at last to consider the exact meaning of the term sacrament when it is restricted to its most ordinary use as signifying a certain type of religious rite or liturgy. We will offer at once the following definition of a Christian sacrament. A sacrament is a ritual act, using a certain form and matter, which both represents some universal relation of human life to God through Christ, and also, in thus representing all life, makes life worthy to be thus represented.

Five of the seven Catholic Sacraments may readily be brought under this rubric. Baptism and Confirmation, which were never separated from each other in primitive thought, together represent a reception into membership of God's family, which in spiritual principle belongs to all human beings as represented in Jesus Christ, but which is made effective in the baptized and confirmed through those sacraments, and through the baptized and confirmed in others also whom the convert. The Sacraments of Holy Order analogously represents and effects a universal priesthood of man toward God, wherein every man through Jesus Christ must offer to God both himself and everything over which his authority extends, and wherein also he has committed to him that ministry of reconciliation towards his fellows which is further represented and effected in the Sacrament of Penance. Finally, Holy Communion represents and effects that universal life of self-offering to God and fellowship with God, which is fully realized in Jesus Christ's own sacramental manhood, and must include all men in so far as through Christ they also are made God's priests and children.

R. I. Wilberforce, *The Doctrine of the Holy Eucharist*, London: Mozley, 1853, pp. 8–9, 15–18.

CONSECRATION THE ESSENTIAL CHARACTERISTIC OF THE HOLY EUCHARIST.

An inquiry into the nature of the Holy Eucharist must be founded upon Scripture, and upon that passage of Scripture by which this solemn rite was authorized as well as explained. The authority of him by whom they were spoken, the interest of the occasion on which they were employed, the sententious weight of the expressions themselves – all give to the *words of institution* an importance which few other passages even of holy Scripture can claim.

'Jesus took bread and blessed it, and brake it, and gave it to the disciples, and said, Take, eat, *this is My Body.* And He took the cup, and gave thanks, and gave it to them, saying, Drink ye all of it; for *this is My Blood* of the new Testament, which is shed for many, for the remission of sins.'

The emphatic words of this declaration consist in each case of three parts. 'This is My Body.' 'This is My Blood.' We have here, to speak logically, a *subject*, a *predicate*, and a *copula*; there is something spoken of – 'This' which was taken by Our Lord: there is the affirmation itself – It *is* My Body: there is '*My Body*', '*My Blood*', which in each case is the predicate, or thing affirmed respecting the subject. And this gives us three topics, which must be considered in order; first, the *subject* which is here spoken of; secondly, the *predicate*, or that which is affirmed respecting it – 'My Body', 'My Blood'; and thirdly, the nature of the relation which is affirmed to exist between them. 'This *is* My Body.'

It is obvious, then, both from the practices of the first Christians, and from their doctrines, that they supposed consecration to be the essential characteristic of the Holy Eucharist. They considered the validity of the ordinance to turn upon the setting apart of the sacred elements; they supposed Our Lord to speak not of bread and wine at large, but of *This*, which He held in His hands, and which His ministers after His example are to break and bless. They would not otherwise have supposed that it was necessary that a peculiar class of men should be set apart for the performance of this action, that it could not be effected without a special commission, and that on it validity depended the perpetuation of Gospel blessings.

It will throw further light upon this subject, if we compare the Holy Eucharist with that, which in many respects possesses a corresponding character – the sacrament of Baptism. Both of these ordinances were instituted by Christ Himself; and both have a immediate connexion with those blessings, which He bestows upon His mystical Body. In both there is an inward grace and an outward sign. In both the union of form and matter is necessary to the completeness of that which is outward and visible. But in Baptism the inward part consists only of the benefit bestowed, whereas in the Holy Eucharist, as our catechism reminds us, the thing signified is distinct from the benefit by which it is attended. Baptism, that is, implies two parts only, the outward symbol, and the inward gift; but the Holy Eucharist implies three – the outward sign, the inward part or thing signified, and the accompanying blessing. In Baptism therefore the outward sign has no permanent relation to the inward grace, since the rite has no existence save in the act of administration; but in the Holy Eucharist the outward sign has something more than a momentary connexion with the thing signified. As respects Baptism, therefore, Our Lord used no words which imply that any particular portion of the element employed is invested with a specific character: it was not *this* water, but the element at large which was sanctified to be a pledge of the 'mystical washing away of sin'. And the Church has always acted upon the principle. It is orderly and decent that the water should be set apart with prayer, and that the ceremony should be performed by Christ's minister; but he absence of these conditions does not invalidate the act, either according to the belief of the ancient Church, or according to the existing law of the Church of England. For the setting apart of the element confers only a relative holiness; it is not necessary to the validity of the sacrament; the inward grace is associated with the act, and not with the element; and does not require that the outward part should be brought into an abiding relation with any inward part or thing signified. And for the same reason, the intervention of the minister, however desirable, is not essential. A deacon, in the priest's absence, is as much authorized to baptize as a priest. No doubt it might have please God to assign the same limitations in the case of Baptism which obtained in regard to the Holy Eucharist; but such limitations are not expressed in Scripture, nor has the thing been so understood by the Church. The priestly office, indeed, is essential to the validity of Baptism, because without it there can exist no living branch of Christ's Church, into which new members may be engrafted; but its relation to this sacrament is general and not specific, because Baptism depends upon an act which all Christians may perform, and not upon any consecration which requires a special commission.

Now the reverse of all these things is true of the Holy Eucharist. Here it is not the element at large which is spoken of, but *this bread*, and *this cup*. The intervention of the minister is not matter of decent ceremonial; it is essential to the validity of the ordinance. For valid Baptism is that which is ministered to a competent receiver, but a valid Eucharist is that which is received, after consecration by an authorized priest. It is obvious, then, that consecration is the essential characteristic of this sacrament, since, but for it, the inward part and the outward part cannot be brought together. And this fact is testified by that law of our Church, which renders the services of the priest indispensable in the celebration of the Holy Eucharist, as it was testified by the practice and assertions of antiquity.

Bibliography

Pre-modern Works

Augustine, *In Evangelium Johannis*, Tractate 26.11–15.
Cyril of Jerusalem, *Catecheses Mystagogicae* 20.2–4 and 22.1–6.
Gregory of Nazianzus, *Orationes* 39.17 and 45.23–4.
Hugh of St Victor, *De Sacramentis* 1.9.viii.
Irenaeus, *Adversus Haereses* III xvii 2, 4 and IV xviii 4–6.
Peter Lombard, *Sententiae* d.ii.n.1.
Pseudo-Dionysius, *Ecclesiastical Hierarchy* II, III, IV.
Tertullian, *De Baptismo* 2, *De Corona* 3.
Thomas Aquinas, *Summa Theologiae* III, 55.1.

Modern Works

ARCIC (Anglican–Roman Catholic International Commission) Statements on Eucharist and Ministry, *The Final Report, Windsor, September 1981*, London: SPCK/Cincinnati: Forward Publications, 1982.
Baptism, Eucharist and Ministry (Faith and Order Paper 111), Geneva: World Council of Churches, 1982.
David Brown, *God and Enchantment of Place: Reclaiming Human Experience*, Oxford: Oxford University Press, 2004.

Christopher J. Cocksworth, *Evangelical Eucharistic Thought in the Church of England*, Cambridge: Cambridge University Press, 1993.

B. A. Gerrish, *Grace and Gratitude: The Eucharistic Theology of John Calvin*, Minneapolis: Fortress Press, 1993.

Gordon Jeanes, *Signs of God's Promise: Thomas Cranmer's Sacramental Theology and the Book of Common Prayer*, Edinburgh: T. & T. Clark, 2008.

David J. Kennedy, *Eucharistic Sacramentality in an Ecumenical Context: The Anglican Epiclesis*, Ashgate New Critical Theology in Religion, Theology and Ethics Series, Aldershot: Ashgate, 2008.

Eric Mascall, *Corpus Christi: Essays on the Church and the Eucharist*, London: Longmans, 1953.

H. R. McAdoo and Kenneth Stevenson, *The Mystery of the Eucharist in the Anglican Tradition*, Norwich: Canterbury Press, 1995, 1997.

Paul McPartlan, *The Eucharist Makes the Church: Henri de Lubac and John Zizioulas in Dialogue*, Edinburgh: T. & T. Clark, 1993.

Kevin Seasoltz (ed.), *Living Bread, Saving Cup: Readings on the Eucharist*, New York: Pueblo, 1982.

Bryan D. Spinks, *Two Faces of Elizabethan Anglican Theology: Sacraments and Salvation in the Thought of William Perkins and Richard Hooker*, Drew Studies in Liturgy Series 11, Lanham, MD, and London: Scarecrow Press, 1999.

Bryan D. Spinks, *Early and Medieval Rituals and Theologies of Baptism: From the New Testament to the Council of Trent*, Ashgate Liturgy, Worship and Society Series, Aldershot: Ashgate, 2006.

Bryan D. Spinks, *Reformation and Modern Rituals and Theologies of Baptism: From Luther to Contemporary Practices*, Ashgate Liturgy, Worship and Society Series, Aldershot: Ashgate, 2006.

Bryan D. Spinks, *Do This in Remembrance of Me: The Eucharist from the Early Church to the Present Day*, London: SCM Press, 2013.

Kenneth Stevenson, *The Mystery of Baptism in the Anglican Tradition*, Norwich: Canterbury Press/Harrisburg, PA: Morehouse, 1998.

Geoffrey Wainwright, *Eucharist and Eschatology*, London: Epworth, 1971/New York: Oxford University Press, 1972.

8

Eschatology

CHRISTOPHER A. BEELEY

The theological subject that moderns call 'eschatology' concerns the ultimate aim, purpose and fulfilment of the Christian life. Christianity is profoundly oriented towards a future, heavenly end, the final condition (*eschaton*) of creation that Jesus proclaimed and enacted as the kingdom of God. Although it has occasionally been associated with the four 'last things' (*eschata*) of resurrection, judgement, heaven and hell, Christian eschatology focuses above all on the purification and renewal of creation, the eternal community of the saints in the City of God and the vision of the Holy Trinity, all centred on the final revelation of Christ's glory as the gift of the transcendent God.

The new life that Christians have received through faith in Jesus Christ is itself an eschatological reality: it is the beginning of a state of ultimate blessedness, the fulfilment of which we await with eager longing. As Saint Paul writes, we are saved 'in hope' (Rom. 8.24), as we look expectantly for the final deliverance that God will bring about at the time of his own choosing. By faith Christians are already justified by Christ's death on the cross; meanwhile, we 'boast in our hope of sharing the glory of God' (Rom. 5.2) one day. We place our faith in God's presence and saving work in Jesus Christ, and yet that presence is only partially realized in our own lives and in the world around us. Christian faith thus involves hope in an integral way. If faith is 'the assurance of things hoped for, the conviction of things not seen' (Heb. 11.1), then it is itself a kind of hope, a looking forward to the enjoyment of something that we currently possess only in part.

Hope extends our faith into the whole realm of individual and social action. Our love of God and our neighbours flows from our hope in the renewed existence that God promises and which Jesus lived, died and rose from the dead in order to make available to us through the gift of the Holy Spirit. The end for which Christians yearn is thus not a distant set of events in a future that we can neither imagine nor trust. Rather, our future end already determines the condition of our present lives in Christ and the eschatological state of blessedness has been the aim of God's work of creation all along. Through our hope in God's future for ourselves and the world, we are liberated and inspired to devote our lives to God in gratitude, obedience and worship, and to give ourselves to one another in upbuilding love and service, even as we look forward to the fulfilment of all our hopes in the age to come.

In order to appreciate the full import of Christian hope, it is crucial that we recognize the imperfection and impermanence of our current condition. Even with the grace of Christ and the gift of the Holy Spirit, our lives remain far from complete; the world is deeply broken; and we are in obvious need of further redemption. Christian eschatology serves to disabuse us of any illusions we may harbour about the state of our present world and our abilities to refashion it. Indeed, creation itself exists in an imperfect condition, 'groaning in labour pains', as it awaits the final revelation of God's children, as Paul says. While Christians groan inwardly under the trials and tribulations of this life, the whole creation longs to possess the final freedom that will be ours, when we share Christ's glory in the age to come (Rom. 8.18–22). As the Letter to the Hebrews states, 'Here we have no lasting city, but we are looking for the city that is to come' (Heb. 13.14).

Our individual and social lives are fraught with frustration. We naturally yearn for peace and happiness, for physical and mental health and for the happiness of human society. Yet, our mortal condition is corrupt on several levels. In a functional sense, our cognitive and moral abilities are constantly limited: we are frequently unable to discover the truth with accuracy or to judge rightly in complex situations, despite our confidence in ourselves. More sinister, the human drive for domination and destruction can touch us intimately, however faithful we may be as Christians; as Jesus warns, our enemies can be the members of our own households (Matt. 10.36). In purely physical terms, there appears to be no hope of our survival anyway. We are each doomed to die, no matter how well we care for our bodies, and life on earth will likely be extinguished as soon as the sun uses up its fuel. Faith alone cannot deliver us from all our troubles. Whatever happiness we do experience with God and one another in this life, it necessarily involves conflict as well, since we must overcome temptation, conquer the remains of our sin and deal with the inevitable anxieties of life. In the face of such challenges, the peace of God truly 'surpasses all understanding' (Phil. 4.7). True peace would be an existence so permeated with joy and a society so harmonious and mutually enriching that we would hardly recognize them, given our current state of fragmentation. Such as condition is simply unattainable in our current, mortal condition.

An important aspect of the Christian hope is thus a sober realism about the limitations of the world as it is. Just as we cannot receive Christ's saving benefits at all without facing our brokenness and deep need for God, so too the *eschaton* will come by grace as God's final redeeming act; it cannot be earned, forced or otherwise fabricated by human effort. True Christian hope serves to inspire lives of faith and love now, while also inhibiting the idolatry of our own projects and qualifying our self-regard. In light of God's future redemption, all human progress is limited, and we are even more prone to regress. Modern fantasies of human progress stand in sharp relief to the Christian mindset. The past 150 years show just how pervasive is the temptation to imagine that, at last, humans have attained the capability to perfect our lives and to usher in a truly new society – a fantasy that inevitably proves to be illusory, and which often brings with it evils far worse than the conditions that our efforts sought to improve. Compared to 'the glory about to be revealed to us', our present life is unavoidably beset with suffering (Rom. 8.18), a fact that we avoid at our peril. Our current happiness comes only by faith and in virtue of our hope for God's permanent, final redemption; otherwise, we are being either sorely deceived or plainly idolatrous.

The *eschaton* can only be anticipated within history, but never predicted, caused or explained in historical terms. Christian eschatology is of a different order than the predictions of scientific cosmology. Whether a given scientific theory of the future of the universe may prove to be true or false, such a theory is based on the nature of the universe as we know it and therefore cannot describe the radical transformation and renewal that God has in store for creation. Any true progress that we make in this life, and whatever the future of the physical universe may be, are equally dependent on God's grace. Divine providence is never synonymous with world history or the theory of any scientist, and we are all in need of redemption and final perfection by the crucified and risen Christ. The consummation of creation is the great levelling act that supersedes all human social and political arrangements as well as the order of nature, and it will occur independent of our plans to bring it about. God's promise in Christ thus gives us hope in the midst of our present struggles and the motivation to love God and one another against many obstacles, yet, it also delivers us from our delusions of grandeur and protects us from the dangerous naivety of imagining that we can attain perfect happiness by our own power.

Since the prophets and apostles themselves, it has been observed that we cannot speak directly about the object of our hope. Not only has 'no one ever seen God' (John 1.18), but the promised beatitude of God's creatures transcends the parameters of our knowledge as well. As Paul writes, 'No eye has seen . . . what God has prepared for those who love him' (1 Cor. 2.9, quoting Isa. 64.4), and the author of 1 John comments, 'Beloved, we are God's children now; what we will be has not yet been revealed' (1 John 3.2). Christian eschatology can therefore be expressed only through symbol, fantastic narratives and the other arts of indirect speech. An example of an apophatic or negative description comes in the famous statement that in the end 'death will be no more; mourning and crying and pain will be no more, for the first things have passed away' (Rev. 21.4). We can imagine our life in the perfected creation only by contrast with the sufferings of the present. Similarly, the prophet Isaiah speaks of our final condition by means of hyperbole, as in fairy tale: 'The nursing child shall play over the hole of the asp, and the weaned child shall put its hand on the adder's den' (Isa. 11.8). The state of our existence in God's final kingdom will be so great that it exceeds the normal limitations of our current life. Because we have not yet experienced the realization of our hope, we can imagine it only by stretching and negating the terms of life as we know it, guided by the significations of these things in Scripture. Most biblical teaching about the *eschaton* has this figurative or symbolic quality; it is not a literal forecast of what we should expect to occur in detail, as if it were history written in advance, despite the fact that many have been tempted to take it that way. God's final kingdom is a paradigmatic example of a subject that requires the spiritual interpretation of Scripture in order to understand faithfully. If we took such passages merely literally and not according to the Spirit (2 Cor. 3.6), we would likely miss their real meaning. The things of which we speak belong to the 'eternal gospel' (Rev. 14.6), compared to which our current life in Christ is but a shadow and a type of something much greater.

At the heart of the Christian hope – indeed, the focus and the very substance of that hope – is the final appearance or 'coming' (*parousia*) of Jesus Christ in glory. In short, Christ is our hope. Christian look to Jesus himself for the fulfilment of our lives and the consummation of the universe that God has made. Contrary to popular imagination, Christian eschatology is not a theory about the end of the world or the future of the cosmos as such; still less is it a projection of the world's future from anything we know about its current state of existence. Rather, Christian eschatology refers to the hopeful expectation of God's full presence with his people in his Son, Jesus Christ, by the power of the Holy Spirit. It is only secondarily a set of promises about our future condition and that of the cosmos in light of Christ's final glory. Christians place their confidence in the fact that, having reconciled us with God through his passion and death, Jesus now reigns as the risen Lord, and that we will come to share in his bodily resurrection, becoming a 'new creation' in him (2 Cor. 5.17). The completion and fulfilment of world history lies in the glorification of Jesus Christ, at whose name 'every knee shall bend, in heaven and on earth and under the earth and every tongue confess that Jesus Christ is Lord, to the glory of God the Father' (Phil. 2.10–11). The future of the world is Christ glorified among the saints.

In one respect, our hope is rooted in an event that has already occurred. Jesus' first coming among us was an eschatological event, and all of God's promises have already been ratified in the life, death and resurrection of Christ. Jesus came among us preaching the good news of God's final kingdom; he died and rose from the dead as the first-fruits of the heavenly life in which Christians hope eventually to share; and his gift of the Holy Spirit is the first instalment of that life during our earthly pilgrimage, as we await Christ's final appearing. Yet, while Christ has already conquered sin and death, entered the transformed condition of beatitude in his resurrection and exercises lordship over the entire creation, he nevertheless remains hidden at the present time. His true glory is veiled from our sight, and the redemption of the world is obviously far from complete. The *eschaton* is thus the final revelation of God in Jesus Christ, the full manifestation of the one whom Christians already know by faith and hope.

The Scriptures depict Christ's return as a dramatic, public event, in reverse of his original incarnation. Whereas previously Jesus humbled himself to become human, being born in relative anonymity and even dissuading people from announcing who he was until he had undergone his passion and resurrection, in the final stage of his redeeming work, Jesus will come in power and great glory in the sight of all people (Rev. 1.7), revealed in his true, divine nature. We read that Jesus will descend to earth seated on clouds, surrounded by angels and archangels (Mark 13.26–27) and heralded by the blast of a heavenly trumpet (1 Thess. 4.16). Symbolic as it is, this image stretches the plausibility of the literal sense of the text, for it depicts a localized event, with Christ coming down from heaven, as if it existed somewhere above the earth's atmosphere, and yet, Christ's revelation is to be visible to all people across geographical space, which is impossible according to the laws of nature, as they now exist. Nevertheless, the image vividly conveys the heavenly origin, the regal quality, the divine power and the global importance of Christ's return.

Although many imagine the Day of the Lord as a cause of great fear and anxiety, the witness of the Scriptures is just the opposite. Jesus' final revelation is meant to be a source of profound joy. 'Stand up and raise your heads', Jesus tells his disciples, 'because your redemption is drawing near' (Luke 21.28). Likewise, in the Lord's Prayer Jesus teaches us to pray daily for God's coming kingdom on earth (Matt. 6.10). The conclusion of the Book of Revelation captures the joyful expectancy of the Christian attitude to God's final work: 'The Spirit and the bride say, "Come." And let everyone who hears say, "Come." . . . The one who testifies to these things says, "Surely I am coming soon." Amen. Come, Lord Jesus!' (Rev. 22.17, 20). Far from being a source of fear and trepidation, the final return of Jesus is the fulfilment of all our hopes. It brings to completion the creation and redemption of the saints and the healing of the cosmos as a whole. All creaturely existence has its fulfilment in Christ's coming glory, just as Christians now find their lives liberated, their freedom increased and their actions empowered by the indwelling of the Spirit of Christ.

As the creeds remind us, Christ's return in glory is accompanied by the resurrection of the dead. Christ exists now as the risen Lord, and Christians hope one day to share in Christ's resurrection. As Paul states, 'He will transform the body of our humiliation that it may be conformed to the body of his glory' (Phil. 3.20–21). Here again the Christian hope is richer than is often imagined. Resurrection is not merely the resuscitation of a dead human being nor the extension of human life in its present form. It is the healing and transformation of our whole being beyond sin and death, a change that is both a fulfilment of our original creation and yet also a new, immortal kind of life. How exactly our resurrected state will incorporate our current condition cannot be described, and the nature of the risen body has been debated since the first generation of Christians (see 1 Cor. 15.35). Paul likens it to a plant that grows only when the seed of our current life dies and is buried. Paul's image is one of both continuity and unexpected, surprising transformation, since plants come from seeds and represent their nature, yet they hardly look like seeds: they are much larger and generally more beautiful; they exhibit powers that are only latent in the seed; and so on. Compared with 'the body that is yet to be', which God will give us at the resurrection, our present bodies are considerably less honourable. Our current, 'soulish' bodies are perishable, dishonourable and weak; while our risen, 'spiritual' bodies will be imperishable, glorious and powerful. And whereas our present condition is determined by our lineage from Adam, who was made of earth, our risen condition will be determined by 'the last Adam', Jesus Christ, who is from heaven (1 Cor. 15.37–49). The contrast is fairly stark: 'flesh and blood', our current physical existence, 'cannot inherit the kingdom of God', Paul says, unless it be transformed through Christ's death and resurrection, so that our perishable, mortal bodies become imperishable and immortal (1 Cor. 15.50–53).

The doctrine of the resurrection holds important implications for our understanding of human personhood, much as it does for politics. From the Scriptures and Christian tradition we learn that our risen state represents our true, permanent identity as God's creatures, in a way that we can barely envision now. Compared with our resurrected condition, our identities are only partially realized. We are in the process of becoming ourselves. Rather than assuming that we already know who we are and what we need to be doing, the Christian belief in the resurrection invites us to appreciate that our true selves, individually and corporately, are yet to be revealed, and that they will be the result of the transforming process of finding our lives wrapped up in the risen life of Jesus Christ (see Eph. 4.14–16). The fulfilment of our own selfhood will be marked by our having truly free wills, unconstrained by the desire to sin and stable in our delight in righteousness. Given that our eschatological condition is our true identity, then in faith and hope Christians look forward to becoming more fully ourselves in the *eschaton*, just as human society will be perfected as well.

The resurrection of the body represents our full adoption as sons and daughters of God, for which we currently wait and 'groan inwardly' (Rom. 8.23), and it is the chief consolation of those who mourn the death of loved ones. Yet, it has also been a scandal to many of the standard assumptions about human destiny. The Christian notion of bodily resurrection is very different from the immortality of the soul and its escape from the exigencies of material life, which anchors pagan eschatology. Shocking to many, Christians boldly affirm the continuance and transformation of our bodily life in the *eschaton*. As such, resurrection it is not what we might expect from the course of life on its own terms, but the object of faith and hope in Christ.

In order to share in Christ's resurrection, it is necessary that we undergo God's final judgement of our lives. Again the creeds confess that Christ will return 'to judge the living and the dead' (see Acts 10.42; 1 Peter 4.5). It is not clear how the resurrection of the dead and the final judgement relate to one another sequentially, since an element of purification and judgement seems to be involved in the transformation from mortality to immortality. It is abundantly clear, however, in the prophets of Israel, the New Testament and the great tradition of the Church, that the fulfilment of God's reign involves his judging the nations, delivering his people from their enemies, righting the wrongs of human society and purifying creation of all its evils. From the New Testament we learn that God has entrusted the final judgement of creation to the incarnate Lord Jesus: at his final return Christ will execute God's judgement of all creatures. Christ's judgement, moreover, focuses on concrete ways in which we have lived our lives on earth. Paul declares, 'All of us must appear before the judgement seat of Christ, so that each may receive recompense for what has been done in the body, whether good or evil' (2 Cor. 5.10; see also Matt. 25.31). Revelation depicts Jesus pronouncing the final judgement from a great white throne, judging the risen dead on the basis of the works of their lives, as recorded in certain books (Rev. 20.11-15).

The final judgement is the great reckoning of creation, by which God's truth finally prevails and his righteousness pervades the universe. Christ's *parousia* is both a revelation of Christ's glory and, at the same time, a revelation of the truth of our own lives. At present, the extent of God's elect people is not entirely clear, and they are mixed with those who seem to be among the reprobate. As Jesus warns, the weeds and the wheat cannot be separated until the harvest at the end of the age, when the weeds will be burned and the children of the kingdom will be gathered like wheat into the Lord's barn (Matt. 13.24-30, 37-39). Christ's final judgement reveals before God and the world who we really are, exposing the truth of our lives, which often remains hidden; 'for nothing is hidden that will not be disclosed, nor is anything secret that will not become known and come to light' (Luke 8.7; see 1 Cor. 4.5). The truth of our lives is hidden, not because it is purely inward and invisible; we are judged by our works, after all. Rather, it is hidden, because the meaning of our works is not entirely clear, given the different motives that we can bring to the same task, and also because our ability to understand ourselves and each other is notoriously weak. At the final judgement, Christ will reveal the full actuality of who we are – our thoughts, words, and deeds – in the light of his own glory. Nor is it the case that we are judged by our works apart from faith, God forbid. Rather, because true and lively faith naturally produces good works (Gal. 5.6), Christ's judgement of our works is also a judgement of our faith. The truth that God's judgement reveals is the nature of our lives as we relate to Christ and the resulting quality of our love of God and neighbour. It is in this sense that the Gospel of John depicts Christ's judgement as being determined by whether or not one believes in him now, just as Paul teaches that our salvation, which is an eschatological event (Rom. 5.10), comes by faith and not by works apart from faith (Gal. 2.16). We will be judged according to the fundamental alignment of our lives, which is determined by our faith in Christ and known through our works of love.

The final judgement is an integral part of the redemption and perfection of creation. It is necessary that God purge from the cosmos every trace of sin and evil in order for God to rule throughout creation. Under God's final and total reign, there can be no more sin and death, no more suffering and tears, but only joy, peace and life eternal. Because of the supreme goodness of God and the nature of sin as disobedient opposition to God, Christ's judgement represents an irrevocable either/or decision. In the simplest terms, everyone gets what they want. The saints, those who turn to Christ in faith, hope and love, proceed to a state of permanent blessedness with God and one another, while the damned, those who reject God's mercy in Christ, receive the full consequences of life without God, whether that means eternal suffering or total annihilation. Here again is a point of difficulty in the literal interpretation of the Bible. The Scriptures speak of damnation both as a condition of eternal punishment and torment and also as the complete annihilation of the damned. On the one hand, Paul argues that in the end Christ will destroy every power that opposes him, and that after submitting all things to God the Father, God will be 'all in all' (1 Cor. 15.28), which suggests that there will be nothing left in existence that is opposed to God. On the other hand, there are passages where Jesus himself speaks of eternal torment, of 'the eternal fire prepared for the devil and his angels' (Matt. 25.41; see also Rev. 20.10) and a 'hell, where . . . the fire is never quenched' (Mark 9.48). Although the distinction is important in some respects, the difference is less significant than it may seem, for in either case we are speaking of the unimaginable horror of eternal separation from God. The prerogative of God's final judgement is one of the central tenets of the Christian faith, as is the promise that no evil can ultimately stand in God's sight. The announcement of the coming final judgement is both an admonition to reorient our lives towards God now, lest we face eternity apart from God and also a source of great hope for those who are devoted to Christ but who presently suffer the effects of the world's evils.

While the prospect of eternal damnation is a matter of great seriousness, so too is the hope that, in the end, all may turn to Christ and be saved. Christians are forbidden from wishing that any would be damned, or from speculating who might be, and we are continually called 'to make disciples of all nations' (Matt. 28.28). To the world it may seem odd that the prospect of the final judgement is a source of great joy for Christians. Nevertheless, the reality of God's supreme goodness and the fact that we have turned away from God in preference for the power of sin and death make it inevitable that Christ's judgement will be a 'day of wrath' against those whose lives are concentrated on the love of self, but eternal life and a reward of glory, honour and peace for those who live in the faith of Christ (Rom. 2.5–10).

Although many Christians are accustomed to thinking of our final destiny as an otherworldly 'heaven', the reality is very much richer than that. The object of Christian hope is nothing less than the radical transformation of the world that God has made – the renewal of creation (Matt. 19.28; Rom. 8.21; Gal. 6.15), which Revelation calls 'a new heaven and a new earth' (Rev. 21.1; Isa. 65.17). Rather than expecting to 'die and go to heaven', in the popular sense, Christians believe that heaven comes to us here on earth; we look forward to the renewal of the earth itself and to our future life in it. The renewal of creation is sometimes described in dramatic, cosmic terms: the heavens will be dissolved, burned or rolled up like a scroll, and the things of the earth will be removed in order to be refashioned and restored (Isa. 34.4; Mark 13.25; 2 Peter 3.10; Rev. 6.14). Following this great transformation, the new creation in its entirety will reflect the presence of God, with Christ seated in glory at the centre. In the present age, we are able to perceive God's glory in creation only indirectly, by faith; in the new creation, however, all things will radiate God's glory in their own natural condition, thanks to the presence of the glorified Christ and the purification of our spiritual vision. In the final state of things, all creatures will find their natural fulfilment in the glorification of Christ.

The heart of the new creation consists in a heavenly society gathered around Christ – what the Scriptures call the New Jerusalem, God's eternal city of the elect (Isa. 65.18–19; Gal. 4.26; Rev. 21.2). It often escapes notice how profoundly social our redeemed existence will be. Heaven is a city. Again, our heavenly condition is likened to a great feast (Matt. 8.11; Luke 14.15) or a wedding banquet, 'the marriage supper of the Lamb' (Rev. 19.9). Jesus promises that those who stand by him in his trials will 'eat and drink at my table in my kingdom' (Luke 22.28–30). Heaven is a giant party. Again, our final state will be an eternal Sabbath rest, compared to which life in this world is endless toil (Heb. 4.1–11). In the New Jerusalem, the saints will enter the leisure and recreation of God's own rest. One of the chief implications of our belief in the resurrection of the body is the social condition of the redeemed state, since our embodiment enables and requires us to have commerce with one another. These biblical images speak of the joy, beauty and celebration that Christians look forward to experiencing in the community of the redeemed, in which there is no envy or discontent, but only peace and goodwill among friends.

The concrete representation of God's eternal city in the present time is the Church. In the fullest sense, the Church is an eschatological reality – the mystical body of Christ – and it is only partially visible to us now. Christ's body, the Church, is made up of the complete society of the saints from every age, past, present and yet to come, and it is synonymous with the New Jerusalem or the City of God. At present, the visible Church reflects or signifies the heavenly society gathered around Christ, above all in its celebration of the Eucharist, which includes the reading of Scripture, the preaching of God's word, the prayers and Communion with Christ's body and blood in the bread and wine. The Eucharist is the Church's anticipation of the heavenly banquet in Christ's kingdom, a festal gathering in which we acknowledge the attendance of angels and archangels and all the company of heaven. In an eschatological mode, when we celebrate the Eucharist we 'proclaim the Lord's death until he comes' (1 Cor. 11.26), and Jesus himself said, 'I will not drink again of this fruit of the vine until I drink with you anew in the kingdom of my Father' (Matt. 26.29). The visible Church is the closest approximation of the New Jerusalem that we will ever know, signifying God's kingdom in a way that transcends the cultural, institutional and sociopolitical arrangements of earthly society. And yet, it can never be fully identified with the City of God. In its present existence, the Church is a mixed body of the elect and the reprobate, living in complex relationships of interdependence with the earthly societies in which it exists while it awaits its final redemption at the resurrection.

By contrast with the City of God, we can discern as well the wicked city of the earth, which Revelation depicts in the figures of Babylon and the Roman Empire. In the most basic terms, the City of God and the city of earth are distinguished by their loves or their ultimate aims. The city of earth is oriented towards the love of self, whereas the City of God is directed by the love of God. In the present age of the Church, Christians live as pilgrims in a strange land, journeying often against great opposition towards our heavenly destination, restless until our longing is fulfilled in God's presence.

Since the Old Testament prophets, one of the central motifs of biblical eschatology has been the enemies of God and his people. The New Testament speaks variously of the enemies of the saints, including one termed 'the lawless one' (2 Thess. 2.3) and a figure called 'antichrist' in the Johannine epistles (1 John 2.18, 22), in addition to the fantastic beasts of Revelation (Rev. 13). These images represent one or more false prophet, an apostate Christian, an evil world ruler and the final human enemy of God. Particularly conspicuous is the close alliance of political authority with religious cult centred on the antichrist figure. Although there have been numerous attempts to identify specific people in contemporary history with these mythical figures, such efforts are misguided and have often resulted in the demonization of individuals and whole groups of people. These images serve a truer and more important purpose in Christian eschatology. Throughout the New Testament we read of enmity, wars and persecution at the time of Christ's *parousia*, even among the faithful and in the guise of what is good and Christian. These figures and events illustrate in dramatic terms the real tendency of human power when left to its own devices, its deceptive and widespread attraction, and the universal need for divine redemption right up to the final consummation. As such, they disabuse us of naive fantasies of progressive utopianism, and they enjoin on all Christians the serious business of truth-telling and discernment.

The *eschaton* comes as both the final event of history and the end of history altogether. Because we will share in Christ's immortality and eternity at the resurrection, human history as we know it will come to an end. Yet, contrary to the pagan notion that the aim of life is to escape the constraints of bodily existence, Christianity promises a final state that is characterized by the renewal and fulfilment of creation. In God's eternity, we will no longer be subject to the fragmenting and distorting effects of space and time, even though we will somehow remain in the creaturely dimensions of the new heaven and new earth. The new creation will include all that is good from cosmic history, a symbol of which is the recording of our lives in the Book of Life (Rev. 20.12). One image of the fulfilment of history is the so-called millennium, the thousand-year reign of the martyrs at Christ's return (Rev. 20.4–6). Although it has attracted various utopian speculations over the centuries, this image is virtually impossible to interpret literally in the narrative of Revelation, where it has several affinities with the New Jerusalem to come and poses a number of unanswerable questions. The millennium is eminently comprehensible, however, as a symbolic account of certain aspects of Christ's *parousia*, namely the vindication of the martyrs against corrupt powers and the enjoyment of creation at God's final reign for an unimaginably long time. Such images help us to appreciate that the Day of the Lord will be not merely the last chapter of a long story, but the revealing and transformation of the entire story altogether, as God's future includes the past in an eternally present state of beatitude.

The new creation will transcend our current experience of space as well. What we now experience as a cause of separation and the basis of exclusive possession will somehow become unified, enabling the fellowship of the saints gathered around Christ. In the new creation, human culture and the natural world will be harmonized in an unprecedented way. The New Jerusalem in Revelation includes within itself the Garden of Eden fulfilled and restored. Through the middle of the city the river of the water of life flows from the throne of God and Christ the Lamb, and on either side stand the trees of life for the healing of the nations (Rev. 22.1–2), an image from Genesis that symbolizes the bounty of the natural world (Gen. 2.10–14). Similarly, Isaiah envisions a new harmony between humans and other animals on God's holy mountain, where the wolf lies down with the lamb, the nursing child plays over the asp's hole, and 'the earth will be full of the knowledge of the Lord as the waters cover the sea' (Isa. 11.6–9). Physical nature and human culture will be holistically integrated within God's glory, as all of life is fed with the water that flows from Christ's throne and the nations eat the fruit of the trees. The new creation will thus be the true, perfected relationship of the cosmos with the one who created and redeemed it and is now its Lord.

In a way that we can hardly imagine, all times and places, all individual and social life, will be integrated into a rich and beautiful society as all of history and all creaturely life are brought to fulfilment. In this regard, the *eschaton* is much more than simply living beyond our deaths; it is the summation of everything good that we have ever known. The image of the New Jerusalem descending from heaven to earth (Rev. 21.2) vividly displays the gratuitous character of the final establishment of God's reign, in keeping with the graciousness of Christ's first coming and of God's initial covenant with Abraham. The new creation is not the natural or inevitable end of the world on its own terms; nor is it a goal towards which creatures could direct themselves by their own efforts. Rather, it is a pure gift of God, just as the first creation was. Even though all who are 'in Christ' are in a sense new creations already (2 Cor. 5.17) by the indwelling of the Spirit, Christians yearn for the fullness of the new creation that is yet to come, when God's glory will finally permeate all creaturely life.

In the terms of Jesus' own teaching, our final existence is defined simply as the kingdom of God. Jesus' proclamation that 'the kingdom of God has come near' (Mark 1.15) is a summary of his gospel. God's kingdom, meaning God's active ruling sovereignty more than a realm within which God rules, is nearly synonymous with the notion of God itself, since God's active power, lordship and healing love are essential aspects of God's very being. In the incarnation of Jesus the kingdom of God has already come near – it is 'at hand' and 'among us' through faith in the crucified and risen Lord. And yet, it has not come fully throughout the world or even in the lives of individual Christians, as is only too evident. God has begun to reign in the hearts and lives of those who follow Jesus by the gift of the Holy Spirit; but that reign has only just begun, and its fulfilment will involve both the 'quantitative' completion of evangelizing the nations and bringing all to faith in Christ (if that is possible) and the 'qualitative' change involved in the *parousia* of Christ and the transformation of the new creation. In the fully realized kingdom of God, all of creation will be perfectly ordered to God's will, with nothing opposed to the divine purpose, no evil, suffering, sin or death to be found anywhere. Jesus himself displayed this quality of life in his healings and nature miracles, his meals shared with sinners and the outcast and his exorcisms and other demonstrations of divine power over the forces of evil.

The revelation of God's glory at the *parousia* leads to the vision of God the Holy Trinity. At the centre of the new creation is the glorified Christ, who reveals to the saints the splendour of God himself. In shocking terms, Paul writes that, although we are able to see God only dimly in the present time, in the age to come we will see him 'face to face' (1 Cor. 13.12). The most radical aspect of the Christian hope is the conviction that one day we will see God in his very being, or the divine essence, as far as our creaturely capacities will allow. It is a staple element of Jewish and Christian faith that God cannot be seen directly. 'You cannot see my face; for no one shall see me and live', God tells Moses (Exod. 33.20), and Jesus plainly says, 'No one has even seen God' (John 1.18). As he goes on to explain, the incarnation provides a vision of God in the face of the human Jesus (John 1.18; 14.9), yet, that vision is still indirect (1 Cor. 13.12; 2 Cor. 4.6). At the *parousia*, however, the saints will at last see God directly – 'we will see him as he is' (1 John 3.2; see also Matt. 5.8; Rev. 22.4) – in a vision that far exceeds our current capacities. The vision of God in the *eschaton* will be the fulfilment of every act of worship that God's people have performed, first in the Temple and more recently through the incarnate Christ. The beatific vision involves us in the inner life of the Trinity in the most intimate way imaginable. As we behold God, we enter into Christ's relationship with God the Father by the power of the Spirit, becoming sons and daughters in the Son. We see the Trinity as an object of vision, as it were, by becoming immersed in the divine life itself and entering into the Trinity's own self-knowledge and self-love.

In keeping with the theme of the new creation, the vision of God will include the vision of everything else as well. When we see God face to face, we will likewise see God's creatures more clearly than ever, seeing and loving them in and for God, just as the love of God always involves the love of neighbour. We could characterize the fallen state of our current existence precisely as our inability to see God in all things. Even now we can observe that our knowledge of ourselves and each other is increased, not decreased, by our knowledge of God, and divine grace promotes, rather than inhibits, our creaturely capacities and freedom. In the *eschaton*, we will be delivered once and for all from the distractibility by which we are prone to idolatry. Our final knowledge and love of all things in God conveys well the sense of Paul's statement that, in the age to come, God will be 'all in all' (1 Cor. 15.28). By participating in God's being, all of creation will become what it was intended to be and share in the divine glory that fills the vision of the saints.

As we know and love God and all creatures in God, we too will become that which we have sought by faith and now see face to face: we will be divinized and made to be like God himself. Having begun the process of divinization in this life through faith in Christ and the indwelling of the Holy Spirit, we will one day participate fully in God's own qualities of immortality, incorruptibility and boundless life, which is the purpose for which we were made. Our divinization is a sharing in the transformation of Christ's own humanity, so that when Christ is finally revealed in glory, 'we will be like him' (1 John 3.2). Surpassing the greatest joys that we have known on earth, we will enter a state of endless growth and fulfilment by partaking in God's very being and coming to exist in union with the Trinity.

Introduction to the Sources

The chief source of Anglican eschatology is Scripture, as it has been interpreted through the living tradition of the Church, particularly the major works of the patristic period. The Apostles and Nicene Creeds are key expressions of this tradition, both of which speak of Christ's return 'to judge the living and the dead', the resurrection of the dead and the life of the world to come.

During the turbulent years of the Reformation, popular apocalypticism in England included the identification of Antichrist with the Roman papacy. Nevertheless, debates over justification by faith and the nature of the Church dominated early Protestant thinking, and eschatological themes hardly appear in the Thirty-Nine Articles of Religion or the Edwardine–Elizabethan Homilies. Traditional eschatology did enter the liturgy of the Church through Thomas Cranmer's adaptation of early and medieval liturgies, beginning in the 1549 Book of Common Prayer. Thanks to their reprinting in the 1662 edition, many of Cranmer's prayers have entered the liturgical mainstream of the Anglican Communion.

The heyday of modern Anglican eschatology came in the seventeenth and eighteenth centuries. With a few interesting exceptions, such as Lancelot Andrewes, we find a vivid expectation of Christ's coming kingdom in writers as diverse as conformist Jacobean clergy, Puritan divines and Anglican evangelicals. As a beneficiary of the Elizabethan Settlement, John Donne brought to bear the full richness of the catholic theology that the Renaissance humanists and the Reformers had recovered for the English Church. A devotee of Augustine and the Greek fathers, Donne's poetry and sermons glow with eschatological yearning. Similarly, George Herbert ends his major set of poems 'The Church' with a series on the last things (included here), a group of poems less emotional and verbally acrobatic than Donne's work, yet more stable in their profundity. Later in the seventeenth century, the great Puritan Anglican Richard Baxter made eschatology central to his devotional bestseller, *The Saints' Everlasting Rest*, which views the entire Christian life as a preparation for eternal rest in with God. In a different mode, Baxter's contemporary Jeremy Taylor made the preparation for a holy death the spiritual centre of his own devotional classic,

Holy Living and Holy Dying, a work that shows less direct eschatological concern, due perhaps to Taylor's interest in defending the Anglican establishment and his heavy reliance on classical learning. Not surprisingly, the Evangelical Revival produced theologians for whom Christ's future coming in glory mattered deeply. In his sermon honouring King George III's recovery from illness (excerpted here), John Newton compares the king's 'advent' to St Paul's Cathedral with Christ's impending Advent and the unspeakable glory that lay in store for his followers. Equally vivid are the Advent hymns of Charles Wesley, which stand among the greatest in all of English hymnody. Ministering as they did to the poor and the disestablished, the Wesleys made the hope of participating in Christ's heavenly glory a central theme of early Methodist spirituality.

Like most Western churches, Anglicanism saw an eclipse of traditional eschatology in the late eighteenth and nineteenth centuries, which resulted in a long process of secularization. Following earlier Latitudinarian and Deist challenges to revealed religion, Enlightenment figures shifted the focus from allegedly superstitious beliefs in the consummation of history and the coming of Christ to an emphasis on human morality and interiority. Most famously, the liberal Broad Church movement of the nineteenth century, inspired by the work of F. D. Maurice, eschewed the otherworldliness of traditional eschatology in preference for this-worldly social reforms. For Maurice the incarnation, and specifically the kingdom of Christ, mattered supremely, but it was a kingdom to be realized in the world as we know it. Nineteenth-century historical progressivism left little room for the transcendent counter-culturalism that eschatology provided before the Enlightenment and after World War One. The statement of the 1922 Doctrinal Commission of the Church of England, chaired by William Temple, gestures towards a recovery of classical doctrine, yet its effect is limited by the lingering Hegelian system of Temple's intellectual formation.

Christian eschatology is notable for its imaginative and symbolic character. It is no wonder, then, that imaginatively gifted theologians like the poets Donne and Herbert and the great fantasy writer C. S. Lewis produced such outstanding examples of modern Anglican eschatology. Communicating in images more effectively than in abstract concepts alone, the High Churchman Lewis integrated classical and modern concerns in a synthesis that outshines many of the more recent attempts at reconceiving the Christian hope. Examples of this imaginative work on Christian hope are *The Great Divorce* and *The Last Battle*.

Sources

Thomas Cranmer, *A Short Introduction into Christian Religion (Catechism) 1548*, Oxford: Oxford University Press, 1829, pp. 145–6.

Now the kyngdome of God commeth vnto vs two maner of wayes, first by his word and faithe, whan the gospel is preached vnto vs, that our Lorde Jesus Christ, deliuered vs from synne, death and hel, by crosse, death and resurrection. For by the preaching of his word we do lerne to put oure truste in God and to loin God.

And thys knowlege and faith in Christ, increaseth from tyme to time, not only in theim that haue but newly begonne to beleue, but they also which many yeares haue professed Christ, do profyt in the same faith more and more. For their faith and loue towardes God, by the dayly preachyng of the gospel is confirmed and made more strong. Secondly, the kyngdome of God shall come to vs at the laste daye when the euerlastynge glorye and kyngdome of God shalbe reueled, whan at the lute daye we shalbe raysed from death to lyfe, and be receyued into the kyngdom of heauen, where we shalbe made perfytely iuste, holy and safe for euer, whiche thyng so long as we be here in this worlde, is hyd from vs, and appereth not clerlye vnto vs, but at that last day shal appere to all men, that excedynge ioye, which no tonge is able to expresse. As saith saint John in his canonical Epistle.

Yet it appereth not, what we shalbe, but we know that whan it shal appere, we shalbe lyke vnto hym, and we shall see hym, euen as he is.

Collect for the First Sunday in Advent

Almighty God, give us grace, that we may cast away the works of darkness, and put upon us the armour of light, now in the time of this mortal life, (in the which thy son Jesus Christ came to visit us in great humility;) that in the last day when he shall come again in his glorious majesty to judge both the quick and the dead, we may rise to the life immortal, through him who liveth and reigneth with thee and the holy ghost now and ever. *Amen.*

Collect for the Sixth Sunday after the Epiphany

O GOD, whose blessed Son was manifested that he might destroy the works of the devil, and make us the sons of God, and heirs of eternal life; Grant us, we beseech thee, that having this hope, we may purify our selves, even as he is pure; that when he shall appear again with power and great glory, we may be made like unto him in his eternal and glorious kingdom, where with thee, O Father, and thee, O holy Ghost, he liveth and reigneth ever one God world without end. *Amen*

Collect for All Saints' Day

ALMIGHTY God, who hast knit together thine elect in one communion and fellowship, in the mystical body of thy Son Christ our Lord; Grant us grace so to follow thy blessed Saints in all vertuous and godly living, that we may come to those unspeakable joys, which thou hast prepared for them that unfeignedly love thee, through Jesus Christ our Lord. *Amen.*

From the 1549 Communion Service

We commend unto thy mercye (O Lorde) all other thy servauntes, which are departed hence from us, with the signe of faith, and nowe do reste in the slepe of peace: Graunt unto them, we beseche thee, thy mercy, and everlasting peace, and that at the day of the general resurreccion, we and all they which bee of the misticall body of thy sonne, may altogether be set on his right hand, and heare that his most ioyfull voyce: Come unto me, O ye that be blessed of my father, and possesse the kingdom, whiche is prepared for you, from the begynning of the worlde: Graunt this, O father, for Jesus Christes sake, our onely mediatour and advocate.

ALMIGHTYE and everlyvyng GOD, we moste hartely thanke thee, for that thou hast vouchsafed to feede us in these holy Misteries, with the spirituall foode of the moste precious body and blond of thy sonne, our saviour Jesus Christ, and haste assured us (duely receiving the same)! Of thy favour and goodnes toward us, and that we be very membres incorporate in thy Misticall bodye, whiche is the blessed companye of all faythfull people: and heyres through hope of thy everlasting kingclome, by the merites of the most precious death and passion, of thy deare sonne. We therfore most humbly beseche thee, O heavenly father, so to assist us with thy grace, that we may continue in that holy felowship, and doe all suche good woorkes, as thou hast prepared for us to walke in, through Jesus Christe our Lorde, to whome with thee, and the holy goste, bee all honour and glory, world without ende.

From the Burial of the Dead in the 1549 Book of Common Prayer

O LORDE, with whome dooe lyve the spirites of them that be dead: and in whome the soules of them that bee elected, after they be delivered from the burden of the flesh; be in joy and felicitie: Graunte unto this thy servaunte, that the sinnes whiche he committed in this world be not imputed unto him, but that he escaping the gates of hell and paynes of eternall derkenesse: may ever dwel in the region of lighte, with Abraham, Isaac, and Jacob, in the place where is no wepyng, sorowe, nor heavinesse: and when that dredeful day of the general resurreccion shall come, make him to ryse also with the just and righteous, and receive this bodie agayn to glory, then made pure and incorruptible, set him on the right hand of thy sonne Jesus Christ, emong thy holy and elect, that then he may heare with them these most swete and coumfortable wordes: Come to me ye blessed of my father, possesse the kingdome whiche hath bene prepared for you from the beginning of the worlde: Graunte thys we beseche thee, o mercifull father: through Jesus Christe our mediatour and redeemer. Amen.

O MERCIFULL god the father of oure lorde Jesu Christ, who is the resurrection and the life: In whom whosoever beleveth shall live thoughe he dye: And whosoever liveth, and his beleveth in hym, shal not not dye eternallye: who also hath taughte us (by his holye Apostle Paule) to bee sory as men without hope for them that slepe in him: We rnekely beseche thee (o father) to raise us from the death of sin, unto the life of righteousnes, that when we shall departe this lyfe, we maye slepe in him (as our hope is this our brother doeth) and at the general resurrection in the laste daie, bothe we and this oure brother departed, receivyng agayne oure bodies, and rising againe in thy moste gracious favoure: maye with all thine elect Saynctes, obteine eternall joye. Graunte this, o Lorde god, by the meanes of our advocate Jesus Christ: which with thee and the holy ghoste, liveth and reigneth one God for ever. Amen.

John Donne, 'Resurrection', in John Donne, *The Complete English Poems*, A. J. Smith (ed.), New York: Penguin Books, 1971, p. 308.

Moist with one drop of Thy blood, my dry soul
Shall – though she now be in extreme degree
Too stony hard, and yet too fleshly – be
Freed by that drop, from being starved, hard or foul,
And life by this death abled shall control
Death, whom Thy death slew; nor shall to me
Fear of first or last death bring misery,
If in thy life-book my name thou enroll.
Flesh in that long sleep is not putrified,
But made that there, of which, and for which it was;
Nor can by other means be glorified.
May then sin's sleep and death soon from me pass,
That waked from both, I again risen may
Salute the last and everlasting day.

George Herbert, *The Country Parson, The Temple*, John N. Wall Jr. (ed.), New York: Paulist Press, 1981, pp. 312–16.

[Death.]

Death, thou wast once an uncouth hideous thing,
Nothing but bones,
The sad effect of sadder grones;
Thy mouth was open, but thou couldst not sing.

For we consider'd thee as at some six
Or ten yeares hence,
After the losse of life and sense,
Flesh being turn't to dust, and bones to sticks.

We lookt on this side of thee, shooting short;
Where we did finde
The shells of fledge souls left behinde,
Dry dust, which sheds no tears, but may extort.

But since our Saviours death did put some bloud
Into thy face;
Thou art grown fair and full of grace,
Much in request, must sought for as a good.

For we do now behold thee gay and glad,
As at dooms-day;

When souls shall wear their new aray,
And all thy bones with beautie shall be clad.

Therefore we can go die as sleep, and trust
Half that we have
Unto an honest faithfull grave;
Making our pillows either down, or dust.

[Dooms-day.]

Come away,
Make no delay.
Summon all the dust to rise,
Till it stirre, and rubbe the eyes;
While this member jogs the other,
Each one whispring, *Live you brother?*

Come away,
Make this the day.
Dust, alas, no musick feels,
But thy trumpet: then it kneels,
As peculiar notes and strains
Cure Tarantulaes raging pains.

Come away,
O make no stay!
Let the graves make their confession,
Lest at length they plead possession:
Fleshes stubbornnesse may have
Read that lesson to the grave.

Come away,
Thy flock doth stray.
Some to windes their bodie lend,
And in them may drown a friend:
Some in noisome vapours grow
To a plague and publick wo.

Come away,
Help our decay.
Man is out of order hurl'd,
Parcell'd out to all the world.
Lord, thy broken consort raise,
And the musick shall be praise.

[Judgement.]

Almighty Judge, how shall poore wretches brook
Thy dreadfull look,
Able a heart of iron to appall,
When thou shalt call
For ev'ry man's peculiar book?

What others mean to do, I know not well,
Yet I heare tell,
That some will turn thee to some leaves therein
So void of sinne,
That they in merit shall excell.

But I resolve, when thou shalt call for mine,
That to decline,
And thrust a Testament into thy hand:
Let that be scann'd.
There thou shalt finde my faults are thine.

[Heaven.]

Oh who will show me those delights on high?
    Echo.   *I.*
Thou Echo, thou art mortal, all men know.
    Echo.   *No.*
Wert thou not born among the trees and leaves?
    Echo.   *Leaves.*
And are there any leaves, that still abide?
    Echo.   *Bide.*
What leaves are they? impart the matter wholly.
    Echo.   *Holy.*
Are holy leaves the Echo then of blisse?
    Echo.   *Yes.*
Then tell me, what is that supreme delight?
    Echo.   *Light.*
Light to the minde: what shall the will enjoy?
    Echo.   *Joy.*
But are there cares and business with the pleasure?
    Echo.   *Leisure.*
Light, joy, and leisure; but shall they persevere?
    Echo.   *Ever.*

[Love. (III)]

Love bade me welcome: yet my soul drew back,

Guiltie of dust and sinne.
But quick-ey'd Love, observing me grow slack
From my first entrance in,
Drew nearer to me, sweetly questioning,
If I lack'd any thing.

A guest, I answer'd, worthy to be here:
Love said, You shall be he.
I the unkinde, ungratefull? Ah my deare,
I cannot look on thee.
Love took my hand, and smiling did reply,
Who made the eyes but I?

Truth Lord, but I have marr'd them: let my shame
Go where it doth deserve.
And know you not, sayes Love, who bore the blame?
My deare, then I will serve.
You must sit down, sayes Love, and taste my meat:
So I did sit and eat.

Richard Baxter, *The Saints' Everlasting Rest*, Filiquarian Press, 2007, pp. 21–6.

Chapter Four *What this Rest Containeth*

Now we have ascended the steps, may we look within the veil? May we show what this Rest containeth, as well as what it presupposeth? But alas! how little know I of that whereof I am about to speak, Shall I speak before I know? But if I stay till I clearly know, I shall not come again to speak. . . .

There is contained in this Rest, a cessation from motion or action; not of all action, but of that which bath the nature of a means, and implies the absence of the end. When we have obtained the haven, we have done sailing; When the workman hath his wages, it is implied he hath done his work; when we are at our journey's end, we have done with the way. All motion ends at the centre, and all means cease when we have the end.

This Rest containeth a perfect freedom from all the evils that accompanied us through our course, and which necessarily follow our absence from the chief good. . . . As God will not know the wicked so as to own them; so neither will heaven know iniquity to receive it: for there entereth nothing that defileth or is unclean; all that remains without. And doubtless there is not such a thing as grief and sorrow known there. Nor is there such a thing as a pale face, a languid body, feeble joints, unable infancy, decrepit age, peccant humours, dolorous sickness, griping fears, consuming cares nor whatsoever deserves the name of evil.

This Rest containeth the highest degree of the saints' personal perfection, both of soul and body. This necessarily qualifies them to enjoy the glory and thoroughly to partake of the sweetness of it. Were the glory never so great, and themselves not made capable by a personal perfection suitable thereto, it would be little to them. There is necessary a right disposition of the recipient, to a right rejoicing and affecting.

The more perfect the sight is, the more delightful the beautiful object. The more perfect the appetite, the sweeter the food. The more musical the ear, the more pleasant the melody. The more perfect the soul, the more joyous are those joys, and the more glorious to us is that glory.

This Rest containeth, as the principal part, our nearest fruition of God, the chiefest good. And here, reader, wonder not if I be at a loss, and if my apprehensions receive but little of that which is in my expressions. If, to the beloved disciple that durst speak and enquire into Christ's secrets, and was filled with his revelations, and saw the New Jerusalem in her glory, and had seen Christ, Moses and Elias, in part of theirs; if it did not appear to him what it shall be, no wonder if I know little. When I know so little of God, I cannot know much what it is to enjoy him. When it is so little I know of my own soul, . . . , how little must I needs know of the infinite Majesty, or the state of this soul when it is advanced to that enjoyment! If I know so little of spirits and spirituals, how little of the Father of spirits! . . .

As all good whatsoever is comprised in God and all in the creatures are but drops of this ocean, so all the glory of the blessed is comprised in their enjoyment of God; and if there be any mediate joys there, they are but drops from this . . . O the full joys offered to a believer in that one sentence of Christ's! I would not, for all the world, that one verse had been left out of the Bible: 'Father, I will that those whom thou hast given me be with me where I am, that they may behold my glory which thou hast given me.'

Jeremy Taylor, 'On Holy Dying', *The Whole Works of the Right Revs Jeremy Taylor*, Vol. III, Reginald Heber (ed.), Hildesheim: Georg Olms Verlag, 1969, pp. 267-70, 276.

Nature calls us to meditate of death by those things which are the instruments of acting it; and God by all the variety of his Providence, makes us see death every where, in all variety of circumstances, and dressed up for all the fancies, and the expectation of every single person.

Death meets us every where, and is procured by every instrument, and in all chances, and enters in at many doors: by violence, and secret influence, by the aspect of a star, and the stink of a mist, by the emissions of a cloude, and the meeting of a vapor, by the fall of a chariot, and the stumbling at a stone, by a full meal, or an empty stomach, by watching at the wine, or by watching at prayers, by the Sun or the Moon, by a heat or a cold, by sleeplesse nights, or sleeping dayes, Thy water frozen into the hardnesse, and sharpnesse of a dagger, or water thawed into the floods of a river; by a hair, or a raisin, by violent motion, or sitting still, by severity, or dissolution, by God's mercy, or God's anger, by every thing in providence, and every thing in manners, by every thing in nature and every thing in chance. *Eripitur persona, manet res*: we take pains to heap up things useful to our life, and get our death in the purchase; and the person is snatched away, and the goods remain. And all this is the law and constitution of nature, it is a punishment to our sins, the unalterable event of providence, and the decree of heaven. The chains that confine us to this condition are strong as destiny and immutable as the eternal laws of God.

Since we stay not here, being people but of a dayes abode, and our age is like that of a flue, and contemporary with a gourd, we must look some where else for an abiding city, a place in another country to fix our house in, whose walls and foundation is God, where we must finde rest, or else be restlesse for ever. For whatsoever ease we can have or fancy here is shortly to be changed into sadnesse, or tediousnesse: it goes away too soon like the periods of our life; or stayes too long, like the sorrows of a sinner: its own wearinesse or a contrary disturbance is its load; or it is eased by its revolution into vanity and forgetfulness; and where either there is sorrow or an end of joy, there can be no true felicity: which because it must be had by some instrument, and in some period of our duration, we must carry up our affections to the mansions prepared for us above, where eternity is the measure, felicity is their state, Angels are the Company, the Lamb is the light, and God is the portion, and inheritance.

Charles Wesley, 'Hymns', in J. A. Hodges and A. M. Allchin (eds), *A Rapture of Praise: Hymns of John and Charles Wesley*, London: Hodder & Stoughton, 1966, pp. 55–6, 69–70, 120.

Love divine, all loves excelling,
Joy of heaven to earth come down;
Fix in us thy humble dwelling;
All thy faithful mercies crown!
Jesus, Thou art all compassion,
Pure unbounded love Thou art;
Visit us with Thy salvation;
Enter every trembling heart.

Come, Almighty to deliver,
Let us all Thy life receive;
Suddenly return and never,
Never more Thy temples leave.
Thee we would be always blessing,
Serve Thee as Thy hosts above,
Pray and praise Thee without ceasing,
Glory in Thy perfect love.

Finish, then, Thy new creation;
Pure and spotless let us be.
Let us see Thy great salvation
Perfectly restored in Thee;
Changed from glory into glory,
'Til in heaven we take our place,

'Til we cast our crowns before Thee,
Lost in wonder, love, and praise.

Lo! He comes with clouds descending,
Once for favored sinners slain;
Thousand thousand saints attending,
Swell the triumph of His train:
Hallelujah! Hallelujah! Hallelujah!
God appears on earth to reign.

Every eye shall now behold Him
Robed in dreadful majesty;
Those who set at naught and sold Him,
Pierced and nailed Him to the tree,
Deeply wailing, deeply wailing, deeply wailing,
Shall the true Messiah see.

The dear tokens of His passion
Still His dazzling body bears;
Cause of endless exultation
To His ransomed worshippers;
With what rapture, with what rapture, with what rapture
Gaze we on those glorious scars!

Yea, Amen! let all adore Thee,
High on Thine eternal throne;
Savior, take the power and glory,
Claim the kingdom for Thine own;
O come quickly! O come quickly! O come quickly!
Everlasting God, come down!

Come, thou long expected Jesus,
born to set thy people free;
from our fears and sins release us,
let us find our rest in thee.
Israel's strength and consolation,
hope of all the earth thou art;
dear desire of every nation,
joy of every longing heart.

Born thy people to deliver,
born a child and yet a King,
born to reign in us forever,
now thy gracious kingdom bring.
By thine own eternal spirit
rule in all our hearts alone;

by thine all sufficient merit,
raise us to thy glorious throne.

Rejoice, the Lord is King!
Your Lord and King adore;
mortals, give thanks and sing,
and triumph evermore.
Lift up your heart,
lift up your voice; rejoice;
again I say, rejoice.

Jesus the Savior reigns,
the God of truth and love;
when he had purged our stains,
he took his seat above.
Lift up your heart,
lift up your voice; rejoice,
again I say, rejoice.

His kingdom cannot fail;
he rules o'er earth and heaven;
the keys of earth and hell
are to our Jesus given.
Lift up your heart,
lift up your voice; rejoice,
again I say, rejoice.

Rejoice in glorious hope!
Jesus the Judge shall come,
and take his servants up
to their eternal home.
We soon shall hear
th'archangel's voice; the trump of God
shall sound, rejoice!

John Newton, 'The Great Advent: A Sermon Preached in the Parish Church of St. Mary Woolnoth, On April 23, 1789, The Day of General Thanksgiving for the King's Happy Recovery'. *The Works of the Rev John Newton,* **Vol. 2, New York: Robert Carter, 1844, pp. 419–24.**

In this life they can know but little of the particulars of that happiness which God has prepared for them that love him; but in general they know, and this suffices them, that they shall see him as he is, and shall be like him. They love him unseen, and while he is yet absent from them, the expectation, founded

ESCHATOLOGY

upon his own gracious promise, that he will shortly descend *himself*, to receive them, and to avow them for his own, before the assembled work, is the food and joy of their hearts, which sooths their sorrows, and animates them under every difficulty they arc exposed to, at present, for his sake.

Oh! the solemnity, the terrors, and the glories of that approaching day! Then they who have slighted his mercy, and abused his patience and forbearance, will tremble. Then many whom the world has admired or envied, many of 'the kings of the earth, and the great men, and the chief captains, and the mighty men,' shall call, (alas! in vain,) to the rocks and mountains to fall on them and hide them from his presence. But they who love him and long for his appearance, will say, 'Lo, this is our God, we have waited for him, we will be glad and rejoice in his salvation.' May we, my brethren, have grace to use all diligence, that we 'may be found of him in peace, without spot and blameless'.

They know that he who will descend to receive them was once a man of sorrows and a companion of grief. And though this too little affected them in the time of their ignorance, it has been otherwise since they have derived life from his death, and healing from his wounds. They have sympathized with him in the agonies which he endured, in Gethsemane, and upon Mount Golgotha. They remember that his face was defiled with spitting, his head crowned with thorns, his back torn by scourges, his hands and feet pierced with spikes; that he made his soul an offering for their sins, and was crucified for their sakes. Thus, 'he loved them, and gave himself for them'. Thus he delivered them from approaching wrath; and this love has won their hearts. And they are waiting his return from heaven; that, when they shall see him as he is, with all his angels, and with all his saints, they may join in nobler strains than they can at present reach, in songs of praise to Him who redeemed them to God by his own blood.

But, though they have much to praise him for in this life, they have much more to expect when he shall descend. Their privileges are great while here. They are already delivered from guilt and condemnation, they have access by him to a throne of grace; they have fellowship with him by faith, and joys which a stranger intermeddles not with; 'But it does not yet appear what they shall be.' They are still in a state of warfare and trial; they are exposed to many troubles, to reproach, opposition, and temptation; they are still straitened and hindered, in their best attempts and desires, by an indwelling principle of evil. They are sowing in tears; but, when their Lord shall descend, they expect to reap with joy. He is coming to wipe away all their tears, and then they are assured they shall weep no more. The days of their mourning shall cease for ever. He has prepared for them a kingdom, 'incorruptible, undefiled, and that fadeth not away.' In that kingdom they shall shine forth, each like the sun in the firmament; an immense constellation of suns!

The manner in which the Lord will descend, can be but faintly illustrated by any circumstances borrowed from the pomp of this day. When the King enters St. Paul's, his arrival will be announced by the voice of the multitude, the discharge of cannon, and the deep-mouthed organ. But what are these, when compared with the voice of the archangel, the shout of all who love his appearance, and that trump of God which will shake the creation and raise the dead?

When all mankind shall be ranged before this Great Judge, he will own and vindicate his people in the presence of assembled worlds, and pass an irrevocable sentence of exclusion and condemnation upon his enemies; and then, He will say to those on his right hand, 'Come, ye blessed of my Father, inherit the kingdom prepared for you,' then He will present them 'before the presence of his, glory with exceeding joy;' then time shall be no more; they will no longer measure their existence by the revolutions of the sun and the moon; they will enter upon an eternal state. With this event the apostle closes the description in my text. Here he stops – the rest is too great for language to express, or thought to conceive. He can only say, 'and so we shall for ever be with the Lord.' Who can expound this sentence? We must leave this world, and be admitted into the inheritance of saints in light, before we can fully understand the import of these few words.

Again: we shall be for ever with the Lord. Oh! That word *for ever*! Even to be with the Lord, and to possess a happiness commensurate to the utmost grasp of our capacity, if it were only for a month, or a year, or an age, or a thousand ages – the thought that this happiness must at length have an end, however distant the termination might be, would cast a damp upon the whole enjoyment. But to know that the happiness is eternal, that they who are once with the Lord shall be with him for ever; this is, if I may so speak, the heaven of heaven itself. Such honour awaits all the saints; for thus hath the Amen, the faithful and true Witness, already declared, 'Him that overcometh will I make a pillar in the house of my God, and he shall go no more out': 'Thy sun shall no more go down, neither shall thy moon withdraw itself: for the Lord shall be thine everlasting light, and the days of thy mourning shall be ended.'

William Temple (ed.), *Doctrine in the Church of England: 1922 Doctrinal Commission of the Church of England*, London: SPCK, 1938, pp. 202–6.

(A) General Considerations

The interest of most modern people in the 'Last Things' has an emphasis and perspective different from that disclosed in the New Testament. To-day the predominant concern tends to be with the personal destiny of individuals. People ask: What is the destiny of ourselves or (still more) of our friends? That concern is indeed present in the New Testament (*e.g.*, 1 Thess. iv.13–18), but it is subordinate. The predominant concern is with the fulfilment of the purpose of God – so manifestly not yet fulfilled on the historical plane. The destiny of the individual is a subordinate part of the whole purpose of God. We are convinced that if we are to think rightly in these matters we must recover the perspective of the New Testament: we must begin with the world-purpose of God, and must see everything else in that context. The Gospel knows no private or merely individual salvation: the faithful departed shall not 'without us' be 'made perfect'; and so neither shall we without them. The world-purpose of God is wrought out partly through history; but for its complete and full working out it requires not only a 'new creation' of man, but a 'new earth' and 'new heavens'. Inasmuch as eschatological beliefs and doctrines are concerned, of necessity, with matters in respect of which 'eye hath not seen, nor ear heard', these beliefs are inevitably expressed in symbolical language. Often the different pictorial images employed will be inconsistent with one another. Their pictorial character having been once clearly grasped, there is no need to attempt to combine them into one picture. Moreover, the several pictures often represent tendencies of thought which are not, as they stand, compatible; we may seek to reconcile the elements of spiritual value found in these, but we must not expect to achieve this perfectly until we have that knowledge of the world to come which is only to be gained by entrance into it. Thus, there is important spiritual truth conveyed alike by the doctrine of the general 'Last Judgment' and by the doctrine of the particular judgment of individuals at death; and while we may hope to make progress towards a reconciliation of these several truths, we cannot expect to have full knowledge of the relation between this life and the life to come while we still have direct knowledge only of the former.

From the point of view of a person looking before and after, neither a beginning nor an end of Time can be imagined, and yet the time-process can only be exhibited as significant in so far as it is imaginatively presented as a drama, with both beginning and end. But it appears vital to maintain that the time-process has a more than merely temporal significance, and that God achieves something through it. The world-outlook of Scripture, which sees in the process of events in time the working out of a divine purpose, appropriately sets at the beginning of things a parable of Creation, and at their end a parable of the End of the World.

The New Testament Scriptures, taken as a whole, are dominated by the thought of the approaching 'end'; by the conviction that the new 'Age' is 'at hand'; that its 'powers' are already at work; and that human life, here and now, stands in immediate relation to the judgment, the Kingdom of God, Heaven and Hell, and the Life of the World to Come. It is this conception of life as being, so to speak, poised on the edge of judgment which gives to the New Testament outlook its notes of finality, absoluteness, and urgency. In the Pauline Epistles the gift of the 'Spirit' is already an 'earnest' or first instalment of the new order; in the Fourth Gospel the phrase 'eternal life' denotes similarly the present gift of a new supernatural life which is to endure for ever.

In a literal sense, the *denouement,* which in the New Testament age was expected, did not take place, though many scholars have urged that there is authority in the New Testament, and notably in the Fourth Gospel, for the view that there was a real *Parousia* of the glorified Lord in the coming of the Spirit. Traditional orthodoxy has tended nevertheless to take the scriptural imagery of the Last Things and the hoped-for *Parousia* or 'coming' of Christ semi-literally, but to explain that the *time* of the coming has been postponed. This explanation already begins to be suggested within the New Testament period (*cf.* 2 Pet. iii.3 *sqq.*).

Inasmuch, however, as the moral urgency of the eschatological message (and, from one point of view, its real heart) is to be found largely in the assertion of the *immediate* relation of human life, here and now, to its consummation in eternity, to the solemn realities of judgment, and to the triumph of God, a truer perspective (it may be suggested) is to be secured by taking the *imagery* in a symbolical sense, but by continuing to affirm, with the New Testament, that 'the time is at hand'.

The 'time' is, in this sense, *always* at hand; and from this point of view the spiritual value of the eschatological drama is best grasped when it is understood, not as a quasi-literal description of a future event, but as a parable of the continuous and permanent relation of the perpetually imminent eternal order to the process of events in time.

Moment by moment, the waves of time beat on the shores of eternity – it is not only the last wave in the series which washes those shores. Moment by moment, 'the world hasteth to pass away'. Moment by moment, we stand in the twilight of the dawn 'The night is far spent, the day is at hand' (Rom. xiii.12). The supernatural is for ever pressing in upon the natural, the eternal upon the temporal. It is at all times true that the supreme and decisive verdict on human affairs is the verdict of God, before whom 'all things lie naked and open'. Despite the solid-seeming permanence of the natural order, the thought of which prompted the Old Testament author to write that 'One generation goeth, and another generation cometh; but the earth abideth for ever,' there is a deeper truth expressed by the words of St. John: 'The world passeth away, and the lust thereof; but he that doeth the will of God abideth for ever.'

But this account of the matter does not cover the ground. There is indeed a continuous process whereby, in accordance with the divine ordering of the universe, 'things are what they are, and the consequences of them will be what they will be'; and in this ordered sequence the divine judgment may be in part discerned. But there is still more to be said: the divine judgment, which is thus always operative, is specially declared in certain events, such as, for example, the fall of Jerusalem, a doom upon which is pronounced in the Gospels. Moreover, on any view, human history on this planet must have an end; upon its course as then completed, as upon every separate episode, the judgment of God must be 'made manifest' (Rev. xv.4). It is the ultimate judgment of God upon human affairs, as thus conceived, which gives to human history as a whole its meaning as the sphere of the accomplishment of the divine purpose; and it is of this truth that the traditional imagery of the Last Judgment is the pictorial symbol.

As to the question whether, or in what sense, there will be a 'Last Judgment', conceived as an *event*, supervening upon the conclusion of this world's history, the Commission is united in believing that it is impossible to pronounce; but we are agreed in the conviction that in the world to come the judgment of God on our earthly lives will be made manifest alike to our neighbours and to ourselves, and the meaning of God's 'strange work' in human history will be disclosed.

The recognition that every moment is pregnant with eternal issues is in no way contrary to the conception of the Judgment as the culmination of history.

The Revised Catechism, Church of England, 1982.

VI. THE CHRISTIAN HOPE

57 What is the hope in which a Christian lives?

A Christian lives in the certain hope of the advent of Christ, the last judgement, and resurrection to life everlasting.

58 What are we to understand by the advent of Christ?

By the advent of Christ we are to understand that God, who through Christ has created and redeemed all things, will also through Christ at his coming again, make all things perfect and complete in his eternal kingdom.

59 What are we to understand by the last judgement?

By the last judgement we are to understand that all men will give account of their lives to God, who will condemn and destroy all that is evil, and bring his servants into the joy of their Lord.

60 What are we to understand by resurrection?

By resurrection we are to understand that God, who has overcome death by the resurrection of Christ, will raise from death in a body of glory all who are Christ's, that they may live with him in the fellowship of the saints.

61 What, then, is our assurance as Christians?

Our assurance as Christians is that neither death, nor life, nor things present, nor things to come, shall be able to separate us from the love of God which is in Christ Jesus our Lord. Thus, daily increasing in God's Holy Spirit, and following the example of our Saviour Christ, we shall at the last be made like unto him, for we shall see him as he is.

Therefore I pray:

May the God of all grace, who has called us unto his eternal glory by Christ Jesus, after that we have suffered awhile, make us perfect, stablish, strengthen, settle us. To him be glory and dominion for ever and ever. Amen.

From *An Outline of the Faith, commonly called The Catechism* in The Book of Common Prayer, 1979, according to the use of The Episcopal Church.

The Christian Hope

Q: What is the Christian hope?
A: The Christian hope is to live with confidence in newness and fullness of life, and to await the coming of Christ in glory, and the completion of God's purpose for the world.

Q: What do we mean by the coming of Christ in glory?
A: By the coming of Christ in glory, we mean that Christ will come, not in weakness but in power, and will make all things new.

Q: What do we mean by heaven and hell?
A: By heaven, we mean eternal life in our enjoyment of God; by hell, we mean eternal death in our rejection of God.

Q: Why do we pray for the dead?
A: We pray for them, because we still hold them in our love, and because we trust that in God's presence those who have chosen to serve him will grow in his love, until they see him as he is.

Q: What do we mean by the last judgment?
A: We believe that Christ will come in glory and judge the living and the dead.

Q: What do we mean by the resurrection of the body?
A: We mean that God will raise us from death in the fullness of our being, that we may live with Christ in the communion of the saints.

Q: What is the communion of saints?
A: The communion of saints is the whole family of God, the living and the dead, those whom we love and those whom we hurt, bound together in Christ by sacrament, prayer, and praise.

Q: What do we mean by everlasting life?
A: By everlasting life, we mean a new existence in which we are united with all the people of God, in the joy of fully knowing and loving God and each other.

Bibliography

Pre-modern Works

Augustine, *The City of God*.
Gregory of Nazianzus, *Orations*.
Gregory of Nyssa, *Address on Religious Instruction/Catechetical Oration, On the Making of Man, On the Soul and the Resurrection*.
Irenaeus of Lyons, *Against Heresies*.
Joachim of Fiore, *Exposition on the Apocalypse*.
Origen of Alexandria, *On First Principles*.
Thomas Aquinas, *Summa Theologiae*.

Modern Works

Karl Barth, *The Epistle to the Romans*, Oxford: Oxford University Press, 1933.
John Calvin, *Institutes*.
John Donne, *Sermons*.
C. S. Lewis, *The Great Divorce*, London: HarperCollins, 1997 and *The Last Battle*, London: HarperCollins, 1998.

Jürgen Moltmann, *Theology of Hope*, London: SCM Press, 1970.
Reinhold Niebuhr, *The Nature and Destiny of Man*, New York: Scribner's, 1955.
Karl Rahner, *On the Theology of Death*; tr. C. H. Henkey, New York: Herder & Herder, 1972.
Albert Schweitzer, *The Quest for the Historical Jesus*, London: Black, 1945.
Jeremy Taylor, *Holy Dying*.
Dumitru Stăniloae, *Orthodox Dogmatic Theology,* Brookline, MA: Holy Cross Orthodox Press, 2005, 2 vols.
World Council of Churches, *The Christian Hope and the Task of the Church*, Geneva: World Council of Churches, 1954.

Select Bibliography

The following selection of texts provides the student with an introduction to the basic subjects, personalities and dynamics of Anglican theology. These texts can furnish the student with a solid beginning in the exploration of the richness of the Anglican theological landscape. However, in no way do these selections represent this vast and ever-expanding territory either in an historical or contemporary fashion.

A. M. Allchin, *Trinity and Incarnation in Anglican Tradition*, Oxford: SLG Press, 1977.
Paul Avis, *The Identity of Anglicanism*, London: T. & T. Clark, 2007.
Mark D. Chapman, *Anglican Theology*, London: T. & T. Clark, 2012.
Rowan A. Greer, *Anglican Approaches to Scripture: From the Reformation to the Present*, New York: Herder & Herder, 2006.
Henry R. McAdoo, *The Spirit of Anglicanism: A Survey of Anglican Theological Method in the Seventeenth Century*, London: A. & C. Black, 1965.
Charles Miller, *Richard Hooker and the Vision of God: Exploring the Origins of 'Anglicanism'*, Cambridge: James Clarke & Co., 2013.
Paul E. More and Frank L. Cross (eds), *Anglicanism*, new edition, Cambridge: James Clarke, 2008.
Arthur Michael Ramsey, 'What is Anglican Theology?' *Theology* 48, no. 295 (January 1945), pp. 2–6.
Arthur Michael Ramsey, *From Gore to Temple: The Development of Anglican Theology between Lux Mundi and the Second World War 1889–1939*, London: Longmans, 1960.
Geoffrey Rowell, Kenneth Stevenson and Rowan Williams, *Love's Redeeming Work: The Anglican Quest for Holiness*, Oxford: Oxford University Press, 2001.
Stephen Sykes, *The Integrity of Anglicanism*, London: Mowbray, 1978.
Stephen Sykes, *Unashamed Anglicanism*, London: Darton, Longman & Todd, 1995.
Stephen Sykes and John Booty (eds), *The Study of Anglicanism*, London and Philadelphia: SPCK/Fortress Press, 1988.
Arthur A. Vogel (ed.), *Theology in Anglicanism*, Wilton, CT: Morehouse Barlow, 1984.
Rowan Williams, 'What is Catholic Orthodoxy?', in R. D. Williams and Kenneth Leech (eds), *Essays Catholic and Radical*, London: Bowardean Press, 1983, pp. 11–25.
Rowan Williams, *Anglican Identities*, London: Darton, Longman & Todd, 2004.

Index

Andrewes, Lancelot 14, 15, 24, 58–9, 64, 127, 129, 247–8, 251, 260, 291
Anglican Communion xi, 7, 17, 24, 153, 172, 174–5, 177–8, 191, 250, 259, 264, 267, 291
Anglican Covenant 153, 178
Anselm of Canterbury 5–6
Aquinas, Thomas 52, 91, 197, 203, 245, 246
Arianism 40, 42, 59
ascension 106, 122, 247, 249
Athanasius 42, 56
Augustine of Hippo 196

Barth, Karl 37–8, 40, 54
Baptism 57–8, 64–5, 67, 101, 106–8, 112, 125–6, 134, 145, 168–9, 173–4, 184, 197, 208, 214, 219, 228, 237, 244–52, 254, 256–66, 268–74, 276–8
  of Jesus 38–41, 47, 53, 66, 123–4, 249
Basil of Caesarea 38, 42, 45, 50, 55, 254
Baxter, Richard 250, 252, 291, 298
Bible 14, 31–2, 35, 59, 88, 91, 169, 179, 192, 245, 251, 260
Boethius 54
Book of Common Prayer 24, 35, 155, 199, 206, 251, 265, 291, 294, 307
Book of Homilies 24, 196, 199, 203–4, 206, 221, 225, 291
Buchanan, Colin 244, 258–60, 264
Bull, George 215
Butler, Joseph 91, 99

Calvin, John 179, 192, 205, 208–9, 245–7, 250–1, 255
Chalcedon, Council of 42, 48

Chicago-Lambeth Quadrilateral 174, 176, 180
Cranmer, Thomas 155, 196, 199, 200–8, 221, 247–50, 253, 259, 264, 266, 291–2
Creed 14, 32–3, 112, 155, 168, 172, 177, 191, 284–5
  Apostles' 155, 250, 291
  Athanasian 29, 31, 36, 155
  Nicene 36, 123, 155, 174, 291
crucifixion 8, 11–12, 78, 84
Cyril of Alexandria 57, 94, 113, 249

Dix, Dom Gregory 92, 106, 257
divinization 109, 291
Donne, John 58, 291–2, 295
DuBose, William Porcher 59, 67

ecclesiology 155, 160, 164–5, 167, 170, 175, 177, 196, 209, 216–17, 222, 259, 264
Elizabethan Settlement 57, 91, 291
episcopacy 171, 177, 192
Eucharist 23, 85, 88, 90, 107, 112, 126, 134–5, 169, 198, 205, 219, 244–52, 254–61, 263–8, 271–2, 274, 276–8, 287, 288

Farrer, Austin 59, 72, 91–2, 103
Forbes, William 211–12

Gaden, John 244, 256–8, 264, 272
glory 28, 32, 35–6, 44, 63, 69, 74, 79, 83, 85–6, 93–4, 102, 106, 108, 119, 132, 137, 140–3, 145, 147–8, 168, 187, 189, 233, 235–7, 248, 261, 280–7, 289–94, 298–304, 307–8
Gore, Charles 24, 29, 59, 91, 101–2, 166–7, 252, 258, 261

Gregory of Nazianzus 44, 49
Gregory of Nyssa 44, 49, 55–6

Hammond, Henry 212–14
Herbert, George 210–11, 256, 258, 291–2, 295
homoousios 42
Hooker, Richard 13, 24, 36, 57–9, 90–2, 127, 160–2, 179, 196, 204, 206–9, 221, 227, 244, 247–52, 255, 259, 263, 267
Hort, F. J. A. 27
Huntington, William Reed 172, 180, 190
hypostasis 46, 48–9, 51, 54, 81

Illingworth, J. R. 59
incarnation 60–2, 70, 82–3, 86–93, 102–7, 113–14, 119, 121–2, 124, 127, 171, 275, 283, 290, 292
Irenaeus of Lyon 36–44, 46–8, 50, 55

Jerusalem 1, 20, 22, 79, 98, 164, 287–9, 299, 306
Jewel, John 13–14, 156–7, 163, 166, 178–80, 199, 203–4
John of Damascus 56
judgement 107–8, 285–7, 297, 306–7
justification 127, 148–9, 196–200, 202–22, 227–9, 237–8, 291

Keble, John 15–16, 165, 180
Kingdom of God 73, 101, 106–7, 132, 261, 274, 280, 282–4, 288–90, 305

Laud, William 7, 162–4, 179, 186, 213, 221
Lewis, C. S. 292
lex orandi, lex credendi 262
liturgy 10, 15, 112, 158, 162, 170, 189, 199, 202, 252, 258, 261, 266, 271–2, 276, 291
Logos 42, 67, 69, 70–2, 81
Lux Mundi 59

Mascall, Eric 92, 108, 255
Maurice, F. D. 11, 127, 149, 167–70, 172–3, 175, 180, 292
mission 85, 88, 122–4

negative theology 43, 45–6, 53
Newman, J. H. 59, 127, 148, 165–6, 180, 187, 216–20, 222, 237
Newton, John 292, 302
Nicea, Council of 42, 48

ousia 40, 42, 48–9, 54, 81
Oxford Movement 126–7, 165–7, 216, 263

parousia 107, 282, 285, 288–90, 305
perichoresis 56–7
persona 17, 54, 299
pneumatology 18, 261
prayer 2, 5–6, 10, 66–7, 77, 82, 84–6, 89–90, 92, 109, 148, 169, 175, 204, 209, 222, 233, 235, 247, 251–2, 256–7, 271, 277, 308
Pusey, E. B. 127, 145, 165, 248, 252

Quick, Oliver 244, 254–6, 263, 274

Rahner, Karl 51
Ramsey, Michael 9–12, 31, 171–2, 180, 192, 248, 261
reason 9, 15, 17, 23–4, 27, 33, 61, 99–101, 113, 135–6, 146, 159–162, 204, 214, 221, 224, 230, 234–5, 242
Reformation 5, 155–8, 164–5, 168, 190–1, 193, 197–200, 206, 208, 212, 215, 221, 245–6, 249–50, 252, 255, 258–9, 264, 267, 291
resurrection 2–3, 9–10, 12, 19–21, 28, 39, 78, 82, 84–5, 88, 106, 122–3, 125, 170, 214, 262, 270, 272, 274, 280, 283–5, 287–8, 291–2, 294–5, 306–8
revelation 4, 10, 18–19, 22, 27, 30, 32, 37–8, 40–1, 50, 53, 69–70, 91, 99–101, 106, 220, 231, 241, 280–1, 283, 285, 290, 299

salvation 7, 26, 58–9, 68–9, 93–4, 99, 127, 129, 140, 142, 145, 154, 157, 159, 167, 179, 182, 184–6, 193, 197–8, 203, 207, 210, 213, 215–16, 219–220, 222, 230, 241, 262, 265, 267, 286, 300, 303–4

INDEX

sanctification 126, 147, 149, 196–9, 204–10, 212–14, 216, 218–21, 229, 253

Schleiermacher, Friedrich 37, 217

Scripture 2, 11, 13–17, 21–4, 26, 30, 32, 44, 50, 55, 78, 86, 88–9, 99–100, 112, 135, 146–7, 149, 153–64, 172, 174, 177–9, 182–6, 191–4, 203, 212, 221, 235, 238, 264, 270, 276, 278, 282–3, 286–7, 291, 305

sin 8, 32, 39, 65–6, 68, 78, 93, 96, 98, 111–12, 114, 124–7, 129, 136, 138–40, 143, 145, 148, 150–1, 167–8, 188, 197–8, 200–1, 203, 205, 207–8, 210–13, 215, 219–20, 228–30, 232, 235, 237–8, 242, 245, 248, 251, 270–1, 273, 277, 283–7, 290, 294–5, 298, 300–1, 303

substantia 48, 52

Taylor, Jeremy 6–7, 25, 91, 95, 213–14, 221, 231, 244, 250, 252, 254, 260–1, 263, 269–70, 291

Temple, William 170–1, 219, 239, 255, 292, 304

Thirty-Nine Articles 24, 35, 87, 154–6, 176, 192, 199, 204, 291

tradition xi, 3–5, 11, 13–17, 20, 22–4, 31, 36–7, 43, 51, 78, 107, 111–12, 159–60, 166, 173, 192, 198, 200, 206, 213, 215, 221, 245, 247–8, 253–4, 256–7, 261, 263–4, 284, 291

transcendence 32, 43, 45

via media 158, 209, 220

Waterland, Daniel 58

Wesley, John and Charles 127, 137, 217, 248–9, 251, 258, 292, 300

Whichcote, Benjamin 127, 135

Whitgift, John 158–9, 161, 179–80, 183

Wilberforce, Robert Isaac 244, 252–4, 255, 263, 276

wisdom 9, 26, 28, 80, 84, 114, 116, 129, 145–6, 229, 231, 235, 267, 270

Wisdom of God 32, 42, 46–7, 63, 92–4, 161

Word of God 22, 38–40, 47, 57, 91, 102, 149, 156, 159, 172, 174, 184–5, 188, 191, 222, 232, 234

worship xii, 2, 10, 15, 25, 30, 32, 35, 75, 78–80, 83, 85, 88–9, 100, 112, 126–7, 130, 156–7, 169, 173, 175, 196, 231, 245, 248, 250, 252, 256, 260, 267, 275, 280, 290